Gift of

Dr. Chester R. Wasson

# CONSUMER BEHAVIOR:
## A Managerial Viewpoint

# CONSUMER BEHAVIOR:
## A Managerial Viewpoint

Chester R. Wasson, Ph.D.

Austin Press
Educational Division of
Lone Star Publishers, Inc.
P. O. Box 9774
Austin, Texas 78766

Library of Congress Catalog Number 74-84177
ISBN: 0-914872-02-08

PRINTED IN THE UNITED STATES OF AMERICA

# CONTENTS

# LIST OF ILLUSTRATIONS

**Tables**

# PREFACE

*Consumer Behavior: A Managerial Viewpoint* represents an attempt to meet the need of those making marketing decisions to understand how the most basic principles of the behavioral disciplines can help them competitively. The emphasis is on application to competitive action and the book is for the tool user. Consequently, the focus is on explicit translation of the most basic behavioral knowledge into its significance for marketing action and not on the research background of the tools discussed.

For the most part, discussion is confined to those principles of behavioral science with a demonstrable direct application to managerial decision in exchange situations of any sort. In turn, each of these is given the prominence deemed appropriate to the importance of its utility in solving major managerial problems. In many instances, this will mean giving far more consideration to the specific principle than it receives in behavioral literature or in current research interest. In other cases, it will mean giving it much less discussion than is accorded it in academic circles, or even none at all if no matter of strategy is involved.

Many of the students using this book will have had some kind of prior exposure to psychology, sociology, social psychology, anthropology, and/or economics. But for the others who have not, and even for those who have, the review of some of the elements of these disciplines may be in order, and the slant given this review may be quite new to many. Their prior exposure will have been, in many cases, to a quite different emphasis on the subjects and principles discussed, and seldom will there have been any explicit connection made with their application to exchange situations.

In addition, some of the review presented here will be needed to bridge the watertight separation between the disciplines. Seldom has the most fundamental knowledge of one of the disciplines, such as psychology, for example, been made a part of the presentation or logic of one of the others, such as economics. Too much of the material on consumer behavior which has been made available for class work carries over this same neglect of disciplinary cross-fertilization, with the result that the behavioral aspects of pricing, for one major example, have been ignored and the implications for product differentiation and management have been slighted. Thus the central managerial problem of competitive strategy has hardly been touched upon. This work seeks to remedy this imbalance.

The approach taken seeks a broader application of behavioral knowledge than does that of most writers and seeks to demonstrate how every kind of marketing decision can benefit from the use of the same set of behavioral concepts—the industrial and commercial, and even the nonprofit, noncommercial exchange choices, as well as decisions concerning transactions at the final-consumer level.

To accomplish all of this in a work brief enough for a single term course means some major omissions, of course. Any attempt to add to it by familiarizing the student with any substantive exposition and evaluation of the details of current research would go beyond the limits set, and would, moreover, be more likely to confuse than enlighten.

Because much of the discussion concerns the most basic fundamentals of behavioral knowledge available from most elementary texts in psychology, social psychology, anthropology, and the like, specific references are made only to especially important research results not so available. On the other hand, there has been no hesitation to refer to the experience of actual business when it reveals tendencies not investigated on some campuses, provided that the experience seems well validated and is explainable on the grounds of well-established behavioral knowledge. In some instances, also, the author has been fortunate enough to have knowledge of the results of unpublished proprietary research which has had to meet the test of direct application in the marketplace, and use is made of this knowledge.

The basic approach of this book is my own, based on an adult lifetime interest, observation and thought, and over a decade of teaching in this area, and any errors or omissions are completely my own responsibility. I must acknowledge, however, my debt for valuable comments and suggestions made by two colleagues whose opinions have earned respect—Harold Kassarjian of UCLA and Richard Shreve of Northern Illinois University.

Geneva, Illinois                                                    C. R. W.

# PART I.
# Consumer Behavior and
# the Exchange Process

BY DEFINITION, CONSUMER BEHAVIOR is the behavior of people in a market type situation. Any study of consumer behavior would therefore have to be a study of all of those aspects of our knowledge of human behavior which apply in any situation containing some of the elements of marketing or exchange.

Chapter One takes a look at the individual differences in consumer reaction which can be observed, at the nature of the exchange process itself, and at the nature of the product or offering which is the hub around which the transaction revolves.

Chapter Two considers the possible sources of the differences in the choices made by consumers under seemingly similar situations and the goals of consumers in the exchange process.

# The Role of the Consumer
## in the Marketplace and
## in the Exchange Process

TO GET PERSPECTIVE on the role of the consumer, let us examine a situation with which we are all familiar: a supermarket shopping expedition. Let us imagine that we have entered our favorite store to do our weekly shopping, and have started down the aisle pushing a grocery cart. Ahead of us are a young mother and her three preschool age children—a toddler who rides in the shopping basket, and a girl and boy who walk alongside. We decide to take note of some of the items she picks. She passes the preserves and jellies and stops to pick up a large jar of peanut butter (not surprising, kids really like peanut butter). At the end of the aisle, she selects a jar of strawberry preserves from the special sale display and walks on.

Turning down by the cereal gondola, our housewife (let's call her Thelma) passes the many brands of dry cereals and stops to pick up a large box of quick-cooking rolled oats. She moves on to the back of the store, stops at a demonstration stand, and eats a free sample of a brand new frozen food product. A friend of hers—a woman of about the same age (also with three small children in tow)—happens to stop for a sample at the same stand. They exchange comments on the taste of the new product, and they chat a bit about their husbands who work at the same office. Thelma picks up a package from the stand and puts it in her cart. The second housewife (Debbie) does not.

The walk on together and continue shopping. The cake mixes are next. Debbie picks a package of chocolate cake mix—Thelma waits until they reach the bakery stand and picks up a ready made chocolate cake. Moving down the aisle, they both pick the same brands of strained foods and cereals for babies. (Unlike Thelma, Debbie had picked a dry cereal instead of oatmeal for the rest of the family.)

In the next aisle—detergents—both women pick large boxes, but Thelma chooses soap, while Debbie selects a well-advertised brand of heavy duty detergent. Thelma tells Debbie that, with her new water softener, she can use old-fashioned soap, such as the kind her mother used, to get problem laundry—even shirt collars—clean without rubbing. Debbie explains that because she has no water softener, she needs detergent to cut the hard water.

Both women pick up cans of concentrated orange juice—Thelma picks the store's own brand, Debbie chooses the most highly-advertised brand on the market. We notice then that almost every product in Debbie's basket is a major advertised brand, but most of Thelma's are the store's brand.

They arrive at the checkout counters together and since both have baskets piled to the brim, they go in different lines. We take a third line to avoid waiting. All three of us are through the lines and out on our way to the parking area at the same time.

As the women approach their cars, they meet a third housewive—a neighbor and obviously a good friend of both of them. Her car is loaded with bags from another supermarket. She explains that she does most of her grocery shopping at the other store where prices are lower—she says her husband works hard and needs meat every day. It turns out that the husband of the third woman is a foreman in a lithography plant, while the husbands of the other two are both middle management executives in a manufacturing plant. At that moment, we get into our own car and drive off, thinking about what we have seen.

We think back to the two housewives—alike in many ways—who had similar shopping lists, but nevertheless made different product selections. We think also about the location of products in the store where the women shopped, and remember the difference in the space allotted to various brands on the shelves, obviously reflecting a difference in the volume of goods sold. These facings remain the same from week to week which indicates that customer demand is relatively stable and predictable. If that were not the case, the store manager would be uncertain as to how to divide the shelf space between kinds of cereals, for example.

At the same time there were obvious differences between the product selections made by the first two women, as compared with those made by the friend they met in the parking lot. Those differences were such that they caused her not only to buy different food but to seek out a different store in which to buy these foods. The reason for that difference seems fairly clear—one family was working class and the other two were middle class.

This may be the explanation for the one difference, but we can't explain the differences between the first two housewives—why one bought a cake mix, the other a cake, one tried a new product on its first presentation, the other did not. We cannot say why one tended to buy heavily advertised products, the other one had less tendency to do so. Both of these housewives belonged to the same social class, the same social groups—at least in part, were exposed to the same advertising, had similar families and apparently somewhat similar backgrounds. But their buying differed.

## Who Needs to Know About Consumer Behavior

For us, as curious observers, to attempt an explanation for all this is merely an academic exercise. But it is a matter of great importance to many other people—in fact, an understanding of this aspect of consumer behavior is necessary if our industrial system is to work efficiently. Getting those supplies onto the supermarket shelves in the right proportions involves a great deal of advance planning by a number of people: by the food packagers and distributors, by the executives who control the chain of stores, and by the store manager himself. Knowing which products will be accepted and which rejected is of extreme importance to the manufacturer who must often spend millions of dollars in product development and even new plants, years before consumer preference can be registered at the checkout counter.

In fact, it is clear that anybody who had anything to sell needs a considerable understanding of the rules governing consumer behavior and the way these rules work out in practice.

When we say "anybody who has anything to sell" we are taking in a great many people—in fact, we're including almost everybody dealing with others who are capable of making a choice. On the superficial level, we are talking about everybody that is in the process of manufacturing or producing a service, of distributing goods at any level, of offering something for sale to the final consumer at a presumed profit. In addition, even people involved in activities not done for profit need an understanding of consumer behavior. For example, symphony orchestras operate at a deficit, but nevertheless must keep that deficit low by attracting as many listeners as possible, and attempt to wipe out the deficit by offering something to those who have money to give over and beyond what the tickets cost. The State University lives largely off the public purse. Tuition is only a small part of its income, yet the university must devise a set of offerings which appeal to enough students of the right sort to fill its classrooms and to gain the public support necessary to back up its request for legislative appropriations.

Moreover, selling does not always involve an exchange of money. In fact, one of the cliches of current usage is to say that "I buy that" or "I don't buy that" with regard to some proposed idea. Unlike most cliches, this term is a reasonably accurate one.

Thus, the lobbyist who is trying to do an honest job to represent his client with regard to a legislative proposal in Congress or the state legislature has to do a selling job on the legislators to get their votes. The school board that needs a new bond issue passed at the next election has a harder selling job, quite often, than the automobile manufacturer does with his new models. Indeed, it is not exaggerating to speak of even the courtship process as a selling process.

## The Exchange Process

In some ways, perhaps, the courtship situation is a very useful way of looking at another aspect of the so-called purchase situation. The young man must persuade the girl of his choice that what he has to offer in terms of lifetime companionship is what she is seeking. She, too, has a selling job on the other side—that what she has to offer is what he is seeking.

Indeed, all purchase situations, if we look at them carefully, are two-way exchanges. In the supermarket, what is exchanged, usually, is simply the money for the product. But more is given in return than the mere purchase price. Brand loyalty—the very fact that we buy the same brand from week to week, and indeed in the same sizes—is another element in the price we pay. The occasional customer who comes in and buys only once is not a very profitable customer for most sellers in today's market. This continued patronage is also a price we pay for getting what we want. The very fact of that patronage is a form of communication to those that are selling to us, and to those from whom the seller gets his goods, that this is what we are seeking in the market.

For this reason, we are going to talk about the exchange process rather than simply the purchase situation. The exchange process involves an offering by one side in return for something from the other side—from one who is indeed making a counter offer of money, time, search costs, goodwill, or whatever. In other words, any situation in which the process we sometimes call "persuasion" is involved is a situation in which we need to understand the principles of what we will call consumer behavior.

This brings us to the question of what we mean by consumer. Consumer behavior is obviously one kind of human behavior. However, it just as clearly does not include all kinds of human behavior, since we have defined consumer behavior as that behavior encompassed within the exchange process, the offering of some valuable product or service by one person in return for some kind of valuable consideration from the other person. Many kinds of human behavior involve no such interpersonal action, but any kind of social interaction inevitably involves what is called consumer behavior.

**Who Is the Consumer?**

Who is this person we call a consumer, and who is the seller? How do we distinguish between the two?

In one sense, there really is no distinction between the seller and the buyer. Both parties are buying something and both parties are selling something. But in a dynamic sense, there is a perceivable difference. The seller is the one who takes the initiative and makes the first offering. The consumer is normally the one who responds to that offering in some way.

But it is a little more complicated than that. Is the consumer simply the customer who hands over the cash for the jar of peanut butter? Or, is the consumer the child who eats most of it? Is the consumer the housewife who buys the dog food, or Snoopy, who eats it?

In literal terms, the word *consumer* is a derivative of the verb "to consume," which means to destroy or use up. This would seem to define the consumer as the person (or the dog) who does the final act of ingesting the food or wearing the clothes. However, the person who chooses the product is also considered to be the consumer. Johnny may insist on peanut butter sandwiches for lunch but is very unlikely to distinguish between brands of peanut butter. His mother may be perfectly willing for him to eat peanut butter, but reserves the choices of brand and package size for herself. We need to understand what happens at the two levels, both at the level of a customer who does the actual purchasing and at the level of the final consumer, who may be somebody else. "Consumer," then, can refer to one person or a complex group of persons. We will not understand consumer behavior unless we understand the process by which a product goes from final purchase to final use and what, indeed, is being bought in this final purchase process. We need, in other words, to understand the consumption or *use-system* and how it involves various people in various kinds of consumer roles within the system.

*The Consumption or Use-System*

Johnny eats peanut butter sandwiches. He does not normally, at least when his mother is looking, eat peanut butter straight from the jar, and even if he does, it involves more than just getting some peanut butter into his mouth. To him, peanut butter is one element that goes on a slice of bread along, probably, with some jelly. If it is for his school lunch, it may be packed in some sort of moisture retaining plastic bag in which to carry and keep it. In other words, consumption of a product involves the use of more items than just the product alone, and requires a step-by-step procedure of some sort.

Perhaps the simplest way to see this is to look at a purchase made by the first housewife we followed—her purchase of a box of rolled oats. Nobody eats uncooked rolled oats, that is, nobody human does as a rule. It has to be cooked. Furthermore it is served with other items—milk and sugar, for example—to be palatable to most people. Moreover, the cooked porridge is normally only part of the meal, not the whole meal or even the whole dish as such. And in order to prepare it for eating as a breakfast cereal, the housewife needs to bring in other products, other kinds of capital goods in effect—such as a cookstove and pan—bought to make preparation possible. The oatmeal uses a dish for service, and must be supplemented by milk and sugar (in containers of their own) and accompanied, usually, with fruit or fruit juice, in a set of habitual routines. Moreover, in the United States oatmeal, as a porridge or cereal, is served only in the morning for breakfast. It is not normally perceived as a suitable food at other times of the day. Thus a cultural imperative governs the system, in part.

Let us look at the way in which Thelma uses that box of oatmeal she bought.

The procedure is illustrated in a use-system flow diagram (see Figure 1-1). Note that there are a series of steps which involve elements that will not vary much from day to day, and which have become a habitual procedure for Thelma—a certain time of day for rising in order for her to prepare for later serving of the product, an assortment of other goods which must accompany the serving of this one product, a system of preparation. Some of those accompanying goods—milk, probably; sugar, possibly; grapefruit or orange juice, almost certainly—were bought on the same day as the oatmeal. Other elements that were in the service probably were not. She may have bought a large supply of napkins weeks earlier. The table, the furniture and the chairs in which the family sat to eat the meal were probably bought years before. All, however, are factors in this one purchase act.

Thus, Thelma needs an assortment of goods to go with the oatmeal, each with a place in a set of known procedures for a single use-system—such as a breakfast cereal.

But even for a simple item like rolled oats, there are other possible use-systems: as an ingredient in oatmeal cookies, for example, or as a cleaning absorbent for furs, or even for helping preserve eggs in storage. Each of these will involve a different use-system, and the goal of that use-system is a different set of satisfactions. Thus, from the consumer's standpoint, oatmeal is not one product, but several different products, each with its own use-system.

## Figure 1-1.  Oatmeal Use-System (Quick-Cooking Type)

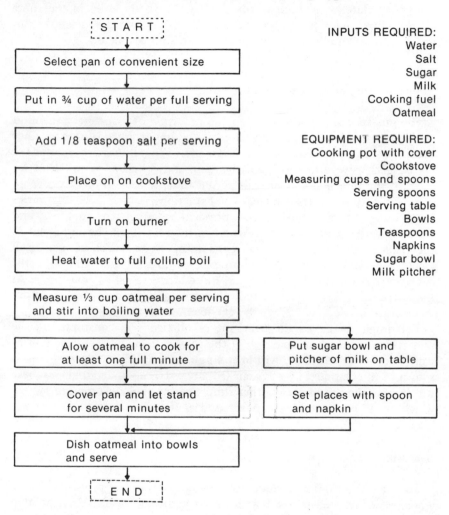

START

| Select pan of convenient size |

| Put in ¾ cup of water per full serving |

| Add 1/8 teaspoon salt per serving |

| Place on on cookstove |

| Turn on burner |

| Heat water to full rolling boil |

| Measure ⅓ cup oatmeal per serving and stir into boiling water |

| Alow oatmeal to cook for at least one full minute |    | Put sugar bowl and pitcher of milk on table |

| Cover pan and let stand for several minutes |    | Set places with spoon and napkin |

| Dish oatmeal into bowls and serve |

END

INPUTS REQUIRED:
Water
Salt
Sugar
Milk
Cooking fuel
Oatmeal

EQUIPMENT REQUIRED:
Cooking pot with cover
Cookstove
Measuring cups and spoons
Serving spoons
Serving table
Bowls
Teaspoons
Napkins
Sugar bowl
Milk pitcher

PERSONAL ROLES:

Gatekeeper        Mother        Financier (s): Father or both parents
Producer

Final consumers: all family members

Thinking back over our supermarket trip, we remember now that almost nobody bought only one item except some children who were barely able to reach up to the counter to pay for a candy bar with a dime they clutched in their hands. Nearly everybody, even in the short express line, had purchased several items. The item itself is an assortment or bundle of satisfactions, as we shall see below.

## Assortment as the Goal of the Purchase Act

For this reason we need to keep the *principle of assortment* in mind throughout the book. The assortment is the important goal in consumer purchase behavior. The reason is simple. We all have a myriad of needs, and if we attempt to satisfy them individually, we will fall far short of the total amount of satisfaction that we seek. For this reason, every product is an assortment of satisfactions, which probably varies from one customer buying the physical product to another, and certainly varies from the person who has the role of purchasing agent to the person who does the final consuming. The purchase act itself usually involves acquiring a number of things at one time—in the supermarket a number of foods and quite a few so-called non-foods. At the automobile dealer, it normally involves gaining a source of future mechanical services as well as the car itself.

This might be called the principle of efficiency in consumption, the aim of which is to gain as much of the total satisfaction being sought as can be conveniently done within a single purchase act. Even so, as is shown in the Oatmeal Use-System (Figure 1-1), any individual purchase will involve the use of many other things within the consumption system which would not normally be purchased at the same time.

### The Roles of Consumers in a Use-System

Such a consumption system involves not only other products, but a whole set of learned motor reactions. In addition, as has been pointed out elsewhere (Wasson, 1974) this consumption system and all other consumption systems involve people in a number of social or family roles. These roles are those of *designer and gatekeeper, financier, producers* and *disposers* of the output (or *final consumers*) and may be defined as follows:

*Designer and gatekeeper*: The individual or individuals who specify the specific imputs and the physical form the output will take. These are the people who make the final choice of brand and product type for each element in the system, constrained by the limits set by those putting up the funds and by the known tastes and desires of the end users who are their consumers. In the case of the evening dinner at home, for example, this is the role of the housewife; in the factory, the design engineer; in the symphony, the conductor; in the medical situation, the prescribing physician. It is the key positive role. The roles of all others are negative—they exercise a veto, or a modifying influence.

*Financier*: The person or persons who determine the budget and disburse the funds to acquire the system imputs. Such inevitably limit the inputs in terms of the amount allocated and may exercise a more direct veto on the specific input, but do not, in their finance role, prescribe the inputs themselves. In the traditional one-worker family, this has been, or course, the wage-earner family head. In the factory, the controller governs the expenditure level; for the Community Chest, the Board; in a governmental consumption unit, the Appropriations Committee.

*Producers*: The person or persons who carry out the production procedure itself. In the case of the family dinner, the housewife usually doubles in this role, doing the cooking and serving up the meal. In the factory, of course, this is the work of the production organization itself—foreman, workers, etc.

*Disposers of the output, or final consumers*: These receive and dispose of the product. In the case of the family meal, this is all members of the family, of course, including the housewife who planned and produced the meal, father who paid for it, and Suzy and Pete who did little more than gulp it down. For the community organization, this is the role of the caseworker's client; in governmental services, the ordinary citizen for much of the effort; in the medical situation, the patient. The factory, too, has its group of consumers—the customers who buy the output to devour in the production of what they expect to sell, either as another factory further along the line to final consumers, as merchants building an assortment to meet the needs of their customers, or as institutions (such as schools, hospitals, governments) utilizing the output to develop a set of directly intangible services.

It should be noted that some or all of the roles can be combined in one person, or may be entirely separate. Thus the physician may be the designer when he prescribes the infant's diet, mother be the producer but not the gatekeeper-designer, father may supply the purchase funds, and baby play no other role than that of consumer.

From the viewpoint of those selling to him, the designer occupies a key role. His specifications determine whose products may be incorporated in or barred from the product he is designing. In any selling situation, he must be identified and his tastes and desires planned for, even though he may never directly purchase any of the product or sign the purchase order itself. The tastes and prejudices of the architects must be kept in mind when designing building products although they may purchase nothing that goes into the structures they design. The perceptions of instructors in an academic area must be kept in mind when designing a textbook, although they will never buy a copy themselves.

But the designer-gatekeeper's choices are not completely free from the influence of the others in the consumption system. They must be within the cost restraints set up by the financier of the system and also within what he considers a proper kind of design. When the Production Department is separate from the designer, the department is operating a consumption subsystem of its own. The design is just one ingredient in the production system for the physical end product for which the Production Department is responsible and it will desire to fit it into a system with which it is familiar. Finally, since the sole purpose of the whole system of systems is the satisfaction of final consumers, the desire-set they perceive as being granted by the design must fit their expectations as well as possible. Even the dog food must be attractive to dogs if dog owners are to buy it.

Any established role in any organization implies an established set of behavior patterns—a set of habits of thought and action which define the status of each individual member in the group. Anything which requires that this role be changed and downgraded is likely to meet resistance. Housewives proud of their role as family chefs did not accept instant coffee which allowed no leeway for individual skill differences in the making of their favorite beverage. Likewise, typesetters and printers have resisted the introduction of computer typesetting which renders typesetting little more difficult than mere typing.

On the other hand, any introduction which fits easily into established motor and perceptual habit patterns is speedily adopted. Black-and-white television changed no person's perception of his role and required no change in entertainment habits. It was an overnight success. Since any consumption system is just such a series of linked perceptual and motor habit systems, the acceptability of any product offering is dependent on its fit into established systems and the resistance met by any new product will be proportional to the extent that its use requires reorientation and learning of habitual patterns of thought, action, and role and value perceptions.

The problem of product design and promotion is further complicated by the fact that any physical product normally fits into several different use-systems, the system varying from consumption system to consumption system because of the differing tastes, habit patterns and value systems of those playing the key roles in each (Wasson, 1974).

It should be clear that, in such a consumption use-system we may conceive of the consumer as simply another production system, building a different set of satisfactions for another set of consumers down the line who may physically consume the product itself or simply incorporate it into their own product. In a sense, Thelma was a producer who consumed the rolled oats as a supply item in furnishing the product—breakfast—that she was producing.

When looked at in a totally objective light, then, the use-system concept makes no distinction between a housewife buying for her family breakfast and the factory purchasing agent buying upholstery materials to put into a car. Both processes can be diagrammed in exactly the same manner, and both involve a set of roles of exactly the same type for the people involved. People do not become less human or step into a different psychology when they leave home and get to their offices. This does not signify that at the office the same person might not make a different decision with regard to purchasing an item similar to one bought for his personal use. His role could be quite different. Since he is buying for a different consumption system, he may purchase a different brand or even a different kind of product to meet a similar kind of satisfaction.

What does seem to be implied is that in studying consumer behavior, no clear line can be drawn between the consumption role of the housewife buyer and that of the purchasing agent for General Motors. It is fortunate that this is so. So many of the identical items are sold to both final consumers, as we generally define the term, and to various kinds of commercial, institutional and industrial buyers by the same firms. Scott Paper Company sells toilet paper to families and the same kind of toilet paper to factories, hotels, office buildings and others. It does not use the same channels and the selling appeals employed may be quite different. But the physical product being sold is the same and the reactions of the people buying do not greatly differ in the two situations. Only the situations and the roles differ. Likewise, Firestone may sell tires to the taxi company or to you and me.

It is, therefore, worth considering the various kinds of buyers that would be involved in the market and how the purchasing situation itself might differ and cause different choices by different kinds of customers or consumers.

## The Differing Kinds of Buyers

Textbooks tend to distinguish between consumer markets and industrial markets. However, many quite dissimilar kinds of markets are comprised in the term "industrial markets." In one quite important type, the purchasing element itself is not important, but the influence extremely so—the professional market.

The ultimate consumer market takes no real definition. It simply consists of families and individuals buying for their own use.

In addition to the ultimate consumer market, many products, even in the same form, must appeal to the professional market, institutional market, and a group of other markets that have somewhat different buying structures but could be loosely classified as industrial and governmental markets, commercial markets, and agricultural markets. The great bulk of what we know as the agricultural market is, in individual sale dollar volume, closely approaching that of the industrial market itself. In fact, many agricultural enterprises are larger than many small industrial plants.

There is, of course, a considerable gap between the kind of purchasing done by an individual consumer and that done by the other kinds of markets. The quantities bought by the final consumer are usually smaller and the number of people who must be satisfied by a single purchase usually fewer in number. Purchases are usually made to satisfy a psychological need. In other words, buying could be done to satisfy one's aesthetic sense. Status or fashion elements can sometimes be a major determinant of the final consumer's perception of value.

All the other markets normally involve purchase of much larger quantities.

Of all the markets normally classified as industrial, none is more unique than the *professional market* which could also be labelled as a *gatekeeper market*. This is a market made up of people who do not themselves consume much or any of the products, the use of which must be sold through them, but who determine what other people will buy—the physician who prescribes the drugs in case of illness, the architect who specifies the material out of which the building will be constructed, the professor who determines which textbook will be used in his classroom. This is a market in which performance, from the specifier's point of view, is the most important characteristic in a product. Price is a relatively minor consideration as a rule. This market is not, however, by any means fashion free. Even the physician may prescribe a particular drug because it is in medical fashion at the moment, provided, of course, it does the job also. Nor is this market completely brand-ignoring. Physicians will trust some drug houses more than others. For example, Wallace Laboratories owns the patent for a tranquilizer known as meprabamate and sell it under their own brand name of Miltown. But more meprabamate is prescribed under the trade name Equanil, made by another drug company, because Wallace Laboratories is also associated with a company that makes a proprietary "liver pill" and physicians, as a profession, distrust companies in the proprietary drug business.

The *institutional market* is made up of hotels, hospitals and other organizations producing primarily some kind of service and buying products that are similar to or often identical to those in normal household use, but in larger quantities. In great part, they are not particularly interested in promoting the manufacturer's brand name, and will often specify that even soap be wrapped with their name on the wrapper. They are, however, much easier to persuade to adopt some kinds of new products which involve labor saving because their major cost is labor and they are quite willing to change their consumption systems if such a saving can be shown—something ordinary consumers are not normally ready to do.

Most of the other markets that we classify as industrial, with the possible exception of the agricultural market, involve a great many people in the purchase decision process. In this respect, of course, they are not completely different from the local household. It is true that the housewife may decide on what brand of concentrated orange juice she is going to buy, but when the family buys its new automobile it is quite likely that every family member of driving age will have a voice in the selection of make.

It is generally thought that all *industrial buying* is done on a coldly objective basis. This is by no means completely true. Executive ego, for example, can be a factor in a great many purchasing situations in companies. The rather plush appearance that most top executive suites exhibit will be hard to justify on a balance sheet. The extent to which businesses rushed to computer operations before costing out the alternatives is a matter of history. The history of marketing research consulting shows that the consulting firms which are most successful at the moment are those which are riding the wave of whatever catchword is currently popular in the business world. In other words, we are dealing with human behavior, not machine behavior, in industrial buying also. Clearly, what is being bought—the real product purchased—is more than a physical artifact or objective service.

## What Is Product and What Is Product Demand?

The exchange transaction is centered around a product, a service, or more usually a group of products and services. This is what the buyer is seeking and for which he is willing to sacrifice some of his resources. To most of us the word "product" connotes something quite physical and tangible: an automobile, a loaf of bread, or a jar of peanut butter. But is this what the customer or consumer, whether it be the final customer, consumer or the purchasing agent, is seeking? We will see that this is not the case.

Johnny is not concerned where that spread he calls peanut butter came from. In fact, if he is very young he will not associate it at all with the peanuts he sometimes gets in his candy. To him it is something that feels smooth, tastes good, and fills him up when he is hungry. Peanut butter is for Johnny a small group of personal satisfactions: a flavor, a texture or tactual sensation, and a feeling of satisfaction.

To his mother, peanut butter is a somewhat different bundle of satisfactions which she has bought to feed to Johnny. It is a food which not only satisfies his hunger drive, but furnishes many of the nutritional elements he needs. Furthermore, it is a food that he prefers, and so it makes Johnny happy. It is simple and easy to serve. Thus, she is purchasing a complete set of satisfactions at the same time, but a different set than Johnny expects to get.

Thus, even the simple step of purchasing a jar of peanut butter satisfies two desire-sets—the mother's desire-set in her role as housewife and mother, and her son's desire-set as final consumer of the peanut butter. The two desire-sets differ because the roles of Johnny and his mother are different in the use-system for which the peanut butter is being bought.

What is being bought is really a bundle of intangible services or satisfactions and the key to insight into consumer behavior must be a clear understanding of what it is that the buyer is giving up some of his resources to obtain—a bundle of satisfactions and the value he attaches to this bundle and to each element in this bundle.

The physical design of the product or service provides some of the satisfactions being sought. The new station wagon can take care of family transportation. A take-out hamburger can quiet the physical pangs of hunger. A Beethoven recording can satisfy the need for aesthetic enjoyment.

However, the value of the physical element of design may depend heavily on the social context of the moment. A billowy, bespangled evening gown which gives the society matron a feeling of confidence in her taste and appearance this year may find its way to the trash barrel next year because it is obviously dated and no longer an acceptable style. The sporty new Benzorati car may be a source of extreme satisfaction today. The same design may be considered disgracefully dated and traded in for a different physical design four years later when the accepted style has changed. Design was a physical element with a positive value in the first case but negative in the second case because the social context in which it was being bought had changed even though its value as a transportation implement remained the same.

Often, the physical design of the product does not, by itself, provide satisfaction enough, particularly in the case of durable mechanical goods. The customer expects to get a parallel service network, and ready repair and part availability included in the Benzorati that he buys. This service is not part of the tangible design of the vehicle but is nevertheless an essential element in the maker's successful distribution strategy.

In addition, the customer may not really consider his Benzorati to be better, more comfortable transportation, or to have better service provisions than any of a number of other less expensive cars he might have bought. But he may feel that this sporty new model is worth the extra expense because it will impress the secretary he is trying to date, and its dazzling and obviously expensive origin will impress the neighbors with his financial success. The makers of Benzorati could do nothing to develop such social status values through any of the tools of advertising or selling available to them. These are the result of social attitudes developed in the society around the buyer as a result of various market forces over the years.

The makers would, of course, exploit the fact itself to the greatest extent possible and, if they could, reinforce it in the firm's advertising, marketing and even its production plans. Distribution would be limited to a selected number of very strong dealers who would be careful never to hint that they would sell the car in a cut price "deal." Certain of the more obvious design characteristics might be discreetly worked into the design of lesser models as time passed, in order to transfer some of the prestige aura to these models but care would be taken that the lower price models would never be confused with the top of the line. These moves, however, would be purely defensive to retain a value already perceived by the customer, however he personally views these values.

Every buyer of the Benzorati is getting at least four services in the bundle he purchases: socially acceptable design, a strong distribution and service network, transportation, and prestige. Not all buyers, however, will perceive these services as having identical values nor will these be all the services which they seek in their purchase. One man may not be interested in the prestige element inseparable in the offering, but loves fine mechanisms and recognizes the Benzorati as one of the most carefully built mass production cars, with an extremely comfortable ride and with what is best described as an edge in quality usually called "silky." Another customer may view the design as really vulgar and a detriment to its value but he likes the economical attribute of the car—its low maintenance cost and low depreciation—and calculates it as the best buy for his driving schedule that he has. A fourth man may find the prestige element so highly negative that he feels that he cannot afford to buy the car. As a psychiatrist charging high fees, he feels that his customers would resent seeing him driving around in such a vehicle and so seeks another car, at least as well built and at least as valuable, but which does not have the name of being a prestige make.

The physical product bought would be the same in all these cases. But the bundle of satisfactions purchased will differ for each one and the same level of value would be arrived at by putting higher values on different characteristics. Nor have we done anything like a complete survey of the number of kinds of product value packages represented by a single model of the Benzorati. If we were to really research the buying motives of another three or four buyers we would probably reveal three or four more sets of values being sought. Few of the buyers would have assigned the same price or value to all of the services which the Benzorati is capable of offering. And many would buy despite certain attributes which others considered as high value.

Moreover, many prospects whose desire-sets were somewhat similar may have chosen something else, other than an automobile. Looking for prestige, for example, one buyer may settle for a well-publicized gift to the symphony hall instead, with his name listed on a suitable bronze plaque. The man seeking design excellence may have finally decided on a sailboat. Thus, "competition" is a complex of many kinds of physical offerings.

The customer, then, is seeking a set of satisfactions. Some of these satisfactions are designed into the physical product. Some of the most important of those sought-for satisfactions in the desire-set may not really be a part of the physical design at all. Any perfume chemist could duplicate the expensive "Secret Wish" perfume for less than four dollars an ounce, so well that even the most expert nose could not tell the difference in smell, but the substitute without the label would not smell the same to the youthful seeker after romance. To her, the "Secret Wish" label has acquired certain associations of glamour and sexuality which really have little to do with the pleasant smell produced by the essences within the bottle.

Any product is, therefore, simply a set of consumer accepted subjective values which differ from one buyer to the next. Whatever price is sought for this offering must not exceed the total value to the purchaser of all the contained and associated services he expects from this buy—all these services rendered by the physical aspect of the offering, by the psychological values he perceives in its use or possession, and by those additional prestige values he believes the reference group attaches to the owner of the items sought. The price is also paid because of the physical aspects of the distribution network, because of the quality of the purchase aid service given by those who are helping the consumer in his shopping expedition, and because of other elements of the total offering situation created by the manufacturer and his distributors.

## What Is Price?

Since product is value, the opposite side of this value is that which must be given up by the buyer, the consumer—that is, the price he pays in order to acquire these values.

Price would seem to be the easiest item in the transaction to define. Superficially it is the dollars and cents that changes hands in a commercial transaction. However, even ordinary everyday usage recognizes price as covering a wider degree of phenomena than this. The buyer of the Benzorati knows that in buying a prestige make such as he has purchased, he will find the number of dealers much smaller and points of service much more widely scattered than if he had bought a lower priced automobile. This is part of the price he pays in order to acquire the other characteristics he seeks. The purchaser of Steuben glassware must expect to travel to one of only seven places in the United States to inspect the designs he wishes to buy. This, too, is part of the price he pays to get an exquisitely fine piece of handblown glassware.

There are many other aspects of price which will be discussed further on when we get into the question of buying motives. However, it is best to say here, that the general usage, which recognizes the term "price" to include anything which inhibits the purchase in an exchange, is much more accurate than the common economic usage of referring only to the monetary side of the various inhibiting factors.

Both the product and the price, therefore, are themselves part of the forces which decide the choices made by consumers in any exchange situation. We shall next consider some of these influences and the possible sources of knowledge which may help us understand how they work.


## Summary

1.   Consumers, although subject to similar influences, nevertheless make divergent purchase choices.

2.   Despite these differences, the experiences of sellers indicate that such choices, in the aggregate, are relatively stable over time, and thus predictable.

3.   Since sellers must plan offerings well in advance of consumer purchase, they need to understand why and how consumers will react in any purchase situation.

4.   Every purchase involves a two-way transaction—an exchange of some of the resources of the buyer for some of the goods and services offered by the seller. The term "exchange situation" rather than "purchase situation" is, therefore, a more accurate description of what takes place.

5.   The exchange process is part of any kind of social interaction— not just a description of a commercial operation. The same rules of human behavior apply, whether we are dealing with a person or an organization seeking to attract any kind of personal resource held by someone else (money, time, effort, votes, and so forth) in return for some kind of offering.

6.   The person whom we designate as the consumer in such a process is any person, organization, or other group which takes any part in influencing the purchase decision, including those who simply purchase, and those who perform the final act of physical consumption.

7.   Whatever is purchased is only one of many items needed to complete a use-system which encompasses the other items, often involves other people, and always is structured in terms of an habitual procedure of preparation and use.

8.   The goal of the use-system is a set or assortment of intangible satisfactions. The satisfactions sought may differ with the role of the individual in the use-system.

9.   Any complete use-system involves a complex of roles for the various persons involved: the roles of designers and gatekeepers, of financiers, of producers, and of disposers (or final consumers) of the output. The key decision role is that of designer or gatekeeper who, in some kinds of situations, may not be directly involved in either the purchase act or the final consumption.

10.  When analyzed in this manner, all purchase situations, including even the most complex industrial procurement, must obey the same rules of human behavior.

11.  There are really many types of consumers: final consumers of personal items, industrial buyers, institutional buyers, agricultural consumers, and the unique type of gatekeeper-designer—the professional advisor. The latter may make no purchase on his own or share in the purchase in any way, but nevertheless be the sole chooser of what will be bought.

12.  The price the buyer pays is much more than money. Other considerations may be even more important—those of time, effort, and the pangs of compromise between what is desired and what is possible.

## Chapter 1, Exercises

1.  Select some relatively homogeneous neighborhood of about four city blocks—preferably one you know. Tabulate the makes and models of automobiles parked there in the evening. How many different kinds do you find (makes+models+age)? Why the differences?

2.  Select a convenient supermarket. Ask the manager how many items he stocks (products+brands+sizes). Check the number of items in general purpose detergents, in breakfast cereals, in coffee. Why the variety?

3.  Consider three of your most important recent purchases (a major garment, an automobile or motorcycle, or any other item costing more than $25). Diagram the use-system for each.

4.  For each such purchase above, list all of the benefits (physical performance, personal, social, etc.) you would have liked to have been able to get in each case (your entire desire-set). How many of these were you able to fulfill in a single purchase? Why not the others?

5.  Select any major industrial firm well known to the general public, which sells some kind of finished products, at least in part. Look up their product line in *Moody's* or *Standard and Poors* directory (your library probably has both). How many kinds of customers does the firm seem to serve?

6.  The exchange process has been defined as a two-way process. What does the symphony patron get in return when he makes an extra donation? What does the Red Cross volunteer give? What does she get in return? What does the developer who builds a house for a customer get from the homebuyer besides money? What does the instructor and the school get from the student besides the tuition? What, besides money, does the automobile dealer get from the car buyer?

7.  Name at least five kinds of professional advisor-gatekeepers. For what products are they an important influence on the market?

8.  List all of the possible satisfactions which some buyer or another might possibly gain from the purchase of:
    an automobile
    a home
    a sailboat
    an evening dress
    a restaurant meal with a date
    a stereo recording system

9.  For each of the above, which ones would *every* potential buyer be seeking? How many could any one offering or brand furnish physically?

10. Besides the difference in money price, what other kinds of prices must a Cadillac owner pay which a Chevy or Vega buyer does not?

**2**

Consumer Choices and
the Factors Influencing Them

CONSUMER BEHAVIOR AS PREDICTABLE IN THE AGGRE-GATE

SIMPLIFIED MODEL OF THE EXCHANGE PROCESS AND COMPETITION

DIVERGENT REACTIONS OF DIFFERENT CONSUMERS UNDER SIMILAR CIRCUMSTANCES

POSSIBLE ROLES OF INTERNAL DIFFERENCES AND EXTER-NAL INFLUENCES

SOCIAL INFLUENCES: FAMILY NEEDS AND CLASS MEMBER-SHIP

THE PURCHASE SITUATION AS A MATCHING OF DESIRE SETS AND OFFERING ASSORTMENTS UNDER EXTERNAL INFLUENCES

THE DESIRE SET

PLAN OF THE BOOK

## Consumer Behavior as a Predictable Choice Process

WE HAVE DEFINED consumer behavior as the way people act in an exchange process. Looking back over our simple examples in the last chapter, we can note that this process obviously has a number of characteristics:

1.  The process always takes place in a context of choices to be made—choices between sources of supply, choices between kinds of products, choices between brands in the category. We might note that there seem also to be some kinds of choice between the needs which have to be satisfied at the moment.
2.  The choices by different customers who seem to be subject to similar influences are, nevertheless, noticeably different.
3.  The choices seem to be the result of a number of external factors, at least in part, and probably some personal internal factors as well.
4.  Individual choices over time must be relatively stable and consistent—definitely not erratic—and, therefore, should be predictable individually as well as in mass.

Consistency and regularity in a choice made could only result from the operation of some sort of formal relationships between the forces influencing action, the internal reaction mechanisms of the customers, and the subsequent result of this interaction. The first approximation of the exchange process could thus be viewed as a four-point framework as in Figure 2-1. Individual potential consumers become aware of their own needs and those of the other members of the purchasing unit for which they serve as purchasing agent and gatekeeper. At the same time, they become aware of various communications concerning objective means of fulfilling the needs in these desire-sets. These desire-sets are then translated into specific shopping lists based on past experience, acquired tastes and new knowledge. The desire-sets so defined, they seek out and choose sellers with offering assortments which come closest to meeting the assortment they have decided upon, rejecting competitors whose assortments are less compatible. In return, they

**Figure 2-1.  Simplified Framework (Model) of the Exchange Process**

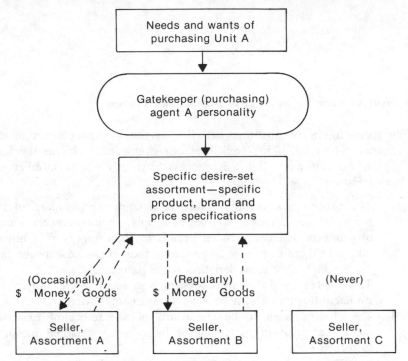

sacrifice some of their resources as a price to obtain the components of their desired shopping lists. The desire-set may well contain some elements not perfectly matched by any assortment offered. When possible, they will occasionally seek out other assortments containing these desired goods. There will also be other assortment offerings on the market they do not consider adequate for their desire-sets, and they will not patronize them at all. (But other consumers will find their desire-set values better matched by this third group.)

It would appear from this that we need a knowledge of the kinds of external forces which can have an effect on consumers, on the way in which these influences work, and on the role of the internal psychological mechanisms in translating external and internal forces into specific kinds of reactions—into shopping lists, for example. We would look to psychology for useful information as to the nature and methods by which these forces work within the individual. But we need to extend our search beyond the limits of individual psychology into the field of social psychology, anthropology, sociology, communications research, and economics in order to get the complete picture.

Our brief supermarket example, of a type any of us could easily observe, indicates the need for an understanding of the internal forces by showing how people in similar situations make different choices. Thelma and Debbie chose different brands of some products, different products for similar purposes. The shopping behavior of housewife number three indicates that some elements of social class structure may play a part. The results of their choices indicate that, in some cases at least, external business communications such as advertising, display and sampling can have an effect, but a different degree of effect on different people. Since the purchase situation is precisely the subject of economics, we would hope that the economist could give us some help.

Let us return to our supermarket example in the first chapter to see what our observations of the three women shoppers might suggest as to the kinds of knowledge we need to understand consumer behavior, and the sources from which we might obtain that knowledge. One aspect of that observation was that there were noticeable differences in the shopping behavior of the three housewives that we met. In the case of at least two of the housewives, the social backgrounds and family composition were so similar that they could not account for the differences in behavior—which leads us to conclude that some of the differences were due to internal factors of some sort, and therefore should be within the province of the psychology of the individual.

### The Differences in Reaction of Different People
### Under the Same Circumstances

Both Thelma and Debbie chose the same source of supply for the weekly shopping. Quite clearly, they had somewhat similar assortment desires and the choices each made indicated considerable similarity of menu goals. However, Thelma chose oatmeal for her breakfast food while the second housewife chose a prepared cereal. Thelma chose to buy an already baked cake while Debbie chose a cake mix, even though both desired the same flavor. Thus, in the matter of the cake, at least, Thelma was shopping for a somewhat different use-system than was Debbie. Presented with a chance to try a new product, Thelma purchased the innovation; Debbie chose not to. While both desired frozen orange juice, one bought an advertised brand, the other did not.

Had we had more time and more depth of observation, we might very well have noticed quite a few other differences in the buying behavior of these two women with obviously similar needs and backgrounds. But we do notice that one is more willing to try an innovation, the other apparently less willing. One appears to be more responsive than the other to external communications influences such as heavy national advertising. One apparently chooses to get the same end result, a baked cake, with less labor than the other, while choosing a breakfast food needing more preparation. Nor are these differences any greater than, or even as great as, many of the differences we notice between different individuals in similar situations all around us every day.

Such differences are obviously the rule, not the exception. No one store satisfies the assortment desires of all the people in any sizeable community. Even to do a good job of meeting the needs of one well-defined set of segments of the local market, any well-managed supermarket stocks from 7,000 to 8,000 items, and some as many as 15,000 or more. Any one customer never buys more than a few hundred of these items. Nevertheless, a large fraction of the buyers find it necessary to shop more than one supermarket in any given week to get the assortments they need.

Nor is this phenomenon purely a food store matter. Every major shopping center must have several department stores, each with its own core of customers, but each also, by itself, unable to meet the full assortment needs of many of the customers, no matter how homogeneous the local community served. Indeed, the very existence of multiple brands in every kind of product category is testimony to the divergent needs of buyers of all types.

It is obvious that some people are much more ready to accept the new than are others. This is true also of some industrial buyers, despite their asserted technical knowledge and objectivity. New products never reach their full potential market immediately. Furthermore, some people seem to be much more susceptible to external communications on a particular offering than others. Why do some individuals respond more readily to such external stimuli than do others? Why do some people accept the sales messages directed to them, others ignore them?

It is also clear that the two women had somewhat different perception as to the value of a brand. How did they acquire these value perceptions? No one is born with them.

Some of the differences, of course, need no interpretation from psychologists. One factor in Thelma's choice of soap was the fact that she had a water conditioner that reduced the need for detergents. And her statement indicates that another factor in her use of soap was her own mother's previous favorable experience with it and thus came from social sources. Thus, we have another set of factors in this situation that seem somewhat certain—that these housewives are responding to some social influences. To learn how these are exerted, we would expect some help from social psychologists, sociologists, or anthropologists, or all three (depending on where you put the dividing line between these disciplines).

## The Various Kinds of Social Influences

Some of the similarities between the first two housewives obviously have their origin in social factors. Both seem to have the same kind of family composition and a number of their purchases obviously reflect the needs of that family. In fact, all three housewives, in addition, were playing the same role, that of purchasing agent, not only for their own desires, but for that of the desires of the rest of the family. Because both of the first two housewives had small children, both of them were obviously aiming toward a menu adapted to children's tastes: chocolate cake, not angel food cake, peanut butter in quantity, baby food to take care of the baby (the fact that both bought the same brand suggests that this may have been a brand either suggested or prescribed by an outside professional, their pediatrician). The third housewife went to the store she did because it had the kinds of meats at the prices she desired to meet the needs of her husband. Thus one of the influences involved is that of the family of which the person is currently a member.

But there are also other kinds of family influences, some of them visible in the situation and some of them possibly not. We are all members of the family in which we grow up. In Anglo America this is not the same family of which we become a member after marriage. Thus Thelma noted that she picked the soap her mother had used, a value she had obtained in the family situation at home. We can assume that some of her other tastes and even some of her use-systems came from a similar source.

There is some hint that their class memberships were also a factor in their choices. The third housewife, for example, apparently laid much more stress on meat in her menu planning because that was her husband's desire. Her husband had a different kind of occupation, that of a supervisory skilled worker of the upper-lower class, as compared with the middle management positions held by the husbands of the other two women—a position giving them status in the middle class. This was reflected in the menu choices she made and this in turn influenced the store she would choose.

The choices offered by the store were also a factor in the situation of the choices they made. The assortments of the store which we visited were such that they attracted Thelma and her neighbor Debbie, whereas the assortment of a different supermarket attracted the third housewife.

But there are other business influences. Within our supermarket, we found a prominent display stimulated purchasing of a product that obviously was already a part of the diet. In another instance, a sample demonstration occasioned a trial of an entirely new product by one of the two first housewives, but not the other. And the consistency with which one housewife bought the most heavily advertised brand and the other one tended to avoid them, indicates that business communications such as advertising have some kind of effect in the choices that are made, but that the effect is different for different people.

Most of the purchases obviously took into account the needs of others for whom the housewife was playing the role of purchasing agent and also as gatekeeper (in determining the brands). But in thinking back over the situation, we noted that both of the housewives made another purchase which apparently met a personal immediate need even though it related to their role in the family. Both of them, we now remember, picked up the current issue of the supermarket woman's magazine, a product in which the rest of the family members quite probably had no interest and so did not include in their desire-sets. Thus, some of the shopping occurred in response to a form of internal personal stimulus for which the magazine provided some kind of satisfaction.

### The Consumer Purchase Situation—An Analytical
### Framework, or Model

We are now in a position to consider a more detailed version of the consumer purchase situation than we had in Figure 2-1. It is clear by now that the purchase situation starts with an awareness of two sets of needs: needs of the purchasing unit for which the gatekeeper is handling the procurement, and the gatekeeper's own personal needs relevant to the particular shopping effort. These become inputs to the gatekeeper's own internal reaction mechanisms and are shaped both by the person's own individual personality and by a number of external influences, including the culture and subcultures of which the individual is a member, the reference groups that they look to for their standards, the face-to-face groups such as family and close friends and associates who serve as sources of information for their buying, external authority figures such as physicians and others who define and prescribe what will meet their needs, market communications themselves— salesmen, advertising display, demonstrations, and so forth—as well as publicity, and finally the factors of the availability of the various choices which might meet their needs.

The result is a translation of the satisfaction desire-set into a specific shopping list, an assortment of types of goods and services, and specific brands of each type, at specific price levels deemed sufficient. This assortment is then matched against the price and product assortments available from various competitors and the one which comes out closest will get most of the business regularly. Specialty items—a rare coffee or wine vinegar, for example—not available at one's usual supermarket, may be obtained by occasional purchases from another supplier whose assortment is not otherwise deemed quite as good a match of the desire-set shopping list. Other competing sellers, whose assortments are considered poorer matches by this specific gatekeeper, will probably be ignored completely, even though they are main sources for other gatekeepers. Figure 2-2 depicts this more detailed analytical framework.

In fulfilling these needs, the customer is always making a choice between various assortments. First, the assortment of outlets which might be used to obtain the various products in the package they desire. Second, once at that outlet, they are making further choices: choices between brands, between types of products which might fit the same need, between forms of those products, all in terms of their fit to a specific satisfaction desire-set sought, translated into a shopping list.

## The Desire-Set Assortment—The Determining Factor in Consumer Reaction to an Offering

Every exchange situation revolves around a specific assortment of multiple satisfactions sought by the buyer—a desire-set even when only a single specific item is the visible result of the purchase. This desire-set is what brings about the exchange between the buyer and a specific seller, among all of those making competing offerings. Let us consider two typical shopping operations: first, that of John Counts, a young accountant, and, second, that of Arpa Inc., an auto parts supply manufacturer selling to both the OEM (original equipment) markets and the auto after-market with a very broad line of automobile parts. Counts has decided he needs a new business suit and Arpa is deciding on their yearly contract for a major production supply of their abrasives (papers and grinding wheels, and so forth).

## John Counts Shops for a Suit

The yellow pages in John's telephone directory have several columns of listings of men's clothing stores and, in addition, the area is well served with five major department stores and their branches. However, John does not consider any stores but those in a single shopping center

**Figure 2-2. More Detailed Depiction (Model) of the Exchange Process**

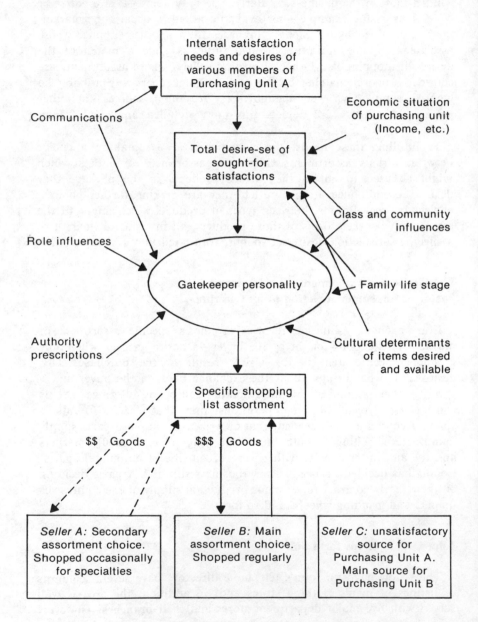

which is located relatively near his home. Thus, the first service he buys is the *location* which the store had chosen when it set up shop. Before he starts out he has also decided approximately how much he is going to pay for a suit. Although he knows that he can buy a suit for as little as $65 in the shopping center or in one of the shops he passes on the way to it, he has no interest in suits in this price class. He knows from past experience that the quality of tailoring does not meet his needs for relatively durable good grooming. Sixty-five dollar suits do not keep their shape long enough for the kind of wear he gives a suit. He thus has already made a choice of the *price line and quality product* services offered by stores. He knows he will have to pay in the neighborhood of $125 for the kind of suit he wants. When he reaches the shopping center he goes briefly through one of the better department stores of the three located in the center, and also checks over what might be available in two of the four men's shops in the center. He disregards the other two department stores because he finds that the styles do not suit his taste nor does he find the kinds of assortments that he desires.

He bypasses one of the other men's shops because he found that it caters largely to a high school clientele and does not carry suits of the sort he considers appropriate for his needs. The other shop, he has found, does not give very much help in his shopping and even at times does not clearly label what is included in a special sale and what is not.

Thus, even before he makes a serious effort to purchase, he has already relied on the availability of six different services in his desire-set: store location, price line, and product quality, styling and assortment services and sales aid. In addition, he has already bought a seventh. He visited the particular shopping center because it had at least three stores he considered as possibilities and knew that he might have to look over the assortment of all three. In this sense, he has also bought a *shopping complex* service. After briefly looking over the stock in the chosen stores, John finally settled on Erday's and goes back to make a final choice among the styles that had already been pointed out to him by a very helpful sales clerk. The suit he finally chooses is one that he thinks sets off his appearance favorably and is appropriate to everyday wear on his job. He has thus put a value on a *personal fit* and *in-style service* and also on a degree of *social approval* of the nature of his purchase. He uses his credit card for the purchase because this is somewhat easier than giving a check and he does not normally like to carry around with him the kind of cash required for such a purchase, even though he has no intention of letting the credit billing run into time payments. He has thus made use of only one of the two values available in the credit end of the business, the ease of not carrying cash. He has rejected the ability to defer payment.

The clerk boxes the suit and hands him a bill of sale which indicates that John has bought a physical object described as a suit—a combination of cloth, buttons, trimmings, cut and tailored in a certain manner. But what John has really paid for is the convenience of a store located close to home and to the other stores in the shopping center, a price line and quality of a sort he desired, an ability to inspect a large assortment in order to obtain the kind of fit and appearance he considers best, the purchase aid of a sales clerk and part of a credit service. All of these were in the original desire-set and and most of these decisions were made consciously.

Furthermore, this assortment of services was in itself really a single product which the store management had designed and put together. It had not merely bought an assortment of suits and hung them on racks. Long before John made his shopping trip, the store had carefully researched location in relation to the kinds of customers which it had hoped to obtain, carefully chosen each item with relation to a particular clientele, and trained its sales clerks in sensing the needs of individual customers. Thus, it was no accident that John made his purchase at this particular shop.

Although we tend to think of industrial purchasing as being a different sort of operation, when we analyze it we can see that it has parallels with the individual consumer purchase.

### Arpa Inc. Contracts for Its Year's Supply of Abrasives

Arpa is quite aware that there is practically no physical differentiation in the grinding wheels, papers and other abrasives produced by the different companies. All of them are made by pretty much the same processes and all do a good job of removing metal in a finishing operation. Moreover, all brands charge the same price. Yet, although there are at least six potential suppliers for Arpa abrasives, the purchases are carefully divided between only two of them in a very meticulous ratio—60 per cent to Baker Company and 40 per cent to Fox Company. Clearly, Arpa sees some kinds of differences among the six different suppliers in terms of its desire-set, and even differences between the two from whom they purchase.

When we talk to Carlson, Arpa's purchasing agent, and ask him why, he points out that Baker has the most complete distributor stocks in the area and can expect to deliver on short notice in any emergency. He, therefore, is reasonably certain that, no matter what he might suddenly need, Baker will have available the kinds and qualities of abrasives that he uses to keep the production lines running. Baker gives the best availability service in the area. In addition, Baker salesmen and their technical representatives, who are available for consultation on special production problems, have been very helpful in the past in showing Arpa how to use abrasives to reduce cost. Their *engineering service*, in his opinion, is as good as such a service can be and, for this reason, he gives Baker a preferred position as an abrasive supplier and a "participation" percentage as high as the company is willing to give a single supplier.

However, it is the company's policy never to depend on a single supplier. A strike against the supplier, interrupted deliveries due to transportation difficulties, or other contingencies could shut down Arpa's plants if they depended on just one source. Therefore, Arpa goes to Fox Company for another 40 percent of their supplies as *insurance* against production line cut-offs. Fox's distribution is not as good as Baker's, and although their engineering service is sound it is not quite as brilliant as Baker's. Indeed, Carlson would be perfectly willing to give Fox 50 percent if they would just improve these two elements to approach the performance of the Baker Company.

Thus, as Carlson tells us, their desire-set contained more than the need for good abrasives. They were looking for a group of intangible services which were the product of the Baker and Fox sales departments—a well-organized system of distributors and technical services under the control of their sales operation. The physical product was no different, in Arpa's opinion, but the desire-set included other things that in some ways were more important than the physical product itself.

The desire-sets of both John Counts and Arpa included far more than the physical items being purchased. In the case of Arpa's purchase of abrasives, the deciding factors in the choice of the particular brand were a set of intangible services completely divorced from the physical product itself. In the case of John Counts' suit purchase, some of the reasons for his choice were embodied in the design of the products at the factory: the style, the pattern, the quality of tailoring, and so forth. Others were created by the store management itself: the store assortments, the sales service, the store location and credit arrangements. In some industrial goods such as process equipment, for example, the reason for choosing a particular product might very well be the physical design, and in some consumer products such as beer and soap the choice of product might well prove to be the result of well established advertising associations.

Whichever is the case, the buyer is looking for these as much as he is for the product itself and he will pay whatever premium he thinks worthwhile to get it. This premium may be money or more frequent patronage, as it was in the case of Arpa.

Thus, what the factory ships out from its inventory is not the complete product in terms of buyer value. The buyer is as much interested in the elements created by the sales department—the distributor relationships, sales promotion efforts, and in the case of mechanical goods, in the service network. The well-known success of the Volkswagen in the American market was primarily the result of recognizing the need for a really good service network before launching sales in any territory. The failure of a number of other much more attractive European makes in the early invasion of the American automobile market resulted from a failure to establish just such service networks.

An exact match between a buyer desire-set and an assortment of goods and services is seldom or never achieved by any one seller. Part of this is due to some kind of incompatibility of these various elements in the desire-set as was the case in Arpa's need of assurance of supply. Some is due to the inevitable compromises made necessary by mass production, preventing the myriad of custom variations necessary to match the highly varied desire-sets of different individual buyers. Indeed, some buyer desire-sets may be so poorly matched by any of the offerings extant that they are in constant search for a better match of product offerings and their desire-sets. No matter how broad his line, no seller can satisfy all of any market, or satisfy well all those to whom he sells. This is why new competition is always possible, whether in the market or in politics. An offering carefully designed to meet the needs of the buyer on the fringes of the segments served by a number of other sellers can always create its own market segment.

## Plan of the Book

The remainder of this book will outline what we know about the way consumers, both as individuals and as groups, come to possess their highly varied desire-sets. We will try to show the psychological and sociological bases for the extreme variation between individual consumers and also for the high degree of comparability and harmony of needs which make possible the development of a single design for a lot of people. The next four chapters will sketch the most important highlights of our knowledge about the individual and the development of his tastes, desires, motives and choices, illustrating the marketing significance of the major psychological findings presented. The section following will deal with the individual consumer as a reflection of the external forces which shape the content of his learning and the making of his decisions—the forces of the general culture and subculture in which he exists, the standards he acquires in his various roles as a member of specific social groups and social class, the influence of the family and current family status and of other face-to-face groups on the content of his desire sets.

The fourth section will consider the strategies by which consumers make their choices, both of established products and of new introductions, including fashions and fads.

The fifth section will translate the meaning of these behavioral patterns into the specifics of market management, showing how they affect the seller's actions in the matters of the positive product and product availability side of his offering, the communications intended to inform the consumer of these products and product availabilities, and the negative avoidance or price side of any offering.

Finally, the epilogue will raise some questions of marketing conduct the student must answer for himself.

## Summary

1.   The problem of choice is at the heart of all consumer behavior, and the kinds of choices made by any one buyer tend to be consistent, but the choices of different buyers are divergent.

2.   The exchange process clearly starts with some kind of list of purchasing unit needs. These are then translated by the gatekeeper and purchasing agent into a shopping list assortment and bought from the seller whose offering assortment comes closest to the assortment on the shopping list.

3.   Consumer desire-sets differ so widely that any one seller must offer a much broader range than any one buyer purchases, and even then he can satisfy only part of the market.

4.   To explain the predictability of individual choices and the diversity of the choices of different people, we need to tap the knowledge of several behavioral disciplines.

5.   Psychology can help us understand those choices which arise from internal personality factors.

6.   Sociology, social psychology, and anthropology help us comprehend the nature of the influences which come from outside the individual.

7.   A reasonably complete model of the exchange process starts with the needs and wants of the purchasing unit (themselves the result of both internal and external forces), resulting in a desire-set of sought for satisfactions. These are in turn translated into a specific shopping list by the gatekeeper, as shaped by his own personality under additional

external influences. This desire-set assortment is then purchased from one or more sellers according to the assortments they offer.

8. Even for a single product or commodity, the desire-set normally contains elements in addition to those embodied in the physical product, whether the purchase be for the simplest of consumer items, or for a complex bit of industrial machinery.

## Chapter 2 Exercises

1. Select two supermarkets under different ownership, located closely enough together to be competitors. Observe the general appearance and character of each store, its breadth of lines, use of store brands, customers, apparent promotional and price policies. How do the two stores differ in character and in the nature of trade they seem to have? Do the two seem to draw the same kinds of customers? If not, why do you think the patronage differs?

2. Make the same kind of observations and analysis for two different department stores in the same shopping center.

3. Think about those of your acquaintances you think you know fairly well. If something new comes along, are there any among them who you think are most likely to be the first to try it? In all kinds of products, or in just some, and if so, which ones? Are there any who seem usually to be among the last to try in any one purchase area?

4. Among your friends and acquaintances, are there any who generally buy only the well-known and established brands? Are there any who seem to pay little attention to brand?

5. Think over which supermarket is your favorite for foods. Why do you pick that one?
    Which restaurant for a meal? Why?
    Which clothing store? Why?

6. If you were to move into a strange community, how would you go about finding a food store you would like? Why?
    What would you look for in a motorcycle or automobile dealer? In a clothing store?
    If you ski, what do you look for in a ski resort?

# PART II.
# The Psychological Endowment
# of the Individual Consumer

PART I DESCRIBED some of the observable differences in consumer reactions which need to be understood and predicted in any kind of market planning. Consideration was also given to the possible internal and external stimuli shaping the response of a given consumer to a specific marketing situation. Since identical external forces result in divergent consumer choices, any study of consumer behavior must understand what psychology has learned about how the adult consumer has come to develop his own individual personality—his own unique reactions to market offerings.

How did the once helpless baby, incapable of any decisions, develop into an adult with definite preferences in nearly every marketing or exchange situation?

He learned, and what he learned was largely a set of specific habits and habitual response tendencies or biases we label as attitudes. Learning of habits is a lengthy process, and undoing any habit is an even more lengthy process. Thus attitudes and any other habits are highly resistant to change.

External communications or other stimuli aimed at changing consumer habits must cope with the consumer's tendency to filter out and ignore all but the tiniest fraction of every kind of stimuli, and to interpret those which he does admit to his attention in terms of habitual perception patterns.

**3**

Consumer Reaction Tendencies
and the Factors
Influencing Them

INBORN TENDENCIES

    Reflexes
    Drives
    Stimulus Needs

CONDITIONED REFLEXES

THE MYTH OF PUSHBUTTON BEHAVIOR

DRIVES AS INTERNAL STIMULI

MOTIVES AS CONDITIONED DRIVES

COMMON CLASSES OF MOTIVES

    Certainty and Familiarity
    Attachment and Affiliation
    Dependency and Social Approval
    Independence and Desire for Personal Achievement
    Escape from Unpleasant Feelings
    Hostility and Aggression
    Adherence to Set Standards of Value
    Identification

ALL HUMANS SHARE one trait in common—they are active and reactive to both the world around them and apparently also to some kinds of internal drives. From the moment of birth, the most obvious characteristic of the healthy baby is his activity during waking hours—his constant attention and response to items in his environment, and also to some kinds of internal tensions.

As the consumer matures, he continues to react to both external and internal influences. Strong experimental evidence, in fact, has shown that the need for relatively constant external stimulation is basic to existence. Individuals who are experimentally deprived of all sources of external stimuli tend to, in common parlance, "go to pieces" (Bexton, et al., 1954).

Such activity and reactivity, however, is not random, even in the baby. Nor is it uniform, even in adults. As people mature, they obviously tend to exercise a great deal of selectivity in the stimuli they react to, and the same stimulus will call forth different reactions in different people, except for the simplest of inborn tendencies—the common congenital reflexes.

## The Inborn Reaction Tendencies

Some of our actions are born with us, in the form of simple muscular, natural *reflexes*—responses to outside stimuli. Any baby whose lips are brushed makes a sucking motion automatically. If the soles of his feet are tickled, he lifts and spreads his toes automatically. When an unexpected loud noise occurs, baby and adult alike react with something known as a startle response: a sudden flexing of the muscles, a forward thrust of the head, shoulders and arms, and a tension of the legs—a preparation of the individual to defend himself. When the doctor strikes one's leg just below the knee with a rubber hammer he produces the knee jerk familiar to all of us from physical examinations.

These are reaction mechanisms with which we are born and which come as a result of some external stimulus. There are many of them and most of them tend to be a means of self protection. We touch a hot surface and our hand immediately pulls away before we even think of it. These natural reflexes become conditioned through various kinds of learning, to form a part of the reaction of individuals in any exchange process. A great many of the reflexes are the source of our emotional reactions. The startle responses and withdrawals form the basis of the adult emotion of fear, or of a tendency to avoid the risk of trying new products. However, although we all come equipped with about the same set of reflexes, the degree of our sensitivity to various stimuli can vary substantially.

Some of our other actions take place without any obvious external stimulus of any sort. We eat because we feel hungry. The feeling itself comes from inside us and will be there regardless of whether or not there is any food in front of us. We have a number of quite easily identifiable *drives* of this sort; among the more important are thirst, hunger, sleep, and the pain we feel when our hands get too close to a fire.

In addition, we have a number of other forms of inborn tendencies toward action that are not so easily defined and to which different psychologists prefer to give different names. Some psychologists call this other set "stimulus needs." Whatever they are called, there is no real controversy concerning their existence. One of the most important of these is the obvious need for some kind of *continuous sensory stimulation*, the need for some outside reason for reacting. Stimulation itself, however, is not enough. We need a change in stimulus or, as some psychologists define it, we need *stimulus variability* (Kagan and Havemann, 1968). Under this term are included reactions some psychologists have named as activity and manipulation drives, and curiosity.

Many kinds of marketing efforts—fads and fashions in particular—succeed because of this drive for stimulus variability. Brand switching among classes of goods with relatively minor satisfaction differentials is also the result of the consumer seeking some degree of novelty.

Another "stimulus need" seems to be a drive for continuously higher degrees of *complexity in the stimuli*. There is also considerable experimental evidence to indicate that human beings and animals need some form of *physical contact* during their developing years. And, finally, it is obvious that very early in life children begin to show a desire for some kind of *certainty* in their environment and in the actions taking place around them.

Just where the congenital stimulus needs leave off and the needs which seem to be acquired by learning begin is not known for certain. *Desire for companionship* and *affiliation* with other human beings seems to develop very early. Nearly all develop some form of *depen-*

*dency* on the presence of others. At the same time, there seems to be the opposite drive for some kind of *independence and achievement.* All of us like to *escape from unpleasant* feelings, and some form of *hostility* is a universal trait.

Most inborn tendencies, however, are important only as building blocks out of which the personality is shaped through learning—through various kinds of conditioning. There are unquestioned differences in individuals at birth. At least one very thorough piece of limited research indicates that the learning process itself faces quite a different reception from different individuals from shortly after birth until well into adulthood. There are also unquestioned differences in the sensitivity of people to various stimuli. We have only to note the fact of color blindness among an appreciable percentage of the population, for example, and the difference in the ability of people to respond to various frequencies of sound and to music, while others are tone-deaf, to realize that there must be many kinds of differences between individuals which have their origin in the congenital mechanisms with which we are born.

Nevertheless, it is true that most of what we are and many of our differences in tastes and reactions are the result of experiences which cause us to learn various and quite divergent reactions to various specific stimuli.

Except for the reflexes, none of our other tendencies are attached at birth to any very specific external stimuli. It is only through learning that such associations and attachments are developed. The process by which we develop them is called *conditioning.* We can understand consumer behavior only to the extent that we understand the way in which the rather simple mechanisms or tendencies toward reactions with which we are born become, through a process of learning, the complex sets of motives toward action which every adult possesses.

## Reflexes and Conditioned Reflexes

A newborn baby reacts with a startle response to an unexpected loud noise in the vicinity. His reaction is no different from that which an adult exhibits in the same circumstances. But an adult will also exhibit the same behavior if he picks up his newspaper and reads that the loaf of bread for which he has been paying thirty-five cents now costs sixty cents. The baby, looking at the same page, will have no specific reaction of any sort. The adult, in other words, has now broadened the startle response to include reactions to symbols on a page and, of course, to many other things, such as a sudden victory by a visiting team which was thought to be unquestionably outclassed, or a headlined warning that the plastic insulation he had been told was safe is a serious fire hazard. The process by which we come to attach many of these original reactions to various kinds of events is known as conditioning and our inborn reflexes are the basis for many kinds of adult emotional reactions.

The classic experiments which established or demonstrated the process of reflex conditioning were those of Pavlov, the Russian psychologist. In the early part of the century, Pavlov demonstrated that he could cause a dog to react to an irrelevant stimulus, such as the tick of a metronome, in the same way that the animal responded to the feel of food in his mouth—that is, with a copious flow of saliva. Before conditioning, the dog would salivate only at the sight or taste of food. The experiment consisted of repeatedly introducing a conditioned stimulus (ticking metronome) at the same time an unconditioned stimulus (food) was offered to the dog. The dog got to the point where the salivary glands would start excreting saliva at the sound of the metronome without the food. Thereafter, if the dog received food at least part of the time when the metronome was sounded (and the interesting part of the experiment was that it need be only sometimes) his salivary glands would continue to excrete saliva whenever a metronome was sounded.

Pairing the food with the sound established a *conditioned reflex* and by continually pairing sound with the food, at least part of the time, this conditioned reflex was strengthened and kept alive, a process the psychologist called *reinforcement*. Although any such reflex can be conditioned to respond to almost any kind of stimulus—at least any kind that is not directly negative or which causes pain for example—some degree of reinforcement is also a necessity for the continued existence of the conditioned reflex. Otherwise the response tends to disappear after a time in which no reinforcement is received. The initial conditioning sets up a degree of expectations and unless these expectations are fulfilled occasionally, the conditioning is cancelled.

We see much the same phenomenon in the market place. Advertising that makes broad promises may build up a set of consumer expectations which cause people to buy the product initially but also will cause them to cease buying when the claims are not fulfilled. This is one reason that a mail order catalog, for example, is one of the most accurate pieces of promotion ever devised by commercial organizations. When a picture of a product appears in a mail order catalog, that picture must look exactly as the product will be perceived by a normal buyer and the language itself must promise nothing that cannot be delivered. This is the only way to keep the customer.

Mail order selling can survive only by permitting the customer to freely return anything he has bought. The customer whose experience with the product does not live up to initial expectations is not at all hesitant about making use of this return privilege. Thus the mail order seller is constantly aware of something that other sellers sometimes ignore: the buyer who has been led (conditioned) to respond to an offer by a form of advertising, will cease to respond, and in this case even respond in a negative way, when those expectations are not met.

Indeed, the kind of conditioning we seek in the market place, that of continuing patronage, can only be established by the perceived performance of the product itself. Any marketing strategy which relies on mere promotional claims without reinforcement by product performance is sooner or later self-defeating.

Reflexes are not the only inborn tendencies that are conditioned by experiences and forces of various kinds around us. Our drives are also conditioned. Indeed, they become associated with specific stimuli only through various kinds of conditioning processes.

However, the final results of conditioning of drives in an adult are not the simple mechanisms exhibited in a conditioned reflex. They are usually a complex of processes which are known as *operant tasks* (such as the response to an advertisement) and the process of reaching them is known as *operant conditioning*. Before we discuss these, however, let us look at the way the results of the earlier experiments in conditioned reflexes influenced the way people view the responses of individuals to promotion and propaganda of any kind.

## The Push Button Model of Consumer Behavior

A popular view of human behavior might be called a push button or puppet model. The early experimental work on the conditioning of reflexes led almost directly to a widespread and erroneous picture of the learning process and behavior in general. This common model is best labeled the *push button* or *puppet model*.

Under this conception of human behavior, we can shape people's actions and attitudes by simple conditioning of reflexes and thereafter can call forth these reactions whenever desired by simply pushing the right button or pulling the right string. That is, the human being has no choice in the matter and reacts automatically to external influences.

If we accept the view of the classical economist, all we need do to make the consumer buy is to set a low enough price. This will automatically cause him to buy. The beginning student in marketing too often believes that all we need do to solve a business problem is to appropriate enough money for advertising and under the deluge of this torrent of communications the consumer will be conditioned to buy whatever it is we have to offer him.

There are many other variations of this misconception of human behavior and there was a period in which they were widely accepted in business. The general model is expressed in psychological terms by the symbolism S-R, meaning that *stimulus evokes response*. It is no accident that John Watson, the leading American exponent in the 1920s of "behaviorism" (as the emphasis on the conditioned reflex was then known), was hired, at the peak of prominence, as a consultant to the largest advertising agency in the United States.

However, advertising agencies, and anybody else who has tried over a period of time to sell the public on anything, have learned that pushing the right button or pulling the right string not only does not always bring forth the desired reaction, it does not get any reaction at all most of the time, or the string-pulling may even bring about a negative reaction. The reason is that a large portion of our behavior is governed not by our reflexes but by our internal drives, and many of our actions take place as a result of some kind of internal drive.

### The Importance of Internal Drives

What many overlooked at the time when the S-R model was in fashion, was that Pavlov made certain that an intense drive for food was present in the subjects of his experiments. Indeed, practically all experiments in conditioning start out with a subject—dog, rat or pigeon—whose drive has been aroused and is in force. The hunger drive is most easily manipulated and so is commonly used. Pavlov did not start with dogs who had just eaten a full meal. He started with dogs who had been intentionally deprived of food for some time.

The reason for this is simple: A satisfied drive does not respond to a stimulus of any kind.

Action, therefore, on most things originates inside the individual, excluding reflex actions such as the knee jerk. It starts with a tension which we call a *drive*. The individual gets hungry and becomes active in order to find some means of eliminating the tension we call hunger. Activity ceases when something occurs which relieves this hunger tension. Generally, of course, relief is obtained by taking in some food through the normal channels, through the mouth into the stomach. However, anything that removes the hunger tension extinguishes the drive. A hungry rat that is injected with a nutrient solution apparently gets the same pleasant reaction as one who gets visible food (Epstein and Teitelman, 1962).

Reflexes and drives are two different sorts of phenomena. A reflex is a specific reaction to a specific external force or event and it is automatic. Most such reflexes seem to fulfill some form of defensive survival need. The startle response, for example, is a preparation to fight. A withdrawal response to any form of pain is, by its automatic nature, a means of keeping to the absolute minimum any danger that is causing pain. The tendency of the pupil of the eye to narrow when the light becomes brighter is a way of defending the retina against too much exposure to light. Even the tendency of the baby's lips to make a sucking motion when brushed is an aid to his gaining food at a time when sucking is the only way he can satisfy his hunger drive. (Perhaps the fundamental nature of this sucking reflex explains why it is so difficult to retrain people not to smoke cigarettes even though they know smoking to be a positive danger to their continued physical existence.)

## The Nature of Drives

A *drive*, on the other hand, is not an act but a condition—a condition of tension within the individual. It is not in itself a stimulus to action, but it is the cause of restless searching for a cue or stimulus that will relieve the tension. Because reflexes are observable and noncontroversial, there is no difference of terminology among psychologists in this area. But a drive is something we can not see—we see only its results. The term "drive" is, therefore, a label for an unseen source of rather diffuse activity. Psychologists differ on the usability of certain kinds of labels. Some psychologists prefer to include as *drives* only the well-established congenital drives about which there is definite evidence: those of *hunger, thirst, pain,* and so forth. They would reserve terms such as "motives" to define the tensions that are equally effective in adults but which are the result of learning of some kind, as are *wishes* and *desires*. Other psychologists speak of the recognized congenital drives as *primary drives*, and speak of *secondary drives* as those resulting from some sort of learning and conditioning process. From the standpoint of those who are interested in consumer behavior, the distinction is not important.

In its initial form in the baby, a drive has no definite focus. It is only through learning that the infant, as it grows, comes to perceive that certain objects fulfill certain drives—these objects then become goals toward which the drives have a motive to approach. Only then does a drive become focused on the possible possession of a specific object or event as a recognized means to relieve his inner tension.

A human being of any age—whether baby or man—will respond with a knee jerk reaction automatically whenever the physician taps the area just below the knee with a rubber mallet. But when suffering the pangs of hunger, the newborn baby just gets restless and cries. By contrast, the adult man may seek out a specific meal or, if he makes a vocal reaction of any sort, he may say to a companion, "I'm hungry, let's stop at McDonald's for a hamburger." The baby's cry is not the equivalent of the man's proposal—it is just a pain reaction. The man's reaction, by contrast, is goal-oriented.

A reflex, in other words, always results in a specific response at any age. A drive does not. A drive is a situation of internal tension, not an action response. It is a sense of deprivation or imbalance in need of relief or satisfaction, and it exists apart from any external force. The initial reaction is just restless, unfocused activity until something external occurs to relieve the tension. In the case of the hunger drive, some source of nutrient relieves the tension. Once satisfied with food, the tension disappears. The drive is extinguished. It is aroused again only when the conditions (body chemistry in the case of hunger) give rise to it again.

Satisfaction of the drive gives pleasure, the pleasure of released tension, and this becomes a source of conditioning—of learning to approach or seek out whatever satisfied the drive in the first place. But it does not give rise to this approach reaction immediately, only when the drive is again aroused to an active state. Thus, the man is motivated to seek food only when hungry, and then seeks out the hamburger stand because he has learned that such a meal relieves his hunger (and also, incidentally, satisfies a number of other motives at the same time—or else he might have appeased his hunger in some other way he has learned will satisfy the same tension).

Thus, reactions to drives differ from reflex reactions in at least two ways. In the case of a drive, all of the stimuli effective in evoking an approach reaction are learned. There is no initial specific congenital reaction mechanism which can be conditioned or re-conditioned. Furthermore, the approach reaction is intermittent—a drive is not always potentially active, a reflex is. The learning that takes place in connection with a drive is not a simple single muscular reaction, but a whole process, in psychological terminology—an *operant task*. Even the pigeon's pecking for corn is a series of procedures: a feeling of hunger, an approach to the button, the peck itself, the retrieval of the corn kernel which appears, the swallowing of the corn. Only then is the hunger satisfied.

The food that we seek is not the stimulus for the hunger reaction but a *clue* that the internal hunger stimulus will be satisfied. As noted above, we learn to associate many kinds of goals with the same drive and we will seek out a hamburger stand at one time when we are hungry, and in a different situation (perhaps on a date) we may seek out a steak dinner in an expensive restaurant. The hunger drive is present in both circumstances, but other drives also are involved in both. We may seek out the hamburger stand because we have goals or activities in mind which will require some time to accomplish and we do not want to take much time to eat. On the date, we may be concerned primarily with the social aspects of the meal, and also be seeking a situation in which we can relax and not be preoccupied with other things.

Furthermore, given the same combination of goals or drives, other people may seek quite different solutions than the hamburger stand or the restaurant. One simply stops off in his kitchen, and pops a frozen dinner into an electronic oven to get a meal as quickly as he would have at a fast food outlet. Or, a third person who has foresight of the need to save time brings his lunch. Obviously, what we are dealing with in any person, more than a few weeks beyond his birth, is a set of learned reactions that come as a result of the drives. A term commonly used to refer to both primary and secondary drives is the word *motive*. In general, a motive can be defined as a goal that, *through learning*, has acquired *value* for the individual.

## Motives

All of us have an infinite number of potential motives affecting our behavior. There are a few special classes of motives which seem to be rather general in their nature, but which can, in any given individual, be manifested in various ways.

One of the most important motives that we all seem to have is a desire for *certainty* and *familiarity*. This, of course, is coupled with a desire to avoid the unknown and the uncertain. Like all motives, the strength of these desires will vary from one individual to another, since they are partly the matter of learning. Thus one person may be willing to take a great many chances to explore the unknown while another will cling to a product that is quite unsatisfactory rather than try an alternative unless he has very strong evidence that the new product is certain to give the results that he desires.

Recent research gives strong evidence that some of this difference in reaction to the new and unknown is congenital. A thorough longitudinal study of personality of children, which focused on the same children from the age of two weeks and continued until they reached teenage, has revealed that individuals have quite stable patterns of reaction to new experiences of any sort. Some children, generally characterized by their mothers as "good babies," accepted new foods without question and approached strangers on first sight. Others rejected the food almost to the point of starvation before they would try something new. They shrank and hid from strangers. Some of the children proved to be between the two opposite types during the whole period of the study. Their reaction was to at first reject and avoid the new but to gradually accept and become accustomed to it over a period of time (Thomas, Chess and Burch, 1970).

Whether congenital or learned (or more likely a mixture of the two in most people), the desire for certainty seems to operate strongly for most people at times. It is probable that only the degree of desire differs greatly.

Since marketing is essentially concerned, in considerable part, with getting people to accept something unusual and new, this general tendency toward desire for certainty and familiarity could be a very important aspect of the way in which new products can be launched. Later material will discuss some of the factors involved in getting people to accept the new.

Another group of factors, extremely important in learning, has been characterized by psychologists under the headings of *attachment and affiliation motives*, *dependency motives*, and *social approval.* It is certain that conditioning plays a part in all of these, starting with the relationship between the baby and its mother. The mother becomes a perceived source of satisfaction of hunger and thirst, and relief of pain, as well as many kinds of pleasant sensory stimulation. It would be strange if a desire for the mother's presence did not become one of the first motives the infant acquires. Later on, the child learns to associate the acquisition of many kinds of satisfactions with the presence of other members of the family. Through the principle of generalization of stimulus (which will be discussed later under *learning*) the individual finally acquires a desire to be affiliated with others, to be close to people, perhaps to join clubs, to be a member of other groups, and to take part in and to look for other goals centering around pleasant social relations. Psychologists now believe that sex motives among human beings are in part a result of this kind of conditioning. Sex in humans does not manifest itself in the same manner as it does among the lower animals—as an intermittent thing depending on the time. The sex act itself is often due as much to a desire for companionship and affection as to the natural impulse itself.

Similarly, the baby early learns to associate various symbols and actions of adults around him with approval of his behavior. A kiss or a pat on the cheek may serve as a reward for certain kinds of behavior. As he learns the use of language symbols, he discovers that the kiss or pat on the cheek classifies acts connected with the word "good." Like the other social motives, these become generalized and attached to other people around us, those in the groups to which we believe we belong.

The extent to which such social approval motives figure in much advertising is so obvious that we hardly need to press the point. In fact, a major part of the value the consumer ascribes to many products is due to an inbuilt cue that possessing them will become a source of social approval.

A burlap sack might provide as much warmth as a good-looking dress, but the properly chosen dress, unlike the sack, can be seen as a source of approval of those around us. Even businesses themselves have been known to change their methods of operation for reasons unconnected with profit, but directly connected with the problem of having a socially approved "acceptable" kind of business. One firm, for example, which had built a fairly high degree of success by the heavy promotion of consumer credit, labored for years to find a way to transform their business into one that was primarily cash (and inherently less profitable thereby) because the pure credit operation carried with it a certain degree of social stigma.

It would be strange if people did not become conditioned to some degree of *dependency* on others to satisfy their drives and wishes. The baby is wholly dependent for the first year or two of its life on the mother or other members of the family for the satisfaction of its wishes and drives. It cannot feed itself, or protect itself from the cold, or escape from the pain caused by an unfastened safety pin except through the help of others. Even though parents normally discourage too much dependency as the child grows older, a great deal of the dependency motive is bound to persist. There are few of us so independent that we will not lean on others for advice and financial help, or for recommendations as to the possible sources of satisfaction of some of our motives. When changing to a different make of car, we frequently draw on the experience and knowledge of others, and the diffusion of any really new innovation is accomplished largely through a chain of word-of-mouth advice and assurance from close associates.

A quite opposite motive that parents try to instill in children with various degrees of success is *independence* and with it a *desire for personal achievement*. Social approval is brought to bear to get children to please parents by acting like a "big" boy or girl. Children are given tasks to perform on their own and are praised for achieving these tasks independently. The degree of success to which people are conditioned to so respond will vary from person to person, partly because of the degree of success of the family, partly because of social class situations. The child that grows up in a family of eight children necessarily achieves some degree of independence if he is to get his motives satisfied at all. Social class and culture, as well as family, have a great effect on attitudes toward achievement.

A very broad set of motives can be grouped under the heading of *escape from unpleasant feelings*. The reaction to something painful to touch is an inborn quick muscular withdrawal from the contact. Later, as the child learns to fear or dislike many things which initially are neutral to him, he learns to develop various other kinds of physical or symbolic avoidance reactions. The use of credit for purchases is often a means of escaping from the unpleasant fact of paying a full price immediately. The dribbles of installments can be much less painful.

The individual early finds that the need to satisfy his own wishes often comes into direct conflict with the desires of others to satisfy their own wishes, and one of the problems of growing up is learning to accommodate oneself to the desires of others. He learns that he cannot always get what he wants when he wants it.

As a result, *hostility* is at times a motive of every normal person, though its presence may not be acknowledged. A person may even desire to inflict worry, discomfort, and pain on others, and may resent their achievements or possessions. Hostility often leads to a type of behavior called *aggression*. Hostility is frequently a factor in the resistance to the introduction of new types of products, particularly ones that are not already familiar to society. For example, women who first started to wear pant suits, even tastefully designed and attractive outfits, found themselves barred from better restaurants in many places, while the clothing being worn by some women who were admitted to the same establishments was far from what was generally considered modest. For years, owners and drivers of small cars were made aware of the resentment felt by others who were driving larger and more powerful vehicles. Whenever they passed a slower moving larger car, the latter would be savagely accelerated to regain the lead.

In one sense, social disapproval is a generalized form of individual hostility and does, of course, manifest itself in hostile reactions by those around the individual.

Those trying to sell or introduce the radically new often meet with directly hostile reactions. Thus, the early county agents who attempted to persuade farmers to use some of the modern agricultural methods were not accepted by the farmers, and the farmers' hostility was generalized and extended towards the state agricultural college with which the agents were connected. This feeling of hostility persisted among large numbers of farmers as late as twenty years after the first introduction of the county agents, in spite of the achievement of a considerable degree of success on their part in getting farmers to adopt new kinds of farming methods and equipment.

Hostility reactions are particularly important to those who are involved in "selling" political candidates or political ideas at election times. A major problem of every school board is the hostility of organized groups of voters who are against increased taxation for any reason, whatever its benefit, and often do not understand the need for certain types of schooling in the classroom. The resulting sales problem requires more advance planning than it usually gets.

A set of motives that may be related to hostility are those under the psychologist-coined heading of *domination*—a desire to be in a position to force other people to behave in accordance with one's own wishes. This often is manifested in adults as a generalized desire for power or symbolic proof that we have power, a desire for signs that other people are respectful and can be dominated. Without question, some of the motives loosely called "status" motives come under this heading—the motive to acquire goods as symbols of higher rank in the community than is enjoyed by others around the buyer: to own the most expensive car, for example, as a proof that greater buying power has been acquired; to wear the most dazzling frock when attending the opera; or to be a member of an exclusive country club which many others are not permitted to join.

It is probable that many people so motivated have some degree of anxiety concerning whether or not they really have the kind of power they seek to symbolize, whether they really are living up to the material standards of the community. These are the people to whom advertisements directed toward a conformity pattern are probably most effective.

All of us, as we reach adulthood, acquire something that is called a *set of standards* or *values*. That is, we acquire motives that lead us to act according to concepts of what society expects of us and what we expect of ourselves. Early sociologists referred to this concept as the "mirror-self," and psychologists tend to refer to it as the *ego ideal*: our notion of how we would think and behave if we were as perfect as we would like to be.

For many people, these standards are acquired through the process of *identification*. Among teenagers in the adolescent period, this normally means the process of identifying with others in the peer group, of conforming as closely as possible, in many superficial characteristics at least, to those with whom we are in daily contact at our own age level.

For teenagers, as for others, the standards usually come to us through a process of identifying with other people whom we admire— athletic heroes, actors and actresses, or others whose glamorous or power positions we aspire to obtain. For all of us, any groups to whose status we aspire can be a powerful influence, and many of the things that teenagers do and much of their buying is centered on the general aspiration of any teenager to be accepted as an adult.

There can be little doubt, for example, that teenagers get into smoking habits because they associate smoking with adulthood, especially since the first contact with smoking is seldom really an enjoyable experience in and of itself (except to the degree that learning to smoke builds on the sucking reflex we have as new-born babies, and is thus an extension of infantile behavior).

Most of these standards are acquired, of course, through the face-to-face groups of which we are members, such as peer groups among teenagers, our parents, our community at large and the class of which we are a part. These standards tend to lead us to hope to acquire the visible material symbols of the status of the group to which we aspire.

It is common for people in such a situation to "go overboard" to acquire such symbols. The freshman newly arrived on the campus of a school away from home will immediately buy all the various symbols that he sees as associated with the school and with those who are upper-classmen, to adopt new hair styles in accordance with what is popular among those in his own classrooms, to acquire various school symbols, identifying them with the new groups rather than with his home town and home people. He will try to furnish his quarters, when he has a choice, with the kinds of furnishings that these people have and in general to alter his manner of dress and personal habits to accord with those he sees among others with a slightly higher status.

Such aspirational ideals and values are the basis for a great deal of selling and even for a degree of exploitation of those in one of the more critical transitional times of life, the period between late adolescence and early adulthood. Even without commercial exploitation, the young woman in this period of her life is the heaviest buyer and user of cosmetics, and is by far the biggest part of the market for dress clothes, according to the standards of her time and group. This is also the period which makes her the potential buyer of goods which are touted to her as symbols of the established young married woman she may aspire to be—the sterling silverware and the various household furnishing items such as fine china, and pots and pans, that are alleged to make her a good housewife and "gracious hostess," when and if she gets married. To some degree, these efforts also exploit an attitude toward woman's role in our society, giving high rank to her role as housewife.

All motives or classes of motives are based on some form of generalized attitude toward people and events or objects. The line between motives and attitudes is not a clear one, but we can make the distinction that a motive is one of the active forces impelling a specific action, usually rooted in a generalized attitude which is simply a favorable or unfavorable tendency toward action in a specific direction for a whole class of situations.

## Summary

1.  The human being is born with a number of tendencies toward reaction to stimuli in his environment.

2.  Some of these tendencies, called reflexes, consist of automatic responses to external stimuli.

3.  Others, designated as drives, are simply a type of general internal tension or restlessness which can be satisfied through some kind of external stimulus, but not, initially, by any one specific stimulus—hunger, for example, is relieved when the body receives nutrient in any form, through any means.

4.  A third set of congenital reaction tendencies, stimulus needs, is more difficult to define than either reflexes or drives. These include the need for change in the environment.

5.  These simple congenital reaction tendencies are modified into the complex of reaction tendencies exhibited by adults through various forms of learning or conditioning.

6.  Only the congenital muscular reflexes are automatic responses, called forth at any and all times by the appropriate stimulus. The complex of motivating forces built on the drives and stimulus needs are operative only when aroused through increasing deprivation. Even then, the kind and degree of response will vary from one individual to another. The consumer is no puppet, responding to the pull of a string or the press of a button.

7.  Specific motives are the result of learning to perceive specific products or services as possible sources of satisfaction of one of the drives. They may be emotional or cognitive in nature, usually both.

8.  The number of possible motives is infinite, and they vary from one individual to another. However, certain general classes of motives seem to be practically universal: desires for certainty and familiarity,

for attachment and affiliation, for dependency and social approval, for independence and personal achievement, for aggression and domination, for adherence to specific standards of action, for identification with others.

9. Some of these blend into the more generalized form of reaction tendencies we call attitudes.

## Chapter 3 Exercises

1. A common cliche refers to the difficulty of finding a gift for the man "who has everything." Why is this a problem? Why should such a person value a gift?

2. *Advertising Age* runs a monthly summary of new product introductions. Skim back through the issues of 4 or 5 years ago and pick out 20 major ad campaigns (headlined in the news section) and product launchings which seemed to be treated as outstanding at the time. On the basis of currently observable and obtainable information, how many appear to have been as successful as touted, how many have disappeared and been forgotten? If they were so great, why did consumers not respond?

3. A World War II veteran who had been with an artillery battalion which was sent to Hawaii for advanced training noted that most of the men in his outfit would steal pineapple from the surrounding fields, and knew enough to cut bananas green and let them ripen. But out of the 100 stateside reared men in his battery, only 5 could be induced to even try a taste of a papaya, and the veteran was the only one who even thought to ask about the mangoes which grew on the trees of the little farm hamlet in which they were stationed. What common drive or motive would account for the difference in attitudes toward these tropical fruits?

4. Quite a few foods have the reputation of taking quite a bit of getting used to before a taste for them is developed. What motive seems likely to cause people to continue trying and using such foods, beverages and tobacco, which are seldom physically pleasant at first)? What motive accounts for the later enjoyment of such products?

5. List some products or other kinds of offerings for which the motive for acquisition and usage seems to be one of escape? Can you name some which would serve such a motive for some people as well as one which is more physically or socially functional for others?

6. It has been claimed that when black-and-white television first became popular, some families who had no set nevertheless purchased antennas and installed them on their roofs. What general class of motive might account for such behavior?

7. What class of motive or drive could account for the ready sale of sweatshirts with school names and seals and the use of school or fraternity decals on the rear windshields of cars? Can you name other products whose sale is heavily dependent on this motive?

8. Observers have noted that children frequently exhibit some seemingly contrary behavior. When they make a path up a steep bank, it seems almost always to be straight up, and at the steepest part. They take a "short-cut" to school which requires climbing up such banks and over other obstacles which consume at least as much time as they might save, and much more energy. What class of motive would seem to account for such refusal to take the easy path?

9. Golf seems to be a game of pure frustration. Even the pros are often in trouble, blow a shot, or miss what appears to be an easy putt. Nor is getting on a course either cheap or easy. Players often have to wait for hours for their turn. Yet golf is a growing sport, and widely popular already. What motive seems to explain this kind of consumer behavior?

10. Name some offerings whose purchase motive seems to be mainly due to the motive of hostility and aggression. For these same offerings and industries, what motives other than these could account for the interest of some of the purchasers?

11. One of the more obvious aspects of the fashion phenomenon is that of "over-adoption"—or the tendency of some individuals to follow a fashion ill-suited to their personal needs. In women's garments, for example, the "micro-mini style" dress (extremely short skirts) looked good only on women whose legs were unusually long and slender, and whose bust development was not pronounced. Yet they came to be worn by the too-chubby, the bandy-legged, and the knock-kneed, as well as many with obviously mature figures. The long-skirted, full-bosomed "prairie style" which succeeded it for a time was well suited to the woman with a mature figure, but came

to be worn also by even flat-breasted youngsters. What motives can you give for this over-adoption phenomenon?

**4**

# Attitudes: The Personality Factor
# in Consumer Choice

ATTITUDES AS THE DELINEATOR OF PERSONALITY

DIMENSIONS OF AN ATTITUDE: DIRECTION AND STRENGTH

ATTITUDE FUNCTIONS

Instrumental or Utilitarian
Value Expressive
Ego Defensive
Knowledge Integrating

THE LEARNING OF ATTITUDES

THE COMPONENTS OF AN ATTITUDE: BELIEF, EMOTION, ACTION

BALANCE OR COGNITIVE DISSONANCE THEORY

Approach/Avoidance Reactions and Cognitive Dissonance

ATTITUDES AS INFERENCES

RELATIONSHIP BETWEEN ATTITUDES AND ACTION

CONDITIONS LEADING TO ACTION

Hierarchy of Needs
Knowledge of Means
Incentive
Perceived Credibility of Success
Absence of Anxiety

IF SOMEONE WERE TO ask you, "What is thus-and-so like?", how would you describe him or her? You might, of course, focus on appearance: "Well, kind of tall, with reddish hair, and blue eyes." But if your questioner persisted, "But what kind of person is he?", wouldn't you respond in terms of something like, "thrifty, a sharp dresser, but never quite the first with the most extreme styles, likes sports cars, collects jazz records, not much interested in sports."? If so, you are describing his personality in terms of sets of attitudes—in terms of the ways you expect him to act in various kinds of specific situations. Indeed, the term *attitude* and the term personality trait are very closely related although some authors make a distinction, noting that some reaction tendencies denoted as personality traits are not directed toward specific objects, nor do they usually imply acceptance or rejection of objects (Britt, 1949).

Attitudes, on the other hand, are directed toward specific classes of objects or situations, and do contain elements of acceptance and rejection. They are, however, a very basic part of the individual's personality, and most of what the consumer is can be viewed as a bundle of those mental habits we label as attitudes. In our opening supermarket illustration, we noted that the specific brand and product purchase decision was shaped by the personality of the gatekeeper, and by this we meant that the specific choices were strongly influenced by the attitudes of whoever occupies this key role in the purchase process.

What do we mean when we say that a man is "thrifty," that he has a "thrift attitude?" We mean that he is the kind of man we would expect to pay close attention to gasoline mileage and to the repair experience of car owners as important considerations in the purchase of a car. We would know that he would shop around whenever making any substantial purchase. We might expect him to buy very few clothes at one time, and to get the maximum wear out of whatever he purchases. We would be certain that he knew all of the out-of-the-ordinary places to buy, the places where he would get the most out of his spending.

We might describe another person, perhaps his wife, as one with an attitude of "little patience with thrift" (perhaps as a negative learning reaction to childhood deprivation). We would expect her to avoid purchases which might be labeled as obviously inexpensive, to be suspicious of bargains and insist on considering first her main desires in relation to a product, and to look at the price tag only incidentally. She might pay much more attention to the kind of service she got at the gasoline service station and pay little attention to the price she paid for her gasoline.

Attitudes, thus, denote some kind of observable consistency in the actions people take and in the kinds of choices they make. They appear as some kind of generalized habit pattern, habits with both an emotional and a cognitive or belief content.

## What Is an Attitude?

Attitudes are certainly the most important habits the consumer has. Like all habits, they simplify the decision process, place the consumer in a position to act without a time-consuming search and careful weighing of all possible alternatives every time he has a purchase to make, and thus enable him to maximize his satisfactions.

Attitudes differ from motor habits, however, in that they are not set procedural action sequences. They are, instead, a set of guidelines or standards for the making of choices in specific types of situations. They define which kinds of action choices are worth considering, and thus set limits on any search effort or cogitation concerning alternatives.

All but a minute fraction of our choices are based on these habitual attitudes including, of course, most of our decisions in any exchange situation. Much of the job of any seller is either to reinforce an attitude favorable to him or to attempt to change one which is less favorable.

Patronage loyalty and brand loyalty are attitudes, as are matters of personal taste, personal perceptions of value, perceptions of what is relatively important and worth spending money for, and how much should be spent, and so forth.

An attitude is probably best defined as a predisposition to evaluate some purchase, product, service, symbol, object, or other stimulus in a favorable or unfavorable light. An attitude is thus a predetermined tendency, ahead of any need to act on any specific matter, to choose to act in a given direction and to avoid actions in the opposite direction. The terms "bias" and "prejudice" are descriptions of attitudes. They are a form of readiness to act in one certain way, and are always a combination of a set of beliefs and a set of feelings in some degree of harmony with these beliefs.

## The Dimensions of Attitudes

Not all attitudes are of equal importance or are equally entrenched in our personalities. Some are relatively simple, relatively trivial, and subject to easy change—such as the preference for a specific brand of laundry detergent among a number of brands we do not consider very different. Some are quite complex, heavily weighted with emotional content, and deeply imbedded in a complex of the individual's reaction patterns. One such complex attitude is that of a chain cigarette smoker toward his smoking habit.

Attitudes thus are characterized by at least two important dimensions —those of direction and strength. With regard to any particular purchase or choice of any relevant kind, they can be positive, neutral, or negative. The strength of an attitude can vary from the very lightly held, subject to easy change (such as the choice of a particular brand of paper towels) to the opposite extreme of very deep commitment, almost completely resistant to change.

Direction is obvious, if we know the attitude. Sherif and his colleagues have suggested a useful way to measure commitment— determining the ratio of the latitude of acceptance to the latitude of rejection (Sherif, et al., 1961).

The latitude of acceptance can be measured by the number of alternatives deemed acceptable, and the latitude of rejection by the number of alternatives considered unacceptable. Alternatives neither accepted nor rejected define the area of noncommitment. The narrower the latitude of acceptance, and the less the area of noncommitment, the greater the commitment to the attitude, and the more resistant the attitude to change. An obvious corollary is that it would be easier to shift an alternative from the noncommitted column to the acceptable than from the rejected to the acceptable. This is one reason why it is easier to develop a market niche for a completely new market entry—by definition, part of the area of noncommitment in most cases—than to get consumers to switch to a rejected known brand. It is also another reason why products whose reputation has declined are best dropped and a completely fresh market entry made under a new brand label.

Phrasing the principle in less abstract terms, the fewer the number of brands considered acceptable and the greater classed as unacceptable, the more the difficulty of switching brand loyalty. In this terminology, convenience goods are those categories toward which the buyer has very little attitudinal commitment and specialty goods those toward which he is deeply committed to one specific brand and quality.

### The Functional Aspects of Attitudes

As with all of our psychological tendencies, attitudes exist because they serve the general purpose of maximizing the holder's satisfactions or defending him from pain of some sort. All of any consumer's attitudes can be classified under four specific classes of function (Katz, 1960): utilitarian (also designated as adjustive or instrumental), value-expressive, ego-defensive, and knowledge-integrating.

*Instrumental* or *utilitarian* attitudes are adopted primarily to save search effort, through capitalizing on either direct or vicarious experience, in order to obtain the optimum level of satisfaction with the available resources of time and effort. Among the more common types of utilitarian attitudes would be those of patronage loyalty, brand loyalty, and some kinds, at least, of taste preferences. We discover, largely through trial of conveniently located supermarkets, that one in particular carries the qualities and types of meats and produce we prefer, at reasonable prices, and the major brands of packaged foods we like, so we generally patronize that market for our weekly shopping and pay little attention to the offerings in other stores. We find the general merchandise assortments at a given department store generally fit our tastes and pocketbook best, and so look there for what we want before shopping at any other outlet. We come to prefer certain colors or color combinations in garments in terms of the way they enhance our appearance, and tend to pass over items not in this range.

Most such instrumental attitudes evolve out of experience with differences we discover in the offerings available to us. But such attitudes as brand loyalty may develop even when the available choices may possess absolutely no objectively perceivable differences, and become quite firmly established. This was demonstrated by W. T. Tucker in a carefully designed experiment with identical loaves of bread (Tucker, 1964).

In the Tucker experiment, forty-two randomly chosen housewives in the same section of the city agreed to participate in an experiment on "how women went about purchasing when they moved to a new location and were faced with unfamiliar brands." On twelve successive occasions, each was visited at her home and offered her choice of one of four loaves of bread, presented side-by-side on a tray. All loaves were of the same single type of bread, all were packaged identically, and all four were from the same batch of baking. The only difference was in the "brand" label—a single capital letter, L, M, P, and H. Each time the housewife was offered the loaves, the position had been rotated (according to a Latin Square design), so that no brand was in the same position two times in a row.

No suggestion was made or implied about any possible difference in the quality of the loaves offered. She was simply asked to choose one, and a notation was made as to her choice. Nevertheless, exactly half of the forty-two subjects confined their choices to a single brand, for at least three successive choices, sometime after the start—in most cases after preliminary trials of the other "brands." Once she had made such a choice three times in a row, her loyalty was tested by taping a penny to the brand she had selected least often, and an additional penny added each day she did not switch to this premium brand. No housewife switched when the first penny was added. Six housewives later switched, for amounts ranging from two to seven cents (maximum possible, seven cents). Eight housewives never switched, indicating that their brand loyalty had acquired substantial strength, despite lack of any discernible objective difference in brands.

One interesting finding was that at least five of the remaining twenty-one housewives had developed, not a brand loyalty, but a position loyalty—they always chose the loaf with the same position on the tray. The loyalty of three of these was also tested. Two switched for premiums of one and two cents, respectively. The other switched to a different nonpremium position after three cents was added. This experiment indicates that consumers may develop some kind of brand loyalty (or other attitude) without any substantive basis in experience, probably to conserve search. Such an attitude proved, in this experiment at least, to be just as strong as one with an objective basis. This is another reason for being first on the market with an offering.

Most brand loyalty, of course, is based on some kind of perceptible difference in available offerings, and we would expect the strength of the loyalty to vary with the degree of such perceivable differences. This seems to accord with the results of a study made by Banks. A panel of 465 housewives was asked to state individual purchase intentions concerning seven common household items, and then after three weeks their actual purchases were compared with their predicted purchases. Among the seven items studied, purchases were the same as predictions much oftener for coffee than for peanut butter, potato chips, mayonnaise and salad dressing, catsup, scouring powder, and ice cream (Banks, 1950). Coffee also happens to be an item in which the taste differences between brands is generally perceived as quite substantial, and has an objective basis in major differences in blend and degree of roast. Scouring powder ranked second in brand intention performance, and this also is a product for which perceived brand differences can be substantial, on an objective basis. The other items are generally offered with little noticeable difference between brands.

Instrumental and utilitarian attitudes such as store patronage and brand loyalty do tend, like all attitudes, to involve some emotional content, once established. But that emotional content is doubtless much less than for the next two functional classes of attitudes: attitudes serving a positive value-expressive function, and those serving an ego-defensive purpose.

*Value-expressive* attitudes help the individual to give positive expression to the type of person he conceives himself to be. Thus consumers tend to have a positive attitude toward purchases identifying themselves with specific groups or a specific social status—purchases which say "this is who I am." The teenager adopts the hair style and mode of dress currently popular with his or her peers (primarily to distinguish himself from earlier teen groups, and from his family, thus asserting his independence). The social climber works hard to gain the exclusive country club membership, buys a prestige make of automobile, moves to the "right" neighborhood, perhaps serves a premium liquor or wine—all as a means of proclaiming, to himself as well as to others, "See! I have arrived." The young adult male smokes cigarettes to show he is now a virile adult, or smokes a pipe, perhaps, to show he is a contemplative intellectual.

Those who have really arrived may actually engage in antistatus consumption, to demonstrate that their position is so well known they do not have to display it. In a luncheon conversation, a wealthy man remarked to the author that "I have never driven anything but a Cadillac since I first got my license at seventeen, but I think I'll get a Ford the next time. The last time I was out at the country club, there were only Cadillacs on the drive." This, too, was a value-expressive attitude, a way of saying, "I have always been there—I don't need to show it."

*Ego-defensive* attitudes serve to promote acts and other purchases which help to protect the individual from unpleasant objective truths about himself, or the realities of his life situation. Both definitive studies and long observation have shown that residents of the ghettos of our large cities are better customers for the premium-price brands of many items of personal consumption than are people with much greater purchasing power. It is the ghetto customer who buys the premium brand shoes, far oftener than the middle class customer. It is he who furnishes the market for the premium brands of hard liquor, especially the more prestigious Scotch whiskies. It is the woman with all of the svelte lines of a well-inflated balloon who spends heavily at the beauty parlor, the man well endowed around the middle who gets the best of custom-tailored clothes. Such purchases are a way of asserting to oneself, "I am not poor, I am not unattractive!"

Lastly, *knowledge-integrating attitudes* are responsible for acts and purchase behavior based on a search for information giving simplified organized meaning to the rather chaotic anarchy of the world around us, and the information we receive from it. The aim is to group under some label (often a too highly simplistic one) the varied offerings we see. Thus it was that during the late 1960s and the 1970s, large market segments would respond enthusiastically to any food label which said "natural," rather than man made. Vitamin C pills which were of rose hip origin brought twice the price of those which claimed no such "natural" origin, despite the fact that all vitamin C is chemically identical, and natural vitamins get just as much processing as do the man made type. "Low calorie" is always a magic touchstone to reach the dieters' market, even when the term really signifies very little aid for the corpulent. In politics, the simplistic labels of party, or of such factional designations as "liberal," "conservative," "socialist," and so forth, have served to shortcircuit careful thought.

## The Sources of Attitudes

With the possible exception of the bias with respect to learning situations already mentioned (Thomas, et al., 1970), attitudes are not part of any consumer's congenital equipment. They are learned. The feelings, beliefs, and attendant reaction tendencies are developed through associations of actions with need satisfactions—through experiences in what caused pleasure and thus is worth approaching, and what occasioned pain and should be avoided. Much of this learning is linked with thought and beliefs acquired through social communications with important people in the consumer's world (Lambert and Lambert, 1964).

A great many of the instrumental attitudes grow, as mentioned, out of direct experience with alternatives. But even these may result from a single trial at the suggestion of trusted associates (especially when faced with a new situation, such as finding shopping facilities in a new locality), and subsequent experience with a single alternative or narrow set which reasonably satisfies.

After that, the principle of satiation would operate to exclude further trial. Even in the case of direct experience, consumers stop far short of trial of all feasible alternatives if reasonably well satisfied with an early experience. In the Tucker bread choice experiment cited above, one housewife persisted with the first loaf she tried, and three more of those who became brand loyal did so before trying all four "brands."

Even many of the utilitarian attitudes, however, are the result of social conditioning, transmitted by conditioning of face-to-face groups as part of the general culture or the subculture. Such is the case of the great majority of taste preferences of all sorts, and of the general attitude toward spending priorities. Indeed, what the culture transmits is mostly a set of attitudes and use-systems. The individual first uses the item to conform to the group around him, or to gain social approval. Continued use creates familiarity, and a number of experiments have demonstrated that, when starting from a neutral position, familiarity alone will establish a favorable attitude.

Classical experiments by Maslow and Krugman demonstrated the effect of familiarity. In the Maslow study (Maslow, 1937), fifteen students took part in a ten-day series of two-hour sessions, during which they engaged in a number of activities including viewing a number of paintings by fifteen well-known artists, and spelling correctly the names of Russian women. During the last few sessions, they were offered something different, without warning, and requested to express some personal preference. In one of the experiments, the participants were asked to choose between the paintings they had been seeing and paired paintings by the same artists. In the case of the paintings and in the other activities, there was a general (but not universal) tendency to prefer the familiar.

Krugman (1943) had three students who preferred classical music and rarely listened to swing music play three swing records—toward which they were neutral—once a week for eight weeks. Likewise, he had three students with a strong liking for swing music play three recordings of classical music (they neither liked nor disliked) for the same period of eight weeks. At the end of that length of time, both sets of students had gained a favorable attitude toward the category of music against which they had been prejudiced.

Both ego-defensive and value-expressive attitudes are also clearly of social origin. The symbolic value attached to purchases and other actions which the individual uses are defined by external groups. Cadillac and Mercedes-Benz do not build prestige into their cars—society grants them that status.

In fact, Cadillac was just another of the more expensive cars until after the Great Depression of the 1930s removed the Pierce-Arrow and Peerless from the market, and caused Packard to downgrade its standing in a desperate search for economic survival at a time when expensive vehicles were not in demand. The Ford Motor Company can testify to the fact that it took more than mere company marketing effort to add Lincoln Continental to the prestige list. Essentially, value-expressive offerings get their definition as such through association with their possession by groups to which the consumer aspires to belong. (See the later chapter on reference groups.)

Likewise, knowledge integrating labels gain their meaning and orientation from reference groups.

The attitudes we thus acquire through learning are probably almost as numerous as the purchase and other reaction motives they give rise to and with which they are associated. Attitudes may concern extremely large topics like those of spending and world affairs, religion, or racial relations or they may refer to a small topic like the way suburban housing should look. Whatever their topic, and whatever their content, attitudes are extremely durable and persistent partly because they involve some of the more basic emotions as well as rather complete systems of belief and the action that results from the combination of belief and emotion. They can be changed only by changing both the beliefs and the emotions and also the habits of action which are associated with both. Changing attitudes, therefore, is the very complex reeducation process of major habit change, some of the problems of which will be discussed later. An important aspect of attitudes in general and of motives, is what is sometimes known as dissonance theory or balance theory.

## Balance or Dissonance Theory and Attitude Change

We have a great deal of experimental evidence to indicate that individuals do a great many things to convince themselves and others that they are rational and *consistent in their beliefs, emotions and actions*. Balance theory or dissonance theory rests on the assumption of the relatively universal applicability of this attitude. According to this concept, people strive to maintain a relative degree of consistency between their feelings on any subject or item, their beliefs concerning that subject, and their actions with relationship to it. When this balance or "homeostasis" is disturbed in any way—that is, when one of the elements is thrown out of line with either of the two, the individual tends to adjust the other two to bring them into line and into a new balance, or to restore the original condition of the element that was forced out of line.

The balance sought is between the three elements of *belief* (or *cognition*), *emotion* (or *affects*) and the *action* toward which both of these motivate the individual. If something forces an individual to change his beliefs, he must either change his feelings and subsequent actions to correspond, or repress the evidence as inadequate in order to protect the feelings and actions (Festinger, 1957).

For example, when authoritative evidence that smoking is extremely dangerous to health was presented in such a manner and with such insistence that smokers could not ignore it, very few stopped smoking, and most of those quitting backslid, according to at least one survey (Kassarjian and Cohen, 1965). Stopping the smoking habit proved too difficult, when the incentive was avoidance of a problem some distance in the future. To achieve balance, some smokers denied the validity of the evidence, regardless of the weight of its scientific backing (29 percent of the smokers in the Kassarjian and Cohen survey did so). The others strengthened their emotional support of the habit by various rationalizations (excuses): "There are lots of hazards in life," "I can die of lots of things," "Not much of a threat to me." Or they compared smoking to even worse alternatives: "Better (to smoke) than being a nervous wreck," "Better than taking pills," "Better than excessive drinking." Some simply commented: "can't stop," "like to smoke," "no guts," "lack of self control," and so forth.

Such defenses did not fully reduce the dissonance. Three out of five respondents obviously still were uneasy. In their discussions of teenage smoking they stated, "Teenagers who smoke are . . . not smart, ruining their health, showing off, foolish, crazy, misinformed," and so forth, indicating a considerable remnant of inner tension between their beliefs, emotions and their action in continuing to smoke.

Changes in belief are not the sole initiating force for dissonance, of course, although the principal one open to sellers, through advertising. A change in the emotions felt can force a need to reevaluate beliefs, or a forced change in action can bring a change in beliefs and/or emotions to be more in line with the action taken. Heavy smokers who previously have failed in attempts to break their habit find it quite possible to quit when faced with a diagnosis of incipient lung cancer or with a mild heart attack.

The powerful effect of emotional influences were visible in the abrupt switch of automobile preferences in the fall of 1973. Until then, the large, heavy automobile had remained the darling of a majority of automobile buyers, with "large" getting larger each model year until the Detroit definition of "compact" meant a larger car than the standard model of the previous decade. Then the Arab oil embargo gave emphasis to impending oil shortages—warnings of which had been publicized, but ignored, at least two years earlier. Suddenly, people feared for their freedom of movement and sharp rises in fuel costs made them aware of one of the disadvantages of size. Belief in the ultimate desirability of the biggest and most powerful disappeared overnight, as fear of rationing and the pinch of gasoline prices switched buyers to smaller vehicles and almost stopped the sale of the larger models for a time.

There is strong evidence, both experimental and observational, that action itself, even when artificially induced or forced, can modify the attitude structure by forcing both beliefs and feelings into line with the action undertaken. Subjects induced to defend a position they oppose tend to shift toward the position defended (Cohen, et al., 1959). The well-known disreputable market practice of "bait-and-switch" works on the principle of employing a mouth-watering bargain offer to lure the unsuspecting to commit themselves to active consideration of a purchase, then switching the customer to an obviously more attractive model, at a price he would have rejected outright originally. And the Tucker bread experiment showed that those who became "brand loyal" under rather artificial experimental conditions came to perceive major differences in the bread. When the premium pennies were put on the rejected brand, one subject is reported to have remarked, "No wonder you put the special on Brand P—it's the worst one of all."

On a somewhat less critical scale, the use of sampling in new product introduction is an attempt to use action (trial of a new and different brand or product) to influence both beliefs and feeling backing a previous brand attitude, by reducing the purchase risk to zero (and perhaps adding the minor social pressure of personal demonstration). It should be noted that the experiments on familiarity forced the subjects to take some action (pay attention), over a span of time.

Balance theory is especially important in the exchange process because nearly all purchases involve some kind of conflicting attitudes and motives. Any exchange requires the sacrifice of resources we value in order to acquire something else which we may value somewhat more. Thus, it becomes important to us in any such situation, but particularly in one that involves a major sacrifice such as the purchase of a car or home, to bolster our belief and feeling that we have acquired a much greater value than we have given up.

One of the pieces of experimental evidence for this balance theory was the study of some sixty-five people who had bought new automobiles within the previous month and a half, and another group of sixty people from the same neighborhood who had not bought new cars for at least three years. A survey of the kind of automotive advertising they had been reading showed that the owners of old cars showed no preference between makes in the kinds of advertisements they read, but of the new owners, two-thirds had recently read advertising describing the virtues of the car they had already purchased, and only one-third had read any advertisements for competing makes (Ehrlich, et al., 1957).

As this would indicate, a great deal of the advertising for major purchases may be directed as much to those who have already bought and need a message of reassurance as for those whom we hope to convert to new purchases.

But there are deeper implications than this for those who are introducing new products which have any capability of affecting the attitude of the individual, particularly products which affect the emotional attachments that individuals may have for their own conceived role in the groups of which they are members. Thus, convenience foods which seem to downgrade the skill of the housewife as a cook met considerable resistance at first, primarily because of the perceived downgrading. Sellers not only had to change the housewife's belief about the necessity of doing much of the work herself, but to change her feeling and her attitude about her whole operation. In some cases, this meant redesigning the product for somewhat less convenience or designing the product to include attributes which might be interpreted as reflecting favorably on some other aspect of the person's life. For example, the first angel food cake mixes that came out contained all the necessary ingredients, including dehydrated egg whites which are the primary ingredient of angel food cake. But one of the manufacturers discovered that by leaving out the egg whites, and advertising the cake as one with which you could "add your own fresh eggs," it not only gained a substantial share of the market, but also could charge a higher price. Presumably, in this way, they may have assuaged the housewife's feelings that she was not participating enough in the process.

Similarly, another manufacturer was unable to sell a fully automatic clothes washer that automatically adjusted the timing of the various elements in the cycle to correspond with the kind of load put in it, apparently because it deprived the housewife of any feeling of having an acceptable role in doing the wash. At an earlier time, another manufacturer was able to gain some market advantage by building a "suds saver" mechanism into his washer—a provision for recapturing the soapy water from one load of wash to use in the next load immediately following—advertising to the housewife that she could "save on hot water," thus relieving her possible guilt feelings at spending so much of the family's resources to do an automatic job.

### Predicting Action From a Knowledge of Motives and Attitudes

Both motives and attitudes are phenomena that we must infer from outside evidence. We cannot see into the subject's mind and no system of questioning, scaling or tests will give a fully objective measure of what the underlying motives or attitudes are, except in the case of purely instrumental attitudes.

Because instrumental attitudes tend to have a relatively low emotional content, their holders are usually able to give a conscious cognitive response to well-designed questioning. But many operating motives have a substantial affective content, of which the holder may be quite unconscious.

Moreover, even what is normally an instrumental attitude, such as patronage loyalty, may be a value-expressive one for some people. One consumer may patronize a prestige department store such as Marshall Field or Saks Fifth Avenue because the products, prices, and quality assortments of these stores come closest to his or her desire-set. Another, however, may buy in the same stores because these are the places "to be seen in." They may buy the merchandise because the Field or Saks label is the one which connotes the status they aspire to. In such a case, patronage loyalty will be value-expressive and carry the high affective content of such an attitude.

Generally speaking, the motives attached to such noninstrumental attitudes, with their high affective content, are not held at a conscious level. For such, all of the available methods (and one is tempted to predict that any possible methods) depend largely on the interpretive ability and analytical insight of the person directing the study. Usually, the heading of "motivation research" in any research text will detail a number of techniques which have proved useful when applied skillfully and the results applied solely on a mass statistical basis to discover widely held attitudes and behavioral goals. As detailed in a later chapter, the advertisers of Marlboro cigarettes used the knowledge gained in such a study of smokers' goals and attitudes to design a successful penetration of the cigarette market. But it is true that equally reputable researchers have come up with quite opposite recommendations concerning the same kind of product, using similar psychological methods.

Even when we feel we have a reasonably good knowledge of the attitudes, we cannot know how any given individual will react in a specific situation. There are four reasons for this. First, actions of any importance are seldom due to the operation of a single motive or attitude. Most are the resultant of the simultaneous operation of a number of attitudes and motives, some of which may be in direct conflict with others. Indeed, as already noted, the exchange situation always contains the inherent conflict between desire to obtain the product and the desire to avoid the sacrifice involved in getting it. Second, the actions of an individual are governed by the motive which is dominant at the moment—one which is the least well satisfied of all of those that might be operating within the situation. Only such aroused motives have any meaning with regard to activity. The third reason is that the complex of values, capabilities and knowledge which all of us have varies from one individual to another. As a result, different individuals will react in quite divergent ways to what seems to be the same situation, acting under what seems to be the same set of attitudes and motives. Activated by a power-seeking set of attitudes, one man enters business, the other goes into politics. One may buy a Ferrari, another take up big game hunting.

Moreover, wholly different attitudes may lead to the same action. One man may buy a prestige automobile to impress his neighbors. Another may have no bent toward status seeking of any sort, but purchase the identical model because he simply enjoys fine mechanisms of any sort.

Fourth, individuals differ greatly in their knowledge of alternatives for satisfaction of any sort, and thus will make different kinds of purchases for this reason alone. Attitudes are purely a directional bias or tendency, and the direction points to many kinds of possible purchase behavior.

The very fact that an attitude is not definitely focused on a particular kind of purchase action is the very meat of market opportunity, however. Whenever we can identify segments in the market with a strong set of attitudes and motives not already firmly fulfilled, we can hope to design a product and accompanying set of communications to gain a market niche, as happened in the Marlboro case (see Chapter 6). It was the knowledge that many women had guilt feelings about their social acceptability during the menstrual period which led to the development of vaginal sprays, which, however doubtful their objective utility, assuaged the guilty feelings and gave the desired confidence.

### The Hierarchy of Motives

As noted quite a bit earlier, most of our reactions as consumers are intended to satisfy a number of ends at the same time. A woman buys a coat to keep warm but also, perhaps, to look well dressed and to have something that makes her seem attractive, according to her standards. She may be thrifty in her attitude and thus seek a style which accomplishes these purposes but also which is not so extreme as to appear out of style several seasons hence, and is made in such a way and of such materials that it seems likely to last for those several seasons. The extent to which she will try to satisfy all of these will be limited also by the resources she has available to spend for this item and at the same time fulfill several other needs she feels must be met, such as shoes for the smaller children, tuition for her college-age son, or even the money necessary to go on next summer's vacation or to replace the family car.

Exactly how these and other varieties of motives involved in the same situation add up, will in turn be affected by the person's knowledge of tailoring fabrics, her acquaintance with the alternatives available in the other stores in town, and with the complex of tastes she has acquired through learning over her lifetime. Moreover, she may have a desire for a coat to meet all these motives, but not exercise it because at the moment she feels that her wardrobe is adequately stocked and that it is extremely important that her daughter's ballet lessons continue in spite of the considerable cost.

Differences in skills and abilities alone would result in quite different sets of actions to meet the same motive among different people. The desire to gain social approval and admiration of the associates and neighbors might, for example, lead one person to spend a great deal of money on carefully chosen clothes and another one to more or less neglect his appearance altogether and devote a great deal of time to landscaping his lawn. A third person might, instead, devote a great deal of time to conspicuous volunteer work in the community rather than satisfy his motives through spending patterns. A fourth might aim for community recognition through diligence in some musical skill or writing ability, or by running for office.

There is no magical connection between motive or attitude and subsequent spending behavior or lack of it. The very fact that we have so many possible operative motives requires that some of them be quiescent for the time being and others take precedent. The result is that all of the various motivational dispositions that we have are arranged in some sort of internal personal hierarchy. We seek to satisfy the topmost one in the hierarchy—that one that is the least satisfied. This motive then drops down the list and is replaced by another unsatisfied one. Thus it is that two individuals with similar motives, but different situations with regard to satisfaction, would react differently to an offering.

Before any motive results in behavior at least five conditions must be met:

1. We must have knowledge of means for satisfying that motive.
2. There must be no conflicting motive that is stronger or higher in the hierarchy.
3. There must be some incentive. We must see that undertaking the

action and making whatever sacrifice it requires will return a
greater value to us than we lose.
4.  The chance of success must be credible.
5.  There must be an absence of inhibiting anxiety.


## Gaining Knowledge of How to Satisfy a Motive or Attutide

One of the purposes of a great deal of marketing activity is to
increase people's knowledge of how they may satisfy particular motives
or attitudes. Thus a car dealer's advertisement in a time of gasoline
shortage and high prices may stress the good gas mileage of the cars
that are being offered, to draw attention to what is assumed to be a
dominant motive at the time. Another ad may imply, by its illustrations, something that is never stated verbally about how well the
product (a cigarette, for example) will satisfy the motive or need to be
approved as virile, as the Marlboro ads did and still do.

Obviously, from what has been said, the motive must be high in the
hierarchy in order to be chosen for satisfaction. The family may have a
fairly strong desire, for example, for a new automobile, but this may be
outranked by the need to meet tuition for the teenage children in
college.


## The Hierarchy of Motives—Key to Action

For an attitude to be a determinant of action, it must be at the top
of the hierarchy. Whatever attitude is least well satisfied will take
precedence and then, when satisfied, will give way to those lower in the
hierarchy. The consumer then turns his attention to fulfillment of the
next attitude in the pyramid.


## The Importance of an Incentive to Act

The need for incentive is overlooked by many would-be sellers in the
market. The potential buyer must see some promise of getting substantially greater satisfaction out of one offering than out of another
offering which competes for the same resource. Just what incentive will
appeal will differ from person to person, depending on what values he
puts on meeting the various motives involved in a given offering, but
the "me-too" product that offers no substantial benefit to any major
market segment is always doomed. The promised unique selling propo-

sition must have real perceivable values—must be viewed as really unique and desirable.


## The Need for Credibility of Benefit

It is not sufficient for the consumer to perceive the product as possibly satisfying a motive or fitting an attitude, or to perceive the possibility of a substantial added benefit as an incentive. Because he must sacrifice resources of some kind, he must also believe that the chance of gaining the desired end is relatively high. Thus, when the first home permanents were introduced to the toiletries market after World War II, it became crucial for the Toni Company to convince the women of the United States that the do-it-yourself wave was a true permanent, as lasting and attractive as the one they got at the beauty parlor. Until then, all true permanents had been beauty shop products, given at the hands of a trained operator. In order to gain this credibility, Toni spent its entire net receipts over a three year period, in advertising of almost unprecedented intensity, to get across just this one point: that a woman could do it herself, with attractive results.


## The Inhibiting Effect of Anxiety

A high degree of anxiety in any situation tends to inhibit behavior which has a perceivable degree of risk. Perhaps no period in one's life is more anxiety ridden than the adolescent period, when one passes from a stage of dependence on others to a stage in which a high degree of independence must be exhibited, yet knows that he lacks much of the knowledge of the adults whom he hopes to imitate. The result is a period in which conformity to the peer group becomes the highest of motives for most teenagers, and presents the greatest of problems for parents who hope to guide their actions, including their spending, into what they consider wise channels. Anxiety is a normal consequence of any role transition period through which a consumer passes many times in his life (see Chapter 7).


## Other Personality Influences on Behavior

The fact that personality enters into consumer decision is so obvious that marketing agencies are swept from time to time with enthusiasm for some form of personality segmentation measures of such behavior, under the banner of various catch phrases (motivation research and psychographics are two of the more recent). Except in the area of attitudes, and even there within limits indicated above, none of the methods touted has lived up to its billing. Although a substantial amount of research has been poured into attempts to correlate personality measures with buying, none has proved very fruitful for managerial use.

There are at least three fundamental reasons for these failures. First, the psychological measures of personality, and the concepts of the traits measured, were developed for quite different, nonmarketing goals—to suit the goals of the clinical psychologist. It would be pure happy accident if they fit the needs of marketing. Second, even if we could find some personality traits which correlated highly with kinds of buying behavior, we have no census of customers classified by personalities, and thus no clear way of segmenting our market approach. (Indirectly, of course, specific media attract specific groups of customers with some commonality of personality, although we seldom know exactly what this commonality is, in psychological terms.) Finally, it is difficult to perceive how a personality trait which was not also an attitude, or at least had given rise to a specific attitude, could affect marketing choices. By definition, all other traits have no characteristics of direction with respect to choice alternatives. It is the direction of the consumer's attitudes, and the goals he hopes to attain, which determine his market choices, and thus define market segments. These alone give much aid in planning products and assortments, and in guiding promotional communications.

Since attitudes themselves are the result of a complex learning process, the role of all marketing effort is to educate the consumer in some manner, and thus requires an understanding of the learning process.

**Summary**

1.  Differences in personal choices are due primarily to personal differences in the complex of attitudes which make up the individual's personality.

2.  An attitude is an habitual predisposition to evaluate a class of potential benefits or acts in a favorable or unfavorable light. Like all habits, attitudes serve to conserve energy by setting advance limits on search effort and cogitation.

3.  All attitudes have two important dimensions: direction and strength. Strength can be defined as the ratio of the number of alternatives which will be acceptable to those not accepted.

4. An attitude can serve one or more of four types of functions: instrumental or utilitarian, value-expressive, ego-defensive, or knowledge-integrating.

5. Instrumental attitudes normally develop out of objective experiences, out of learning which alternative sources of satisfaction optimize benefits or minimize unpleasant results. Included are most of the brand loyalty and patronage loyalty attitudes.

6. Value-expressive attitudes help the holder give positive expression to the kind of person he is, to convince himself and others of the status he believes he has.

7. Ego-defensive attitudes lead to choices intended to shield the person from the realities of himself and his situation.

8. Knowledge-integrating attitudes help the individual organize his knowledge of the chaotic world around him by furnishing useful labels for incoming information.

9. Attitudes are learned, some through direct experience; most, in part at least, through social conditioning and familiarization.

10. All attitudes have three components: the cognitive element of beliefs, an affective component of emotional involvement, and the action which normally results from the combination of the two.

11. Balance theory or cognitive dissonance theory holds that people try for consistency between the three elements of belief, affect, and action. Thus a change in any one creates an inner tension or drive which can only be reduced by bringing the three into a new alignment or balance.

12. According to balance theory, an attitude may be changed by acquisition of new information which influences the beliefs, by events changing the emotional content, or by inducing action counter to previous tendencies.

13. While the seller usually finds it easiest to work on the belief component through advertising and sales effort, some forms of promotion such as sampling also work to induce action as a means of attitude modification.

14. All purchases involve at least a minimal degree of mixed approach-avoidance reaction, and the compromise can be substantial for large purchases. Consequently, one function of advertising is to reduce after-purchase cognitive dissonance.

15. Sometimes the dissonance is so great as to make necessary design modification to offset tensions such as guilt feelings.

16. Neither attitudes nor specific motives can be observed or measured directly, but must be inferred from a mixture of test methods.

17. Even when measured skillfully and insightfully, knowledge of the motive or attitude does not enable prediction of specific individual

action. Most actions involve a mixture of motives, some conflicting. In the case of such conflict, the motive highest in the needs hierarchy tends to govern. Further, a number of alternatives may satisfy any one motive or attitude, and quite divergent attitudes may, in different individuals, lead to the identical action. However, sound information on widely held attitudes can be useful in revealing successful communications or product strategies.

18. All of the individual's attitudes are structured in some kind of temporary hierarchy, with the least well satisfied at the top. Once satisfied, the drive becomes inactive, giving way to the next one in order.

19. In order to result in action, any attitude or drive of any kind must meet five conditions: possession of knowledge of some means of satisfaction, absence of conflicting motives higher in the hierarchy, presence of substantial incentive for action, a belief in the chance for successful satisfaction, and an absence of inhibiting anxiety.

20. While there are many kinds of personality traits in addition to those connected with attitudes, none of the others seems to be of any value in explaining purchase choices.

## Chapter 4  Exercises

1. Describe thoroughly the personality of some close friend, as you see it. In how many situations could you predict what purchase choices he would make? If you had never seen his living quarters, do you think that you could describe reasonably well how they might be furnished, and how well  kept? If so, what would give you the clues?

2. Compare the attitudes which would lead one man to purchase a Jaguar sports model, and those of another man who might purchase a Mercedes-Benz diesel-powered sedan. Are there elements of similarity in the two cases? What elements are dissimilar?

3. Name five specific examples of offerings which most buyers would seem to be acquiring for value-expressive motives. Cite examples of customers who might well buy the same offerings for utilitarian reasons.

4.  List five specific offerings which might very well be purchased for ego-defensive reasons, and give the circumstances under which such would be the case. Under what kinds of circumstances would the same offerings be purchased for value-expressive reasons? For utilitarian motives?

5.  Find five words commonly used in advertising and other kinds of promotion which seem to be attempting to exploit the knowledge-integrating function.

6.  If cognitive dissonance theory is as valid as some of the evidence indicates, changing an attitude completely depends on changing all three components of that attitude: belief, emotion, and action. Which marketing and promotional tools are most effective in the case of each component, and how do they operate to accomplish their purposes?

7.  If we can describe people we know in terms of a set of attitudes, as the text claims, why should it be so difficult to study and identify specific attitudes, as the text also claims?

8.  The text lists five conditions which must be met before an attitude leads to appropriate action. Which of these can advertising, selling, or other promotional tools hope to affect? How? Which are not likely to be affected by any form of marketing communications? Why?

9.  In a discussion of fashion later in the text, some attention is given to the phenomenon of the classic: the style which is always in good taste whatever is popular at the moment, one which never changes much. Sellers can always identify such classics—the plain pump in women's shoes, the knee-length dress, auto designs like the 1947 Studebaker, specific colors, such as off-white in automobiles. Some consumers obviously concentrate largely on such designs. What attitudes would lead to such behavior?

10. Consider the various body models available in the automobile market. (Don't forget the pick-up truck, which is often a family passenger vehicle as well.) Describe the attitudes which seem likely to lead to the purchase of each.

# Learning to Behave
# the Way We Do

OUTLINE OF CHAPTER FIVE

HUMAN BEHAVIOR AS LEARNED BEHAVIOR

LEARNING CONTENT: HABITS AND APPROACH/AVOIDANCE
PATTERNS

THE CONDITIONING PROCESS

    Conditioned Reflexes
    Operant Conditioning

EXTINCTION OF RESPONSE PATTERNS

STIMULUS GENERALIZATION

STIMULUS DISCRIMINATION

LANGUAGE AS A LEARNING DEVICE

    Language and Brand Family Response
    Drawbacks of Language Symbolism
    Instructional Learning—Learning Through Language

LEARNING BY IMITATION

THE LEARNING CURVE AND THE EXPERIENCE CURVE

LEARNING TRANSFER: HOW LEARNING BUILDS ON
LEARNING

    Positive and Negative Transfer
    The Difficulty of Habit Change
    Mediated Transfer

FORGETTING

FACTORS WHICH AID IN NEW HABIT ACQUISITION

It is not an exaggeration to claim that understanding consumer behavior involves understanding the process and nature of learning. In a very fundamental sense, the exchange process is centered on some aspect of learning. The aim of the seller is either to establish a new habit in the behavior of the buyer or to prevent the change of an old one which is favorable to him as seller. The content of the habitual reactions of any adult consumer are always a product of a long learning process. Only by understanding how learning works, what aids it, what interferes with it, and what the sources of that learning are, can we hope to stimulate new learning among potential consumers.

The ability to learn is basically what distinguishes man from many of the lower forms of animals. Any knowledgeable bird watcher can look at an abandoned nest in a tree and tell you what species or bird built that nest. He will recognize instantly the shallow mud-daubed nest of the robin and be able to confidently predict that wherever you find such a nest you can be certain that it was built by a robin. Even if the robin is raised without ever being instructed in nest building, the nest the bird builds will look the same as that of every other robin. The nest building pattern is an inherited instinct.

But one cannot look at a house and tell you what race or type of man built it or lives in it. Indeed, even two brothers may live in different kinds of dwellings and a man may choose a different dwelling in one part of the country than he had lived in elsewhere for most of his life. Likewise, the American takes a coffee break, the Englishman a tea break. The coffee the American drinks will vary from one region of the country to another. Coffee blends most favored by those along the southern gulf coast will be rejected by those who live in the Great Lakes area. The specific physical location has nothing to do with these taste preferences, of course. The cause is the conditioning which led to these learned tastes.

Two men go out to dinner. One orders a stein of beer, the other a glass of wine. Both aim at a similar satisfaction goal—the relaxation induced by a moderate amount of alcohol—but they choose different means. This, too, is a matter of learning, starting with a foundation of reflex actions and unfocused drives with which each was born, and building on these with progressive layers of taste habits as they grew up in different environments, culminating in adult attitudes of product preference.

Learning is of three basic types: acquisition of information, development of taste biases through familiarization, and formation of habits of thought, perception, and action. Acquisition of simple items of information (such as the availability of a new brand and its claimed benefits) is usually the matter of a single lesson. Gaining familiarity takes time and continued exposure, but need not involve any real effort on the part of the consumer. Indeed, probably the greatest proportion of our taste preferences of all sorts are formed in this manner. The face-to-face groups with which we associate bring us into contact with items involved, and this continued contact breeds the familiarity which, as already noted, can lead to preference, provided we start with a neutral attitude. If the point of origin is one of dislike for the item, extended contact tends to breed rejection, and to generalize this rejection to all similar items. In one experiment, for example, subjects were exposed to samples of several kinds of paintings for five sessions. One of the categories exhibited was floral paintings, and the initial reaction to this type was one of dislike. At the end of the experiment, the dislike of the whole floral category increased (Krugman and Hartley, 1960).

Clearly, then, whenever matters of taste and preference are involved in product acceptance, the strategy is to obtain frequent exposure over an extended period of time, under circumstances providing favorable associations.

The real learning problems, however, and the ones whose understanding is the subject of most of psychological learning theory, involve the formation of new habits of action, feeling, perception, or thought. This is normally a prolonged process requiring effort, practice and time on the part of the individual. Such habit formation, and usually the even more difficult habit change as well, is the critical factor in new product acceptance of any kind.

## Formation of Habits Under Mixed Approach/Avoidance Conditions

Habit formation is really the final goal of all learning. Only by reducing all but the most minute fraction of our responses to internal needs and external stimuli to some form of automatic response can we hope to attain the optimum degree of goal satisfaction. So we undergo practice to build the complex muscular reaction procedures we call skills. We traverse habitual roads to reach habitual destinations. We shop the same stores, week after week, to fill our shopping needs, consume an habitual diet with a restricted range of possible foods, habitually choose certain specific brands for each of our purchases. Most important of all, we build a whole panoply of habitual biases toward action in unique situations—biases we call attitudes.

Only through building such a complex of habits can we reserve the tedious, time-consuming task of arriving at that balanced decision between alternatives for those few occasions in which habit is not a useful guide. The result is that most of consumer behavior consists of habitual reactions. The job of the seller is one of three habit-centered tasks: (1) reinforce an existing habit which operates in his favor, (2) lead the consumer to undertake the effort of developing a completely new habit, or (3) attempt the most difficult task of all—give the consumer adequate incentive to change an existing habit in his favor.

Habits can be divided into two sorts of reaction experience. One kind leads us to *approach* or search out certain kinds of stimuli—certain objects, people, or services which we both believe and feel will result in what we perceive as some form of pleasure. The other set of habit patterns are *avoidance* reactions. We seek to escape from situations, goods, services, or people which we believe or feel, or both, will cause us some degree of discomfort.

Most of our actions, and all of those in the exchange process, are a result of *mixed approach/avoidance* situations. Gaining most of the things we desire in this world results in some mixture of both pleasure and pain. In the exchange process, the pleasure comes from the use of the product or service we seek. The pain is a result of the sacrifice we must make to gain our goal—the price we pay in effort as well as money to make the acquisition. Whether we participate in the exchange process at all or not depends on whether we believe or feel that the pleasure we gain from it is greater than the pain we must suffer in order to obtain what we seek.

The classical laboratory version of the mixed approach/avoidance reaction is the situation in which a pigeon is first taught that by pecking a button it will gain a grain of corn. Since the corn is seen as a cue that its hunger will be appeased, the pigeon quickly learns an approach reaction to the button as a means of guaranteeing itself something to eat and thus the pleasure of a satisfied or appeased hunger. Once this new reaction is established and the pigeon has learned to recognize the button as a secondary object of its drive to relieve hunger, the plate on which he must step to peck the button is electrically charged so that he receives a shock when stepping on it.

The pain of the shock initially conditions the pigeon to avoid that area, including the button which yields the corn. However, the longer he avoids the area the hungrier he becomes. At some point his hunger reaches such intensity that he will ignore the pain stimulus to peck at the button and get his corn. In marketing parlance, we can say that the shock is the price he pays to get something to eat and the degree of the shock he will ignore is the measure of the degree of hunger he is willing to endure before accepting the conditions of the exchange.

As human consumers, our avoidance reactions do not normally involve matters of electrical shock. They do involve, however, the expenditure of various personal resources with which we are loathe to part. In a normal commercial transaction, we must give up some monetary resources which we could use for other purposes if we so chose. We may also have to spend time in searching and shopping for a particular brand or a particular style that we desire. This, too, is a price, since time is the most limited of all of our resources. Finally, since the object of our search is always some kind of an assortment, either an assortment of benefits embodied within a particular object or an assortment of goods to be obtained from a single source, we must nearly always pay some design-compromise price. We must be willing to accept less than we desire of certain of the satisfactions within the assortment in order to obtain a full measure of others for which we have a greater desire. We learn to accept design compromises, to choose the car that has less acceleration than we might occasionally desire, in order to have one which costs us less when we stop to refuel it. We learn to accept value compromises—to buy a home that has somewhat less spacious grounds than we might desire in order to have property which is more easily maintained with less time expenditure, or to have available funds to promote the college education of our youngsters. We learn to accept assortment compromises at the store— to buy a brand that is our second choice rather than our first because other items which are more important to us are handled in the market at which we are shopping, and we prefer not to spend extra time traveling to a second store to pick up the one additional item.

The fact that all exchanges are mixed approach/avoidance reactions accounts for the high degree of segmentation of markets and makes possible the entry of new brands in an already established market. Since a great number of those who are buying the product, in any given set of offerings, have had to compromise on some factors that they would prefer, and since the nature of mass production precludes the design of products to meet every possible variation of tastes, there will always be large numbers in the market who could be attracted by a new design which comes closer to meeting their optimum compromise. In general, these people will be at the fringe of the segments served by various brands and the new segment will be composed of former purchasers from a number of segments.

The same principle, of course, holds for the entrance of a new merchant into any market which a number of merchants already serve. If the newcomer can develop a merchandise mix which fits the needs of substantial numbers of people who are not fully satisfied with the assortments offered by any of the other merchants, he will have adequate reason to enter the market.

Thus, successful competition consists of developing a specific niche in the market, of creating an offering which comes closer to meeting the needs of a substantial number of potential buyers who are not currently reasonably satisfied with the kinds of compromises they are making. Those who are at the core of the segment attracted will then be immune to attraction by other sellers since they have come close to satisfying the desires that cause them to make the search and to foresake their previous sources of satisfaction.

If the product or service being offered is quite different from those already on the market, the seller will nearly always have to undertake an educational effort. He will have to find some way to teach considerable numbers of consumers to view his offering as a cue to the kind of satisfactions that they seek. Such learning will usually be needed no matter how unsatisfied consumers may be with current offerings. To succeed in this educational effort, the seller needs to understand how the customer came to acquire the tastes which led to the kinds of design compromises he is making and the forces that can aid in his learning to acquire new tastes, or can hinder the process of this learning, or "conditioning," as a psychologist terms the process.

## The Conditioning Process

In order to succeed, the educational situation must contain three elements:

1.  The existence within the individual of some kind of aroused drive or motive to obtain some new goal which he desires.
2.  The individual must have an existing behavioral pattern to which a new stimulus can be attached in such a manner that two things will happen: he (the person who is learning) perceives that he has obtained his goal, and he is led to act in a manner desired by the initiator or seller.
3.  Some distinctive stimulus within the situation which the learner

perceives as being capable of being connected with the kind of behavior to which the stimulus is sought to condition him.

It is important to recognize that all learning starts with some form of inner drive or motive and cannot take place without it. It is not true that freezers can be sold to eskimos at Point Barrow in the middle of the winter for the purpose of freezing fish. They have an adequate means of doing so already and would not be aware of any need to improve on what the weather does very well for them.

A sale of any sort, and particularly any sale of a new kind of offering, starts with motion within the buyer toward a goal. But there also must be some kind of behavioral pattern which can be built on—some behavior already capable of use in leading toward the goal sought. The process of learning consists of developing an association between this already established behavioral pattern with the new stimulus, whether the established pattern be some initial reflex or other congenital response, or some previously learned response. The purpose is to get the consumer to make an habitual association between these newly offered goods or services and the response which he already perceives as capable of obtaining the goal he seeks. All conditioning builds on some kind of response of the individual—some reflex, some random action, or some previously learned behavioral pattern of some sort which can be rewarded and thus reinforced.

Psychology recognizes two major types of conditioning: the conditioned reflex and operant conditioning. The mechanism of learning is the same, although the initial response is of a different type. A *conditioned reflex* is set up when the initial impulse is a completely automatic muscular response to a specific external physical stimulus of some sort—such as the knee jerk we are all familiar with, or the startle response on which a great many of our emotions of fear and anger are based through learning. In *operant conditioning*, the initial impulse is an undefined internal feeling, an internal tension which we designate as a *drive* when it is congenital, or a *learned motive* when it is of learned origin built on these original drives.

As already noted, such a drive or motive does not, in its initial form, result in any one specific kind of action. In the laboratory, the experimenter depends on random movements, stimulated by the internal restlessness, to eventually cause the subject (animal or bird) to undertake the desired kind of behavior at some point—the pecking of a button in the case of the pigeon or the entering of the proper arm of a maze in the case of a rat. At the moment that the subject comes forward with the desired behavior, it is rewarded with something that is seen as appealing—normally food, whose perceived value has been raised to a fairly high level by previous deprivation. By this means, an initial association is developed between the form of reinforcement (the food in the case of the laboratory animal) and the behavior which seemed to provide this reinforcement or reward.

In the case of human beings, even in the laboratory, the starting point is usually some already known form of behavior rather than a dependence on some kind of random probing. Instructions are given which normally lead to the kind of behavior desired, and when this behavior is forthcoming, a reward is given. In some simple laboratory situations, this reward, of course, can be some sort of physical reward such as food or money, but, more usually, a great deal of the reinforcement that we as humans get is a form of inner satisfaction of accomplishment. Generally speaking, the hoped for reward for much of our behavior is some form of attention from those around us, which we have come to feel as pleasurable.

Consider the complex of our eating habits. As babies, when first hungry, we simply became restless and cried and someone, usually our mother, brushed our lips with a nipple of a bottle or of the mother's breast. This touching of the lips evoked the universal reflex with which all of us are born—an attempt to suckle on what touched the lips. This in turn led to partaking of nourishment and cessation of the tension we had felt. As time went on, we came to associate people with the release of our hunger pangs. The fondling we received in contact with people came to be associated with the pleasurable satisfaction coincident with the appeasement of any drive.

It is possible, of course, that the fondling itself is pleasurable, as the goal of some kind of congenital drive for association with other people in the case of human beings. Monkeys who were reared by furry dummies—"surrogate mothers"—learned to cling to these inanimate mothers as monkeys do to real mothers, but grew up to be neurotic, indicating a need for real contact (Harlow and Harlow, 1962).

Whether or not born with some kind of desire for human contact, we later do come to associate the pleasure derived from food eaten to appease hunger pangs with the people who offer us the food. As a result, we also come to value human associations of various kinds as a pleasurable thing in itself. Thus, we build a myriad of dietary habits, and also a multitude of social responses, starting from two congenital sources, a congenital hunger drive and consequent pain reaction, and a congenital reflex which causes us to close our lips and suck on things that brush them. We have built a whole series of learned "operant tasks" or habits based on these two simple beginnings.

The distinguishing feature of all of our habits and all forms of operant conditioning is that the initial stimulus for the action comes from within the individual. We do not eat simply because somebody has shown us some food. We eat because we feel an inner drive, the satisfaction of which depends on ingestion of some kind of nourishment. We may, of course, learn to react to the smell or sight of specific foods as a reminder, a cue, that we are hungry and desire to eat, but the inner stimulus must still be there.

All exchange situations involve such habits or operant tasks and, thus, all sales start with the buyer even though the seller may and does take the initiative in making an offer. He is simply hoping that what he offers will be perceived by the customer as a cue that the drive that he desires to satisfy will be appeased. The habits or operant tasks that we learn, therefore, might be defined as a set of associations of numerous stimuli as cues that the undertaking of certain procedures, and the acquisition of certain kinds of artifacts or products and services, will satisfy certain inner drives or motives that we have. Most of the motives themselves, of course, are learned motives.

## Extinction of the Response Pattern

There is considerable evidence that the associations, once formed, are never completely obliterated. The response pattern, however, can be suppressed or "extinguished" by negative conditioning—by associating a pain reaction rather than a pleasure reaction with a desired response.

The ease with which extinction can be carried out depends in part on how consistently the response has been rewarded in the past. A response which has always been rewarded may be extinguished with a single adverse reaction. But a response which has been reinforced or rewarded only part of the time may take a great deal of adverse reaction to extinguish. Since no expectation was developed that reward would always be forthcoming, the lack of it is not perceived as unexpected.

Thus it is that products which deliver something less than consistent performance often maintain loyalty of customers in a sort of perverse manner, despite their lack of consistency, if there is no better alternate during the time they are in use. Ford's Model T occupied a rather high place in the affections of its owners for a long period of years, from 1908 to at least 1925, despite the need for almost constant mechanical adjustments to keep it operating. One of the more expensive sports cars on the market has a pretty well established reputation for proneness to expensive repairs, yet is considered one of the most sought-after makes on the market. Of course, a product can attain this position only by giving a very high degree of differential satisfaction of some sort, initially, relative to the competition on the market at the time it is entered. It is true, nevertheless, that the mere existence of inconsistent behavior on the part of any product or any idea or procedure is not enough to cause buyers to switch immediately to some new offering which promises, but hasn't proven, better performance.

On the other hand, a single negative reaction can extinguish a response that has been consistently rewarded. And, of course, a negative reinforcement in the beginning can establish a negative or avoidance response, which makes establishing a later positive response much more difficult, or even well-nigh impossible. Thus, a newly introduced product which stumbles because of a defect noticeable to the users usually cannot be revived on the market by simple removal of the defect.

## Stimulus Generalization and Stimulus Discrimination

If we had to learn all that we know by responding specifically to every stimulus exactly as it existed, we would probably not learn very much in this life. Fortunately, all kinds of conditioning, even among lower animals, involves a process of generalization. In the original Pavlovian experiments in conditioning a dog, for example, the dog would salivate originally to the sound of a certain bell, but would salivate also to the sound of a bell with a different tone or even a buzzer. If the sound was very similar to that of the original bell, the degree of salivation was quite large. As the difference in the sound stimulus increased, the amount of salivation decreased. Thus, by this *principle of generalization*, we learn to respond to a wide class of stimuli perceived as being similar. When we taste a McIntosh apple we also have learned, at the same time, to try other apples that look similar and even those apples of a different color. We do not have to be conditioned to every new variety that comes on the market.

However, we can and do learn also to *discriminate*. In Pavlov's later experiments, he presented no food when the bell or buzzer was of a different sound. After a period of time, the dog learned to salivate only to the single sound tone of the original bell and not to other sounds.

This, too, is important to us as consumers. We learn to discriminate between qualities of products that are presented to us and to pay less for those that are of lesser quality or even to refuse them. The degree of discrimination is a learned characteristic and will vary greatly from one individual to another. The brewmaster at a brewery, for example, can distinguish the taste of different batches within his own brewery. Blind taste tests of beer drinkers, however, have shown that their discrimination between makes is so imprecise that they cannot recognize their own brand without the label and often will assign a lower flavor rating to it if they are unaware of its source.

Both discrimination and generalization are important to the consumer. He almost never meets precisely the same situation in any major purchase decision as he has met in the past. It is his ability to generalize—to respond to a complex situation which is not exactly like any met before but simply contains some similar components—that enables him to make a useful decision.

### Language as a Source of Learning

Language plays a key role in the way we generalize our learning and is even itself a conduit for learning. Language labels are an important factor in all of our reactions. The names we give things are concepts. They enable us to see similarities where we might miss them otherwise, and may even cause us at times to perceive similarities where they do not objectively exist. Whether for good or ill, they help us to organize the universe around us. Thus the success of one brand helps the introduction of others, and eases the acceptance of other items under the same brand.

But the force of language labels as a source of response generalization can also cause us to avoid products we would otherwise try and like. For instance, some years ago a United States meat packer developed and put into test a new processed meat product. The research analysts found the user panels were uniformly high in their acceptance of the unlabeled product. But even before any attempt was made to sell it, the analyst predicted that, once the package was labeled as the law required, the product would fail. Sure enough, when introduced and put on supermarket shelves, the entire initial stock gathered dust and had to be cleared out at ridiculously low prices. The product, which tasted like the best of corned beef, was *corned mutton.* Mutton is not considered an acceptably flavored meat in the American cuisine, so the word "mutton" on the label created an immediate avoidance reaction.

The tendency to generalize our responses to cover a whole family of stimuli is quite obvious in the market place, in the phenomenon of brand acceptance over a whole family of products. We buy Old Emperor peaches and find them to our liking, so we have no question about the quality and value of the pears when Old Emperor introduces them under its own brand. The peaches have already established for us an expectation of quality and value.

Of course, some of this transfer of the response from an old stimulus to a new one can backfire if the seller is not careful to maintain a consistent level of quality and value across all of the products under the brand name. One good example of this was the loss of adequate consumer traffic by two major regional chains in some parts of the midwest, because a great many customers came to perceive the featured store brands as not being consistently good values. In some of the same areas, a third chain has managed to dig itself in for a leading niche in the market partly because it does have a strong store brand policy at three different quality and price levels, with consistent quality within each level.

Brand acceptance is just one example of a very important aspect of human learning and behavior—the learning of language symbols and other images, and of relationships in which the individual has faith. The use of language is the major element in the ability of the human being to learn faster and learn more than any other animal. A great deal of initial learning takes place through language alone. We buy a new kit that has to be assembled, or a new product that requires some manipulation which is different from any that we have had before, and we start out with an instruction sheet—nothing more than some language on a sheet which tells us how to proceed. If this instruction sheet is well done, we will often do an acceptable job the first time around. If the procedure is at all complex, of course, as most mechanical procedures are, the first job is usually a relatively awkward one as it would be under any circumstances.

The use of language symbols has some drawbacks, however, it may cause us to perceive similarity in products which have very little actual similarity. Both an MG sports car and a Cadillac limousine are automobiles covered by the same symbolic language classifications. As a result, there is a tendency to speak of each of them as having "a share" of the same market and sales executives may base plans on this kind of share measure. Yet, it is clear that the man who buys the sports car is not in the same market as the man who buys the Cadillac limousine—the uses each has in mind are not alike. On the other hand, a pickup truck is classified as a truck regardless of its use. Yet for many families it is one of the transportation vehicles used for family affairs and its main auxiliary service purpose may not be that of a truck in the usual sense at all, but a means of mounting a small traveling abode known as a camper. To the extent that it is a family passenger vehicle, it may very well compete with the station wagon models of the same or another make and be, in a sense, part of and have its share of that market. Yet, because we call it a truck, we put it in the same category as the large over-the-highway semitrailer rig capable of hauling twenty or more tons of produce.

Similarly, we apply labels to stores and carry in our head some sort of image or set of expectations of the kind of products we expect to find there and the level of quality, even before we visit the store. Indeed, we go much beyond that. We may very well form our own mental image of the store on the basis merely of the layout and the typography of its advertisements. We have acquired a certain expectation set concerning the compatibility of a given quality and type of merchandise and the way in which the store publicizes its business and conducts it. Generally, of course, we are correct because the image itself is based on past experience with the same firm, and on a tendency for both firms and people to be consistent in their behavior.

### Instructional Learning—Learning Through Language

Language is also a means of learning in its own right—learning by instruction. The concept of conditioning tends to carry the connotation of learning as a process that starts from the outside. But much of our conditioning originates from some internal motive which causes us to search out a means of satisfaction, and the only reward is success in the search. Among the sources we seek out are instructions of various sorts—printed procedures for accomplishing some end. The most familiar single such source is the cookbook—the perennial favorite of all books—with its assortment of recipes, or detailed language descriptions of ingredients and procedures for preparing almost anything edible in any way imaginable. And of course, food recipes are to be found in many other sources—they are staple features in every newspaper, and a major attraction in many magazines.

The drive for stimulus variability—seen in the desire to vary the menu—is one of the obvious motives for seeking out this specific kind of aid to self-instruction. Another motive can be social approval—to be able to serve an attention-getting dish to friends and guests. Or sometimes social approval is the indirect motive—as in the desire to lose weight in order to be more attractive. Or we may look for low-calorie dishes for an avoidance motive—to get to a weight level less dangerous to our health.

Whatever the motive, a new and interesting recipe is always such useful news that this becomes one means of inexpensive promotion. The U. S. Department of Agriculture regularly issues information on good seasonal buys in foods, and often issues recipes, primarily to help producers sell what is currently plentiful on the market. Because consumers are eager for such instructions, they get printed in the newspapers. Likewise, commercial food and beverage companies can often bring their products to consumer attention and stimulate trial by similar devices.

Nor are foods and beverages the only products for which consumers seek out instruction, and for which there is thus a readily available publicity channel of which sellers can avail themselves. Every Sunday paper, and every home and handicraft or mechanics magazine, carries editorial material on new products and old, facilitating both sides of the exchange process by teaching the buyer.

Indeed, some form of instructional learning is a key element in the adoption of and diffusion of innovations. The early innovators are those most likely to seek out news of and instruction in the new. When possible, of course, they often seek out this instruction from other people. But whatever the source of instruction, most of the knowledge comes in language form. Much of the instruction necessarily is in printed form—largely in periodicals covering their trade, business, or other special interests.

A great deal of instructional promotion of many products is done on a person-to-person level, however. Examples are the county agricultural agents and home demonstration agents, the principal catalysts in bringing about the great twentieth century agricultural revolution in the United States. Another is the drug company "detail man"—a salesman whose main duty is not to take orders, but to instruct physicians on the uses and limitations ("side effects") of the remedies manufactured by their employers. Much industrial selling is also instructional in nature, including the work of the salesman and of the technical representatives sent out by makers of major industrial supplies, such as abrasives, dyes, textile fibers, plastic resins, and other technical materials and supplies used in volume.

Formation of some of our principle attitudes is the result of language guidance, using our desire for social approval. Repeated admonitions such as "that is not wise!" and "that is not the way to act!" serve as an adequate negative reward to lead us in the direction of the approved habits. Other instruction, however, is in the form of direct or indirect demonstration, making use of another avenue of learning—that of imitation.

Imitation plays a role in attitude formation also. We learn to imitate the direction of opinions and attitudes of those in the reference groups whose association we value—to imitate the tastes in food, beverages, clothing, spending patterns, and so forth, eventually conforming to the same general patterns in such matters.

All such habit formation requires repeated practice, building up to automatic efficiency by following a pattern recognized as the learning curve.

## Imitation as a Major Source of Learning

A great deal of what any of us learns is acquired by imitation. As children in any culture, much of our play is centered around imitations of one aspect or another of adult behavior—use of tools that adults use, crude imitations of adult activity such as "playing school" or "playing store," or following out the pseudo activities seen on the television screen. On the farm or in any rural civilization, children early develop skills in some of the agricultural tasks. In the modern suburb, children who are deprived of many opportunities to observe the adult work-a-day world eagerly flock around any adult engaged in some meaningful task, such as spading a garden, asking to "help."

Much of this activity is spawned by a desire to acquire a more prestigious role, to be an adult. Lacking membership in the group they consider to be higher in status, they try to act as adults do. As we shall see later, this longing to play a higher role is an important element in the buying behavior of people of all ages who are in a role transition period, of which childhood is only the first.

## The Learning Curve

Most of the operant tasks or habits we acquire are complex procedures. They build on already established reactions of one kind or another, but often involve much more precision than we have given those individual component tasks and always involve coordination between them in a way with which we may be totally unfamiliar. Both long observation and laboratory experimentation have established that the learning process proceeds along a curve known as the learning curve (see Figure 5-1A). Efficiency of performance during the learning period is quite low initially. When we are learning to type, for example, we are slow and inaccurate, but as we continue to practice, both our speed and accuracy will increase and approach some sort of plateau. There are variations in this learning curve. For example, it may reach a plateau rather early and for a time no increase in efficiency occurs, then suddenly the curve takes an upward spurt as a new kind of skill is attained (see Figure 5-1B). It is also believed, but not demonstrated, that the initial reaction to a wholly unfamiliar task is for rather slow improvement in response at first, and then a speed-up. (The plateaued

## Figure 5-1. The Learning Curve

A. The Classical Form:

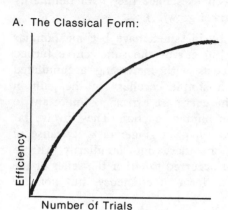

B. The Plateaued Learning Curve:

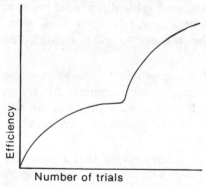

(A pattern underlying the pyramided life cycle of some basic inventions such as the automobile—see Figure 12-5. Sales approach the first plateau as consumers accept the initially perceived benefits, then resumes a new growth as they learn to find new uses and benefits.)

curve, incidentally, resembles a pyramided product life cycle curve. The resemblance is not pure coincidence. With some new products, consumers themselves discover unforeseen uses once they gain familiarity with the offering, leading to new market growth.)

In recent years, economists and businessmen have become familiar with a corollary form of this learning curve—the same curve turned upside down to show decreasing costs with increasing accumulated experience in production. This is a simple corollary of the gain in efficiency. Both interpretations of the curve are extremely important to sellers. All learning curves start with human reaction. They involve far more than mere efficiency of operation of a single task. Because of stimulus and response generalization, increasing familiarity with a product will reveal uses that had not occurred to either the seller or the buyer initially. This is, of course, a form of efficiency, but not one measured in terms of dollar cost.

These learning curves have a crucial lesson for those introducing new products and processes in manufacturing, construction, and the like. Where a product is a component being used in the production of some other product—for example, a new building material requiring somewhat different procedures than previous ones, this learning curve means that the initial use of the new material or a new process will not yield the expected efficiencies early. The calculated value differences between a new process and an old one may not be attained for quite some time, due to the need for those using the process to gain accumulated experience.

From the competitive standpoint, the accumulated experience curve also means that the first seller in the market can maintain his initial advantage if he continues to aggressively pursue both product developments and production improvements, simply because of his accumulated production experience.

The final corollary is that the costs of producing the initial runs of a product are far in excess of what they will become later, and it behooves the early introducers of a new product to watch their costs and keep their prices declining in line with these costs. Otherwise, they will eventually attract more competition than the mature market will support due to the increasingly attractive level of profits resulting from learning curve advances in production costs.

Not all learning requires a long process. There are many instances in which a task is learned in an entirety in a single trial. In these cases, what has happened is that the trial builds on fully learned components of previous experience. What has taken place is a true transfer of learning, of which more will be said below.

## Learning Transfer—How Learning Builds on Learning

Learning can and does build on previous learning. In one sense, this is simply an extension of the principle of stimulus and response generalization. Learning can also interfere with new learning under other circumstances. The principles of transfer of learning are particularly important in product design, especially in the case of new kinds of products.

*Positive transfer* of learning occurs when there is a similarity of the stimulus and the response association. One everyday example is the way those who grow up using the handle bars of tricycles first, and then the handle bars of bicycles and maybe motorcycles, have little trouble learning how to use the steering wheel of an automobile. Although the steering wheel does not look like a pair of handle bars, it is manipulated in much the same way and gets essentially the same results in guiding the direction of the vehicle. Another form of positive transfer occurs when the stimuli are quite different but the response procedure is the same. Thus, the introduction of the touch-tone telephone really involved no great amount of learning for most urban families. They had grown up in a civilization in which a great many people had learned to use ten-key adding machines and other similar push-button devices. To make a phone call by using the same general approach to a similar keyboard instead of by conventional dialing was no great leap and there is no evidence that the introduction of the touch-tone telephone was, for the average consumer, any large innovation requiring any learning of new motor habits.

Learning can also interfere greatly with new learning—the phenomenon of *negative transfer* of learning. A good example is the case of changing designs in water faucets. The change from twisting a handle to pushing it can cause a great deal of interference with the new learning. Indeed, any learning which requires a procedure quite the opposite of one previously used can create a great deal of difficulty among people who are thoroughly familiar with the old procedure. An excellent example was the length of time it took to get the electric typewriter accepted, a period spanning virtually a full generation of stenographers. One reason, without any question, was the negative learning involved for the experienced stenographer in using the new machine. Taught to rest her fingers on the middle row of keys on an ordinary manual machine, she found that this procedure caused type bars to be actuated. She had to relearn her hand position habits, to hold her hands in such a manner as to never touch a key unless she intended the type bar to strike.

Just how much the learning of a skill will interfere with the acquisition of a new skill is illustrated by an old psychological experiment (Hunter, 1912). Rats were placed in a simple T-maze starting at the bottom. At the point where they had to turn either to the right or to the left, they got a cue from a light. If the light was on, food was to the right. If the light was off, they found food to the left. They learned this relationship on the average in 286 trials. Then the pattern was reversed, food was at the left when the light was on and to the right when it was off. It took 603 trials to relearn and master the new pattern, or well over twice the time it would have taken to learn the new pattern in the first place had the old one not existed. Rats have no more difficulty in reversing habit pattern than people do.

As personal observation will show, changing a habit requires a prolonged unlearning effort to first destroy the automaticity and efficiency of the old, followed by a fresh start on a new learning curve to construct the new response pattern, with some kind of in-between period of consolidation necessary. The process might be diagrammed as shown in Figure 5-2.

**Figure 5-2.   Conceptual Model of the Habit Change Process**

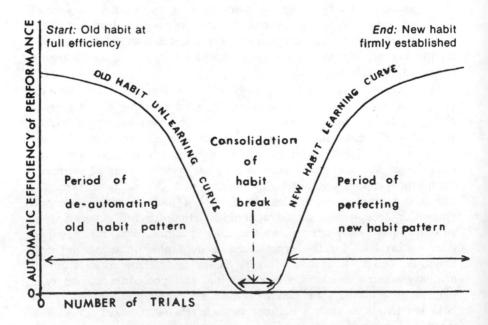

Because of negative transfer, it is extremely important that initial product design cause the least possible change in motor habits and also in habits of perception. It is probably no accident that the name "horseless carriage" was so accurate a description of the first automobiles. Certainly, the similarity of design of the first automobile to that of the horsedrawn carriage did not hinder the rapid rise to prominence of the automobile industry, which took off on a rapid market growth from the very first.

It is easy to find many examples of new products or new product models in which some degree of negative transfer blocked early acceptance of the new because of the learning difficulties involved in some minor aspect of the design. In the boats using water jet propulsion when it was first introduced, making a turn required that the steersman use exactly the opposite maneuver from that used in making a turn with motorboats having the other kinds of propulsion— he had to speed up the motor to get adequate force to deflect the boat rather than dropping the power as he normally would, because steering was done by deflecting a fixed jet stream. This error in design was one of the major factors which caused the initial introduction to fail and probably limited future acceptance, more than would otherwise have happened, when it came back on the market (with a much better gimbaled jet, one which did not require the habit change).

Similarly, the fact that the typist had to hold her hands off the keys of an electric typewriter rather than rest them on the middle row (as on a manual machine), while probably an unavoidable element in the design, unquestionably hindered the acceptance of the electric typewriter among skilled typists for more than twenty years.

Another aspect of learning transfer that has been used by advertisers, consciously or unconsciously, is that of *mediated transfer*, consisting of the use of unconscious association between two language or other image symbols and the association of one of these symbols with the product itself.

Mediated transfer has been demonstrated in the laboratory by first teaching students to learn a pairing between a nonsense syllable and a real word—the pairing, for example, between the nonsense syllable LAN and the real word Detroit. Once a number of such pairings have been taught, any attempt to pair the same syllables with a different word usually proves difficult—we get negative transfer. However, if we ask the subjects of the experiment to learn a new response—the real word, *traffic*, with the nonsense syllable LAN we get no negative transfer and quite often some positive transfer. The reason: most of us associate Detroit with automobiles, and automobiles with traffic. Even though we may not be aware of this association, we find it much easier to associate the nonsense syllable LAN with traffic after we have learned to associate it with Detroit.

A striking instance of a successful advertising campaign making use of such mediated transfer was the introduction and subsequent continued success of the Marlboro cigarette, described in more detail in the next chapter. Building on research evidence that virility is the major motive among smokers, the firm used a campaign linking the brand with illustrations of models fitting the "virility" stereotype.

The final aspect of transfer of learning is that the learning process itself builds on learning of any kind. Laboratory tests have shown, for example, that monkeys, given problems to solve, get better and better at solving new and different problems. Students given laboratory tests with nonsense syllables learn each new list much more quickly than the previous one. While these experiments have obvious meaning for education in the formal sense, they also have a corollary implication on the marketing scene. Every new product requires some new kind of learning, even if it is no more than association of a new brand with those that are among the acceptable. Studies of acceptance of new innovations (to be discussed later) showed that, in general, people most likely to be among the early innovators are those who have successfully exposed themselves to many kinds of change in their lives, and many kinds of learning, to a far greater degree than those who adopt later.

But while learning builds on learning, learning can also interfere with learning. It can actually make us forget.

### Forgetting

Psychologists are now inclined to believe that all learning is more or less permanent and does not fade away with the passage of time. But they also know that what we have learned can be interfered with by new kinds of learning, or that the new learning process may be repressed by what we already know. When the habits and knowledge we have already acquired become "rusty" because of the establishment of new habits and new knowledge, psychologists label it "retroactive inhibition" of learning. From a marketing standpoint, this means that the acceptance of products requiring new habits probably tend to speed the decline of the old products which they had displaced by making it difficult for even those who had established habits in their use to reuse them again. Anyone who has transferred from a manual to an electric typewriter, and then, after becoming accustomed to the latter, was forced to switch back to manual, is aware of how difficult it was and how strange it seemed to have to use the finger force needed to operate a manual.

However, it is also true that well-established habits can interfere with the acquiring of new ones. What the psychologists refer to as *proactive inhibition*, teamed up with negative transfer, may make it difficult to learn a new set of habits aimed at a similar set of satisfactions already associated with a well-established set of habits—the better established, the slower the learning. In addition, even when the new habits have been thoroughly acquired, old habits are likely to interfere and break in at any time.

This is one reason why it is often easier to sell a new process to a new firm in any industry than to get an older one to change over, even when the new process has a very substantial economic advantage over the old one. It was Kaiser Steel which bought the rights to the oxygen converter, while the much larger and older U.S. Steel and Bethlehem Steel continued to build the far more expensive and less efficient open hearth furnaces, until forced to change by competitive costs.

This explains why it is easier to train the new generation that has not yet learned to smoke to completely abstain, than to get an habitual smoker to break his habit. Together with the learning curve advantages of the highly skilled, this is one reason why those who have not yet cemented a new habit well within their established actions are more easily sold on trying and working with the new product than those more thoroughly skilled in the use of the old.

In this connection, skill is related to what the psychologist calls "overlearning," meaning practice well beyond the point which is necessary merely to learn the task. It is always true that overlearned habits are the most difficult to suppress, overlearned knowledge the least likely to be forgotten.

## Factors Which Aid Acquisition of New Habits

One of the most important elements in acquisition of new habits and knowledge is an extensive storehouse of previous habits and knowledge. This is the reason why good merchants, research analysts, and other creative personnel often acquire more and more skill and efficiency as the years go by, are able to produce a desired result in a very small fraction of the time taken by a less experienced, albeit brilliant, colleague. It is also obviously a factor in the slope of the learning curve.

A number of specific factors aid in the establishment of new associations:

1. Meaningfulness and/or logic in the task to be learned
2. Familiarity with the stimulus

3. Guidance in the learning process
4. A powerful motive to learn
5. Rewards and punishment
6. Novelty or other form of distinctive stimulus that tends to catch our attention and make an especially good impression

### Familiarity with the Stimulus

We learn easiest those tasks which include elements with which we are thoroughly familiar. The child who grows up in a musical home has much less trouble learning to play an instrument, even one not in the home, than one who has never been exposed to a musical environment. The cabinet maker who is skilled in the use of a number of hand tools has little difficulty in adapting to hand manipulated power tools.

In general, the less the learning gap between the new habit to be acquired and the old one which it must replace, the less difficulty in gaining acceptance of the new process or habit. Thus, in selling industrial equipment to relatively undeveloped nations, it has been found that the highly automated plant seldom is useful. What works best are simple batch processes long discarded as much too primitive in the more developed nations, but which are less of a jump from hand methods.

Likewise, in introducing revolutionary new products, it is well to keep their initial designs as close to the designs of what they are intended to replace as is possible without sacrificing too much of the advantages being offered. Today's farmers buy tractors capable of drawing long strings of planting tools, as much as 80 or 100 feet in length, or of harvesting 1,000 acres of crops as easily as the farmers of fifty years ago harvested 20. But the tractors first introduced simply performed essentially the same work as a good team of horses in good condition. It is doubtful if today's mammoth machines would have had any measurable acceptance during that period.

### Meaningfulness

The need for meaningfulness, or some logical pattern, in what we are asked to learn is really a corollary of the fact that we forget rather quickly those elements of what we are being taught which seem to us to be nonessential or lacking in meaning. Thus, it becomes important, especially in the case of new products which require rather complicated instructions, that the logic of the operation be as much a part of the instructional process as the details of the operation itself.

## The Value of Guidance

We do not have schools because people could learn in no other way, but simply because the guidance furnished by a skilled instructor will speed up the process appreciably. In the world of business, whenever a new product or process is introduced to an industry, it is generally true that the firms doing the introduction furnish skilled technical guidance to those seeking to install a new process. The initial introduction of the now familiar textile, rayon, really accomplished very little in the thirty years from 1894, when first developed, up until 1924. Then the principal chemical companies involved in yarn production decided to abandon the attempt to associate rayon with silk (under the misleading name *artificial silk*) and to teach the textile mills, that would have to use it, how to handle it well. Within the next fifteen years, rayon displaced silk almost completely in the women's dress industry. Since that time, no major chemical has been introduced to industry without extensive skilled technical guidance to customers. And even going products, used in quantity by industries, are marketed by the major firms with continual availability of technical assistance to the buyer.

## The Importance of Motive

The stronger the motive to acquire a specific set of satisfactions, the more readily we learn. The lesser the motive, the less likely we are to undertake the formation of new habits. In the market place this means that any new offering must be perceived by potential customers as granting a very substantial added degree of value in attaining their goals. The "me-too" product is certain to fail for this reason alone. It also means that there will be a relatively ready acceptance, even of products requiring rather new habits, if there is a high degree of dissatisfaction with the means of attaining the sought-for goals with products currently on the market, and if people have already attempted to gain the sought-for satisfaction without the product.

## Feedback

Feedback is a relatively new term in our language, with a very simple meaning: information on how well something is progressing. In the case of learning, feedback is some measure of how much we have already learned. Learning takes place much more rapidly when feedback is quick and obvious. For most of us, this means success is greatest with products which yield a high degree of obvious satisfaction immediately, instead of after a period of time. The fertilizer which imbues the lawn with a deeper green in days is more eagerly sought than the plant food with a slow release over time.

### Rewards and Punishment

Perhaps the oldest motives used in education of all sorts are the motives of reward and negative reward, or punishment. The greatest rewards that we can normally get from the learning of new habits are the attainment of the specific satisfaction goals which we seek. Those goals may be objective acquisition of whatever we have sought to buy, or they may simply be an internal feeling that those around us approve of what we are doing.

Punishment, of course, is a different kind of reward. It is a reward of pain for doing something we should not be doing. Thus, American motorists kept buying heavier and more cumbersome automobiles, which required more and more fuel, until the critical events of the fall of 1973 brought to their attention the declining sources of energy in the world and the wastefulness of their habits. Then the shortages of gasoline at the pumps and the steeply rising prices together inflicted an immediate pain that was very easy for them to understand. Demand switched overnight to smaller and more economical vehicles.

Most of the rewards and punishments which guide our learning are not so directly physical or tangible. For the most part, they consist of various signs of approval or disapproval of those whose affiliation we value. Much of it is not directly expressed, so that we must infer it from minor cues in the actions of those around us, such as a minor grimace or smile, or some even more subtle sign of approval or rejection. Even the basis for the signs we do recognize must be guessed at. ("Even your best friends won't tell you.")

Some of our inferences as to such rejections or approvals exist only in our imaginations, arise purely out of fears or ambitions. The result could be an unnecessary effort to ward off a rejection which will not occur. This is especially likely to happen among those in a high state of anxiety during a period of role transition, when we have the least knowledge of how we are expected to act. (Discussed later in much more detail.) Sellers can and do capitalize on such fears at times.

*Novelty and Attention*

Attention to the learning process is an obvious prerequisite to any kind of learning and it is by no means automatic. A major method of gaining attention is the use of novelty. This builds on our desire for stimulus variability, for a departure from the already too familiar. Many of the devices considered effective in advertising are essentially attention getting devices—the use of the unusual illustration, for example, the use of color ads in a magazine in which very few ads are run in color, or the use of black-and-white print ads in issues in which nearly everything is in color.

We tend to learn quickest those things which are most distinctive and get our attention. This is one reason why advertisers will pay a premium for the first or last pages of advertising in a magazine. We have learned that those things that stand out most are either the first or last in a series.

Gaining attention, indeed, is anything but automatic, and an understanding of attention is the first essential to communicating with the consumer.

## Summary

1.  Practically all adult consumer behavior is learned behavior.

2.  Learning is of three types: mere acquisition of information, establishment of preferences through exposure and familiarity, and the formation of habits.

3.  The end result of learning is a series of habits of mixed approach/avoidance reactions—of reactions to offerings and situations in which benefits can be obtained only after paying some kind of price.

4.  In psychological terms, learning is a conditioning process—the development of new response patterns through the association of new stimuli with other congenital or learned established patterns, by means of reward and reinforcement.

5.  Conditioning can occur only when some goal-oriented drive or motive already exists, when some action pattern capable of being used to meet this goal has already been established, and when the stimulus to be attached to this pattern is unique.

6.  Long continued absence of perceivable reinforcement can also extinguish such a conditioned response.

7.  The stimulus to which the response is conditioned tends to be generalized. That is, a response will be made, not only to the very

specific stimulus, but to others which simply resemble it in some manner.

8.  Discrimination in response can also be learned. The individual can learn to limit his response to a very narrow range of generalization.

9.  For human beings, language itself is a learning device, and a given language symbol can be the major stimulus generalized. This accounts for the market value of brand families. This fact may also result in quite different products, objects, services, or ideas being treated alike when in fact they differ radically and do not yield the same benefit.

10.  Another major avenue to learning is imitation—a tendency which is important in the introduction of new products and which accounts for the strength of demonstration as a promotional device.

11.  The learning of habits and skills is a gradual process, requiring a lengthy practice before the pattern becomes automatic and efficient.

12.  Learning builds on learning through a process of transfer and association. Transfer can be either positive (adding to the total) or negative (inhibiting new learning). Mediated transfer occurs when two stimuli with some common association become associated with each other as a result.

13.  Changing any established habit is more than doubly difficult than simply establishing a habit which does not interfere with old ones. The automatic efficiency of the old habit must first be broken down before a start can be made on building the efficiency of the new pattern. This is especially important to the design of new products.

14.  The acquisition of new habits may thus require learning to forget the old, and new habits may interfere with remembering the old ones.

15.  Habit acquisition is facilitated by a number of factors: familiarity with the stimulus, meaningfulness, expert guidance, feedback on progress, use of rewards and punishment, and the presence of attention-getting novelty.

Chapter 5  Exercises

1.  In marketing new products, and even some established ones, the problem of learning a new use-system itself constitutes an avoidance factor above all other prices. What approach factors or

drives could be used to offset this avoidance factor to get people to:

   a.  Try the advantages of a more compact car than they are familiar with?
   b.  Learn to play tennis or golf well?
   c.  Use automobile seat belts as a matter of habit? (Why don't they do so now?)

2. Smoking is clearly a learned habit, a result of operant conditioning based on a combination of inborn tendencies and acquired motives.

   What inborn reflex or drive would seem to be one of the building blocks for the physical side of the smoking process?

   What incentives would seem to account for the continued practice, after an initially not-very-pleasant first experience with smoking?

3. Many product introductions require some degree of learning or even habit change on the part of the consumer. Even some mature products do. Whoever buys a bicycle or motorcycle has to learn how to ride it. Learning to drive an automobile requires some considerable practice. What drives could act as incentives in each case?

4. Really new products often require the complete change in well-established habits. The microwave oven, for example, requires a wholly new approach to meal preparation. What would you expect the initial market acceptance of such a product would be like? Why?

   One of the greatest advantages of this introduction is the speed and thoroughness with which small quantities can be heated or rewarmed. In what type of market would you expect resistance to the introduction would be least?

5. Some innovations—even mere packaging at times—may require some learning to use, and must also depend on written instructions (language learning). Under what conditions is this likely to work best? When may it fail?

6. If the instructions must go beyond mere written instructions, as in the effective use of a sewing machine or a computer system, how is its sale best expedited?

7. If the benefit is not readily perceived by buyers, how can the seller best teach buyers the value of it?

8. Under what condition of general quality in the trade is quality control most critical? Under what conditions is it much less crucial?

9. It has long been demonstrated that the regular use of automobile seat belts can sharply reduce the risk of injury and death in

automobile mishaps. In some countries, such as Sweden, drivers buckle up as a matter of course, even for a short neighborhood trip. But only a few American drivers would adopt the practice when the belts were first introduced into the U.S.A., and even now, a large portion of the drivers neglect the belts. Why?

10. As this goes to press, some very vocal safety proponents are insisting on a very expensive and awkward substitute for the belt system—the air bag. What problems of consumer behavior can you foresee with the air bag?

11. People can and do learn without benefit of any classroom. One President of the U.S.A.—Andrew Johnson—never was in school or class of any kind, yet taught himself so well that he developed into a respected orator.

    What purpose do schools serve in the learning process? What is the instructor's role in the process?

    What meaning does this have for marketing, and in the case of what kinds of products or services?

12. Some businesses sell mainly a forecast service. Among these are investment advisory services whose business is essentially that of forecasting what securities and other investments will be likely to appreciate in value. In general, forecasting is not a very successful process—even the weatherman, who deals only with known natural forces, has less than a perfect record. Investment advisory services do not even do as well as the weatherman. One university study found that a chance series did better than the leading advisory services. Yet these services prosper, because according to the cynics, people "notice the hits and forget the misses". What established psychological knowledge would explain such a phenomenon?

**6**

# Attention and Perception:
# The Consumer's Internal Censors
# of External Stimuli

SELECTIVE ATTENTION

INBORN SELECTION TENDENCIES

    Adaptation and Change
    Contrast
    Relative Movement
    Relative Size
    Repetition

LEARNED SELECTION TENDENCIES: THE FACTOR OF INTEREST

SELECTIVE AND CREATIVE PERCEPTION: INBORN TENDENCIES

    Figure and Ground
    Closure
    Proximity
    The Discriminal Threshold (j.n.d.)
    Context

LEARNED TENDENCIES

    Constancy
    Individual Experience and Emotional Associations

ARE YOU ONE of those people to whom the word "advertising" conjures up a vision of insidiously powerful persuasion? If so, consider for a moment the ads you have seen and heard in the last twenty-four hours or so: the many billboards you passed in driving or riding, the posters and announcements around the school, the multitudinous advertisements of all sorts which make up the vast bulk of the printing in your morning or evening paper, the all-too-numerous spot announcements on your favorite radio programs, the supposedly insistent commercials on the television shows you watched. How many of them can you, at this moment, remember and identify: fifty? twenty? ten? five? Even one? Yet, you were exposed to literally hundreds of them overall—careful studies have indicated perhaps an average of 600 to 800 for a middle-class person. If advertising and other external stimuli are as powerful as they are sometimes thought to be, why did they make so little impression on you?

Nor are advertisements all that you have witnessed in the last twenty-four hours. If you drive to your class, you had occasion to observe many incidents and literally thousands of objects along your path of travel. How much of those can you recall a few short hours afterwards? Even if you merely walk from your dormitory, you passed dozens or even hundreds of people, could have observed them in all sorts of behavior, were a possible witness to a great many incidents and passed many kinds of visual impressions: lawns and their cover, houses and their construction, the nature of the pavement, and many others. How much of that could you describe at this moment?

You will, of course, have to answer for yourselves, but the author's experience with college students has shown that less than one in twenty can remember even a single advertisement to which they have been exposed, and only a few out of hundreds of students can name as many as two. And there is no reason to think that you, as students, are different from the rest of humanity. Some kind of censor or filter clearly is shutting out from your consciousness the myriad possible stimuli attempting to enter and catch your attention. That censor, or rather censors, can be called *selective attention* and *selective perception*.

As this simple self-examination should show you, the push button or puppet model of the consumer is far from accurate. A much better visualization is that of a person with a super-efficient mental secretary who diverts all but the smallest fraction of a percent of the possible messages directed to the eyes and ears of her boss, accepting only those items which she considers to be worthy of his consideration and of direct interest to him. Alternatively, we might say that each of us is equipped with a pair of highly selective filters which admit a tiny fraction of the possible stimuli, and shape and refocus what is admitted (see Figure 6-1).

**Selective Attention**

Our senses could not hope to respond to the infinite number of possible stimuli assaulting them at any given moment—the hundreds of different kinds of sounds so constantly a part of our environment that, by contrast, a really soundproof room seems confining, the literally thousands of wave lengths of light in the lamps or streaming in through the windows in the room in which you sit, the multitudinous details of pattern and texture of the various furnishings that are part of our normal environment, to say nothing of the literally thousands of ads in that inch-thick newspaper you receive Sunday morning.

Some of these intended stimuli are shut out for us biologically. The "silent" whistle which dog trainers use is not silent for the dog. His ears can respond to frequencies as high as 20,000 cycles per second. No human ear can hear such a sound. The hundreds of smells in every room and even on every blade of grass, have meaning to the hound, but to the human nose they do not exist. By contrast, the colorful reds and blues and greens in our everyday costumes have no meaning to the hound. To him it all looks as though it were on monochromatic television.

Perhaps the most dramatic example of selective perception is that built into the inheritance of the bull frog who, sitting motionless on the lily pad, uses selective attention to enable himself to fill his belly with the insects zipping past his nose in the evening air. Science tells us he is able to perform the seemingly miraculous task of pulling insects in from the evening air with his six-inch-long tongue because he observes only two aspects of anything around him: shape and velocity. Unlike the entomologist, he has no way of distinguishing between the different characteristics of the various species and subspecies zipping through the evening air. Were he to do such a careful job of observing the wide variety of color, of wing structure, of legs, and so forth he would go

### Figure 6-1.   The Real Consumer

No mere puppet, responding to the whim of any seller:

But a choosy individual, selecting for attention just those messages and other stimuli directed to his interests, perceiving only those details he finds important, and ignoring all else:

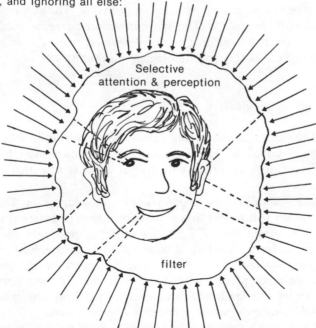

Selective
attention & perception

filter

Infinity of selling efforts and other
stimuli beseiging his attention

hungry, so he merely concentrates on finding convex shapes moving in his direction, notes the speed, and flicks out his tongue for another morsel. Thus, he has an inbuilt biological mechanism which narrows his attention to those elements that enable him to keep himself fed.

Our consumer housewife's selective attention goes far beyond her initial biological equipment, or she too would be unable to feed her family. When she checks over the dozens of pages in the Thursday morning food section of her local newspaper, she spends no precious time comparing, in detail, the hundreds of items listed by all the stores in the area. Her attention stops only at the ads of the Market Basket and Bond's Market chains, for these are the only ones near her home. She notes only the lamb shoulder and Temple orange ads, which seem to her to be good buys and fit into her Sunday menu plans. The ad showing a good buy in pork may be passed by because she is dieting and does not want a meat with much fat, and she doesn't even note the artichoke ads because her family never eats them. The coupon for a new type of frozen pizza, however, does catch her attention because the kids really go for pizza and this might be a useful supplement to her freezer storage.

Only by so limiting her attention to those items which are of interest to her can she hope to have time and energy to take care of the many other activities she must engage in during the day. The end result is the same as that of the frog's. The mechanism in her case is a learned mechanism, and based on her personal learned interests. It is just as efficient, however, as the frog's biological mechanism.

### Inborn Selection Tendencies

Some of the rules for attracting attention are obviously inborn, since they can be observed in babies as early as two days after birth. The most important of these rules is that what attracts attention is *change* of some kind.

The reason for this is the process known as *adaptation*. Our senses tend to accustom themselves to any persistent type of external stimulus. We adapt to a certain level of light, for example, and only notice when that level is suddenly changed. A radio playing in the background in our room soon becomes silent to our ears. An advertisement seen in the same form, the same places, week after week, month after month, soon becomes part of the landscape and ceases to deliver any message. A woman of the author's acquaintance, who was extremely sensitive to smells and very much interested in perfumes, used to change her brand of soap every two to three months, choosing a brand with a different fragrance, simply because the older brand had for the time being lost its ability to transmit a perceivable odor to her nose. Eventually, of course, she would return to the same brand, after her nose had become adapted to the other odors and she could no longer sense them. The previous brand then became the means of getting the needed change.

This is doubtless one reason why many firms unconsciously feel the need for occasional advertising agency changes, to draw on creative personnel who will come up with changed advertising themes or treatments, which thereby become, for the time being, more effective than the previous advertisements, which themselves had proved effective initially under the old agency, but which had lost their message-transmitting power because of the lack of variation.

Change is involved both in the intensity of a stimulus and in its quality. For example, one theory of advertising is that it is better to "flight" ads than to maintain a consistent campaign—to run an intensive series of the advertisement for a period of a few weeks and then drop them completely, or switch to a different theme for a considerable period and then bring them back.

A change in the quality of a stimulus is also effective. If our background music has been composed mainly of Strauss waltzes and a rock and roll record is suddenly interjected, we immediately become aware of the program. A sudden shift in the flavor of a favorite food gets instant notice (and it may not be favorable).

One attention-getting characteristic of external stimuli that is very closely related to change is that of *contrast*. Thus, we notice the dress of a woman which is in sharp black-and-white checks much more quickly than the dress that is in checks of two muted shades of green. We notice the advertisement that is in color when all the other advertisements in the magazine are in black and white, or, conversely, the advertisement that is a stark black-and-white print ad, standing among a lot of four-color illustrated advertisements. A package on the supermarket shelf which has a design very similar to that of other packages would be hard to find. One which stands out in terms of shape or basic color and design will be easily picked out. The district that always goes Republican will attract little attention in the news-papers until it suddenly elects a Democrat.

Another attention-getting characteristic very closely related to change is that of the effect of *relative movement*. An advertising sign using stroboscopic motion is normally a better attention getter than a sign whose message remains stationary, but on a street on which all of the display signs show movement, the one that shows no movement will get the attention.

*Relative size* is another attention-attracting characteristic. It is the headlines, not the smaller print, of the newspaper that catch your eye first. But were the front page all headlines, with only a little box of very small print, it is the small print that would catch the attention first. Likewise, relative intensity is an attention-getting stimulus—the black display type is noticed rather than the less intrusive lighter faces. Again, however, it is really the contrast that catches our attention, so that in a magazine of all heavy-faced ads, one with a set of lighter faces will catch the vision first.

One attention-getting characteristic not related to change is that of *repetition*. The very insistent nature of repeated stimuli may finally break through and penetrate our consciousness. For example, in one study of the effect of advertising for frankfurters by one of the leading packing companies some years ago, it was found that it took close to fifteen repetitions before an effect in the packer's sales could be perceived (Twedt, 1965).

The fact that repetition works would seem to be a contradiction in the process of adaptation. However, repetition seems to be most important in breaking through the barrier to attention whenever the inherent interest in the subject is relatively slight, although not absent. One major item in our internal censorship of external data is our own degree of interest in the stimulus being presented. None of the tricks appealing to our inborn attention-getting tendencies are of much avail if the subject which is being presented to us does not have some response in our own internal interests.

### The Consumer's Individual Interests and Selection

If you are a man, it is unlikely that you noticed anything about any of the advertisements or news articles about women's fashions, in the newspapers you perused in the last week. But if you are a girl, particularly of the ages between eighteen and twenty-five, you may very well remember quite accurately a number of these advertisements. On the other hand, if you are a mechanically inclined auto buff you may have passed by all of the garment advertisements of any type, whatever your sex, but saw and remembered the small notice for next week's auto rally and picked up the back page item about the new model sports car that is appearing on the market.

Only those messages get through our mental secretary or filter which are directed to our personal interests. If they are so directed, indeed, and the interest is very high, few of the tricks of attention getting may be necessary. A small ad, simply selectively headlined to our particular interest, may catch more attention from us than a double-page spread in the center fold of the magazine which has no content appealing to us. It is this personal selectivity that accounts for much of the diversion of the messages directed to us to our mental secretary's waste basket.

One important aspect of attention getting is what is known as the *law of primacy and recency*, which states that out of any series of stimuli we find it easier to remember those which come first (primary) or those that are last in the series (recency). Thus we tend to remember the topic sentence or the last sentence of a paragraph that we read. When there are a number of radio spot announcements that are crammed in between two parts of a program to which we pay attention, we are more likely to remember the first and the last of the series than those in between, provided they have an equal degree of interest to us. The most recent experiences with a product we commonly use may well mean more to us, especially if they are different, than the experiences we had previously.

## Selective and Creative Perception

The world around us is probably just as much the kind of blooming confusion we all experienced as new-born babies. Nevertheless, to us it all seems to have meaning and organization due to the process we call *perception*.

Perception is the process through which we gain meaning from the parts of the universe to which we pay attention, by organizing and interpreting the evidence brought to us by our senses. A person's voice is really a whole series of individual sound waves that we organize into images we recognize as words. Indeed, much of what we receive through our senses is extremely fragmentary. Without some degree of organization, the filling in of details which are not directly seen or heard, we would have difficulty getting any meaning out of what our senses tell us.

As with attention, we have a number of inborn tendencies toward perception, the most important for our purposes coming under the heading of the concepts *figure and ground, closure, proximity,* the *discriminal threshold,* or *j.n.d.* (just noticeable difference), and *context.*

### Figure and Ground

There is no real dividing line between attention and perception, since the very fact that we choose to pay attention to some events around us is in itself a method of organizing our universe, of interpreting what is important and what is unimportant to us personally. The concept of figure-ground phenomena is essentially an attention phenomena. But it is also clearly a case of interpreting what we sense. Figure-ground is illustrated by the fact of your perception of this page. All that it really contains, objectively, are splotches of pigments that absorb light and thus appear to you to be black, and other splotches of white, or near-white, that constitute the paper. You, however, do not see them this way. You perceive letters and words of black against a background of white. "Background" is the everyday term for what the psychologist calls *ground*. You see the letters as *figures*, the page you see as *ground*. this would be true even if the page were printed in reverse with the letters left blank (or white) on a black background. You would still tend to see the letters as figures and the page as ground.

Two common psychological examples of visual figure-ground phenomena are shown in Figure 6-2. Figure 6-2A may appear to you at first to be simply a bunch of irregular blotches of black. However, if you continue to look at this carefully for quite a time, you will see something quite meaningful to you—you will see a word. Look away for a while and look back. Immediately the word is what you see. Figure 6-2B illustrates the fact that ground and figure can easily be reversed at times. As you look at it, at first it may look to you like a bird bath or vase. Look carefully, however, at the center line in this figure and you can see two facial profiles—but note that you cannot see both the vase and the faces at the same time. You must perceive the figure either as the vase or as two faces. One of them has to recede into the background.

This tendency to divide the universe of our senses into figure and ground is built into every aspect of the organism's reception of stimuli—sight, sound, taste, feeling, and so forth. However, once a given perception of a situation is learned, it tends to persist. Look back for example, at the black blotches. Do you not immediately see the word "FILE"? Figure-ground, of course, is typical of all of our sensory impressions. The constant roar of traffic or other noises around us in the city become ground against which we may hear the siren of a police car easily or the hail of a friend from across the street. To the woodsman, the rustle of the trees is ground against which he may hear the cracking of a twig indicating the passage of a deer. News that happens every day is not news (and so it seldom gets printed)—only the unusual and out-of-the-ordinary gets the headlines.

What we perceive as figure and what we perceive as ground tend to be modified by learning and perceptual expectations. The story is told of a woodsman who came to New York and in the midst of the crowds

## Figure 6-2. Figure and Ground: Visual Experiments

A. What is it?

B. A Classical Experiment: Is it some kind of goblet or bird bath?

OR

Is it two facial profiles?

Can you see both at one and the same time?

became quite lonely. Suddenly he heard a familiar sound above the roar of Madison Avenue—the chirp of a cricket—and followed it until he found a cricket beneath the grating. His searching movements attracted a crowd, and when the people saw what was happening they wondered at his ability to hear the chirp of a small cricket against the roar of the city. Then someone dropped a dime on the pavement and immediately everyone turned but the woodsman. To them the sound of the dime was a familiar and important item, the chirp of the cricket mere background.

Figure and ground is usually interpreted in terms of familiarity. It is the ability to separate a mass of impressions into figure-ground that enables us to pick our favorite brand out quickly, from a long line of items in a supermarket. It is also undoubtedly one of the factors in the reinforcing effect of advertisements which reduce our cognitive dissonance. The fact of a recent decision with regard to a major purchase heightens the importance of the advertisements for that particular item.

The figure-ground phenomena can be seen as basically the problem of selective attention. However, not all of our attempts to organize our universe around us, not all of our perceptions, involve simply the division of sensory impulses into figure and ground. Some of them involve the interpretation of what we sense by filling in details which are not part of our sensory experience. We call this *closure*.

### *Closure*

Closure is the tendency to fill in whatever seem to us to be gaps in the information of our senses in order to create a whole that does make sense. One way of seeing this is shown in Figure 6-3. The geometrical elements and the letters we see there are all of them incomplete. Nevertheless, we see them for what they are intended to be: triangles, circles, rectangles and the familiar letters. It is the use of closure that enables most of us to drive at night when we see only fleeting shadows which we must translate into three-dimensional perceptions.

One of the side effects of closure is the apparent tendency of the perceiver to gain a stronger impression from his sensory experiences than he would if he saw the item without the missing detail filled in. Nearly all effective and lasting entertainment is based on some degree of closure. Jokes become jokes only when the hidden meaning is furnished by the listener himself. The effect of closure, carefully used, can be a very powerful method at times of getting across the point of an advertisement which, if made explicitly, would seem superficial and

**Figure 6-3.   Closure: Visual Examples**

Do you have any difficulty recognizing each of the following symbols?

almost pointless. Closely related to the phenomenon of closure is that of proximity.

*Proximity*

Proximity is our tendency to construct patterns of sensory impressions that are seen together or heard together or otherwise sensed in relation to each other. Because of the coincidence of the sensory impressions to which we have paid attention, we tend to organize them into some meaningful pattern. This is a widely used trick in advertising —to illustrate a situation, event or condition to which most of us aspire, such as a happy social gathering, and to pair up with it some specific brand, some product which the seller hopes to have us buy: perhaps a can of beer. Another example is that of featuring a pleasant fragment of melody, a "jingle," with a product which the seller hopes to impress on our minds.

An extremely effective use of combination of mediated association transfer (described in a previous chapter), closure, and proximity were the early Marlboro cigarette campaigns, intended to establish a major niche for what was a revitalized cigarette brand.

This campaign and similar other ones, all based on some sort of masculinity stereotype, proved very effective, and Marlboro rose to be one of the leading brands—one whose image was shown by all research to be that of a masculine type of brand.

### THE MARLBORO STORY: USE OF MEDIATED TRANSFER
### OF LEARNING AND THE PRINCIPLE OF CLOSURE
### TO POSITION A NEW PRODUCT ENTRANT

Gaining a strong market niche in a well-established market for such low-physical-difference products as beer, cigarettes, detergents, soap and other toiletries generally depends on what the advertising fraternity calls "positioning." Achieving any significant perceived internal physical differentiation is rarely possible in the case of many such items of consumer usage, seldom is there much room for adding meaningful external services to the total offering bundle, and distribution of all brands is as intensive as possible. Price cutting, as with all mature categories, will not buy market, but simply imply an inferior product. Since the market is relatively mature, any sales gained must be at the expense of brands already well established on the market. With product, price and distribution not available as possible sources of noticeable difference, communications must bear the burden—generally speaking, advertising, paralleled by appropriate label, packaging and product design, to the extent possible.

"Positioning" might be defined as the establishment of a higher than normal association of the brand with some highly desired attribute in the general desire-set for that specific product category. The attribute with which the seller desires to associate the brand must, first of all, be one which large segments of buyers already hope to gain from the purchase. In addition, it must be an attribute not already clearly identified with any one brand on the market. Unless the attribute meets both of these conditions, no trick of communications technique can hope to establish the sought-for position (or "image," as the process is sometimes not too accurately labeled).

Since the difference cannot be one of physical function, the desire-set attribute involved must normally be some sought-for emotional association.

The successful invasion of the cigarette market by the Marlboro brand furnishes a classic example of such positioning. The task was successful because of the astute use of two basic psychological principles. *Mediated transfer of learning* was utilized to associate the Marlboro name with a research-established attribute in most cigarette smokers' desire-sets—a feeling of virility. The principle of *closure* was used to get the reader to make the association himself, and thus make it convincing.

The Marlboro brand name was one of a number acquired by the Philip Morris Company when it purchased the Benson and Hedges operation, and it was chosen as the vehicle for entry into the then growing filter tip market segment. Preliminary research by Elmo Roper and Associates had disclosed that the little-known brand suffered from an undesirable feminine image. A rather thorough psychological study of smokers, sponsored by the Chicago Tribune, had already disclosed that the strongest single emotional motive for smoking was to gain a sense of virility, or potency. This was, of course, not a motive any smoker would name outright, or even was directly conscious of. It was not a cognitive motive, but an affective one—a feeling.

The Philip Morris Company and its advertising agency, Leo Burnett, Inc., decided to build on this knowledge to position Marlboro as a "man's man's" cigarette. But any copy which stated this theme outright, in any manner, could not hope to succeed in sounding anything but silly. Such a cognitive appeal would not work to establish an affective association. It was necessary to lead the prospect himself to make the connection.

The device used consisted of two parts:

a. Use of the known association of virility with cigarette smoking, by illustrating the advertisements with cigarette smokers in highly masculine, "men only" occupations (cowboys, sailors, and others), reinforced by means of a further stereotype of masculinity—a tattoo on the hand or arm of the model. Although the model shown was smoking, none of the earliest advertisements showed any brand identification for his cigarette in the illustration itself. (The copy portion did picture the Marlboro package, of course.)

b. Use of accompanying copy which made no reference to the main illustration, but simply carried a brief message about Marlboro, with the slogan (sung as a jingle on the aired advertisements) "You get a lot to like in a Marlboro—filter, flavor, fliptop box." The original package was a "hard" pack—the fliptop box. Later a conventional "soft" pack was added, and the "lot to like" became "filter, flavor, pack or box." The advertisement in Figure 6-4 is one of the early series, used after the introduction of the soft pack.

Objectively analyzed, the advertisements thus consisted of two unrelated parts: an illustration of a brawny, he-man type smoking a cigarette, and some copy with a simple message about Marlboro cigarettes. But the two are juxtaposed, and as already shown, human perception tends to relate items in close proximity to each other, to gain some organized meaning for the whole, through *closure*. Since the illustration accompanies the copy, the two must, to the reader, have some meaningful connection, and the obvious connection is that the cigarette must be a Marlboro. Thus the initial association is of the brand with the illustration. The illustration itself, moreover, is one of a stereotype representing a virile "he-man." Thus, through mediated transfer, Marlboro must be a cigarette that is most likely to confer the sought-for virility.

Since the prospect made the association himself, it could be a convincing association, not the silly one that it would have been had the advertiser sought to establish it directly. Subsequent research revealed that such, indeed, was the case—that Marlboro was, and still is, perceived as the most masculine of brands. (Once the position was clearly established, some later Marlboro ads did show the model with a Marlboro pack in hand.)

Thus explained, the psychological devices used would seem to be obvious. Proof that such is not the case lies in a subsequent advertising campaign for a competing filter brand, apparently hoping to emulate the Marlboro success with a different position —that of "the thinking man's cigarette."

This other campaign, however, violated the first of the principles of positioning—it sought to manufacture a position which did not exist in the smoker's mind. No study, then or since, has revealed any association of cigarette smoking, in the smoker's perceptions, with intellectuality. "The thinking man" was not part of the desire-set for the purchase of cigarettes.

Moreover, the campaign sought to state its theme directly. The brand was hailed in the advertising headlines as "the thinking man's cigarette," thus attempting to gain an affective (emotional) association through cognitive copy. (In nearly two decades of advertising, Marlboro has *never* made a direct statement that it is a "man's" cigarette.) Thus the emulative campaign missed the need for a preexisting association which could be transferred through mediation, and the need to make the prospect build the association himself through perceptual closure. The "thinking man's cigarette" campaign never got off the ground.

**Figure 6-4. An Early Marlboro Advertisement**

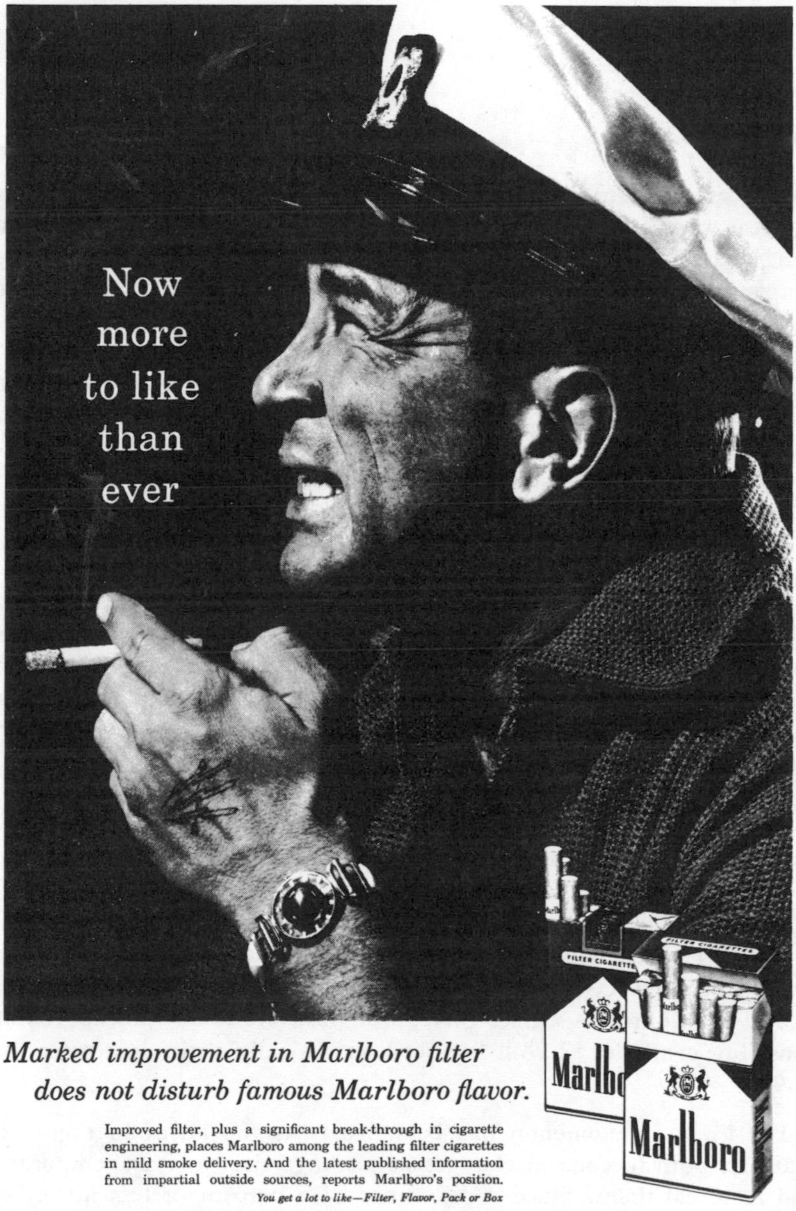
Now
more
to like
than
ever
*Marked improvement in Marlboro filter does not disturb famous Marlboro flavor.*
Improved filter, plus a significant break-through in cigarette engineering, places Marlboro among the leading filter cigarettes in mild smoke delivery. And the latest published information from impartial outside sources, reports Marlboro's position.
*You get a lot to like—Filter, Flavor, Pack or Box*
FILTER CIGARETTES
Marlboro

(Marlboro illustrations courtesy of Philip Morris, Inc.)

Another very important inborn aspect of our tendency to organize our perceptions is that of the discriminal thresholds, or the *just noticeable difference* (j.n.d.).

## The j.n.d. Effect

To a great extent we are all born to do approximations rather than to exercise very close discrimination. Extremely minor differences are perceived as no difference at all. This can be illustrated very easily by a simple personal experiment. Take two piles of paper, each of them holding exactly 100 sheets of the same type, quality and weight of paper. Have someone subtract a couple of sheets from one of the piles while you are not looking. Turn back and see if you can tell the difference. It is very unlikely that you can. Continue this process until you can definitely perceive such a difference. The probabilities are that something close to ten sheets will have been subtracted by that time. Or take a look at the boxes shown in Figure 6-5. Which is the largest of the three? Which is the smallest? Which two are most closely alike? Now turn to the end of the chapter and see the right answer.

The just noticeable difference phenomenon is an extremely important one in marketing efforts of all sorts. As our suggested experiment with the paper indicates, and as the test of perceptual discrimination (Figure 6-5) does also, a *just noticeable difference* is not a tiny or infinitesimal difference. Indeed, with a possible exception of man's sensitivity to light intensity, the differences are often of the order of 7, 8, or 10 percent, except where modified by long arduous training. In the case of visual impressions of light intensity, the differences are still well over 1 percent.

As will be seen later in discussing pricing, the j.n.d. is an important factor in all aspects of pricing and price changes. We do not merely receive the figures as we see them, but translate them into approximations. For example, $2.98 is not seen as basically a different price than $2.94.

The j.n.d. phenomenon has been used, as the boxes in Figure 6-5 indicate, both to conceal changes in package size, at least temporarily, and to reveal them. Since a difference of 5 percent or less in any one dimension is not likely to be quickly perceived, such a difference can be made in each of the three dimensions, and the consumer can be led to

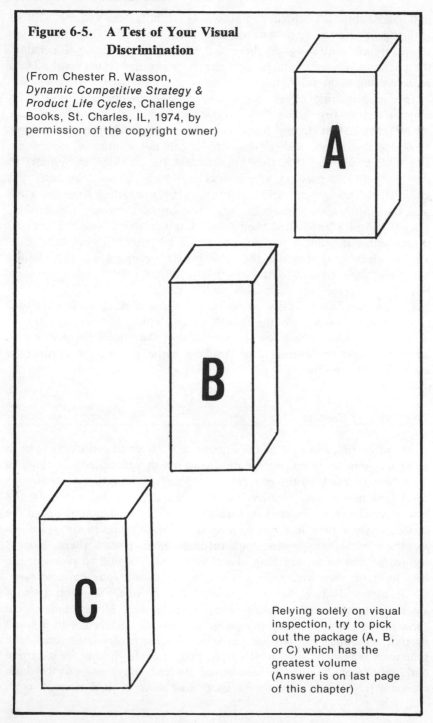

**Figure 6-5.   A Test of Your Visual
                Discrimination**

(From Chester R. Wasson,
*Dynamic Competitive Strategy &
Product Life Cycles*, Challenge
Books, St. Charles, IL, 1974, by
permission of the copyright owner)

Relying solely on visual
inspection, try to pick
out the package (A, B,
or C) which has the
greatest volume
(Answer is on last page
of this chapter)

purchase a product which contains substantially less volume without realizing it. However, as one of the other boxes in this illustration shows, by concentrating all these differences into a single dimension, the package can be made to look much larger and thus emphasize a greater value being offered.

This emphasizing effect, for example, was the method used by a major toiletries firm when their hold on the women's water-based hair spray market was being threatened by a much larger competitor. Realizing that they could not hope to match the volume of advertising and sales promotion that they knew would be mounted in support of the competitor's product which was obviously already in test, the established firm waited until they knew that the invading firm had gone past the halfway mark in preparing their initial inventory for market. They then quickly switched their own container size to one that was 50 percent more in volume and put the entire 50 percent in height of can. The result was that when the new brand appeared on the shelves alongside their own, it was obviously a much poorer buy. The new brand never gained an acceptable market share.

The j.n.d. effect is really another one of the various inborn tendencies we have to reduce the bewildering chaotic complexity of the universe around us into a few simple patterns. In effect, the purpose of all our inborn tendencies is to produce some pattern or context in everything around us.

## The Effect of Context

An interesting example of the unconscious effect of context is seen in an experiment to determine the degree to which people judge quality in a product as much by the general atmosphere surrounding a product as by the nature of the product itself. In the experiment, women's silk hose were shown to housewives with the instructions that they judge the quality of these hose in the same way they normally did in the store—to feel them with their fingers, look through them, stretch them, look at the seams and to do anything else they normally would to pick out the best for their own use. Each housewife was shown four pairs of hose, all of them identical in every respect except one. To each pair of stockings was pinned a small card of perfumer's blotter paper. On three of the pairs, this blotting paper had been moistened with a small drop of aromatic compound capable of emitting a very faint scent, one somewhat below the level which most people could detect. As it turned out, only 6 of 250 housewives tested noticed the scent on the hose consciously. One of the scents used was that of a narcissus type, another was of a type known by perfumers as fruity, and the third was that of a sachet type scent. The fourth hose was not reodorized in any way, so that it had the naturally slightly rancid scent which comes from a mixture of castor oil and sulphates used in lubricating the yarns to facilitate weaving and confer some degree of softness. No mention was made of the fact that a scent might be present on any of the hose. Nevertheless, less than one housewife in twelve chose the natural (unscented) hose as the best in quality and there was a consistent preference for those with the narcissus scent in approximately one-half of all the housewives interviewed. Quite clearly, there was an unconscious bias toward the quality of the product shown in a perfumed context, even though the housewife was not consciously aware of the perfume (Laird, 1932). This specific device of perfuming is widely used in marketing, particularly in the establishment of some kind of contextual brand differentiation in minor convenience items like soap and toilet paper.

Likewise, another experiment indicated that housewives were more likely to perceive bread as fresh when covered with a cellophane wrapper than when wrapped in waxpaper (Brown, 1958).

This tendency to view things within a context is always an important part of merchandising. A mink coat offered in a discount market will not sell as well as one offered in a quality shop. Its quality is not perceived as being the same. The history of the sale of Steuben Glassware shows that the volume of sales went up substantially for this extremely expensive handblown glassware when it was taken over by Corning Glassware and the number of outlets reduced to a mere handful which were then required to show it in very elegant displays.

The importance of context explains why a great deal of attention is paid to packaging of all sorts of consumer products, but the results are not confined to consumer products alone. A company that was making a standard laboratory instrument—a potentiometer selling in the neighborhood of $500—found that when the instrument was put in a well-designed case instead of the standard, rather stodgy, walnut case, they could obtain well over $100 more for the same instrument. The meaning which we give to the contexts or settings and to the perceptions in general are largely a result of learning. To a very great extent we perceive things as we have learned to perceive them.

## Perceptions—Learned Tendencies

If we take a snapshot of a cow head-on from very close up, the resulting picture shows a very strange animal indeed—one in which the head is bigger than the rest of the body. If we take a picture of a disc held at an angle, the photograph shows us an oval. The camera has no perceptions. It only records the images that come to it much as our retina does.

But what we perceive is quite different from the image projected on our own retina. Cows to us look the same whether we are close up, head on or seen from the side at a considerable distance. The head is always in proportion to the body. A plate we know to be round always looks round to us, no matter from what angle we see it.

It is probable that, as babies, we first saw things exactly as the camera does. But through long experience we have learned to know what a cow looks like, or in fact, what any animal looks like, and we never expect the head to be larger than the body, so we always see it in proportion. Similarly, if you were to set out a six-feet-high stake directly in front of a person, and another stake the same size at a distance of 100 yards, 200 yards, or 500 yards, most people will see them as exactly the same size, picking up clues from the surroundings to judge the distance. The camera, of course, shows them to be of various lengths on the flat surface of its film.

This phenomenon is known as *constancy* by psychologists, and this applies to all of the various senses through which we receive our impressions, including any mental impressions or images we may have of various kinds of situations and contexts. We sense things as we expect to sense them, based on past experience, and we approach things with perceptual sets based on prior knowledge and experiences. If we see a fur coat that looks like mink in a discount store, we see it as a low quality coat and probably a fake, even though it could be identical to one sold in the most exclusive shop in town. And since mink coats are supposed to be quality products, we would not buy one in the discount store. Because experience has told my wife that the Silver Duck Supermarket has by far the best steaks in town, she finds the broilers and fryers that she buys there taste better than those she buys at the Pick-and-Save down the street, despite the fact that the broilers in both stores doubtless came from the same production area, even the same producer, and have been raised under identical conditions.

It is this constancy aspect of our perceptions which accounts for much of the value of an established brand. It is also one reason why it is relatively difficult for an emulative product to take over part of the market of an established brand if the real difference in quality cannot be sensed at a very substantial level. If the difference is only a minor one, the product will still tend to be percieved as being inferior by those accustomed to the older brand. In fact, on a blind test, producers of products such as beer, in which the differences between brands are often relatively minor, sometimes find that habitual drinkers of one brand rate that brand lower than others in blind test situations. Such constancies of perception are relatively universal traits throughout a culture in which experiences are common. There are other differences between what we sense and what we perceive which are due to individual factors.

## Individual Factors in Perception

Not all people have the same experiences, and the results of these differences in experience can result in different perceptions of the same objectively similar stimulus. Furthermore, our perceptions can be colored by our emotions and desires at a given time. We often perceive what we would like to perceive or even what we fear. An excellent example of the difference in perception of a specific stimulus has been cited by Martineau (1957). He found that middle-class housewives shown a picture of a baby responded with such adjectives as "cute," "attractive," "appealing." Working-class housewives shown the same photo, however, reacted with such terms as "brat," "nuisance" and the like. Both of them were reflecting their feelings and experiences about the role of housewife. To the middle-class housewife, this was normally a pleasant experience. To the working-class housewife, not a beneficiary of diaper service, family and housewife duties meant frustration instead.

Emotion, of course, was an important component of this reaction. Another aspect of effect of emotion on perception was an experiment in which children of various degrees of affluence were shown coins. It was discovered that poor children remembered coins as being larger than did children from rich families (Bruner and Goodman, 1947). Such experiments suggest that a great deal of care needs to be taken in the use of symbolism in advertisements, most of which are prepared by middle-class-agency artists and copywriters. The connotations and perceptual sets that we have for words, symbols and pictures of all sorts will vary from one group to another.

Product designers face a similar problem. As knowledgeable experts, they are prone to read meaning into design elements which the layman does not perceive at all. One of the errors in the unfortunate design features of Ford's Edsel was a central free-standing grill. To professional designers in the automobile industry, this grill was a symbol of the classic cars of the 1930s such as the Pierce-Arrow and the LaSalle, and also of sports cars such as the Bugatti and Alfa Romeo. But to lay critics, it was a "horse collar," and to most laymen, it conveyed no meaning whatever (Myers and Reynolds, 1967).

Perception is thus as much a part of the personality as the differences in facial appearance. One of the reasons people differ in the way they react to any stimulus of any kind is because they have different perceptions of the meaning of the stimulus.

## Summary

1.   All of us ignore and fail to react to all but a tiny fraction of the stimuli directed to our senses. The reason is the high degree of selectivity in both our attention and our perceptions, based on pre-existing interest and knowledge.

2.   Selective attention enables the individual to reserve his consideration to just those stimuli in his environment which are of current importance in meeting his needs.

3.   Some types of selective attention are inborn: we are naturally deaf to much of the sound range other animals can hear, and sense few of the subtler odors quite apparent to many species.

4.   In addition, certain inborn tendencies govern the characteristics of the stimuli which will gain notice.

5.   One major tendency is attention mainly to change: the individual filters out, by adaptation, any stimulus which tends to persist.

6.   Contrast is a related attention-attracting characteristic.

7.   Relative movement and relative size also attract notice.

8.   Repetition can eventually win attention.

9.   The key factor in attention is the appeal to the individual's currently aroused interests.

10.   Perception is the process by which individuals organize and give coherent meaning to the information to which they do pay attention. This is also a selective process.

11.   The perceptual processes most important to the understanding of consumer behavior are those of *figure and ground*, *closure*, *proximity*, the *discriminal threshold* or *j.n.d.* (just noticeable difference), the effect of *context*, and the principle of *constancy*.

12.   By figure and ground is meant the tendency to focus on certain details of what we sense (figure) and relegate the remainder to the background (ground) to which we pay slight attention.

13.   Closure is the process by which we fill in gaps we perceive in the detail of what we sense in order to give it coherent meaning.

14. Proximity is the tendency to view as a single whole those items of sensory experience which come to us in close association.

15. The j.n.d., or discriminal threshold exists because we experience minor differences of sensory stimulus of any kind as no difference at all. Generally speaking, for most people in most matters of sensory experience, the j.n.d. is of the order of 7 to 10 percent. This is a matter of central importance in product differentiation and in pricing decisions, as well as many other aspects of marketing management.

16. The context in which a stimulus is perceived will color that perception.

17. What we actually sense, physically, and what we perceive mentally are not necessarily the same. Due to the principle of constancy, we sense things as we expect them to be on the basis of past experience.

18. Wide differences in individual perception exist because of equally wide differences in experience as well as differences in the emotional context in which the sensory experience occurs.

19. Because of these differences, often of class origin, designers, copywriters, and other communicators need to be careful about assuming that their own perceptions are paralleled by those in the market segment they hope to attract.

**Answer to Question in Figure 6-5**

If you chose B, your perception is normal, but wrong. B does have more volume than A, because it has the identical depth and breadth, and is 15 percent higher—a noticeable difference because all of the excess is concentrated in a single dimension. But C has slightly greater volume than B. Although it probably seemed equal to A on inspection, each of its three dimensions is 5 percent greater (less than a j.n.d. for most people) and thus has nearly 115.8 percent of the volume of A, as compared with only 115 percent for B. B nevertheless would appear larger than C because it is nearly 10 percent taller (close to their j.n.d.), even though 5 percent less (less than a j.n.d. in *both* width and depth.

Chapter 6 Exercises


1.  Your text gives one famous example of the use of closure to gain conviction for an advertising theme—the Marlboro Man theme. Can you find other examples in current advertising of any kind?

2.  How selective is your attention? Try this experiment. For one day, keep a dawn-to-dusk diary of the advertisements you are actually exposed to:

    Check and mark just those pages of the newspapers and magazines you happen to read, as you are reading them. Then go back and count the ads on the pages you covered (do not read them).

    Count the commercials on the broadcast programs you listen to or see.

    Count the billboards on whatever route you are traveling.

    Total the number of advertising exposures. The next morning, ask yourself which advertisements you remember. Put down this number. What were the advertisements about which you seem to have remembered? What was there in them which caught your attention, and what do you remember about them?

3.  During the 1973-74 impeachment hearings of the U. S. House of Representatives Judiciary Subcommittee, leaks about the testimony were often contradictory, with some Republicans finding nothing really wrong in some of the testimony, and others, usually but not always Democrats, finding the same testimony quite damaging. Yet the testimony of the reporters seemed to indicate that few of the committee were taking a really partisan approach. What aspect of the material in this chapter would explain this discrepancy?

4.  Some advertising campaigns are run for 20 years or more without change, but most advertisers seem to find frequent changes of approach necessary, even to the point of making agency changes at times. What aspect of psychology discussed in this chapter supports the need for changes?

5.  Try this experiment. Take two equal fresh stacks of the same kind of paper, with at least 100 sheets in each stack. (Two fresh reams of exactly 500 sheets each would be even better.) Turn your back and have a friend remove one sheet from one stack. Then see if you can identify the stack. Repeat the process, having him always remove the sheet taken from the same stack, until you can

identify the smaller stack, by sight or by feel. This is your j.n.d. What percent is it of the total?

6. Give some examples of the *figure and ground* reaction that you can observe. (Remember, any form of perception is involved, not just the visual patterns useful for printing in a text.)

7. Is there any product for which you periodically and intentionally change brands or styles or types? Why?

8. Signboards are sometimes designed with one letter or word printed backwards and some trucks have their company name or business printed on the front in mirror image. Why?

9. Find some ads in which the principle of relative size is used to catch attention.

10. No new automobile model ever can be a very important fraction of the cars on the road in the first few months of introduction. Yet many drivers find the relative frequency of the sighting of a new model which is getting popular quite high. What principle explains this tendency to note these few cars among the multitude the driver passes on the road?

# PART III.
## The Social Sources of Behavioral Content

PART II OUTLINED how the consumer's habits, attitudes and perceptions develop, but did little more than indicate the sources of the external conditioning which leads to the specific habits and perceptions of the given individual.

That conditioning results in an adult whose personality can be conceived of as a complex series of learned social roles relative to the reference groups of which the individual is a member or to which he otherwise looks for approval. The reference groups themselves, of which the family is normally the most important, define the outlines of those roles, passing on to him a set of perceptions, of value and correct behavior. The standards themselves originate in the culture or subculture of which the group is a part. Some of the cultural and subcultural differences are geographical in extent. Social class, however, is a very important form of subcultural grouping which is not geographical. Social classes in the same area show many wide differences in matters of taste and preference.

# 7

# The Consumer as a Complex
# of Social Roles

THE MANY ROLES OF ANY INDIVIDUAL AND THE EFFECT ON BUYING DECISIONS

GROUP ROLES AND THE PECKING ORDER

GATEKEEPERS AND THE PURCHASE DECISION

ROLE CHANGES OVER TIME

THE WORKING MARRIED HOUSEWIFE AND THE EFFECT ON FAMILY ROLES

OLDER POPULATION ROLE EFFECTS

INDIVIDUAL INTERPRETATION OF THE ROLE

ANXIETY BEHAVIOR, REFERENCE GROUPS AND ROLE TRANSITIONAL BEHAVIOR

    Role Transition as a Source of Anxiety
    Specific Sources of Anxiety:

        Uncertainty and Rejection
        Frustration and Conflict
        Consonant Dissonance
        Physical Harm

EFFECT OF ANXIETY ON RISK BEHAVIOR

IDENTIFICATION AS DEFENSE AND AS MAJOR MARKET FORCE

ROLE TRANSITION AS A MAJOR MARKET FORCE

In very few of his decisions, and especially in a very minor part of his buying decisions, does the consumer act as an individual, making decisions purely on the basis of his own independent desires and wishes. Most of his purchases are heavily influenced by the role he is performing at the moment as a member of a larger group. Shakespeare was being more than a biased member of the theatrical profession when he observed that "all the world's a stage, and all the men and women merely players." Most of what we do from day to day and month to month is to act out one of the roles prescribed for us by one of the various groups of which, for the moment, we are acting as a member or perceive ourselves as a member.

The term "role" is taken directly from the stage by sociologists and has exactly the same meaning as it has for the actor on the stage. It can be defined as a prescription for our interpersonal behavior with other people, behavior which is associated with a specific socially recognized *category* of person.

As on the stage, the role is basically the same no matter who performs it, but it is also subject to the individual interpretation of the actor. The role goes with a given position and with a specific status assigned to us within the group. This position and status will vary greatly from one to another of the many groups of which we are members, and will also change over our lifetime within a given group, as Shakespeare himself observed. The script for a role defines a relatively broad range of behavior between what is prohibited for a person in that position and what is definitely prescribed.

## Our Many Roles at a Given Moment in Time and Their Effect on Buying Decisions

As marketing research has long shown, we can predict a great deal about the behavior of a person by simply describing him in terms of the many kinds of positions which he holds. He may, for example, be described as a purchasing agent for the local factory, a 40-year-old father of three teenagers, an ardent golfer and member of the local country club, and so forth. If we do a thorough enough job describing the various positions he holds, our knowledge of the roles involved in each will enable us to make a fairly good prediction of how a group of such men will act in a given purchase situation within a given role. Thus, the personality of any individual can be very largely defined in terms of his many roles in the community and society of which he is a part. (See Figure 7-1.)

**Figure 7-1.    The Many Roles Which Make Up the Personality of One Consumer, Mr. Smith**

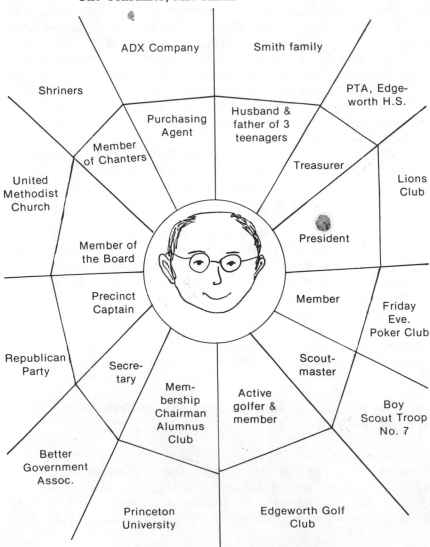

However, to predict his behavior properly, we also need to know in what role he is acting at a given moment. Is he buying a car for himself, for the factory, or for the family, for example, in making an automobile purchase. If he is buying it for the company's sales fleet, he will be expected to pay close attention to the type of car necessary to impress the buyers on whom the salesman will call and at the same time pay equally close attention to mechanical characteristics which make for low maintenance costs on the fleet. If he is buying purely for himself and his own personal interests for commuting to his office, he may very well, if he has very much traffic to dodge and is very mechanically minded, buy a sports car. But if he is buying a car for the family to use for general traveling and shopping, he may very well purchase a station wagon. On the other hand, he may want to have a sports car because of its ease of handling and his love of precision machinery but recognize that it is not very practical in a family with four drivers and thus settle on a different model entirely. Thus, roles can conflict and the decision will be made on the basis of whatever role is dominant at the moment.

If we think back to our beginning example of the three women in the supermarket, we remember that many of their decisions were made with respect to the tastes of other members of the family rather than their own. They were acting, not as individual women, or even as women at all, but as homemakers who were expected to take into account the needs of all the members of the family and not just their own personal wishes. The mother may not particularly have cared for either chocolate cake or peanut butter, but she knew that these would satisfy the younger members of the family. And even though they had little direct decision authority in their status as children, they nevertheless influenced her purchase.

Similarly, in a factory, the purchases that are made by the executives in the company must take into account the feelings and desires of the other members of the plant. The worker on the assembly line may sign no purchase orders on his own, but if the supply of wipers, for example, or the particular tool ordered does not meet his tastes, the purchasing agent will not have done a good job in his role of representing the factory, since any intense dislike by those using the items can disrupt production.

For example, some years ago, one of the major paper companies developed a lintless wiper for use in removing grease and grime from the hands of workers who were working on the assembly line of a major auto manufacturer. Up until then, the company had used a laundry service which furnished cloth towels, taking back the soiled ones for cleaning. When the paper company introduced the paper wipers into the plant as a pilot test, the shop stewards representing the workers immediately protested to the management, insisting that the men did not want to use the new paper product. A resulting compromise made both the towels and paper wipers available to the workers. After the considerable period of use needed to test out the value of the paper wipers was completed, the paper company withdrew its supply of paper wipers. Immediately the executives of the company were again informed by the stewards that the men were ready to strike because they now wanted these paper wipers!

### Group Roles and the Pecking Order

Thus, there are limits in what seems to be superficially an independent decision by anybody who is representing a group. Nevertheless, those in the top status have much more leeway than those on down the line. In every group there is some kind of "pecking order" or status. The term "pecking order" is adapted from the observation of flocks of birds by psychologists. In any flock of birds, such as chickens, for example, the status of the individual in the group is determined by his degree of aggressiveness. Two birds put together will soon establish who can peck whom. The more aggressive one can peck the other one and drive him away, for example, from a choice morsel. The other dare not peck back. If a third bird is introduced, he has to be fitted into the hierarchy. Either he has to establish his dominance as the one who can do the pecking of all others, or accept a second or third position. No matter how large the flock grows, there will thus be a definite hierarchy of who pecks whom.

Human social groups also have a pecking order (figuratively speaking, of course), in purchasing decisions as well as other matters. This order determines who is freest to make decisions, and who may deviate or object, and to what extent. Those at the lowest ranks of the order are expected to conform most rigidly to group norms, and in fact they themselves expect to do so. Numerous carefully structured psychological experiments have shown that whenever human subjects are led to believe that others in the group are conforming to a given decision, most people will conform regardless of how ridiculous the decision might appear to them as individuals in the absence of group guidance. This is doubtless one reason why some people will buy and wear fashions ill-suited to their figures and personalities.

An especially important role in purchase decisions is that of the gatekeeper, who may or may not be a member of the group itself.

## Gatekeepers and the Purchase Decision

In our opening supermarket shopping illustration, we noted that the housewives were shopping, and in some instances making decisions on the spot, for the whole family. Whether or not the family acquired and consumed the new product being demonstrated was determined by the housewife's own reaction to the product at the time of the demonstration. In other instances, the brand of product chosen was made by her, not by all of the members in consultation. She was acting in the role of gatekeeper, controlling the flow of products and brands, and perhaps even product information to the family, and the seller could reach the family only through her. Communications directed to other members of the family would probably be wasted in many cases.

But in making some of her purchases, the housewife may have been acting on the basis of directions from someone else, a person not a member of the family. Her choice of baby food may have been prescribed by the pediatrician, for example. While the pediatrician himself might never purchase a single package of the item prescribed, his choices would be the determining factor in the purchases of many families. Then the pediatrician becomes the gatekeeper, and the housewife's role is little more than that of order clerk.

The housewife's own choices of brand and product, when she is acting as family gatekeeper, would probably be based on much the same factors as if they were made by the family as a whole. Cost would certainly be one important factor, as well as such performance factors as taste and nutrition. But when the choice is being made by a professional advisor outside the group, such as the pediatrician, the first and most important factor in his mind is performance, as he sees it, and in many cases he will not be concerned about price itself to any great degree, except inasmuch as it might limit the capability of the client to obtain the item.

Outside gatekeeper advisors are a widespread phenomenon in marketing. The physician and his medical prescriptions are an obvious one. The college professor and his choice of texts is another. The architect and his choice of construction methods and materials is more important than the choices of the contractor who does the actual purchasing. A major manufacturer of large valves, widely used in utility construction, concentrated a large part of his entire selling effort on a half dozen design consultant firms, not on the utilities themselves. The specifications written into the design contracts determined whose products would be acceptable.

Gatekeepers may be, as the housewife often is, a member of the group itself. In industrial situations, it is important to learn who writes the final specifications in any purchase contract. Even within the family, there may be individuals whose choices govern those of the housewife herself, and she may merely carry out the desires of these other members as a mere purchasing agent. Such was the case of the third housewife in our opening illustration, who noted that she bought her meat at another market because of her husband's dietary desires. Such is sometimes the case in the matter of breakfast cereals promoted directly to young children on television. In the latter case, the brand and type are chosen by a consuming member without the purchasing power necessary to buy for himself. Sometimes, the expert knowledge of a member of the family, or his specific desires may affect the family decision on a major purchase. For example, the knowledgeable teen-ager may actually be the gatekeeper for the family's choice of new automobile, the purchase of which he does not finance.

### Role Changes Over Time

Although we can define much of a person's behavior at any given moment in terms of the various positions he holds and the roles assigned to those positions, his personality will change over time as his positions and group memberships change.

As we implied above, age and sex are roles in themselves. Thus, within the family, the infant begins with the lowest status and has little influence on the choice of the purchases made for him, except perhaps to completely reject a certain food product by refusing to eat it. As he grows older, however, he has more and more say in what he will accept, even before school age. By this stage in his career, advertisers have found that he can exert a great deal of pressure in the matter of products purely for his own personal consumption. When he starts to school, his group memberships themselves reach out beyond the family circle, and his "peer groups" tend more and more to set some of his behavioral standards. By the time he reaches puberty, the child expects, and to some degree is expected, to exercise a considerable degree of independence, at least from family norms. During this period, the peer group is likely to be the dominant influence in his purchase choices.

Later, as a young single adult he has a new set of roles. By this time, many of his contacts are no longer peer group contacts, but occupational contacts, for example, and other various interest groups which may very well cut somewhat across age limits. As no longer an integral member of another family so far as his purchasing decisions are concerned, he makes many new kinds of decisions on his own but by now he is looking to other reference sources for those decisions.

During early adulthood, for example, he becomes interested in what staid academics refer to as the mate selection process. And whether we are talking about a him or a her, one of the major concerns will be his own expectation of the way he will be viewed by possible companions of the opposite sex. If, as is normally the case, he and she eventually come to a mutual decision to form their own family, he passes into another status, that of the newly established family and thus begins another family cycle.

During the early periods of this new family cycle, his main attempts will be to establish a viable household and a great many of his purchase decisions will be radically switched from those of his early days as a young single. Indeed, the role of the person in the family life cycle is a major factor in purchases throughout his life as Figure 7-2 shows. As a young single, his purchases tend to be strongly directed, as we might expect, toward such personal things as automobiles, meals away from home, clothing, and recreation. Expenditures for such family oriented purchases as home furnishing equipment and such age-oriented problems as medical expenses are extremely low. The transition, however, from status of the single to that of the young married more than quadruples the expenditures for home furnishings equipment and better than doubles the medical expenses immediately—probably largely in anticipation of new members being added to the family in the latter case. The personally oriented expenditures such as those for automobile, clothing, and particularly meals away from home, drop drastically.

As responsibilities for family additions come into the picture, the expenditures on meals taken out, and on automobiles, continue to drop, and home furnishings and equipment also decline, as the family has filled most of its immediate needs in that area. The passage of children to the older age groups, however, increases the automobile and clothing expenditure. Then, as the children leave home and we get the "empty nest" families, we find a sudden increase in expenditures for medical needs, due largely to personal problems and again a strong decrease in expenditures for transportation and clothing.

Not all individuals, of course, and not all families, conform to this family life cycle as depicted. Some individuals never marry, some after marrying dissolve the partnership and join the singles culture again. Nature itself takes a hand and breaks up some of the families and leaves us again with singles. In addition, some families do not take on the responsibilities of children after marriage, or take on a very limited responsibility in this respect. Indeed, one of the more important major

**Figure 7-2.  The Family Life Cycle and Selected Consumption Patterns (Urban households, U.S.A., 1960-61)**

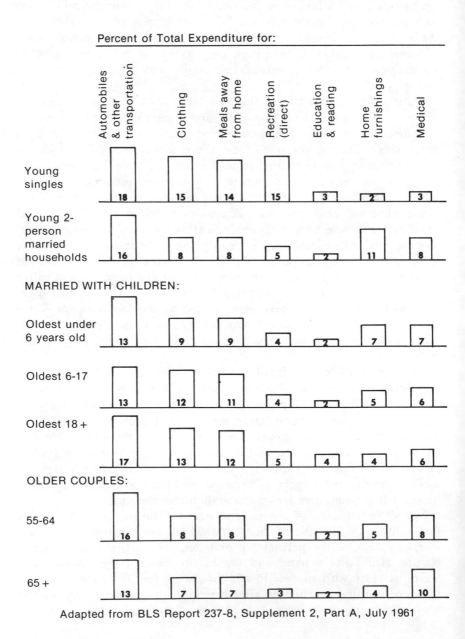

Adapted from BLS Report 237-8, Supplement 2, Part A, July 1961

developments in recent years, with a great many major effects on the marketing system, has been the growth in numbers of the employed housewife and the effects on expenditure patterns of this general tendency toward employment of both husband and wife.

## The Role of the Wife in the Working Housewife Family

The economic role of the wife in American families has gone through a considerable metamorphosis in the last 100 years. Up until early in the twentieth century, a majority of the families in the United States lived on farms, and the wife of the family had a specific group of economic functions of extreme importance in maintaining the family income. She prepared all the food from basic raw materials, made most or all of the clothes—indeed, in the early days even spun and wove the fabrics from which the clothes were made—and performed many of the food producing functions themselves, such as gardening, chicken raising, butter churning, and so forth. As populations moved to the city, however, more and more of these functions were taken over by industry itself and the housewife's production functions shrank, particularly with the development of the many electrical appliances the average household considers an urgent necessity today. Her role then became largely that of maintaining cleanliness in the home and raising the children.

Curiously enough, these two functions together seemed to take up all of the time previously occupied by many of the production functions. For many housewives today it still does, despite the large proportion of the food preparation which is undertaken by industry itself.

However, the role of housemaid began to bore many of the housewives and the costs of buying the many family necessities brought many of these women into the work force, particularly during World War II. As a result, the participation of the housewife in the production of the household's monetary resources has been steadily increasing over the years. Even a part time job outside the home cuts into the amount of time available to the housewife for many of her previous activities. Purchases, particularly in the food field, have changed markedly as a result. Home baking work, from scratch ingredients, was an early casualty. The commercial bakery took over much of the production of bread and cakes and pies. Where the housewife did do any of the baking, she began to use prepared mixes which took much less time.

The working housewife, and those who did no outside work, also tended to buy processed vegetables, especially after the advent of freezing, rather than undertake the preparation-time consuming fresh produce which had long been a staple of the food market. The result has been a steady decline in the fresh produce portion of the food market business, offset by an increase in the sale of the processed and frozen vegetables and fruits, as well as wholly processed meals and dishes.

There can be little question that the growth of "convenience" foods has largely been a result of participation of women in the work force. Sociological studies have shown that as a woman begins to participate in the work force, the importance attributed to her status as a housekeeper declines and the husband even takes over part of the household chores. It is an interesting fact that of the two most important instant products to come out of World War II—frozen orange concentrate and instant coffee—only the orange concentrate met a complete and ready acceptance from the very first. Instant coffee, which was really much simpler to market and use, took quite a period of time to gain acceptance (see Figure 7-3).

The reason for the difference seems to be a greater perception of the importance of skill in the preparation of the coffee. Frozen orange concentrate was simply a substitute for squeezing the juice out of fresh oranges—a process which has never been considered one requiring any special skill and thus met no psychological barrier to acceptance.

Coffee, on the other hand, is a product which is subject to some degree to the skill of the person making it, when prepared from roasted beans. Early studies of the attitudes of housewives toward the use of instant coffee revealed that many women considered the user of such products to be a "lazy housewife." One such study presented two different shopping lists to two different groups of women. The only difference between the shopping lists was the inclusion of ordinary roasted coffee on one list and an instant coffee on another list. When women were asked to describe the housewives who had such shopping lists, the major finding was that the list naming the instant coffee must have been made by a "lazy housewife" who did not care for her husband. But once the housewife's major role began to be that of providing part of the economic sinews of the family, and her role as homemaker declined, instant coffee gained increasingly wide usage. It was now important that the housewives save as much time as possible for the more important homemaking functions and the quality of the instant coffee was no longer seen as inferior.

One of the effects of the working housewife, and of urbanization in general, has been a decrease in the size of the family with children. At one time, the housewife's function as a breeder of children was part of her economic function. She was providing field hands for her husband during the years of their growth. In the city, however, (and also on the highly mechanized farm) the child is an economic liability. One result

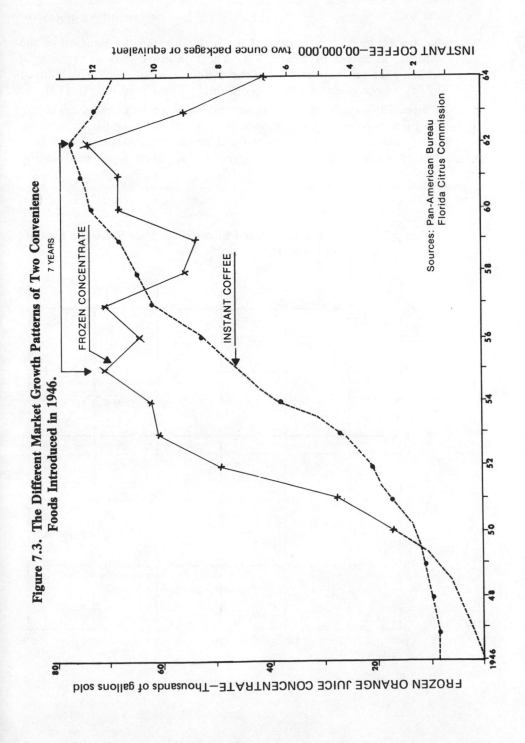

Figure 7.3. The Different Market Growth Patterns of Two Convenience Foods Introduced in 1946.

Sources: Pan-American Bureau
Florida Citrus Commission

has been a long term downtrend in the birth rate since the turn of the century, as shown by Figure 7-4. The downtrend was masked for a while by the postwar reaction to the childlessness of the 1930s, induced by the depression, and a baby boom finally peaked out only in 1957.

Since 1957, the birth rate has declined substantially and is beginning to reach a point where people can talk of zero population growth. Many families have, for reasons far different from those of the 1930s, decided to have few or no children at all. Such a no-child family

**Figure 7-4.  Trend in the United States Birth Rate Since the End of World War II**

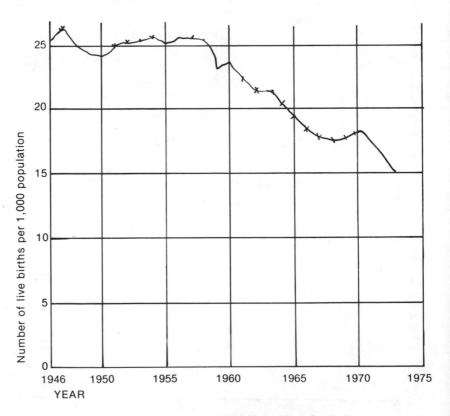

Source: Dept. of Health, Education and Welfare, *Vital Statistics*

becomes a market for a quite different mix of goods. They perceive the role of the family and their role within the family quite differently from those who have children. One of the industries which has suffered, for example, has been that making baby foods. As we got into the 1970s, industries which centered around increasingly higher school populations have felt the pinch—particularly those serving schools. On the other hand, the auto industry benefited, since such families trade in their cars oftener.

One product that has benefited has been the microwave oven. Despite the absurdly misdirected promotion of the latter, the microwave oven is a blessing for a family of only two people in which the wife and the husband get home for supper at approximately the same time. For a small meal or for dishes pulled directly from the freezer, the microwave oven can greatly speed up the whole process of meal preparation without dependence on relatively less-tasty prepared foods. (Parenthetically, it is also an extremely useful product for families with a number of teenage children and adults who must eat at different times and need quick warm-up of meals.) The industry, however, has foolishly overlooked the importance of family roles and has promoted the product as one that can cook a turkey quickly (which families cook perhaps only once a year, and for whom the oven is not at all well suited) or large roasts which no urban family with a working housewife would be interested in. Despite this bad promotion the market has gradually grown to a point where it is becoming a major appliance.

## The Roles of the Older Population

Recent changes in birth rate are being accompanied by medical advances which increase the role of older people in the population. Such changes have also been abetted by various measures which have guaranteed a greater degree of economic security in old age, extremely important in an urban culture in which the older people are no longer part of an extended family with their children. The increased numbers, improved health, and better economic conditions of these older portions of the population are causing a great deal of rethinking about the economic role of people past the retirement age. Many of them are seeking an active role in economic society, and to the extent that they succeed will become an independent consuming segment of considerable size, far more than in the past.

However, the needs and desires of people in these age groups are, as our family life cycles chart shows, quite different from those of younger families. They are no longer accumulating the hardware and software necessary to run a household. On the other hand, they are far more interested in such personal pursuits as travel and recreation. Regardless of medical advances, of course, health needs become an increasingly important problem as years go by, and there is a growing need for many kinds of quite varied institutions to provide the services that older people need. One of the markets that has grown steadily in recent years has been nursing homes for those who are nearing the terminal years. But there is also a growing need, which is only partially fulfilled, for personal service operations far short of the kinds of medical and nursing attention furnished by such a home. Many well-equipped in-town hotels, for example, are being turned into retirement hotels to take care of the household needs of these older families without the cost of heavy accompanying nursing facilities. There is unquestionably going to be an increasing market for a wider variety of kinds of services in this area than has been supplied in the recent past.

### Individual Interpretation of the Role

The roles that we are assigned within a group are by no means rigid prescriptions. They are affected to a great degree by the individual's own conceptions of what the role should be. For example, a study of French housewives uncovered two distinctly divergent orientations with respect to the role of housewife: traditionalists and modernists. Each of these two main types is found subdivided into two other subdivisions: "devoteds" who battle with the toil and are more pleased with the quantity of work than with the results obtained, and another group who might be designated as "blue ribbon" who concentrate more on the quality and nicety of their cooking (Ferber, Blankertz, and Hollander, 1964).

Another difference which developed in the late 1960s in the United States was the attitude toward the role of children in the family. A very large portion of middle-class families were child- and youth-oriented, permitting and even insisting on a great deal of personal independence on the part of the older children. This led to all sorts of demands by the offspring for changes in their roles in school and elsewhere, culminating in the selection of a Democratic candidate for President in 1972 who was essentially their choice and went down thereby to ignominious defeat.

The prime reason for the candidate's defeat was rather simple. The child's role was a subordinate one in the majority of the working class families in the United States, both as perceived by the children themselves and by their parents. Within such families, the child was still considered to have a role subordinate to that of parents and he was expected to take the advice of his elders. This quite large segment of the usual Democratic support deserted its party in pure protest.

The difference in role perceptions from country to country can be quite substantial, too, and they complicate the problems of international marketers in a great many cases. The American housewife is accustomed to the use of a great many mechanical aids—the use of convenience foods, for example, and a wide variety of appliances. But the women in Continental Europe have long considered such habits an abdication of their responsibilities in their roles.

All of these changes in the individual's many roles over the years involve transition periods which can in themselves be the cause of a very important psychological condition—that of anxiety. Anxiety behavior is particularly evident at a number of points in role transition in society, as well as situations in which the individual is trying to conform to reference groups outside of those to which he belongs but toward which he or she has some sort of aspiration.

### Anxiety Behavior, Reference Groups and Role Transition Periods

Uncertainty about the behavior expected in a role gives rise to one of the most overpowering emotions that human beings can experience— that of *anxiety*. Such uncertainty arises during any period of transition from an established role into a new status with an unfamiliar role. Such role transition uncertainty is particularly high during the age of puberty when a teenager is no longer a child and still not quite an adult and is uncertain as to what constitutes correct adult behavior. The necessity to continually move from one well-understood role within the group and within society, to a new and still poorly-understood role, is the source of a great deal of anxiety during any period of transition. This is especially true in an industrialized urban society in which children have few opportunities to participate in adult activities.

Unlike the roles in a well-written play, the roles that we assume within our groups are not spelled out in meticulous detail in any clearly-written script. We have to learn what is expected of us largely by relatively indirect means. It is true that some of what we know about the role into which we are moving can be obtained by observation and in some cases there are books that tell something about the role. But the nuances and important details of these roles can only be inferred from the attitudes and actions we see in the people around us, and these are not always easy to interpret. The resulting uncertainties often lead to one of the most powerful and to a degree the most immobilizing emotions that the human being can experience, that of anxiety. This anxiety, in turn, leads to a very special type of purchase behavior, that of trying to acquire as much as possible of the material symbols which we associate with the role into which we are hoping to move.

Anxiety could be defined as a vaguely unpleasant feeling—some kind of premonition that something very bad will soon happen to us. To anyone who has ever experienced the stage fright that normally accompanies the first attempt to speak or act before an audience, no further description is needed of this emotion.

The most important element of the anxiety emotion is the very vagueness of it, and this makes it difficult to cope with. The words usually used to describe it are such terms as "worried," "tense," "blue," "jumpy," and "edgy." The terms "jumpy" and "edgy" are especially appropriate because the person who is in the grip of anxiety has a lowered threshold to other kinds of emotional responses. He tends to be quite irritable and quickly moves to anger. On the other hand, he may over-react to pleasurable stimuli, going through very wide swings of mood and a very high degree of unpredictable behavior.

If this seems to be a familiar description of the teenager, it is no accident. There is no period in the human life associated with a higher degree of anxiety than that of the adolescent. He is no longer a child and yet not quite the adult he desperately wishes to be. He is leaving the expectations of childhood, and particularly in our modern urban society, entering a world of adulthood with which he is highly unfamiliar and which has a completely different set of expectations attached to his actions. Within the space of a very few years, he is expected to pass from a stage of relatively complete dependence on his family and schools to a period of complete independence, economically and even emotionally. As will be seen below, this tends to result in some very specific kinds of buying behavior on the part of the teenager.

Psychologists list five general sources of anxiety.

1.  *Uncertainty.* Lack of certainty is the source of the anxiety that most of us experience when we take on our first job or indeed, any new job; pass from high school into college, pass from college into the working world, have our first date, enter our first marriage, and so forth.

2.  *Rejection.* Perhaps this starts from the infant's acquired desire for the presence of the mother. For whatever reason, by the time any of us are beginning to make choices, we all have a strong desire for the approval of those around us. Conversely, the fear that we will be rejected by any new group which we are about to enter, or hope to enter, can be an extremely strong source of

anxiety. Anxiety of rejection plays a large part in the dating and marriage period and was, indeed, the principal emotion underlying the "youth movement" of the early 1970s—the fear on the part of the youth of that period that they could not fit into an adult society on their own.

3. *Frustration and conflict.* These may arise when two contradictory motives are present. In the case of the teenager, for example, and indeed in the case of a good many of our other transition situations such as those of early marriage, this conflict may be between the learned motive to strive for independence and the desire, nourished from infanthood, for dependence.

4. *Cognitive dissonance*—the conflict between our emotions and beliefs, or between either of these and our actions or actual performance. Thus, the teenager who thinks of himself as an adult may become upset when he does not find himself able to meet adult standards of performance. The young husband who would like to think of himself as a very satisfactory lover may find himself in a situation he does not understand the first time there is a difference of opinion.

5. *Physical harm.* Probably not the most important source of anxiety from the standpoint of marketing, but it is true that the physical awkwardness that often accompanies the rapid maturation of the adolescent period may contribute highly to the anxiety because of the fear of physical harm that might result.

Of these five sources of anxiety, the most important for marketing behavior are those of uncertainty and rejection, or rather the fear of rejection. These two sources, particularly, are far from being independent.

The many and varied psychological effects of anxiety behavior are too numerous and not relevant enough to marketing decision to go into. However, there is one effect and one major defense that are extremely important. The effect is that of *risk behavior.* Laboratory experiments seem to indicate pretty clearly that the highly anxious person tends to be either extremely conservative in terms of risk taking, or else to take the wildest of risks with very little moderation in between. He also seems to learn very simple tasks related to his anxieties, but to find it very difficult to learn more complex tasks. Since learning is a very important aspect of a new product introduction, this can be crucial.

The most important principal defense against the feeling of anxiety, from the standpoint of the marketer, is that if *identification.* Identification is an attempt by the individual to relieve his anxiety by acquiring some of the more visible characteristics and symbols he associates with an admired person or group that seems free of anxiety—particularly a person that is in the group to which he aspires to belong at the end of the transition period.

One of the interesting aspects of the period of Hollywood's great popularity was the extent to which the mere use of a particular dress design by one of the popular screen stars or starlets caused an instant rush to the stores for that same design. The teenager anxious about her own lack of charm and social skill sought to identify herself with a glamorous heroine who appeared on her local screen.

The easiest way to obtain identification is to acquire some material possessions which are seen as symbols of the role into which the person is moving. The young girl just entering adolescence may seek, for example, to use every form of make-up available—a practice she perceives as an attribute of adult women. The young couple with their first baby may acquire every known book on infant rearing and care to make sure that they are informed parents. (In the case of the second child, none of these things seem to be as necessary.) The young girl of dating age, hoping to land a permanent mate, becomes an easy prospect for all sorts of sales operations aimed at providing her with the material accessories of a "gracious hostess," from pots and pans and cutlery to sterling silver and chinaware, none of which are part of her immediate needs. It is no accident that the heavy users of cosmetics and the major market for women's dress clothes are among those in the adolescent and early adulthood years ending at about age twenty-five.

We make many other role transitions during a lifetime, of course, and many of these result in various forms of consuming behavior centering around our attempt to achieve identification. The young executive on the rise, who is beginning to make a good income, will tend to buy the prestige automobile. The young couple who grew up in high-rise apartments and moves to the suburbs will buy out the local tree and plant nurseries to establish their identity as local suburbanites with gardening interests.

Another aspect closely allied to identification of anxiety behavior, particularly among teenagers, is the attempt to use some simplified way of obtaining the status of independence which happens to be their goal. In effect, this is another form of the use of acquisition of symbols. Studies of peer group behavior among teenagers, for example, have shown that one of the most obvious characteristics of this age group is seen in attempts to appear to be as unlike their parents' generation as possible. This wish to be different usually manifests itself in the teenagers' choice of clothes and habits of grooming, but also in other methods and tastes such as, for example, tastes in popular music. This attitude is clearly an attempt to demonstrate another adult character-istic—independence.

Thus the teenage market for some things of personal taste becomes quite a separate market all of its own. The one generation goes in for jazz and swing and even sweet music, the next generation goes in for rock. But as time goes on and adults take on some of these tastes themselves, or as the teenagers themselves become part of the new young adult population, the taste itself swings in the opposite direction for exactly the same reason. To appear independent, the new wave of adolescents must adopt customs similar to those the previous wave of adolescents had rejected.

## Role Transition as Market Opportunity

Not all of the facets of role transition and of buying behavior during these periods are purely the result of anxiety behavior. Much of the buying behavior during a role transition is a necessary matter of obtaining the items required to carry out the role itself. One often-overlooked aspect of such transition periods is the fact that, when entering a new role, the consumer is much more open to sales efforts than he is when his habits of consumption are already established. The teenager, for example, is establishing new habits of consuming many kinds of personal items, from shaving instruments, in the case of men, to lipstick and menstrual supplies among girls. Because he already has a strong desire for the independence which he is expected to assume, he does not necessarily take with him the habits of consumption from his own immediate family. And because he is going through this period in a very short space of time, often a matter of from one to two years in the case of any given product, he is a different kind of market for the advertiser than the established adult market for the same kinds of items. As a result, very different kinds of promotional media and means must be used.

One writer has likened the difference between the youth and adult market to the difference between fishing in a moving stream and fishing in the pond or lake into which the stream flows. The methods best adapted for catching fish in the lake are not particularly well-suited for working over a stream. In the latter, the best method involves the use of a net which catches the moving fish as they pass a given point (Schiele, 1974). Schiele has pointed out that the standard method of new-product introduction used by the leading exponents of the product manager system—Procter and Gamble, for example—has been that of a very heavy promotional campaign to launch the product, followed by a much lower level of promotion aimed at a general market. This has worked well for many kinds of products in which the purchasing activity is largely that of established households.

But Procter and Gamble has not always succeeded too well in the area of toiletries in which the consumption habits are established in the teen years. For these, a specialized audience approach has enabled competitors to shave a very substantial portion of Procter and Gamble's lead by concentrating their advertising and promotion on the new users. Likewise, the internal tampon introduced some years ago as a substitute for the standard sanitary pads, established a very strong marketing niche with a promotional budget much less than that of the sanitary pad manufacturers, by concentrating its attention on the young girls just starting to use such products. Schick Safety Razor has been able to gain and maintain a consistent foothold in the shaving instrument field in the face of the dominance by giant Gillette, by a continuing and significant promotion to the young new consumer market.

The necessity to catch people in a transition period is not limited to the teenage part of the individual's life cycle. As the life cycle expenditure data shown indicates, each stage in the family life cycle brings in a new type of spending. It is for this reason, for example, that the editorial matter in a number of so-called "home magazines" is aimed primarily at young families. It is during this period that they become the primary promotional target of companies in the home furnishings and appliance fields, making large expenditures which will not be duplicated again during the lifetime of most of them. As Ben Wattenberg pointed out to an American Marketing Association convention, newly wed families are only about 2.6 percent of all households, but they buy 58 percent of the sterling silver flatware, 25 percent of the bedroom furniture total, 41 percent of the stereo and hi-fi equipment, 27 percent of the sewing machines, 16 percent of the vacuum cleaners, 11 percent of the hard surface floor coverings, 13 percent of the electric blankets, and 12 percent of the refrigerators (*Marketing News*, June 1, 1974).

To understand the consumer, we must clearly comprehend the many roles he plays and the changes that occur as he passes from one period to another and goes from one known role to a new and often uncertain role. But we also need to understand the nature of these groups and the roles of these groups in his life and in the learning process—the importance of the reference groups in setting the norms for his behavior.

## Summary

1.   Consumer behavior is role behavior. Most choices made and most action taken relate to the role the individual is playing, at the moment, as a member of the group involved in the purchase.

2.   Every individual occupies different roles in different groups, and thus plays as many roles as he has group connections. The personality of the individual can be defined in terms of his complex of group roles. The role itself is defined by the position, whoever plays it.

3.   The members of every group are organized in some kind of pecking order—some hierarchy or relative status. Those whose status is at the top of the hierarchy are freest to make decisions. Those nearest the bottom of the hierarchy must conform most closely to group norms.

4.   In any purchase situation, the gatekeeper role is crucial to the specific choice to be made.

5.   Sometimes the gatekeeper role is occupied by a group member, by the housewife in the family, for example, in most food shopping. However, in other instances, the gatekeeper is an external professional advisor—the physician who prescribes the drugs or even the diet in case of illness, the architect who writes the materials and equipment specifications for the building design, the professor who chooses the textbook for the course, and so forth. For such a professional advisor gatekeeper, product performance takes precedence over cost, as a rule.

6.   The roles the individual plays change over time—they are not fixed for life. As the infant matures into adolescence and adulthood, his group contacts and memberships proliferate, and with them, his role structure does also.

7.   During marriage, the course of the family life cycle plays a dominant part in a predictable change of roles within the family, with quite different expenditure patterns at each phase of the cycle.

8.   The growing participation of women in the workforce has brought a change in those families with a working wife member. The importance of homemaking skills has been downgraded, as the wife's status is no longer tied solely to her kitchen status. One result has been the more ready acceptance and rapid growth in use of convenience foods.

9.   The sharp drop in the birth rate has paralleled the rise in workforce participation by the housewife, substantially altering spending patterns in other ways.

10.   The growing number of older people in the population, and their improved health and economic situation, have created new roles for people at that stage in the family life cycle, and with these new roles, new markets.

11.  Roles are not rigidly specified and spelled out, but generalized and rather vaguely defined. As such, they are, like roles on the stage, subject to a relatively wide latitude of interpretation, with the spending pattern varying accordingly.

12.  Because the individual's group memberships change over life, he goes through quite a number of role transition periods.

13.  Role transition periods tend to be times of high anxiety. The individual is leaving behind a well-understood role and having to learn a new one with new rules of which he is often quite uncertain.

14.  Anxiety in such situations tends to lead to aspirational overbuying, as the individual seeks to acquire the symbols he perceives as badges of the new role he is entering, and to avoid rejection.

15.  Such role transition periods also offer legitimate market expansion opportunities. During such periods, the individual is starting to consume items not previously important to him. The brands which gain importance at this juncture have a built-in market share advantage.

### Chapter 7  Exercises

1.  In your own family, list all of the significant roles of each parent. What is the purchasing or use-system role in each case? In which roles is that parent a gatekeeper? In what circumstances does that parent have an advisory or veto role?
    What is the role of each in choosing a new automobile? Are others involved, and what are their roles?
    What is the role of each in deciding a place to eat when dining out?

2.  How might the choices of a young couple differ, when choosing a place to eat out, as between the two following situations:
    a.  by themselves
    b.  as parents of three small children, ages 5 to 9, who would go with them

3.  In any group of which you are a member, could you name the person most likely to make an acceptable suggestion on some important action (such as where to go to the beach or go skiing next weekend)? If so, who would be the next most likely? Who would be least likely? In other words, can you sketch the pecking order in your group?

4. Who, in your family, is the gatekeeper determining most brand or similar choices in the following budget groups:
   food
   beverages
   tobacco
   automobile
   vacations
   furniture

5. Is the purchasing agent in a business firm the gatekeeper on all purchasing? If not, on what types of purchases is he likely to be the chooser? On what types of purchases is he least likely to make the final choice?

6. We are moving into an era in which a job outside the home is the norm for the housewife, no longer the exception, for nearly all social classes. How might this change the traditional roles of the parents in important purchasing situations? Why?

7. An increasingly larger proportion of the population is in the over-65 bracket, many of them in good health and with sufficient incomes, although most such incomes will be pension-based in one way or another.
   How will such significant numbers in the "senior citizen" role affect various kinds of markets?

8. List all of the important role transitions any normal middle-class person might pass through in his lifetime (including divorce). For what kinds of purchases might each of these role transitions be affected by the accompanying anxieties in such a period?

9. List purchases which might be sought out as a means of aspirational identification during each such period.

**8**

# The Sources of our Perceptions of Value and Values: The Family and Other Reference Groups

REFERENCE GROUPS AS FORCES FOR THE CONDITIONING OF BEHAVIOR

    Face-to-face Groups
    Aspirational Groups, Both Positive and Negative

THE ROLE OF GROUPS

    Sources of Information as well as Norm References

THE ROLE OF THE FAMILY

    As Developer of Motives of Attachment and Affiliation and Desire
       for Social Approval
    As a Potential Negative Force
    Diminishing Role as Child Matures
    Cultural Differences in Family Organization and the Effect on
       Purchasing Choices

PEER GROUP INFLUENCE

IMPORTANCE OF BEING IN AT THE START OF THE CON-SUMPTION CYCLE

ADULT FACE-TO-FACE GROUPS

ASPIRATIONAL REFERENCE GROUPS

A GROUP OF SEVERAL dozen preteen boys and girls were set loose in a large supermarket with instructions to pick out and take with them, free of charge, any twenty items they chose. To everyone's surprise, although they picked up some watermelon and soft drinks for immediate use, they filled their baskets largely with family food items such as their mothers might have chosen—meats, vegetables, flour, and so forth. They did not pick up such items as camera and toys, as some observers had expected, even though camera and toys were on display on the shelves (Riesman and Roseborough, 1955).

The parents of a bright four-year-old girl were trying to decide what to give their daughter for her birthday, and finally asked her what she wanted. Without hesitation, she replied, "a bicycle." Taken aback, they explained that a bicycle cost somewhat more than they felt they could spend, whereupon she said, "I have the money"—and brought out her bank to prove it. To their astonishment, she proved to have nearly enough. Although the mother had always carefully insisted that part of each allowance be saved, she did not realize how much saving the child had been doing, nor had she consciously trained the youngster in the matter of saving for a goal.

By contrast, consider how frequently the parents' attempt to enforce family standards is met by a growing child's, "But all of the other kids have one." While sometimes a mere excuse, more often it is a truly anguished appeal.

All three of the above are examples of group conditioning of behavior. In the first two, we have instances of one of the stronger results of family influence—of the phenomenon of *anticipatory socialization*. By the latter is meant the learning of roles which the individual will have to assume later in life. In the case of the little girl and the bicycle, we have a combination of anticipatory socialization (in the matter of saving and saving for a goal), and also, without question, aspirational behavior—of wanting a material item associated with the role of older children in the neighborhood, a group to which she did not belong, but hoped to.

Both the shopping and the bicycle incidents reflect the strong influence of the family in setting norms or standards of consumer behavior patterns. On the other hand, the cry of "All the other kids . . .," far too familiar to any parents of preteen or teenage children, reflects the norm-setting influences of outside reference groups as the individual matures—in this case, of the peer groups.

The term *reference groups* is almost self-explanatory. Reference groups are those in which we play a role as members, or aspire to, and thus they are the groups to which we look to determine the standards, or norms, of correct attitude or action in any given situation—to determine what is right, what is wrong, what will work, what may not, what is beautiful, what is ugly, what tastes good and is nutritious, what tastes bad and should be avoided. As adults, we look to many reference groups for these standards—both face-to-face groups in which we play an active role as members, and aspiration groups of which we are not yet full members, but with which we seek to identify ourselves.

Any purchase decision is the result of certain attitudes and motives we possess, certain internal standards as to what is important and how much sacrifice we are willing to undergo to meet a particular internal drive or desire-set. As we have already noted, attitudes and motives are all learned, and the direction and content of that learning can only come from the outside. We develop them by means of some kind of conditioning process through which we are rewarded for the development of group-approved attitudes and motives, and feel ourselves to be negatively rewarded for doing the opposite of what is suggested by these attitudes and motives.

Such conditioning is not random, it comes to us through our various reference groups over the span of our life. Most rewards—both positive and negative—are implied in the actions of those around us. They are seldom explicit instructions or material rewards, but are what we perceive as the attitudes of associates in the reference group, from indirect clues of expression.

The most important of these reference groups are various face-to-face membership groups—groups of which we are a member and with which we maintain a high degree of social interaction. The most important of all such face-to-face groups is the family, or the two families to which most people belong at some time in their life—the family into which they are born and under whose guidance they mature, and the family of choice into which they marry.

But there are other groups of growing importance through the individual's life. As the infant matures into the young child, he begins to come into contact with other people and other groups and to form affiliations of various kinds with these groups—initially with the peer groups, with people of his own age, normally in school. Later he branches out, beyond the mere accidental peer groups of his school room, to form various kinds of friendship groups. As he begins to take on the responsibilities of adulthood, he becomes a member of various kinds of work groups and normally develops some kind of social relationship between part or all of the groups with which he works. At the middle-class level, he may also belong to some form of professional group whose influence can extend far beyond that of the mere matters of his profession.

In addition, other groups, of which he is not an actual member, can be of great importance to the consumer. These may be *aspirational groups*, both of a positive and a negative character. They are *positive* when the norms which they communicate to us lead us to perform certain positive kinds of activities including making various   kinds of purchases. They are *negative* when we refer to them as a standard of what not to do, or what behavior to avoid. Past membership groups can also at times be a source of negative norms.

In the case of these nonmembership groups, social interaction is not part of the picture. We do not deal directly with nor are we influenced by other members in the group whose standards we are hoping to adopt, and we must learn of those standards indirectly from various external forms of communication. Beyond the group are other aggregates that influence us through these groups, to be discussed in later chapters.

All of our groups normally have a role within the context of some social class, and the standards that they pass on are normally those of the social class of which they and we are members. The social classes themselves are part of the over-all pattern of a general culture of wide geographic extent, and this culture itself tends to determine the structures of the groups of which we become members and even, quite usually, of the reference groups to which we may aspire outside the membership groups.

## The Role of Groups

Groups are important to consumer behavior for two basic reasons. In the first place, the groups all inculcate certain general attitudes toward what sort of behavior is acceptable and what is not, what sort of products fit into such behavior and which do not. But they also act as sources of information about products that would solve a need we have, even a very personal need so long as it does not transgress group norms.

The cultural and group norms covering our actions all usually permit a wide variety of alternatives in solving a particular desire-set which may activate a purchase at the moment. Many of those alternative offerings on the market are quite complicated, and making a judgment as to the suitability of each and every one is far beyond the capacity of any individual, especially in such matters as the purchase of major mechanical appliances and items such as automobiles. Even when we are expert in one area, we are usually quite deficient in others. To make a careful survey of all the alternatives, and a thorough analysis of the ability of each possible choice to meet our needs, would be far beyond the capacity and available time of the greatest genius.

The result is that we limit our interests to some particular area of our purchases and attempt, at most, to make ourselves expert only in these small areas. For our other purchases, items of somewhat less interest to us, we approach those within our acquaintanceship on whose expertise we feel we can rely, asking them for advice. Thus our membership in groups has a direct effect on our purchasing, whether or not a group norm is involved. As will be shown later, the acceptance of new products and their diffusion to widespread usage depends on such a network of personal relationships and advice.

Whether for direct advice or for a more general norm to which our purchase should conform, the most important influences in nearly every consumer's life are the families to which he belongs at one time or another, the family of his birth and the later family of his choice.

## The Role of the Family in Consumer Behavior

Nearly every consumer spends more of the hours of his life in contact with other members of his family than with any other single reference group. For the first few years of very early childhood, the family is the only social contact he has, and the family situation and the course of childhood development is primarily responsible for the two basic attitudes which account for the fact that much of the rest of his life will be guided by group influences—the desires of *attachment and affiliation* and a *desire for social approval.*

There is some sketchy evidence to indicate that we are all born with a degree of need for social contact. Whether or not this is so is unimportant to our discussion. The fact of survival in the first few years of life depends on very intimate contact with the parents. It is from them that we receive all nutrients and all protection from pain and discomfort. It is the parental relationship that dispenses the rewards we early come to value, the pats and smiles and other elements we learn to associate with approval, and which are often followed with a material reward. As a result, the human being who does not have a strong motive for attachment and affiliation—the hermit—is such a rare deviant that he is generally considered to be "sick" in some way.

As we become older, we look for the various signs of social approval from the other groups around us. Because, initially, we seek to identify ourselves closely with the family, and we seek signs of social approval from them, any sign of social approval becomes a strong form of conditioning reward.

We develop a given attitude because the attitude is rewarded or at least made familiar by continuing exposure within the group. Among the many attitudes we develop are measures of values and of value. By values, we mean the relative importance we assign to various kinds of activity and various types of decisions and choices. Thus, in one family, the value of good grooming may receive a high degree of approval. The individual who acquires such an attitude early in life often later becomes a person with a highly favorable attitude toward clothing and personal care items. The child reared in the family in which book learning and reading are given an extremely high level of importance will, unquestionably, later in life, become a heavy consumer of various items feeding on the desire to read and inform himself.

At times, of course, the family may become a negative conditioning influence. Specific attitudes, customs and kinds of activities promoted by his family may yield such negative results and frustrations that the individual will thereafter shun any kind of consumer behavior represented by these family norms. This is particularly true when the family norms create conflict and difficulties for the individual as he grows up and becomes a member of other groups in the community. The child reared in a condition of extreme poverty or even of just plain parsimony may experience such frustration of personal desires and of the desires set loose by his membership in other groups that he will thereafter react negatively, as an adult, to any idea of sharp bargaining or economy purchasing.

The structure of the family itself and the role of the individual within it can exert a direct contemporary effect on consumer behavior, as will be noted later in the discussion of culture (previously noted in the discussion of the changing role of the working housewife in the family).

As the child moves out from the toddler stage into school age, the family's influence begins to diminish. He comes in contact with, and later becomes affiliated with, groups outside the family and most particularly with the groups of people of his own age, the so-called *peer* groups. By the time he reaches what is sometimes called middle childhood, the age of nine or ten, his peer group will tend to dominate his life. It is the gang which determines much of what he decides to do. However, the peer group itself begins to split up into various kinds of friendship groups as he approaches adolescence, although the influence of the peer group remains extremely dominant until he enters young adulthood and goes out into the work-a-day world and his own independent existence.

As he goes through the courtship era and eventually marries, as most people do, he starts a family of his own. At this time the structure of his social relationships begins to exert a very strong influence. As pointed out earlier, his role as a member of a newly established household requires a sudden shift in his expenditure habits. If and when children come along, their needs begin to take a high priority in his purchasing pattern, and these needs themselves change as his own children pass through peer groups into young adulthood. Finally, when his children leave home, he again makes another change in habits and is able to gratify more of his own and his wife's personal desires.

Family needs and personal needs alone, however, do not determine family expenditures. Indeed, what are defined as needs will vary greatly from class to class within the population. Furthermore, the structure of the family within the culture will dictate a different purchasing role for the housewife or the husband in one area of the world than in another with a different family system. As will be seen later, purchasing attitudes of those in the *conjugal family* (the immediate nuclear family plus such other in-law relationships as are maintained through life) will be quite different from the kinds of decisions made where the extended family is the basic form of organization.

The *extended family* is definable as that family composed not only of the immediate nuclear family of husband, wife and children or the conjugal family of husband, wife, and children and immediate relatives with somewhat lesser contacts, but also includes uncles, aunts, cousins, in-laws, and other members of various generations on one side of the house all tending to live closely together, ideally under the same roof. The extended family structure is the kind found in many areas of the world outside the most highly industrialized nations in particular. Industrialization tends to destroy such an extended family pattern, because the mobility of the members makes impossible the continued close contact of the various generations and various collateral relatives. Important as the family is, however, it is, as already noted, not necessarily the most important element at every period in life. For a considerable period during the maturation process, the peer group sets the standards for conduct and consumer behavior as the individual is moving into consumptionhood.

## Peer Group Influence and Consumer Behavior

Until the age of four, five, or six, when a child makes his first contact with a school system, the family influence is a monopolistic one. Once the child enters nursery school, kindergarten or first grade, two new influences begin to shape his life—his teacher and his contemporaries or peers, the other children of his age with whom he associates directly. The influence of the teacher is largely one of reinforcing many of the adult influences he finds at home, particularly if both he and the teacher are of the middle class, as most teachers are. The influence of his peers, however, grows increasingly dominant as time goes on. Among his peers, he can, for the first time, evaluate himself in relation to others, and he sooner or later acquires a specific role within the peer group, a role assigned him by other members of the group but which he sooner or later accepts and to which he conforms.

The peer group also gives the child an outlet for a growing desire to acquire independence. It gives him a chance to rebel against some of the restrictions of the adult world. Thus, the peer group helps the child gain an objective evaluation of his own talents and position in society. It assigns him a role to play and provides models the child can identify with and imitate. Peer groups also give the child an outlet for feelings of rebellion at which the adult world may frown. As time goes on, the peer group becomes the standard for his direct purchases and even for his indirect purchases of personal items furnished him by his family. By the time of the early teens, it is one of the peer groups which dominates the choice of much of what is furnished a child by his parents for his personal use. Also, during the adolescent years, many later adult consumption habits and personal item purchases become established.

## The Importance of Being In at the Start of the Consumption Cycle

Because of the growing aspiration for independence and instant adulthood in the teen period, the peer group culture tends to be negative to family and adult standards. The adolescent behavioral norm is one of strong conformity to peer group norms, but these tend in turn to be in direct opposition or negative conformity to the norms of the elders. Since each wave of adolescents soon joins the elders, each new wave has a different negative standard to which it conforms.

As the child moves through the transitional period from puberty to adulthood, he takes on many habits of consumption and many of his brand preferences become relatively fixed. The boy has to shave, or otherwise groom the hirsute growth on his face in some manner, and the shaving materials and tools which he first uses may pretty much bias what he uses for most of the remaining years of his adult life. He may, of course, be switched later by some major improvement in one of these items or by some major appeal. But at that time, he must go through some degree of brand benefit relearning process, whereas as an adolescent he starts out with no preferences and must only learn to use the new—initial learning which he cannot avoid in any case. Similarly, for a girl, this is the period during which she establishes many of her habits in personal care items and sanitary supplies as well as toiletries and cosmetics. Brands and products which establish preferences in this period, therefore, start out with a major advantage among new converts.

As already noted, the effectiveness of product design and appeals directed to this group has been proven by many brands and types of products. Clairol, starting with a very minimal position in the shampoo market, achieved a substantial share for its Herbal Essence brand by directing its appeal specifically to young consumers, and Johnson and Johnson broadened the market for an established product, its Baby Shampoo, by directing its promotion toward teenagers, gaining a strong market share. Similarly, the Schick Safety Razor Division of Warner-Lambert has managed to achieve and maintain a significant foothold in the razor market against the dominant Gillette brand by concentrating its much lesser funds and resources on the beginning young shavers.

Reaching this beginning-use market requires, of course, a persistent, highly focused campaign of more modest proportions than is normal for campaigns directed at restructuring the adult market through brand switching.

The adolescent period, of course, is not the only one in which beginning usage is an important aspect of market penetration. As the adolescent matures into an adult, he makes many new kinds of purchase decisions for the first time. The information he needs and the standards to which he conforms for many of these come through the new kinds of face-to-face groups with which he comes in contact. Indeed, the diversification of his face-to-face contacts begins long before he reaches full adulthood. The peer group of the children in the middle years from nine to twelve is almost the only major nonfamily influence. As he moves through adolescence, however, he still associates largely with his peers, but the groups with which he associates tend to break up into different kinds of interest groups. Once he leaves school, even narrowly age-determined peer membership is not a major characteristic of many of the grups in which he plays a role, of which he is a part, or which help set many of his norms and standards.

**The Many Kinds of Face-to-Face Groups in the Adult**

Somewhere along the way in late adolescence, the budding consumer joins a courtship group of somewhat loosely affiliated single men and women, and in this group he acquires a number of standards of personal consumption covering not only the strictly personal items but probably such purchases as automobiles. Sooner or later, of course, participation in this group usually results in the formation of a new family of which he becomes the head. This, in itself, as already shown, requires a drastic change in his entire spending pattern, as he and his wife seek to acquire the necessary means for establishing a household.

The young maturing adults also enter a new adult world of another sort, the world of everyday work. With very minor exceptions, this involves membership in some kind of work group, an office or a work crew in which the individual must play a role in relation to others. Beyond the absolutely necessary acquisition of new work habits, this group also becomes a source of information on consumption goods and norms for consumption in matters ranging far outside problems relevant to the work situation. The work group is largely an involuntary one. In very few instances does the young worker have much choice as to his companions. Their influence, however, becomes important, since his role depends on his ability to meet the standards of the job as his group sees them. And the many hours during which he is normally thrown in contact with them overshadows the time spent in almost any other group except that of his immediate family.

The work group may be next only to the family in importance, and in some ways it may be even more of an extensive educational influence. Unlike the other groups the young adult has participated in, its membership tends to be quite diverse. Age groups are nearly always somewhat mixed, with all that this implies for diversity of experience and interests. Particularly in an urban industrial society, it is also generally composed of people from a diversity of backgrounds of many kinds, from different subcultures—ethnic, neighborhood, and education—and, to the extent different echelons and occupations mingle, the work group is composed of different social classes (particularly in office work). The effect of this diversity of background and cultures on broadening the interests and information base has been manifested in recent years in the dramatic shifts in the attitudes and interests of the large body of working-class housewives.

*Changes in Working-Class Housewife Attitudes*

Even as late as 1965, the attitudes and goals of the workingman's wife could still be described as they were in a definitive study done in 1959 (Rainwater, et al., 1959): housebound and family-centered (Social Research Inc., 1973). Their five main goals were:

1. Search for economic and physical security (not mobility)
2. Drive for common-man level of respectability and recognition (rather than for higher status)
3. Desire for support and affection from people important to her (primarily family, relatives)
4. Escape from household burdens and chores
5. Urge to decorate, "pretty up" her world—that is, her home

Her world tended to be a narrow one with little variety and few contacts outside her family and relatives. She felt lonely and needed to be closely tied to people. In stores, she looked for friendliness and personalized atmosphere.

She seemed to be wrapped up in her children and would make many sacrifices for them, nonetheless viewing them as a burden. Her main reading material consisted of family behavior magazines, like *True Story*, which she read for escape. Her leisure time was largely spent talking to neighbors, watching TV, and reading magazines. She liked to see youthful girls illustrating advertising. A major interest was food, especially children's products. Asked how she would spend $7,000 a year (at that time, a somewhat high amount for her group), food was the first item she mentioned. Housing was second, and she would spend a lower percentage for this than would a comparable middle-class woman. On furniture, she would spend 35 percent—a full 10 percent more than her middle-class counterpart. Recreation and vacation got scant attention in her budget.

By 1973, however, this pattern had undergone a marked shift, due in large part to the heavy participation of much of this class in the workforce and a growing acceptance of this participation as normal. Much of this increased participation was due to economic pressures, and by 1970, nearly 60 percent of even those mothers with children under six whose husbands earned between $5,000 and $10,000 per year were employed outside the home (Seiffer, 1974). The new group contacts and activity broke her narrow dependence on the family (Social Research Inc., 1973) and broadened her attention to wider community issues of day care, equal pay for equal work, job opportunities, and training for women. Although she did not consider herself a part of the official Women's Liberation movement, she began to broaden her group contacts even more, taking part in many kinds of volunteer community efforts aimed at specific issues of interest to her.

Her spending priorities also shifted. She upgraded many consumer items from "luxuries" to "necessities," primarily items which promised to get her out of the house or out from under the burdens of housekeeping, but also items of personal entertainment and comfort. On the other hand, she had begun to downgrade consumer items which reminded her of homemaker tasks and which seemed to demand work rather than relieve it. These latter were viewed now as less essential and figured less prominently in her replacement plans. Figure 8-1 lists some of the types of consumer items which Social Research, Incorporated, found had shifted significantly in working-class priorities after the mid 1960s.

**Figure 8-1.  Consumer Items Which Have Changed Significantly— Up or Down—in Working Class Priorities in the Years 1967 to 1973**

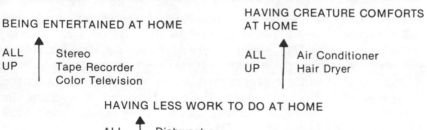

GETTING AWAY FROM HOME

ALL ↑  Baby Sitter
UP     Personal Car
       Bowling
       Dress for Special Occasions

BEING ENTERTAINED AT HOME

ALL ↑  Stereo
UP     Tape Recorder
       Color Television

HAVING CREATURE COMFORTS AT HOME

ALL ↑  Air Conditioner
UP     Hair Dryer

HAVING LESS WORK TO DO AT HOME

ALL ↑  Dishwasher
UP     Garbage Disposal
       Clothes Dryer

HAVING WORK TO DO AT HOME

ALL    Sewing Machine
DOWN ↓ Kitchen Stove

THE HIGH COST OF EATING

DOWN   Weekly Steak ↓

Roger F. Coup, Shirley Greene, and Burleigh B. Gardner, *Working Class Women in a Changing World*, Social Research, Inc., 1973.

Thus it is that membership in the work group, and a realization of commitment to it, has greatly modified the attitudes and consumption habits of the workingman's wife and also has introduced her to new and wider contacts in various volunteer groups, which in turn provided her with wider sources of information.

## Other Adult Groups

As he moves into adult life and becomes an active member of the working community, the consumer comes to join many voluntary groups with interests similar to his own in one respect or another. All of these groups become sources of information and help shape his attitudes. For the adult professional, these groups would very likely include some form of professional organization covering his area of specialty. For professionals and others, there are formal clubs and fraternal organizations, and informal friendship groups, as well as community service operations. These people, too, become sources of contact for product knowledge and product acceptance, both in his field and outside the field of the profession or occupation. As will be seen later in the discussion of product diffusion, it is these face-to-face groups which largely facilitate the spread of the adoption of new products and lend legitimacy to the claims made for them.

Such groups not only set standards but they create an atmosphere for conformity. Many replicated psychological experiments show that, under presumed group pressure, most individuals will agree to many propositions which they would otherwise personally consider silly or obviously incorrect, provided only that they perceive the group as being strongly in favor of these propositions and choices. Indeed, the further an individual is from the top of the role hierarchy in a group, the greater the degree of conformity (Asch, 1959; Crutchfield, 1959; Nosanchuck and Lighthouse, 1974).

Conformity, however, is not limited to the standards of groups with which we are in direct face-to-face contact. Much of the consumption of individuals is governed by their aspirations to membership in groups of which they are not yet full members or even members at all. It is the aspirational aspect of much of human activity which accounts for many kinds of status perceived goods.

## Aspirational Reference Groups

Nearly all of us, as individuals and as consumers, are governed not only by our current status and group memberships but also by our desires to become accepted members of other groups of which we are not yet members and of whose standards we are not fully aware. Much of the play of a seven- or eight-year-old child concerns itself with attempted imitations of adults, a group to which the child aspires but cannot belong for many years. As he grows older and approaches adulthood, the tendency to aspire to adult consumption patterns of some sort becomes stronger. There is little question that the smoking habit, for example, starts as a means of acquiring the first of the materialistic symbols that children see as a mark of adulthood. The heaviest users of cosmetics are not the grown mature women, but the youthful teenager who sees cosmetics and toiletries of any sort as a symbol of adult status. The best prospects for the sale of the prestige cars, particularly the best known of them, the Cadillacs and the Lincolns, are not those people with the greatest amount of wealth, but those who are socially climbing and need to reinforce their aspirations by acquiring the symbols of the group to which they aspire.

The young couple who is just moving from the inner city to the suburbs is a heavy user of garden nursery items, items they perceive as signs of an established home in the suburbs. The young parents on the verge of giving birth to their first child are the major market for books on the rearing of children. It is the star-gazing teenager who apes the well-known characters of stage and screen, as models of what glamorous and attractive young women (or sought-after young men) are like.

Advertisers have long used this aspirational aspect of the various transitional periods in our lives as a means of promoting the quality of their brand or product. For years, a major maker of cold creams featured testimonials of young society debutantes in an attempt to establish the use of its brand among the more general area of society. To a great extent, the success of cigarette brands which stress virility and manhood unquestionably have been due to the appeal of this theme to the youthful beginning smoker.

Thus, both face-to-face and aspirational reference groups play a very considerable role in passing on the norms of standards for the groups to which the consumer belongs and also those to which he aspires to belong. The standards themselves, however, seldom originate within the group itself. In general, they are those of a particular culture and segment of that culture, and it is the general culture that defines the limits of the acceptability of various goods and determines the relative value in the consumption system of all we desire to purchase.

## Summary

1. The immediate sources of nearly all of our norms of attitudes

and action are the reference groups, i.e., those groups in which we play some role, or aspire to.

2. The most important are the face-to-face groups in which we have membership and, of these, the families (both that of origin and that of choice) are two of the most important influences.

3. As the individual goes through life, he joins other groups outside his family and usually acquires aspirations to membership in groups to which he does not yet belong. These latter, too, affect his attitudes and behavioral norms.

4. Groups influence consumer behavior in two important ways. They inculcate general attitudes of acceptable behavior, and they serve as sources of information, shortcutting the process of considering alternative choices.

5. The family of origin develops the desires for attachment and affiliation which serve as the means of group influence and conditioning throughout life. The mere fact of group approval becomes a strong form of reinforcement reward for approved behavior, and disapproval helps extinguish group-disapproved behavior.

6. Families, particularly, and other groups also, may serve at times as negative conditioning influences whenever their norms create conflicts and difficulties for the individual as his group memberships expand.

7. The monopolistic influence of the family of origin begins to diminish as the child reaches school age and joins peer groups. Peer groups dominate in the middle-childhood period and remain important throughout puberty.

8. When the young adult forms his own new family, his expenditure patterns change radically to meet the needs of family formation.

9. During the role transition period of adolescence, the consumer is likely to establish lifelong brand choice patterns for many personal items.

10. Other periods of role transition offer similar market opportunities for other items.

11. Adults take on roles of many kinds in diverse face-to-face groups, of which the work group and the professional group often become major influences. They also may join numerous volunteer groups, all of which serve as sources of information as well as standards of conformity.

12. All consumers pass through many periods during which they aspire to become accepted members of groups to which they are not, as yet, members.

13. Such aspirations result in the purchase of many items which

serve the value-expressive attitude of belonging to the aspirational group.

14.  The standards passed on by all groups come out of the culture of which they are a part.

## Chapter 8  Exercises

1.  List all of the face-to-face groups of which you are or have been an active member.
    What part of your purchasing habits of all kinds have been influenced, one way or another, by each group? Have any been a negative influence, and if so, why?

2.  What purchasing and use habits of your own (good and bad) may have originated in aspirational imitation? Include any skills or special knowledge you acquired with aspiration as the first incentive.

3.  Consider any first time buying or patronage choice you may have made in the last three years: a motorcycle, a car, a stereo set, a supermarket in a new town, your choice of college, where to shop for clothes, when you got there, etc. Where did you go for information you thought you could rely on? Why?

4.  It is a known fact that children growing up in families in which one or both parents are active musicians tend to take up music seriously, although not necessarily with the same instrument, children of tool-using artisans tend to be more tool-oriented, children of parents who read a lot tend to be more literarily oriented, and so forth. Why would this be?

5.  Give examples of peer-group-dominating purchasing which you have observed.

6.  Just the process of growing up puts all of us through a number of transition periods in our lives. But some individuals acquire other kinds of aspirations not connected with the maturation process. Can you think of some?
    In what parts of society are such types of aspirations most likely, and why?

7.  List those products or other offerings whose habitual use nearly

always starts during each of the following transitional periods:
    adolescence
    going away to college
    entering the first career job
    marriage
    having a baby
    breakup of family through death or divorce
    retirement

Culture: The Sources of our
Norms of Value and Values

GROUPS AS TRANSMISSION AGENTS OF THE CULTURE

Cultural Differences and Divergent Marketing Approaches

CULTURE AND THE FAMILY STRUCTURE

The Nuclear Family Versus the Extended Family
Effect on Marketing Decision

GEOGRAPHY AND CULTURE

Major Cultural Outlines Geographical in Extent
Differences in Neighboring Countries

Quantitative Differences
Implied Qualitative Differences

Regional Differences within the United States

Migration of Culture with the Population

Ethnic Differences

A LANDMARK OF downtown Salt Lake City is a statue to a sea gull, memorializing a dramatic incident in the first year of the Mormon settlement. Just as the settlers' first wheat crop appeared to be on the verge of destruction by a swarm of large crickets, a flock of sea gulls appeared and devoured the invaders. To the Mormons, their salvation was little short of heavenly intervention. The nearby Indian tribes, however, would not have viewed the gulls as saviors, but as a calamity. Like many other nonagricultural peoples, they found well-roasted crickets and grasshoppers tasty delicacies and an important source of nutrition. Wheat and other grasses were not so considered.

Our roles and behavior in the groups to which we belong and to which we aspire must conform to the norms dictated by these groups, but the groups do not originate the norms. The groups are the conduit by which behavioral norms and attitudes are transmitted from one generation to another. The total pattern of these norms is the specific culture of which the group is a part. Culture may be defined as the pattern of norms of behavior of all sorts, including customs, beliefs, values and ideals, that a society in any given area develops and passes along to new generations.

Basically, a culture is a set of attitudes—attitudes about value and values, about what is worthwhile and what is worth doing, as well as what is forbidden and not of value. Even the structure of the groups to which we belong is culturally determined, as are the consumer's attitudes as to what has high value and what is bad and should be avoided, what is acceptable behavior, which purchase is desirable and which is not, what is beautiful and what is ugly, what tastes good and what is revolting.

The role of the individual within any of the groups to which he belongs is culturally defined—the role of the sexes within society as a whole and within the smaller membership groups, especially the family; behavior with respect to cleanliness, to debt or obligations, to planning for the future. Clearly, the culture has a direct effect on any kind of marketing effort.

Differences in cultures make it difficult or even impossible to develop a single kind of worldwide promotional campaign for a given product. The culture defines what is tasteful and distasteful in advertising and, even more, it determines which themes will be selected for attention and which will not be understood by those to whom they are directed. It is the culture that determines the acceptable design of the product itself and the importance of the product in the total economy.

In addition to this, the culture exerts a direct influence on the decision processes by which groups make their purchases, particularly the family and industry. Consider, for instance, how the standardized or ideal relationship of members of the family, as well as the composition of the family, differs in various countries of the world and the effect this can have on the way purchasing decisions are made, and even the way in which an ad can be viewed.

One such difference is the difference between the so-called nuclear or conjugal family typical of the highly industrialized nations of the North Atlantic Community of Western Europe and northern North America, and the extended family which is the ideal norm in major areas of the world, including most of Asia, particularly India, and much of South America.

### Family Structure and the Consumption Decision-Making Process

There are a number of possible family relationship structures but two major ones dominate most of the world. The first of these is the small family, or nuclear or conjugal family, typical of the United States, Canada, and the western European areas in particular. In this structure, it is assumed that when the children mature, and particularly when they marry, they will establish a new household of their own, separate from that of the parents on either side. All ties with the former family are seldom completely cut, but the importance of the in-laws diminishes greatly once the new family is established. At the other extreme is the extended family which would consist of, say, the paternal grandfather and his wife, his sons and their wives and children, and any unmarried daughters, all living under the same roof and sharing the total incomes. If the elders live long enough, there may even be the wives of grandsons and their children. In this pattern, designated as "patrilocal," sons stay with the parents while daughters move in with their husband's parents. This is the norm for the ideal family in India, for example (Wilson B. Brown and Ramish Motwani, unpublished manuscript, 1972).

Within such an extended Indian family, the grandfather or father has the highest position and status. He is at the top of the pecking order. His advice is sought and his decisions are final. His decisions, however, are not made without consideration of the other members of the family. His position is more like that of the chairman of the board rather than of a general manager or president—that of going along with decisions made by other members of the family as long as decisions are within the bounds of what he feels are acceptable and so long as he is consulted. Seldom is he likely to veto an action outright. More often, he will make suggestions and modifications or raise doubts about the wisdom of an action. In one way, the system is very similar to that of a large diversified corporation in which the managers of individual operations have a great deal of autonomy, but are always subject to the overview of the corporation itself.

This analogy, however, is far from perfect. Within the Indian system, the family income and assets are generally considered as parts of a single pool. Individuals are not on a specific budget, but each individual has a sense of how much he should spend and the limited range of goods on which he is likely to spend it. Few purchases are made by the purchaser for himself without some degree of consultation with others.

Indeed, the Indian hesitates to make a decision of any sort, within the family or outside, without consulting numerous people for advice—whether it is deciding on a new job, remodeling the house, making a governmental decision or deciding to purchase a minor appliance. The Indian never feels comfortable until he has consulted with numerous other people before making a move—even the purchase of, say, a watch might not be made until a brother, the father and the mother were consulted. Because of this situation, an Indian would be very uncomfortable making a decision by himself. If he lacks personal contacts for adequate consultation, he may seek to "consult the stars" for help and only after the astrological signs are favorable will he dare to move and make a purchase or undertake other actions. When the wife goes to make a purchase for her husband or for the family, it is to the in-laws with whom she now lives that she turns for help to determine which tea brand she should buy or where she should buy it. She will consult her husband's mother and the latter will probably shop with her, whether or not she lives in the same household.

This family structure with its decision-making process leads to much more conservative buying patterns than exist in an area in which the nuclear family predominates. Products have to be satisfactory to several people of very different ages, hence the personal appeal is of little value. New products are slow to be adopted because the individual does not like to stray outside the known, acceptable limits of purchases. When new products are introduced, it is best that they carry recognized brand names and be distributed through established channels, with promotion emphasizing the wide acceptability by all members of the family and population. Price cutting may be taken as a sign of inferior quality and shopping puts the emphasis on durability and quality.

As already noted, this in-family attitude spills over from the family to industry itself, even more than in the United States. The person responsible for making the purchase for a firm must consult many elements within the firm and arrive at some sort of consensus before the purchase is approved. One implication of this system has a great deal of importance to marketing. Many American ads, for example, imply that the wife's problem is to satisfy the husband or the husband his wife. In areas with the extended families, however, advertising themes are more likely to stress the satisfaction of other members of the family of the older generation. The direct accountability of the wife to the husband is not an understood process in such areas. When family members are pictured together in advertisements, it is usually a mother and son, or father and son, or mother and daughter-in-law, rather than a husband and wife.

Family relationships are only one aspect of the culture, of course, although an extremely important one because of the dominance of the family among the various reference groups in which the individual plays a role. The family relationship itself is made possible in considerable part by the specific way of making a living. Probably the dominant part of any culture is the standard way of making a living within that culture.

Anthropologist William G. Summer proposed that the culture be considered in two aspects: the *primary mores*, i.e., the customs surrounding the ways people make a living; and the *secondary mores*, i.e., all the other aspects of their customs, beliefs and attitudes. According to his view, the way people make a living shapes much of the rest of their culture.

Without any question, the extended family found in India and Asia, in general, and in Mexico are possible only within a relatively immobile culture, one that is predominantly agricultural and commercial, but not heavily industrialized. Obviously, the extended family cannot exist if the husband does not follow an occupation close to that of his father and in the same area. Mobility of any sort, geographical or occupational, destroys such a structure. It is no accident that the most highly industrialized nations of the west are also those nations in which the nuclear family has completely taken over the general structure.

As will be seen later, the occupation of the husband is the primary determinant of social class. This is true in India, where the caste system itself defines the occupation the man may pursue, as well as in the West where a man may follow a quite different vocation than his parents did. No caste lines restrict the individual in the United States, but the social status of the individual, nevertheless, is just as truly determined by occupation as in a caste system.

Social class is only one of the various subcultural phenomena. All major cultures of major countries are subdivided into many kinds of subcultures. Within India, these are determined by region and by caste, to the extent that the latter is still operative. Within the United States, the subculture is largely defined by region, by type of residence (rural, urban, or suburban) and by social class. Social class itself is such an important determinant of individual attitude and values that a separate chapter is devoted to it following this one, but it is not the only source of subculture differences within the western world, within the United States or even within a given community.

## Geography and Culture

The basic outlines of the culture generally correspond to some kind of geographical boundaries. Nevertheless, neighboring countries which share a similar language will exhibit substantial cultural differences which show up in purchase and consumption patterns. One of the distinguishing marks of any culture is the dietary pattern. As Table 9-1 indicates, even within Western Europe, there are marked differences in the consumption of major classes of foods and beverages. The British, for instance, eat nearly three times as much meat per capita as do the Norwegians, and although far more fish is eaten by Norwegians than by Britons, the British still consume twice as much meat and fish together. Belgium, the Netherlands, and Germany are next door neighbors, and Belgium and the Netherlands share many interests in common, yet both Germany and Belgium consume half again as much butter and fats per capita as do the Netherlanders, and also about 40 percent more meat. The three Scandinavian countries share a virtually common language, but obviously not the same diet.

The differences in beverage consumption are even more striking, with the Spanish quite obviously the most enthusiastic consumers of soft drinks in Europe, and drinking much less wine than either of their Latin neighbors, France and Italy. The British taste for tea is well known, documented by Table 9-1, and it is clear that the Scandinavians live up to their reputations as heavy coffee drinkers—almost two liters per day among the Swedes.

**Table 9-1.  Cultural Differences in Food and Beverage Consumption Patterns, Western European Nations, 1971**

| COUNTRY | FOODS (In Kilograms/capita/year) | | | | |
| | Bread Cereals | Meat | Fish | Milk & Dairy Products | Butter & Fats |
| --- | --- | --- | --- | --- | --- |
| Belgium | 93 | 69 | 12 | 20 | 31 |
| France | 109 | 82 | 14 | 23 | 28 |
| Italy | 142 | 47 | 11 | 19 | 8 |
| Netherlands | 87 | 53 | 13 | 32 | 19 |
| Germany | 91 | 71 | 13 | 27 | 29 |
| Great Britain | 94 | 117 | 9 | 25 | 21 |
| Denmark | 85 | 73 | 18 | 30 | 35 |
| Sweden | 79 | 63 | 24 | 31 | 39 |
| Norway | 85 | 39 | 22 | 34 | 36 |

| | PURCHASED BEVERAGES (Liters/capita/year) | | | | | | |
| | Total— all items | Natural Mineral Water | Soft Drinks | Tea | Coffee | Beer | Wine |
| --- | --- | --- | --- | --- | --- | --- | --- |
| France | 456 | 32 | 14 | 5 | 251 | 40 | 114 |
| Spain | 241 | 5 | 55 | 12 | 70 | 31 | 68 |
| Italy | 307 | 15 | 25 | -- | 144 | 12 | 111 |
| Belgium | 581 | 23 | 41 | 35 | 348 | 122 | 12 |
| Netherlands | 457 | -- | 40 | 18 | 348 | 46 | 5 |
| Great Britain | 517 | -- | 41 | 306 | 72 | 93 | 5 |
| Germany | 445 | 9 | 31 | 9 | 248 | 111 | 17 |
| Denmark | 744 | -- | 37 | 22 | 588 | 97 | -- |
| Sweden | 799 | -- | 32 | 16 | 695 | 48 | -- |

Source: *European Marketing Data and Statistics*, Vol. 8, 1971, European Marketing Consultants (Publications) Ltd., 125 Pall Mall, London SW 1 England

Underneath these purely quantitative differences are clear differences in menu and meal patterns.

Personal appearance is another culturally determined pattern, as revealed in the consumption of cosmetics and toiletries, reflected in Table 9-2 for seven Western European countires. Although the general stereotype would probably place the French high on the list of users of such beauty aids, the table reveals that more than twice as large a proportion of British women use nearly every item listed, as do their neighbors across the English Channel. Note also that the use of deodorants by men appears to be a much more firmly established part

**Table 9-2. Cultural Differences in Cosmetic and Toiletries Usage, Western European Nations, 1971**

Percent of Women Using:

| COUNTRY | Foun-dation Cream | Face Powder | All-in-One | Eye Shadow | Eye Pencil Liner | Mas-cara | Hair Condi-tioner | Talcum Powder |
|---|---|---|---|---|---|---|---|---|
| France | 39 | 36 | 20 | 24 | 18 | 21 | 13 | 36 |
| Italy | 30 | 44 | 15 | 21 | 34 | 33 | 19 | 78 |
| Germany | 17 | 24 | 30 | 25 | 34 | 26 | 58 | 41 |
| Austria | 12 | 30 | 31 | 23 | 32 | 23 | 68 | 44 |
| Great Britain | 51 | 54 | 42 | 49 | 30 | 46 | 27 | 94 |
| Sweden | 39 | 43 | 32 | 41 | 43 | 62 | 21 | 37 |
| Norway | 45 | 45 | 14 | 31 | 25 | 49 | 13 | 26 |

Percent of Men Using:

| | Talcum Powder | Deodorant | Hair Lotion | Hair Cream |
|---|---|---|---|---|
| France | 22 | 31 | 20 | 11 |
| Italy | 39 | 44 | 19 | 15 |
| Germany | 7 | 48 | 38 | 26 |
| Austria | 7 | 34 | 34 | 12 |
| Great Britain | 35 | 25 | 18 | 32 |
| Sweden | 7 | 57 | 36 | 40 |
| Norway | 8 | 60 | 17 | 36 |

Source: *European Marketing Data and Statistics*, Vol. 8, 1971, European Marketing Consultants (Publications) Ltd., 125 Pall Mall, London SW1, England

of the Scandinavian culture than it is in Great Britain and France.

The ownership of such artifacts of modern civilization as the various kinds of electrical appliances is not only part of the norms of the local culture, but also reflects attitudinal norms in less tangible matters. The ownership of selected electric appliances in four neighboring Western European countries tells much about the Dutch attitude toward cleanliness. Note, for example, the dramatically higher ownership of vacuum sweepers, washing machines and clothes dryers in the Netherlands as compared to neighboring Belgium and Germany (see Table 9-3). Such ownership differences cannot be explained on the basis of income. They reflect different community attitudes and tastes, different standards of approved conduct which can aid or inhibit any sales effort in the area of taste involved.

**Table 9-3. Differences in Ownership of Selected Electric Appliances,
Four Neighboring Western European Nations, 1971**

Percent of Families owning:

| COUNTRY | Electric Cooker | Food Mixer | Toaster | Washing Machine | Clothes Dryer | Vacuum Cleaner |
|---|---|---|---|---|---|---|
| Netherlands | 4 | 53 | 40 | 85 | 53 | 100 |
| Belgium | 78 | 62 | 50 | 57 | 28 | 28 |
| Germany | 72 | 68 | 69 | 79 | 38 | 38 |
| Great Britain | 48 | 36 | 25 | 73 | 23 | 87 |

For example, it has been noted that in the United States, mere added convenience is enough to sell many kinds of products, from instant mashed potatoes to riding lawn mowers. In Germany, it is not—the product must somehow be shown to render some practical advantage. General Electric's International Division sold the German *hausfrau* on automatic dishwashers by demonstrating the better job made possible by the extremely hot water, too hot to use in hand washing. The advantage of boiling water sterilization was the deciding factor in selling to the Germans. But the initial attempt to sell electric blankets, electric can openers, and electric baby bottle warmers (all of which did well in the United States) was rebuffed because no such practical advantage was put forward. The German culture did not approve of buying for purely personal convenience (*Business Week*, 1963).

Regional attitudinal differences of a similar nature have been noted within the United States. One study by the Center for Research in Marketing, based on a number of surveys bearing on the use of leisure time, indicated that people in the Eastern region of the United States "appear to need more excuses or rationalizations" for the way they pass their leisure time than do West Coast customers. "[The Easterner is] almost always ready with an explanation of his motives. He prefers to cast his hobbies in an educational light" (*Advertising Age*, 1966).

Cultural differences of substantial size exist between broad regions of the United States, large enough to show up in expenditure patterns. One such major division of the country falls into four broad groupings: the Northeast, comprising the New England and Middle Atlantic states; the South, reaching from Virginia to Oklahoma, Arkansas and Kansas; the North Central, including all other states east of the Rockies; and the West. Even on this broad basis, there are significant differences in the allocation of consumption spending. Northeastern families spend a higher proportion for food, beverages and shelter, as Figure 9-1

**Figure 9-1. Regional Differences in the Percentage of Spending in Selected Categories of Personal Consumption**

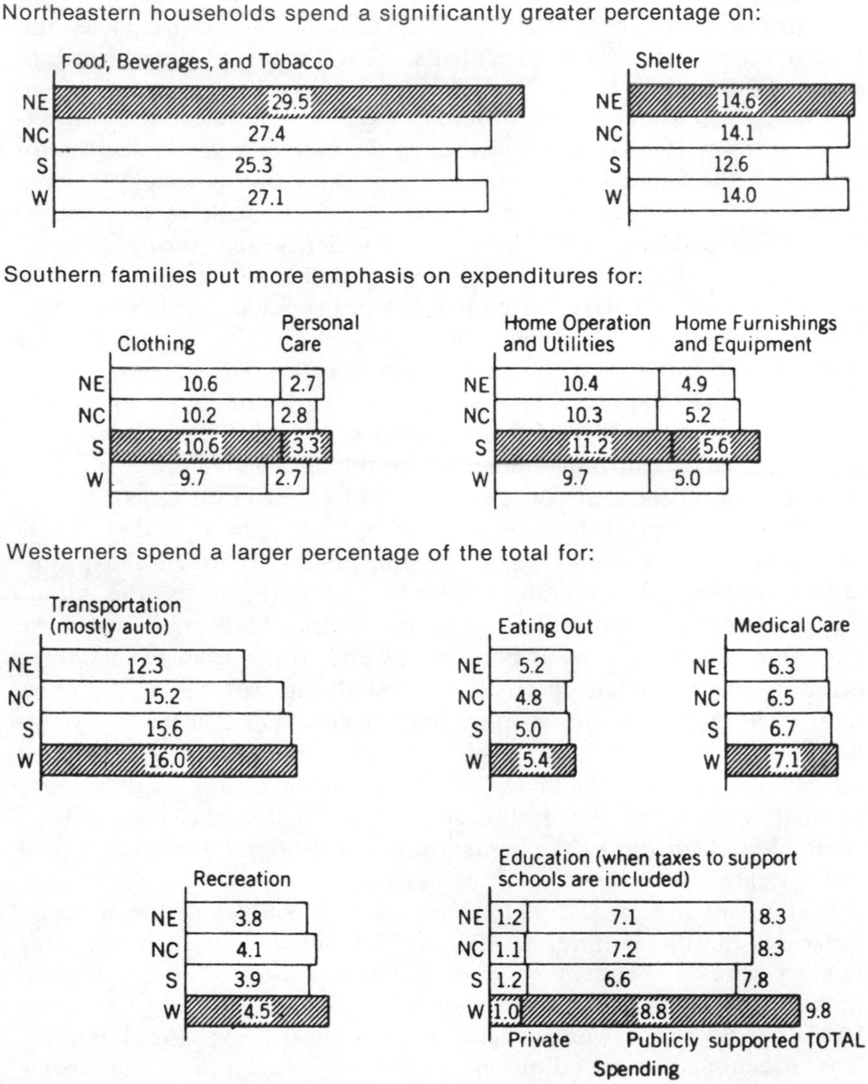

Northeastern households spend a significantly greater percentage on:

| | Food, Beverages, and Tobacco | | Shelter |
|---|---|---|---|
| NE | 29.5 | NE | 14.6 |
| NC | 27.4 | NC | 14.1 |
| S | 25.3 | S | 12.6 |
| W | 27.1 | W | 14.0 |

Southern families put more emphasis on expenditures for:

| | Clothing | Personal Care | | Home Operation and Utilities | Home Furnishings and Equipment |
|---|---|---|---|---|---|
| NE | 10.6 | 2.7 | NE | 10.4 | 4.9 |
| NC | 10.2 | 2.8 | NC | 10.3 | 5.2 |
| S | 10.6 | 3.3 | S | 11.2 | 5.6 |
| W | 9.7 | 2.7 | W | 9.7 | 5.0 |

Westerners spend a larger percentage of the total for:

| | Transportation (mostly auto) | | Eating Out | | Medical Care |
|---|---|---|---|---|---|
| NE | 12.3 | NE | 5.2 | NE | 6.3 |
| NC | 15.2 | NC | 4.8 | NC | 6.5 |
| S | 15.6 | S | 5.0 | S | 6.7 |
| W | 16.0 | W | 5.4 | W | 7.1 |

| | Recreation | | Education (when taxes to support schools are included) | | |
|---|---|---|---|---|---|
| NE | 3.8 | NE | 1.2 | 7.1 | 8.3 |
| NC | 4.1 | NC | 1.1 | 7.2 | 8.3 |
| S | 3.9 | S | 1.2 | 6.6 | 7.8 |
| W | 4.5 | W | 1.0 | 8.8 | 9.8 |
| | | | Private | Publicly supported | TOTAL |
| | | | | Spending | |

Sources: Bureau of Labor Statistics Report No. 237-38, July, 1964, and adapted from other U. S. Government reports on taxation and population.

indicates. Southerners put a higher than average emphasis on items of clothing and personal care, and on home equipment. Westerners are clearly more footloose, spending more on their automobiles, and also on eating out, recreation, and education.

Dietary differences between regions are even greater, as Figure 9-2 illustrates. An interesting sidelight of these quantitative differences is what they indicate as to the quite different Southern attitude toward food preparation. There is a clear bias against convenience foods and toward the use of scratch ingredients. This shows up quite clearly in Figure 9-2 C and D.

These gross average item differences do hint at substantial differences in tastes. This is quite obvious in the case of vegetable consumption, with the South buying much less of the more delicately flavored lettuce and asparagus, and over three times as much of the coarser dark green leafy vegetables (especially collards and turnip greens). Other taste differences lie beneath the quantitative reports. Just how much the approved flavor of coffee differs in various regions is borne out by anyone from the Midwest who has ever tried to find his favorite coffee brand in a New Orleans supermarket. Indeed, one of the problems of any garment chain is the differing attitudes on colors and other details in the different communities around the country. Each store must be carefully merchandised for the local community, and thus each resident manager must be sensitive to local taste variations.

Although cultural differences are usually geographical in their coverage, the culture is basically that of the groups to which the people belong. When they migrate, it travels with them, as the ethnic neighborhoods and cuisines in any large metropolitan area show. The migration of large groups of both blacks and whites from the South to other regions has often upset the merchandising patterns of the areas into which they move. In an upper-middle-class Los Angeles neighborhood, for example, infiltration of upper-class blacks almost destroyed the business in fine vegetables of an independent supermarket. They brought with them the tastes of the South for the coarse leafy vegetables which the local population did not normally consume, and which yielded much lower profit potentials.

Even within a region, the kind of town in which people live makes a difference in the culture, as Figure 9-3 shows. Metropolitan area families tend to spend much more for shelter and utilities, for food prepared away from home and for education and reading, than do families in smaller towns and especially in rural areas. Rural families tend to emphasize spending for clothing, personal care, for home furnishings and equipment and spend nearly as much for food as do families in the major metropolitan areas, even though they obtain some considerable proportion of their diet from home sources.

# Figure 9-2. Subcultural Dietary Differences, Urban Families, U.S.A., by Regions, 1955

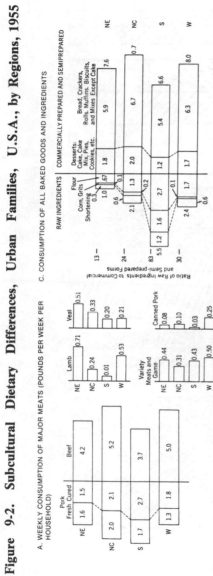

A. WEEKLY CONSUMPTION OF MAJOR MEATS (POUNDS PER WEEK PER HOUSEHOLD)

| | Pork Fresh Cured | Beef | Veal | Lamb | Canned Pork | Variety Meats and Game |
|---|---|---|---|---|---|---|
| NE | 1.6  1.5 | 4.2 | 0.51 | 0.71 | 0.08 | 0.44 |
| NC | 2.0  2.1 | 5.2 | 0.33 | 0.24 | 0.10 | 0.31 |
| S | 1.7  2.7 | 3.7 | 0.20 | 0.01 | 0.03 | 0.43 |
| W | 1.3  1.8 | 5.0 | 0.21 | 0.53 | 0.25 | 0.50 |

B. THE DIFFERING REGIONAL TASTES IN FRESH VEGETABLES (POUNDS PER WEEK)

| | Dark Green Leafy | Cabbage | Lettuce | Asparagus |
|---|---|---|---|---|
| NE | .26 | 0.82 | 1.1 | 0.56 |
| NC | .25 | 0.87 | 1.6 | 0.37 |
| S | 0.82 | 1.3 | 0.72 | 0.07 |
| W | 0.2 | 0.59  0.07 | 0.62 | |

C. CONSUMPTION OF ALL BAKED GOODS AND INGREDIENTS

RAW INGREDIENTS       COMMERCIALLY PREPARED AND SEMIPREPARED

Ratio of Raw Ingredients to Commercial and Semi-prepared Forms

| | Flour Corn, Grits Shortening | Desserts: Cake, Cake Mix, Pies, Cookies, etc. | Bread, Crackers, Rolls, Muffins, Biscuits, and Mixes Except Cake | |
|---|---|---|---|---|
| 13 | 1.0  .67  0.3 | 1.8 | 5.9 | 7.6  NE |
| 24 | 0.6  0.1 | 2.0 | 6.7 | 0.7  NC |
| 83 | 2.1  1.3  0.2 | 1.2 | 5.4 | 6.6  S |
| 5.5 | 2.7  1.6 | | | |
| 30 | 2.4  1.7  0.1 | 1.7 | 6.3 | 8.0  W |
| | 0.6 | | | |

D. CONSUMPTION OF READY-TO-EAT AND BROWN-AND-SERVE ROLLS

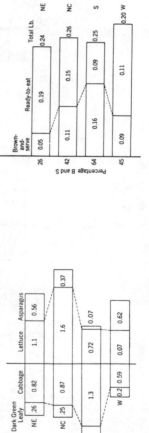

Percentage B and S

| | Brown-and-serve | Ready-to-eat | Total Lb. | |
|---|---|---|---|---|
| 26 | 0.05 | 0.19 | 0.24 | NE |
| 42 | 0.11 | 0.15 | 0.26 | NC |
| 64 | 0.16 | 0.09 | 0.25 | S |
| 45 | 0.09 | 0.11 | 0.20 | W |

Source: Adapted from *Household Food Consumption, 1955*, Reports 2-5, U. S. Dept. of Agriculture, Washington, D. C., 1956.

**Figure 9-3.   Percentages of Total Personal Consumption Spending Devoted to Specific Classes of Expenditure, Metropolitan and Rural Families Compared, U.S.A., 1960-61**

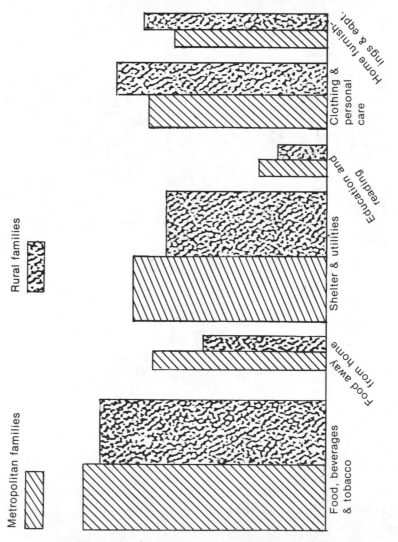

Clearly, the merchandising patterns of stores have to be different in different regions and even within the same region in different kinds of cities. Even within the cities, there are obvious major differences.

Cultural is something which is handed down from generation to generation and children move away from the cultural patterns of their families only very slowly and by degrees. For example, individuals of Italian descent tend to eat heavily of pasta products such as macaroni and spaghetti. Families three generations away from central Europe may still include large amounts of sour cream in their diet.

Occupational and geographical mobility slowly erase some of the boundaries over time, spreading what were originally ethnic tastes into the general population, as well as changing the dietary habits of the ethnic groups themselves. Pizza was an unknown product outside the Italian ghettos two generations ago. Today, pizza is a favorite snack item among groups whose ancestors never came within hundreds of miles of Italy. Southern Californians have learned to enjoy the tacos and other Mexican specialities brought to their attention by the infiltration of Latin-American migrants into their community. Thus geographic and generational mobility causes the cultural differences in diet and in many other matters, within the broad area of the United States, to be much less than the differences between very small and very closely adjacent neighbors in many other parts of the world. Moreover, the United States pattern is substantially different from that in other regions of the world, and marketers have learned that the same kind of promotional campaign or even the same product will seldom have a universal appeal.

## Cultural Factors in International Marketing

The international marketer must be an anthropologist in a great number of respects. Many aspects of life which are a matter of taste in our western culture may take on deeply religious or other moral significance in other parts of the world. Whether or not most Americans eat much or any pork at all is a matter of personal choice and a difference only of emphasis between regions. But to the Mohammedan, pork is essentially a poison, and to the devout Hindu, any form of meat is forbidden because of his religious belief in reincarnation. The Japanese word for the number four, "shi," sounds like the word for death, so the use of four must be avoided in any kind of promotional copy. In Japan, the husbands and wives live separate lives and should not be pictured appearing together in public. To the Japanese, red and white is a happy color combination, but the black-and-white combination is reserved for funerals (*Printers Ink*, 1964). Chinese consider red lucky but the Thai's consider yellow a sign of good fortune. An American manufacturer of water recreation products had to stop shipments of his green-hued items to Malaysia because customers there associated green with the jungle and sickness.

Nor does the seller have to go as far geographically and culturally as the Far East to encounter cultural traps for the unwary advertiser. Green Giant's projected invasion of the British market, with its line of canned goods and a determination to apply American marketing methods, received laudatory and very wide mention in the advertising press of 1962. In its subsequent experience, however, a British advertising executive noted that the campaign to sell canned sweet corn "laid a giant egg. The majority of British people have never nibbled an ear of corn. They love corn flakes, but ordinary corn is what you feed to chickens or animals" (Dutton, 1963). Even the form of a product must often be different in different markets. American attempts to sell asparagus soup in Europe ran into trouble because the American manufacturer made it of green asparagus instead of the white asparagus used in soups in some countries (Stridsberg, 1961). Even in the United States, brown eggs sell for a premium over white in the New England area, and white eggs at a premium over brown eggs in New York City.

### The Effects of Population Concentration on Culture

Such differences have been disappearing slowly over time, due to the high degree of mobility within the United States population and also because geographical mobility has brought the groups into contact with conditions which do not favor certain elements of culture and tend to emphasize the value of other elements. It has already been pointed out that the increase in the participation of women in the labor force has caused a major change in one aspect of the culture, the relative role of the sexes within the family, and the implications this has for marketing of convenience foods in particular as well as many other aspects of consumption. The shift of population out of various rural areas into often far distant urban areas has brought many kinds of shifts within the culture. Those moving to urban areas themselves must often adapt to a new culture.

The very conditions of living within a major metropolitan area or suburban area are vastly different from those in a rural area, and the United States has been undergoing a very rapid shift of population from largely rural living to largely metropolitan living within the last generation. One result of this has been an increased concentration of people in much smaller areas of the country and the growth of what has been called the megalopolis (giant city)—strings of cities and suburbs so close together that an entire region is nearly all composed of a single urban complex. The most obvious of these is the one sometimes called Boswash, to delineate the area running from lower New England down through Washington, D.C.

This growth of extremely large metropolitan areas, or megalopolises, has created a number of problems which came to a head in the oil crisis of 1974. When the population was much more widely scattered, widespread ownership of cars led to no great problems of transportation congestion. The decline of urban mass transit did not appear to be a great problem in the years in which the automobile was destroying this major vehicle of metropolitan transportation. But by 1974, the sudden crisis in the supplies of available automobile fuel brought to a head the results of a traffic congestion in which freeways have become parking lots during the rush hour. It became obvious that the large megalopolises of the modern United States could no longer survive on purely individual transportation, and the rehabilitation of urban mass transit became necessary and a major change in life styles extremely important. The result had already been foreseen by the growth of a number of regional transportation authorities, bringing together groups within metropolitan areas which have been largely hostile politically to any form of political cooperation. Meanwhile, the long distances of travel to and from work have created changes in family structure and recreational outlets.

One major element in any culture is the social class to which the individual belongs. In general, the social class will adhere to many of the superficial boundaries of the culture within which the social class is a part, but the priorities for spending within those limits vary so greatly that the life styles are quite opposite. These social class differences are to be found in every country in the world, including those which claim to have a classless society. The United States is no exception, and the consumption differences between social classes are so important that they deserve separate mention by themselves in the following chapter.

## Summary

1. Most of the consumer's attitudes and other norms of behavior come out of the culture to which he belongs, and the culture itself determines the organizational relationships of the groups which transmit it.

2. One of the major structures defined by any culture is that of the family. In most of the highly industrial nations of the Atlantic

Community, this structure is that of the nuclear or conjugal family, centered around the relationship of the individual couple, husband and wife. In much of the rest of the world, the common family structure is that of the extended family, with several generations on the husband's side of the family living together, whenever possible, and acting as a single cohesive unit in any case.

3. Consumer decision structures and attitudes are quite different under the extended family system from those under the conjugal family, and the kinds of advertising and product appeals which can succeed are totally divergent. Under the extended family system, even highly personal product choices are a matter of consultation with the members of the family, and both personal appeals and appeals to the husband-wife relationship which work well under the conjugal system are meaningless.

4. Major cultures tend to correspond with geographical limits, with differences both between nations and between regions within a nation.

5. Quite marked differences, reflected in sharply different consumption patterns, can be observed between closely neighboring nations, even those sharing a similar language. For this reason, products and advertising appeals must be tailored for the local area.

6. Striking cultural differences can be found even within a country, reflected by quite different expenditure patterns and quite obvious matters as diet.

7. Although most cultures and subcultures can be described in geographical terms, the culture is carried by the people, and migrates with them when they move in any number into distant communities, creating ethnic and other specialized markets within major metropolitan areas, and requiring localization of merchandise planning for optimum success.

8. Eventually, some of the items the migrants bring with them tend to gain adoption in the communities in which they settle.

9. International sellers need to be acutely aware of even the minor nuances and attitudes of the local cultures in all aspects of the marketing effort—in product design details, in labeling and packaging, and in the advertising appeals and language they use.

10. Rural and urban cultures differ even within the same country, and the growth of giant city complexes (megalopolises) has created special cultural characteristics of their own.

11. One major subcultural division in every country is not geographical—that of social class.

## Chapter 9 Exercises

1.  The text makes a clear distinction between the nuclear family form and the extended family form. In practice, there are gradations between, even in the U.S.A. In some situations, relatives cluster together and confer between themselves a great deal. In other circumstances, the nuclear family is almost entirely on its own without significant contact between relatives.

    In what kinds of situations and/or social classes might you expect at least some remnants of the extended family form? Why?

    In what circumstances and/or social classes might you expect the nuclear family to be almost totally independent of relatives in their purchase decisions?

    How would you expect the general nature of purchasing decisions to differ between these two types of situation?

2.  Although France produces both white wines and red ones, the French are more likely to drink a red wine than a white one, while their close neighbors in Germany produce and drink mostly white wines and consume more of their alcohol in the form of beer than of wine (as does Belgium). Why do you suppose this is so?

3.  As far as alcoholic beverages are concerned, Spain is more of a wine-drinking culture than a beer-drinking one. But Spaniards are far more likely than their French neighbors to drink their wine mixed with citrus juices, in a wine punch, and are the champion soft drink consumers in Europe (whereas Frenchmen are top mineral water consumers). Why, do you suppose this is so?

4.  Recent years have witnessed some marked new trends in food usage in the culture of the U.S.A. Among them:
    a. The use of eggs, per capita, has been in a definite downtrend for decades. What cultural changes might be responsible for this? (Consider carefully the use-systems most important for eggs.)
    b. Sales of fresh produce in food stores has been in a steady decline, replaced by the sale of frozen types, canned and other processed forms. What cultural changes might account for this?

5.  List some of the regional differences in diet you are acquainted with. What might be the origin of these differences?

    List some other differences you know of (habits of dress and housing usage, for example, or of music tastes). How do you account for these?

6.  All of the following are dietary items in some important cultures.
    How many have you eaten? How many would you try?
       Fruit soup
       Fish soup
       Raw fish
       Aged fish, raw
       Roasted cricket or locusts
       Fried snails
       Mangoes
       Roast dog
       Roast snake
       Fried intestines
       Grits
       Pickled codfish
       Burdock
       Dandelion greens
       Roast mutton
       Papaya
       Goat meat
       Avocados
       Scrapple (a form of ground
          loaf consisting of slaugh-
          ter scrap and waste such
          as brains, kidneys, etc,
          mixed with about one-fifth
          cereal)
       Cabbage soup

7.  What foods can you name which are now in general use in the
    U.S.A. which were confined to ethnic groups no more than two
    generations ago?

# Social Class, Value Priorities and Taste Discrimination

SOCIAL CLASS: A NONGEOGRAPHICAL FORM OF SUB-CULTURE

SOCIAL CLASS AS PECKING ORDER

OCCUPATIONAL BASIS FOR CLASS IDENTIFICATION

    Lack of Correlation with Income Class

SOCIAL CLASS AND TASTE DIFFERENCES

SOCIAL CLASS, STORE DIFFERENCES AND ADVERTISING CLUES

SOCIAL CLASS AND ADVERTISING COMMUNICATION

THE CHANGING SOCIAL CLASS MIX IN THE UNITED STATES

    Resulting Individualization of Taste Preferences

CONSIDER THE FOLLOWING examples of differences in social class standards. A group of young executives were emerging from their office building, just a couple of minutes after noon, to cross a public street to the company's cafeteria, all of them seeking a light and relatively inexpensive noon meal. As they emerged from the building, they noted a city laborer with a tar cart he had been using to help fill in some of the cracks and pot holes in the asphalt pavement. He had obviously just finished cleaning the heavy smoothing iron used for finishing his work. As the executives watched, the laborer reached back in his hip pocket and pulled out a package containing two large T-bone steaks, and then placed them on the smoothing iron, now reversed and on top of the fire in his cart. The cost of those two steaks alone would have bought two of the already prepared lunches being purchased by the executives. Yet his income was probably substantially below their level.

Consider also a different sort of phenomenon. A mail order company asked its research department to find a method to test the relative demand in a line of dresses about to be sold by the company. The analyst picked a number of different kinds of samples from the company's customer file and sent out a simple questionnaire, together with copies of the pages that were to be in the catalog, asking for the customer choices. As the same time, desiring to check to see if a short cut method might be almost as good, the same questionnaire and the same catalog pages were submitted to the women who held clerical and supervisory positions in the company's head office. Tabulation of the results showed a very close correspondence between the choices of all of the various kinds of customers' samples, but a complete reversal of choices between those made by the customers and those made by the company's clerical and supervisory personnel! The supervisory personnel rated lowest the very items the customers rated highest and gave as their first choice the item that was at the bottom of the customer's ratings, with the other numbers in equally reversed positions. Yet the basic style pattern (that is, the general silhouette) of all of those garments being presented for tests was essentially the same. The only difference was in the general type of garment (a suit dress in one case), and in the details that make one style within a general fashion differ from another.

Finally, consider a third example. A supermarket chain which had a very high degree of success and crowded stores on the south side of Chicago, where its customers consisted of lower-middle and skilled-worker classes, decided to build another unit along the north shore of the same metropolitan area, in a neighborhood with middle- and upper-middle-income families. The choice of location could hardly have been better. It was in an attractive, high traffic location in which the nearest stores were not only some distance away but older and not nearly as well constructed for the current type of merchandising. It had an ample parking lot. Unfortunately, the parking lot soon proved to be far too ample for the volume of traffic the store attracted. The firm's normal merchandising pattern for a south side store did not attract the north shore residents at all. The market's special emphasis, luncheon meats and cold cuts, which brought a lot of business on the south side, were of no interest to north shore residents who did not carry their lunches. The lack of choice of brands in the canned goods section drove away the kind of middle- and upper-class customers who prefer a great deal of individual choice in such matters.

All three of the above examples show the result of a form of subcultural market segmentation that is not basically geographical in nature, the phenomenon of social class. As the examples indicate, social class results in a different pattern of expenditure and a different level or type of taste for many kinds of goods and services; and these various levels of taste and expenditure allocation are, to a very considerable extent, independent of the level of income itself.

There is a very definite pecking order of individual and group status within every known society, including the so-called classless society of the Communist world. Both the individuals within a given status and those outside recognize a specific position for their status within that hierarchy. In the western world, and in modern times at least, occupation and source of income are the principal elements in class distinction, but not the level of that income.

Indeed, occupations generally considered relatively farther down the scale may actually earn greater incomes than those in occupations much farther up the recognized status scale. In one metropolitan area, for example, a journeyman plumber normally receives an individual income of $25,000 a year or more and an operating engineer (the operator of a ditch-digging machine, bulldozer or other construction equipment) has a union rate which translates to $20,000 a year even when he does not work overtime, and he normally receives overtime pay at various periods. By contrast, in the same area, assistant professors and many associate professors whose social status is generally recognized by both the plumbers and the professors as being much higher, normally receive pay well under $20,000 a year and with no provision whatsoever for overtime.

Sociologists have used various kinds of multifactor scales to indicate class, with the standards generally being those of occupation, source of income, type of housing and level of education. But level of education itself tends to be a necessary prerequisite to entering most of the higher status occupations, and the quality of the housing itself results from the class expenditure standards. Consequently, for practical reasons, it is sufficient to use occupational ranking and, in fact, people will recognize quite fine class distinctions between various occupational rankings. A study made in 1947, and repeated sixteen years later in 1963, shows a high degree of stability between the ranking of most occupations in these two widely separated periods, over a list of ninety occupations (see Table 10-1). If we break these ninety occupations down into groups, we note that all of the occupations in the top one-fifth of this list are generally considered intellectual or highly technical in their nature and all of them require a high degree of education. On the other hand, of those in the bottom one-fifth, all but one are considered clearly manual tasks (the exception is that of a singer in a nightclub) and all but the nightclub singer and coal miners are normally considered highly unskilled operations.

These two exceptions appear to be based on the degree of "desirability" of the occupation. In general, a study of consumption patterns will show that there is a sharp cleavage in the way the classes whose occupations are basically manual in nature, whether skilled or otherwise, spend their income, and the expenditure patterns of those whose occupations are generally intellectual and normally described as "white collar" in nature.

When we look over the list in Table 10-1, we will note that the first one-fifth consists entirely of professional, technical, and official positions of one sort or another. The second one-fifth, with ranks from nineteen through thirty-six, is also in the same category, but apparently the positions are considered to carry a somewhat lesser level of responsibility than those in the first one-fifth. The third level, with ranks from thirty-seven through fifty-four, out of ninety, is composed mainly of skilled workers, small proprietors, and lesser professionals. The fourth level consists of more skilled workers, some semiskilled, very small proprietors and clerical, but most of them would be considered "clean jobs." As already noted, the bottom one-fifth is made up primarily of manual workers and one "dirty" skilled job (coal miner),

**Table 10-1. Prestige Ratings of Occupations in the United States, 1947 and 1963**

| Occupation | 1947 Rank | 1963 Rank |
|---|---|---|
| U.S. Supreme Court Justice | 1 | 1 |
| Physician | 2.5 | 2 |
| Nuclear physicist | 18 | 3.5 |
| Scientist | 8 | 3.5 |
| Government scientist | 10.5 | 5.5 |
| State governor | 2.5 | 5.5 |
| Cabinet member in the federal government | 4.5 | 8 |
| College professor | 8 | 8 |
| U.S. Representative in Congress | 8 | 8 |
| Chemist | 18 | 11 |
| Lawyer | 18 | 11 |
| Diplomat in the U.S. foreign service | 4.5 | 11 |
| Dentist | 18 | 14 |
| Architect | 18 | 14 |
| County judge | 13 | 14 |
| Psychologist | 22 | 17.5 |
| Minister | 13 | 17.5 |
| Member of the board of directors of a large corporation | 18 | 17.5 |
| Mayor of a large city | 6 | 17.5 |
| Priest | 6 | 21.5 |
| Head of a department in a state government | 13 | 21.5 |
| Civil engineer | 23 | 21.5 |
| Airline pilot | 24.5 | 21.5 |
| Banker | 10.5 | 24.5 |
| Biologist | 29 | 24.5 |
| Sociologist | 26.5 | 26 |
| Instructor in public schools | 34 | 27.5 |
| Captain in the regular army | 31.5 | 27.5 |
| Accountant for a large business | 29 | 29.5 |
| Public school teacher | 36 | 29.5 |
| Owner of a factory that employs about 100 people | 26.5 | 31.5 |
| Building contractor | 26.5 | 31.5 |
| Artist who paints pictures that are exhibited in galleries | 24.5 | 34.5 |
| Musician in a symphony orchestra | 29 | 34.5 |
| Author of novels | 29 | 34.5 |
| Economist | 34 | 34.5 |
| Official of an international labor union | 40.5 | 37 |
| Railroad engineer | 40.5 | 39 |
| Electrician | 45 | 39 |

Source: Robert W. Hodge, Paul M. Siegel, and Peter H. Rossi, "Occupational Prestige in the United States: 1925-1963," in Reinhard Bendix and Seymour Martin Lipset, eds., *Class, Status, and Power*, 2d ed. (New York: The Free Press, 1966), pp. 322-334, at pp. 324-325.

## Table 10-1 (Continued)

| Occupation | 1947 Rank | 1963 Rank |
|---|---|---|
| County agricultural agent | 37.5 | 39 |
| Owner-operator of a printing shop | 42.5 | 41.5 |
| Trained machinist | 45 | 41.5 |
| Farm owner and operator | 39 | 44 |
| Undertaker | 47 | 44 |
| Welfare worker for a city government | 45 | 44 |
| Newspaper columnist | 42.5 | 46 |
| Policeman | 55 | 47 |
| Reporter on a daily newspaper | 48 | 48 |
| Radio announcer | 40.5 | 49.5 |
| Bookkeeper | 51.5 | 49.5 |
| Tenant farmer—one who owns livestock and machinery and manages the farm | 51.5 | 51.5 |
| Insurance agent | 51.5 | 51.5 |
| Carpenter | 58 | 53 |
| Manager of a small store in a city | 49 | 54.5 |
| A local official of a labor union | 62 | 54.5 |
| Mail carrier | 57 | 57 |
| Railroad conductor | 55 | 57 |
| Traveling salesman for a wholesale concern | 51.5 | 57 |
| Plumber | 59.5 | 59 |
| Automobile repairman | 59.5 | 60 |
| Playground director | 55 | 62.5 |
| Barber | 66 | 62.5 |
| Machine operator in a factory | 64.5 | 62.5 |
| Owner-operator of a lunch stand | 62 | 62.5 |
| Corporal in the regular army | 64.5 | 65.5 |
| Garage mechanic | 62 | 65.5 |
| Truck driver | 71 | 67 |
| Fisherman who owns his own boat | 68 | 68 |
| Clerk in a store | 68 | 70 |
| Milk route man | 71 | 70 |
| Streetcar motorman | 68 | 70 |
| Lumberjack | 73 | 72.5 |
| Restaurant cook | 71 | 72.5 |
| Singer in a nightclub | 74.5 | 74 |
| Filling station attendant | 74.5 | 75 |
| Dockworker | 81.5 | 77.5 |
| Railroad section hand | 79.5 | 77.5 |
| Night watchman | 81.5 | 77.5 |
| Coal miner | 77.5 | 77.5 |
| Restaurant waiter | 79.5 | 80.5 |
| Taxi driver | 77.5 | 80.5 |
| Farm hand | 76 | 83 |

**Table 10-1 (Continued)**

| Occupation | 1947 Rank | 1963 Rank |
|---|---|---|
| Janitor | 85.5 | 83 |
| Bartender | 85.5 | 83 |
| Clothes presser in a laundry | 83 | 85 |
| Soda fountain clerk | 84 | 86 |
| Share-cropper—one who owns no livestock or equipment and does not manage farm | 87 | 87 |
| Garbage collector | 88 | 88 |
| Street sweeper | 89 | 89 |
| Shoe shiner | 90 | 90 |

plus one whose job is certainly skilled (that of a singer in a nightclub) but probably considered slightly socially undesirable.

For purposes of statistical investigation, we can group the various hierarchies into five standard occupational classifications widely used by census and other governmental authorities:

1. Professional, officials and proprietors who make up the upper and middle classes

2. Clerical and sales, who would normally approximate the lower-middle class

3. Skilled workers, who are the aristocrats of the upper-lower classes

4. Semiskilled workers

5. Unskilled laborers who make up the lowest of the occupational hierarchy

As Table 10-2 very clearly shows, the income of these groups is not in any clear linear scale with relation to social class, expecially if we take into account the total family income. It is true that those at the bottom of the social hierarchy, the unskilled laborers, are largely in those incomes below the median level ($8,000 in 1960-61) but it is also true that the majority of the self-employed proprietors, who are in classes above the unskilled, are also below this median and, indeed, almost exactly one-half of the salaried professionals and officials are also. Furthermore, families receiving less than $4,000-a-year income in 1960-61 included over one-fifth of the clerical and sales middle-class people while only one in eight skilled-worker families received so little.

Since there is a very heavy overlap between income level of all of the classes, it is possible to investigate the consumption pattern differences

**Table 10.2.  Distribution of Income Levels for Each Major Occupational Grouping, 1960-61**

| Occupational Group | Percentage with a Family Income of ($000) | | | | | | | | |
|---|---|---|---|---|---|---|---|---|---|
| | Under 3 | 3-4 | 4-5 | 5-6 | 6-7.5 | 7.5-10 | 10-14 | 15 or more | All income classes |
| **White-Collar, Upper and Middle Classes** | | | | | | | | | |
| Self-employed | 14 | 10 | 11 | 12 | 12 | 15 | 13 | 12 | 100 |
| Salaried professionals and officials | 3 | 4 | 8 | 11 | 21 | 28 | 19 | 7 | 100 |
| Clerical and sales | 10 | 12 | 17 | 17 | 20 | 16 | 16 | 7 | 100 |
| **Manual Workers** | | | | | | | | | |
| Skilled | 4 | 8 | 14 | 17 | 27 | 21 | 8 | 0.5 | 100 |
| Semiskilled | 12 | 13 | 19 | 19 | 19 | 13 | 5 | 0.2 | 100 |
| Unskilled | 32 | 17 | 18 | 12 | 11 | 7 | 2 | 1 | 100 |

Source: U. S. Bureau of Labor Statistics, Report No. 237-38, July, 1964.

between classes while holding income steady. This is done in Table 10-3. Note the very sharp distinction in the amount of income devoted to shelter expenditures by those in the white collar lower- and upper-middle classes and those in the lower classes below them. Since incomes themselves overlap, this means that it is quite possible for those in the skilled-worker classes, for example, to be living in the same neighborhood with salaried professionals and officials of quite a different social class, and this is indeed the case. Although the skilled worker devotes about one-third to one-fourth less of his income to housing, his higher pay scale will often make him a next door neighbor to an accountant or a professor, for example.

That does not mean, however, that these neighbors share the same culture—quite the reverse. Indeed, quite often their acquaintanceship is that of mere small talk at best. One of the author's early experiences in opinion polling revealed this quite clearly during the very controversial 1940 national election campaign. Interviewing one family in the middle of the income scale neighborhood, he would be told, "We are for the Republican candidate, we don't know anyone who is going to vote for his opponent." Going next door to a skilled-worker's household, "We are for the Democratic candidate. We don't know anybody who is voting for the Republican."

The reason for such lack of direct contact is not necessarily snobbery in a country like the United States, but rather a lack of mutual

**Table 10.3. Family Expenditures for Consumption by Families of Two
or More in Each Major Occupational Grouping, for Four
Principal Income Classes, 1960-61 (In percentage of total
expenditure for personal consumption)**

| | Families with Income of ($000) | | | |
| --- | --- | --- | --- | --- |
| | 4-5 | 5-6 | 6-7.5 | 7.5-10 |
| A. Food, Beverages, and Tobacco Expenditures by: | | | | |
| Salaried professionals and officials | 21 | 23 | 23 | 23 |
| Clerical and sales | 24 | 24 | 24 | 24 |
| Skilled | 25 | 26 | 24 | 25 |
| Semiskilled | 27 | 26 | 26 | 25 |
| Unskilled | 28 | 27 | 25 | 24 |
| B. Shelter Expenditures by: | | | | |
| Salaried professionals and officials | 16 | 17 | 16 | 14 |
| Clerical and sales | 16 | 15 | 14 | 13 |
| Skilled | 14 | 13 | 12 | 11 |
| Semiskilled | 14 | 13 | 12 | 11 |
| Unskilled | 14 | 13 | 13 | 11 |
| C. Home Furnishings and Equipment Expenditures by: | | | | |
| Salaried professionals and officials | 4.5 | 6.2 | 5.2 | 5.6 |
| Clerical and sales | 4.6 | 4.6 | 4.5 | 5.1 |
| Skilled | 4.9 | 5.4 | 5.5 | 5.2 |
| Semiskilled | 5.0 | 5.7 | 5.5 | 5.6 |
| Unskilled | 4.4 | 5.2 | 6.0 | 6.3 |
| D. Education and Reading Expenditures by: | | | | |
| Salaried professionals and officials | 2.5 | 2.2 | 2.1 | 2.2 |
| Clerical and sales | 2.7 | 2.7 | 1.8 | 2.0 |
| Skilled | 1.3 | 1.4 | 1.5 | 2.0 |
| Semiskilled | 1.1 | 1.4 | 1.7 | 1.5 |
| Unskilled | 1.2 | 1.5 | 1.9 | 1.7 |

Source: U. S. Bureau of Labor Statistics, Report No. 237-38, July, 1964.

interests. As Table 10-3 shows, the further we go down the social scale, the greater the interest in food expenditure and the less the interest in education and reading materials. The contrast in the importance of attention to the intellectual side of life is quite sharp when we examine the reading expenditures of those families with children past high school age (over eighteen years old). The percentage of income devoted to education and reading for such families in 1961, by occupational groups, was as follows:

Professional, technical and official families . . . . . . . 5.9 percent
Clerical and sales families . . . . . . . . . . . . . . . . . . . . . 5.9 percent
Skilled-worker families . . . . . . . . . . . . . . . . . . . . . . . . 3.0 percent
Semiskilled . . . . . . . . . . . . . . . . . . . . . . . . . . . . . . . . . . . 2.9 percent
Unskilled . . . . . . . . . . . . . . . . . . . . . . . . . . . . . . . . . . . . 2.5 percent

Thus one clear pattern emerges, even when we simply have the gross level of expenditures, and that is that the middle and upper classes value the quality of neighborhood and housing more than any of the groups below the white-collar line.

The differences between professional groups and other groups in home furnishing spending are blurred because of the family life cycle influence. As shown much earlier, families buy a great portion of their total home furnishings in the earlier years of married life. The starting salaries for young professionals at the time of the 1960-61 survey resulted in a concentration of young new families in the $5,000 to $7,500 bracket and thus a higher spending rate for home equipment than is typical of established families. Nevertheless, the general trend across class lines for home furnishings and equipment expenditures shows what some in-depth sociological studies of the 1960s had already shown: working-class families put much more emphasis on the material furnishings in the home than do the middle classes.

*Social-Class Differences in Taste*

The tables used to this point reflect only the dollars spent on a class of products, not the kind of products bought within that class. However, regardless of the dollars spent, the specific style and nature of the goods bought are quite different from one class to another. This was illustrated in our opening examples by both the dress preference sample of the mail order house and by the experiences of the supermarket.

Differences in quantity are only a reflection of the differences in taste. At the time of a number of *Chicago Tribune* studies in the 1950s, Martineau found that in architecture, for example, the blue collar lower-half of the market disliked the modern ranch homes and two-story colonials then being bought by the upper segments of the social classes. Neither did they want the severely plain functional furniture the middle classes preferred. The "heavy commercial highly overstuffed styles" were then the choice of the blue-collar families.

The same study showed apparent class differences in the kinds of clothing bought by the women in the various social classes, and in the response to the phrasing of clothing advertising. Upper-upper-class women responded to styles and to fashion advertising characterized by such adjectives as "aristocratic," "well-bred," "distinguished," and tended toward independence from the fluctuations in current fashions. In other words, they tended to buy classic designs. Clothes were viewed as symbols of wealth and high living by lower-upper-class women who sought to combine opulence with quiet elegance. They tended to buy costly clothes which, superficially, did not look expensive. Lower-upper-class women were attracted by advertising using such terms as "chic" and by terms which connoted "sophistication." Clothes characterized by "glamour" were avoided by these lower-upper-class women as something that to them meant "cheapness."

On the other hand, the suggestion of high style repelled middle- and lower-class women as being too extreme. What they sought was respectability, not the impression of breeding. To them, the best styles were those described as "smart," like those worn by movie stars who had "glamour," which meant to them simply "femininely pretty" (Martineau, 1957). Other American studies of class taste differences have been cited by Meyers and Reynolds (1967). In one such study, the design preference of matched panels of women in three different social levels could be classed by designations of *expressive, sentimentalized* or *controlled* as follows:

| Class Preference | Design Preference |
|---|---|
| Upper-middle | controlled |
| Lower-middle | sentimentalized |
| Upper-lower | expressive |

In another piece of research, Paul F. Lazarsfeld concluded, from observations and studies made by his Columbia Bureau of Social Research, that the differences in preferences among upper- and lower-income groups could be characterized as follows:

| Upper-Class Preferences | Lower-Class Preferences |
|---|---|
| Bitter dry taste | Sweet chocolate taste |
| Irregular weaves and fabrics | Rubbery fabrics |
| Less-pungent fragrances | Strong fragrances |

To Lazarsfeld, it seemed that while upper-class people preferred, or perhaps could better discern, the "weak stimuli," lower classes preferred or perhaps directly reacted to stronger stimuli. This seems to have some support from the third study—one of leather grain vinyl upholstery materials for automobiles cited by Meyers and Reynolds: "The lower-income people in the sample tended to prefer the coarse grain vinyls while the upper-income class preferred the finer grain 'crush skiver.' " As Meyers and Reynolds suggested, the preferences for less contrasty and intrusive stimuli are probably the effect of a learned ability to distinguish and appreciate finer differences due to their higher education. As we noted earlier, in the discussion of perception, perception is a matter which is subject to training and experience.

A British study of biscuit (cookie) preference in the United Kingdom showed the class preference extended even to brands of every day food items, and to kinds of stores in which the purchases were made (see Table 10-4). In this study, upper classes gave greater preference to the plain types than did the lower classes, and to four of the brands studied, with one of the brands being chosen almost exlcusively by upper classes.

Tastes, of course, are learned phenomena and do change over time, particularly in matters in which fashion can be important, as it is in building and in furniture. In the *Chicago Tribune*'s studies of the 1950s, only the upper and middle classes found the Scandinavian modern style of furniture attractive. However, by the middle 1960s, these designs, or cheap copies of them, were being featured in advertising of retail outlets whose trade was mainly lower class.

## *Social Class, Store Patronage, and Advertising Cues*

Because of social class and consequent differences in tastes and spending patterns, retail competition is in no sense the kind of conflict situation most people generally think of in relation to the market. Indeed, experience has shown that department stores benefit most when they are near other department stores, and all shopping centers built in the last couple of decades have been multiple department store shopping centers, with a trend to even more in the same area. This is also true of outlets like specialty dress stores. There are really three reasons for this:

1. The first is that the more stores there are in an area, the wider the selection available to the customer and the greater the traffic of customers, to the obvious benefit of the smaller specialty stores in the center. It is also true that many customers are not dedicated to any one

**Table 10.4. Social Class in Great Britain, the Type and Brand of Biscuits (Cookies) Bought, and Type of Store in Which Bought**

|  | Upper Class % | Middle Class % | Lower Class % |
|---|---|---|---|
| Type of Biscuit Purchased |  |  |  |
| *All types* | 100 | 100 | 100 |
| Plain | 71 | 56 | 58 |
| Sweetened | 43 | 31 | 38 |
| Dry | 28 | 25 | 20 |
| Cream | 6 | 10 | 10 |
| Assorted | 20 | 21 | 25 |
| Chocolate coated | 19 | 16 | 15 |
| | | | |
| Brand Purchased |  |  |  |
| *All brands* | 100 | 100 | 100 |
| Weston | 8 | 1 | 1 |
| Jacobs | 12 | 8 | 8 |
| Crawford | 14 | 11 | 7 |
| Peak Frean | 14 | 12 | 10 |
| McVitie & Price | 18 | 20 | 18 |
| Cadbury | 3 | 4 | 1 |
| Huntley & Palmer | 7 | 9 | 0 |
| CWS* | 1 | 2 | 5 |
| St. Michael | 5 | 8 | 8 |
| Loose unbranded | 4 | 5 | 9 |
| | | | |
| Type of Store at Which Biscuits Were Purchased in Previous Seven Days |  |  |  |
| *All types* | 100 | 100 | 100 |
| Supermarket | 25 | 21 | 14 |
| Department store | 9 | 6 | 4 |
| Dairy | 4 | 3 | 3 |
| Chain store | 17 | 19 | 13 |
| Independent grocery | 36 | 48 | 42 |
| Cooperative | 2 | 5 | 12 |
| Bazaar | 3 | 5 | 8 |
| Bakery | 0 | 2 | 2 |
| Other | 3 | 2 | 3 |

*Private brand of Cooperative Wholesale Society.
SOURCE: *Market Research*, No. 1, London, European Research Consultants, 1965.

outlet but often find it necessary to shop in a number of stores to make up the assortment they desire. But these facts alone do not explain why each store may have greater volume with a competitor in the neighborhood than it would by itself. They do not explain why each store attracts a solid core of its own which has little interest in the other stores in the area except for fringe purchases. The reason for this lies in the differences in tastes and spending patterns of the different social classes, and also in the differences in what they expect from the store which they patronize.

2. Stores may carry "overlapping dress lines," for example, in terms of price, but the details of construction and ornamentation of the dresses in the two competing stores will be quite different and each will attract its own social class of customers. The same is true, of course, of supermarkets. Each will attract its customer core based on the type of assortment that it offers and also the variety of that assortment. Furthermore, each develops its own personality—a set of expectations for customer treatment as well as merchandise. This personality sooner or later permeates every aspect of the store's operation, whether the store is aware of it or not, and women come to judge the store by the advertising, making what seem to be extremely accurate judgments based solely on the layout and content of the ads. A rather dramatic example of this showed up in a *Chicago Tribune* study in the 1950s of the advertising of a Kansas City furniture store. Women in both Kansas City and Atlanta were shown copy of the ads run by this Kansas City store. All clues to the identity of the store were blotted out of the copy and the women making the judgments had to go entirely on the physical appearance of the advertisements themselves. Nevertheless, the judgments made about the store's merchandise and its shopping atmosphere were virtually identical in both cities, as can be seen in Figure 10-1. Moreover, when people who were quite familiar with the store were asked about the store, virtually the same profile of judgment was obtained. The class content of the judgments made is quite obvious.

It is possible, of course, for advertising to give an erroneous impression of the store's offerings and service, and thus actually cost it sales. Martineau tells us of one instance in which the furniture buyer from one of Chicago's top department stores clipped a mattress ad from some "borax" store (a store that is highly promotional and tends to puff the quality of its goods well beyond the level of their actual worth). He insisted that it be run in exactly the same form: "Factory Warehouse clearance! Fourteen-car-load special purchase drives prices down to new lows for this quality bedding!" With the ad was an illustration showing flat cars piled high with mattresses, all done with extremely heavy black and over-powering type. The ad did very poorly

**Figure 10-1. Comparison of Judgments About the Personality of a Kansas City Store Made by Housewives in Kansas City and in Atlanta, Based Solely on Advertising**

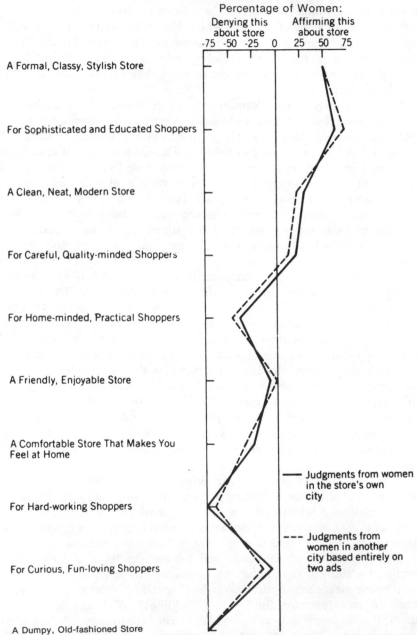

From Pierre Martineau, *Motivation in Advertising*, McGraw-Hill Book Company, New York, 1957. Used by permission of McGraw-Hill Book Company. Page 176.

for the department store, although a similar promotion of mattresses the previous year, in the store's own advertising style, had been quite successful.

Another instance which has come to the author's attention has to do with a local food chain in a southwestern city. The chain was extremely successful, with a steadily rising sales curve for its four quite large, well-merchandised stores. Unlike most food stores, the company used a local advertising agency to prepare its copy, with very little emphasis on price and with very attractive weekly double-page spreads, often spending more space on menu suggestions and on good seasonal buys than on groups of specific special items.

The ad agency, however, began to feel that perhaps it might not hurt to lend a little price emphasis to specials of various kinds and prepared a suggested ad of that sort featuring items which were then seasonally in good supply and especially good buys. The result was a sudden jump in patronage in the sales curve of the store which, in succeeding weeks, resumed the same upward growth from the new level. Quite clearly, the previous ads had conveyed a feeling that the store catered almost too exclusively to upper-middle-class clientele, to the extent that it drove away people who were somewhat below this level but with similar food tastes.

One of the problems in the social-class identification of stores is that as communities change, or as the labor force in general changes, the social class with which a store is identified shrinks and the store may have trouble changing identity to fit the new kind of market. Changing the assortment of goods within the store is relatively easy. However, changing the expectations of people as to what they will find in that store is not done so quickly. One instance that came to the author's attention was a department store in a major eastern city which had built a solid business based on catering to the semiskilled and unskilled workers of the area. By the late 1950s, this group was a declining element in the country as a whole and within the local community, and the store's sales were going downhill as a result. To counter the trend, the store was trying to upgrade its merchandising. However, in the women's clothes section, for one example, the items that they added to the line had no appeal to their old customers and stayed on the racks until the clearance sales. The customers the new lines were supposed to attract still did not come to see what they had.

One of the problems in advertising is the degree to which the symbols we use convey different meanings to different classes in the population. Martineau relates how, in the *Tribune*'s studies of soaps and detergents, women were asked to state the first things that came into their minds when shown the word "baby." The associations given by middle-class women were "darling," "sweet," "mother"—which most of us would think would be the association nearly all women would give "baby." When the replies of the bottom half of the market were tabulated, however—the replies from people who did not use a diaper service or have extra help—they turned up such reactions as "pain in the neck," "more work," "a darling but a bother" (Martineau, 1957, pp. 165-166).

One of the problems of a great deal of advertising is that the copywriters are themselves middle-class people and tend to use symbolism common to their class. Those who are selling or trying to communicate a sales message to the public need to understand the motto of the head of a major mail order firm. He used to say to his dress buyers, "If I like it, do not put it into the catalog."

As one of our examples above indicates, the social-class composition of the population of a community or the nation as a whole does not stand still. Inheritance taxes tend to restrict the growth of those classes at the very top of the social pyramid, or even to decrease their importance in the total market. On the other hand, the constant tendency to attempt to get rid of the less desirable and unwanted jobs in our society tends toward a continual decrease in many of the bottom steps of the pyramid.

*The Dynamics of Social-Class Composition*

In our discussion of social classes so far we have discussed mainly five occupational groups. Sociologists, however, tend to use a six-part classification developed by Lloyd Warner and Paul Lunt and later refined for objective use in the marketing studies that were sponsored by the *Chicago Tribune* in the 1950s. These six classes are as follows:

The four white-collar classes:

Upper-upper class: wealthier older families living largely on inheritance. This is a relatively small part of the total population and one which is, in terms of the buying of most products, not especially important to the market of the mass manufacturer.

Lower-upper class: newly arrived rich, a slightly larger group.

Upper-middle class: professional and businessmen. This is a very substantial portion of the market, although not quite as large as the next class just below it.

Lower-middle class: white collar, salaried workers. A growing and very large portion of the market.

Blue-collar classes:

> The skilled and semiskilled workers of the upper-lower class—a group that is still not quite as large as the lower-middle class, and not increasing in importance.

> The lower-lower class—those in unskilled and relatively menial service occupations. A steadily decreasing portion of the total population.

Figure 10-2 shows the changes occurring in the composition of the labor force. Note that the biggest changes are in the groups in the

**Figure 10-2.   The Shifting Social Class Composition in the U.S.A.: Percentage Distribution of the Male Nonfarm Occupational Groups, 1950 and 1972**

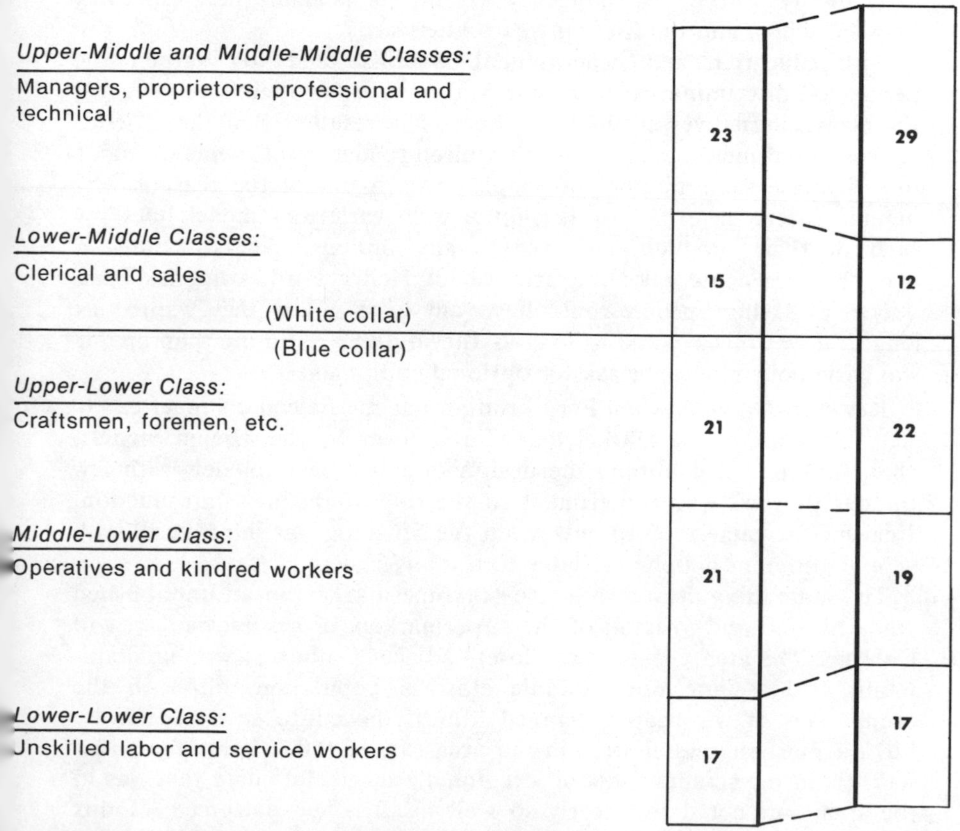

_Upper-Middle and Middle-Middle Classes:_
Managers, proprietors, professional and technical

23            29

_Lower-Middle Classes:_
Clerical and sales

15            12

(White collar)
(Blue collar)

_Upper-Lower Class:_
Craftsmen, foremen, etc.

21            22

_Middle-Lower Class:_
Operatives and kindred workers

21            19

_Lower-Lower Class:_
Unskilled labor and service workers

17
              17

Source: Statistical Abstract of the United States

upper-middle and probably middle-middle classes of the market, who have been increasing steadily in recent decades, and the big decreases have come among the unskilled sections of the population, who have been decreasing in total numbers as well as importance for a full generation.

These changes have obvious implications for the kinds of goods which can be sold and the quality and designs of those goods. Beyond that, however, they have one major implication, explaining much of what is happening in the market place—a greater demand for width of choice in the merchandise available and individualization of that merchandise. The growing classes of workers in the population are in occupations which require at least a fair amount of formal schooling and a great many requiring schooling beyond the mere secondary level. Moreover, the acquisition of jobs, particularly at the professional, technical and official level, normally requires a great deal of geographical mobility during the younger years of the person's life, especially between school and the first ten years afterwards.

Both education and geographical mobility tend to sharpen the perceptual discrimination of people and to broaden their knowledge of the many alternatives available to them. The result is that these better educated and more mobile classes require broader assortments of goods to satisfy the same number of people. This is one of the reasons why manufacturers have had to develop a wide variety of model lines for each of their products and very many options. At one time, a manufacturer could take the attitude of Henry Ford, who has been quoted as saying "people could have any kind of car they wanted as long as it was black" (and as long as they didn't want more than one or two basic body models or ask for optional equipment).

However, by 1960, when Ford brought out the Falcon compact car to help get some of the market being taken over by the foreign models, the philosophy of confining the design to a few basic models with few options proved to be a detriment to the sale of the new introduction. Real success came to Ford only when the Mustang was introduced, with seventy different options available to the buyer.

The same thing proved to be true of supermarkets in an unpublished study by Bell and Wasson of the supermarkets in a suburban area of Chicago. The area chosen, two closely adjacent suburbs, was predominantly middle- and upper-middle class in population, although the occupations of the people spanned almost the entire social scale. By far, the most successful store in the area carried 9,000 items compared to 7,500 in the standard mix of a regionally successful chain that was in the area, but not doing nearly so well locally. The patronage of this independent proved to be primarily families from the middle- and upper-middle-class portion of the population and the emphasis on variety in the store could be seen from the fact that, despite its relatively limited space (12,000 square feet), it carried a broader line of produce than any other store in the area, or indeed than almost any store anywhere in the metropolitan area, as well as a broader line of meats and of frozen foods. All of these items are of particular importance in the purchasing patterns of the middle- and upper-middle-class population.

The drive for individualization of tastes has obvious meaning for those who are designing and marketing products for the mass market, as well as for the merchant. No longer is it possible to specialize in a single design; instead, designs must be so developed that a wide variety of tastes can be accommodated by modular variations.

## Summary

1.  Social class is a subcultural phenomenon in which each class exhibits a characteristic consumption pattern of its own.

2.  Every society has its own class system, with a definite status position for each class in a well-recognized hierarchy of prestige.

3.  Class is nearly always definable in terms of occupation and source of income, but by no means by the income level itself.

4.  In general, occupations requiring large amounts of education or training are well up the status ladder, with those requiring no special skill at the bottom.

5.  In modern industrial societies, particularly in the United States, income classifications are not coincident with class—there is a very strong overlap in income brackets not reflected in the prestige accorded to the occupation.

6.  Middle- and upper-class-consumption patterns show a heavier commitment to spending on housing, reading and education, even at the same income level, than among the blue-collar classes, who place a higher emphasis on food.

7.  Classes differ noticeably in matters of taste, also, regardless of the level of expenditure, and some merchandise designed for one class will not attract the trade of the others. This leads to merchant differentiation on the basis of the class of the clientele served.

8.  Even the kind and layout of advertising can carry class significance, and consumers can make relatively accurate judgments concerning a store, its merchandise, and its service merely from the appearance of the advertising.

9.  Because of the wide differences in class tastes and in the consequent positioning of stores by class, it becomes extremely difficult

for any merchant, once established in a given niche in the market, to upgrade the class of his customers.

10.   Generally speaking, individual tastes tend to be more varied as we move up the class ladder, partly because of the broader and more extensive educational background and experience and the greater mobility of those in the middle and upper classes.


## Chapter 10 Exercises

1.   Rank the following occupations according to their prestige or desirability, as you see it. Have four friends do the same.
     Nurse
     Sales manager
     Operating engineer
        (Operates ditchdigging
        machines, bulldozers, &
        other heavy construction
        machinery)
     Purchasing agent
     Tool and die maker
     Accountant
     Design or project engineer
     Municipal judge
     Company attorney
     Dress shop manager
     Assembly line worker
     Supermarket manager
     Painter
     Electrician
     Stock broker
        customer's man
     Advertising agency
        account executive
     Bricklayer
     Dental technician
     Bricklayer's helper
     Machine tool salesman
     Bus driver
     Salesclerk
     Milk truck driver

    Machinist
    Aircraft mechanic
    High School teacher
    Gas station attendant
How well do the five ratings agree?

2.   Check the pay scales of each, in your locality. How well do these agree with the rankings you gave socially?

3.   Observe two suburbs or two sections of town, as follows: one in which the residents are predominantly professional and business people, the other predominantly upper and middle working class.

    How does the value level of the homes compare? (Census block statistics will give this, or real estate agents can tell you.)

    How does the appearance, architecture and decoration of the homes in the two areas compare or differ?

    Do the same chain supermarkets seem to do equally well in the two areas (the number of cars in the parking lot is one possible clue). If they differ, how do the store's merchandising and promotional policies seem to differ?

4.   Classify the local department or specialty clothing stores according to the apparent social class of their clientele. How do the garment styles compare? How do their advertising policies and layouts compare? How do their merchandising policies compare?

5.   The lower- and upper-middle classes are an expanding proportion population and the lower-lower class is shrinking.

    What industries as a whole might be affected adversely? What professional spectator sports? Which industries and sports stand to gain?

    What other marketing implications can you foresee as a result of of this trend?

# PART IV.
## Consumer Choice Process

THE PURPOSE OF MARKETING effort or any other exchange initiative is to influence consumer choices. Only a very small fraction of such choices are or even could be the result of a decision process in any meaningful use of that term. Any purchase choice represents a possible risk from the standpoint of the consumer, and he adopts various strategies to minimize the risk as he perceives it.

Numerous small purchases are chosen habitually and routinely on the basis of familiarity. The familiarity itself is mostly of cultural origin. Other routine purchases are based on some kind of initial comparison of alternatives, with the choice made then becoming habitual and reinforced by familiarity. A small number of highly significant purchases are chosen on the basis of some kind of investigation and decision on each occasion. What evidence is available indicates that even for such choices, the investigation is limited to discussion with trusted acquaintances considered somewhat more expert than the purchaser, plus, perhaps, some comparison shopping. Thus a great many of the more important choices are the result of the personal influence of acquaintances. This is the primary means by which new products get adopted and diffused throughout the culture.

Extensive research on the adoption of new products reveals that the diffusion of innovations is the result of a chain of personal influence, starting with a limited number of innovators and early adopters, who tend to possess personalities more accustomed to change than the early and late majorities who follow their lead, and ending with a smaller group of laggards. The diffusion process corresponds with the growth phase of the product life cycle, and the length of time required appears to be related to the amount of habit and attitude change needed for product acceptance and use.

Two important kinds of new products are fashions and fads, both the result of the drive for stimulus variability. Fashion is a substantive, moderately high learning product whose fluctuations can be traced to the need for design compromise. Fads are empty, no-learning products whose only benefit is novelty.

# 11

Consumer Choices Among
Established Products

VARIATIONS IN CONSUMER CHOICE STRATEGIES

ROUTINE PROCEDURES BASED ON SIMPLE FAMILIARITY

Importance of Familiar Clues to Quality
Cultural Origins of Familiarity
Original Sources of Cultural Bias
Kinds of Items Purchased on a Familiarity Basis and Their Budgetary Importance

ROUTINE PURCHASES BASED ON INITIAL CONSCIOUS CHOICE

BRAND SWITCHING SUSCEPTIBILITY OF ROUTINE PURCHASES

Products with Substantial Perceived Functional Differentiation: Highly Resistant
Positioned Products: Moderately Resistant
Products for Which a Range of Variations are Familiar: Highly Susceptible
Switching Due to Development of Quality Defects

CHOICES OF PERIODICALLY PURCHASED SHOPPING GOODS

Concious Need for New Information on Alternative Choices
The Continuing Passive Search for Information
The Active Search for Information and Sources Used
Making or Postponing the Purchase
After-Purchase Information Search

CHOICES MADE UNDER CONDITIONS IN WHICH PAST EXPERIENCE IS NO GUIDE

CONSUMER BEHAVIOR AS RISK BEHAVIOR

How DO CONSUMERS go about making choices among known established products? Even the most superficial observation indicates that the amount of planning and comparison varies greatly between different classes of purchases. Some purchases seem to be on impulse—that is, they seem to be made on the spur-of-the-moment—triggered, perhaps, by a prominent promotional display. Others seem to involve comparisons of several alternative offerings, and of the offerings of several sellers. Still others seem to require, in addition, long consideration involving counseling with friends and perusal of formal information sources, including advertisements, before active shopping takes place.

The great majority of purchases are manifestly routine. The consumer routinely keeps a stock on hand, almost mechanically replenishing the stock when it gets low. When shopping, she arrives at the store with either a written or mental shopping list, goes directly to the right shelf location and pulls out the item desired without comparison with other brands on the shelf. What seems to be the basis for this very common sort of routine purchase? One motive for choice—and it can be extremely resistant to change—is simple familiarity.

## Routine Choices Made on the Basis of Simple Familiarity

A leading food manufacturer decided to carve out a major share of the catsup market by launching a tastier, more naturally flavored product. Noting that conventional processing resulted in an overcooked, scorched flavor and loss of aroma, the firm spent millions of dollars to find and perfect a process which preserved the fresh tomato flavor and aroma. The market rejected the new catsup completely. Only when it restored the scorched flavor was the firm able to score a market success with its "improved" catsup (Bralove, 1974).

As our review of psychological knowledge indicated, simple *familiarity* can become a strong motive for preference, and unfamiliarity a cause of rejection.

Only the smallest fraction of purchases are anything but habitual and routine, from routinely used sources. The shopper routinely goes to the same supermarket for most of her weekly supplies, perhaps visits one more, routinely, for certain specialty items. She knows before she starts, without even thinking specially about her choices, what types of items she is going to buy, and usually also the specific brands she desires. She knows where to find them in her usual store, picks them off the proper shelf with little thought as she goes up one aisle and down the other. She will, normally, also keep an eye out for special buys or attractive offerings not on the original list. But these "impulse purchases" will almost invariably be items she expects to buy sometime. She also may note a display of seasonally new goods—the first fresh strawberries, for example. But her attention is drawn to them only because they fit into her general menu plans and also, perhaps, because they offer a change (a "stimulus variation") for her family.

Finally, she may notice a display, or taste an offered demonstration sample of a "new" food item and try it for the novelty (stimulus variation again), but only if the item is in a familiar category, and the initial cost represents an insignificant risk.

How does the housewife settle on a particular brand so routinely, from among the many similar offerings available to her? Why, in many cases, does she exhibit a strong degree of brand loyalty? Careful research has found no substantial level of correlation between brands chosen with as many as fifteen personality and socioeconomic factors. One author concluded that brand loyalty was something of a mystery needing more research (Frank, 1967). Perhaps, but only a little analysis reveals that all of the purchases cited above have one factor in common. What is bought is familiar, is used in a familiar context, and bought within the pattern of an habitual assortment. The only differences or shifts are to gain some degree of stimulus variation novelty, but not too much novelty.

As already noted, one of the best established psychological principles is that if preference starts from a neutral point, mere familiarization can establish a liking, and eventually a strong preference, with rejection of the unfamiliar. The familiar is synonymous with "best," or at least "good," and the unfamiliar is definitely synonymous with "bad," or at least "not to be trusted" or "risky." The catsup incident cited above is only one of a myriad of observable examples of this principle.

For example, although the claim to "farm-fresh" or "old-fashioned homemade taste" may make useful advertising copy, expert flavor chemists have learned that this is just what must be avoided. A commonly recognized problem is one they label "the pineapple juice bias," derived from the discovery that consumers, long familiar with the slightly metallic flavor of canned pineapple juice, find freshly squeezed juice distastefully unfamiliar, "not real" (Bralove, 1974). Similarly with grapefruit juice, laboratory tests with subjects accustomed to using the canned product, with a characteristic "cooked" flavor, show strong dislike for the freshly squeezed product.

Furthermore, consumers come to associate clues to flavor and quality, such as color, with the taste or other desired attributes, and will reject products which have all of the desired attributes, but lack the clues. Indeed, they will go even further and accept products exhibiting the desired clues, even when they clearly lack the attributes supposedly correlated with the clues. Apple growers long ago learned that consumers are so accustomed to judge apple flavor with redness that they will even pay a premium at times for very red varieties with all of the flavor of a stale raw potato, and reject or at least discount flavorful varieties which are pale or yellow naturally.

Almost no butter, as churned, is the deep yellow generally associated with this product—only that produced from the milk of Channel breed cows (Guernseys and Jerseys), and then only for a short period in the spring when pastures are lush and succulent. The supposedly characteristic yellow is due to the fact that the vitamin A in the milk of these two breeds is not the true vitamin A, but a simpler product (which has equivalent value nutritionally) known as provitamin A, or carotene. Most butter, however, comes from Holstein herds, whose milk contains true vitamin A, which is colorless, and thus produces a white milk. So every creamery in the United States has, for decades, been a major customer for manufactured carotene coloring to bring the butter up to consumer appearance standards. In Iran, where white butter is what is familiar, yellow butter, which is imported from Denmark, must sell at a substantial discount (Riker and Besharaty, 1969). This practice never deterred the dairy industry from lobbying to keep margarine from being colored the same way—a defensive tactic which succeeded for three-fourths of a century.

Oranges, too, must be the right "orange" color, which only limited varieties really are. Most of the juiciest varieties are a pale yellow, with spots of green even when dead ripe. But to sell well, they must be dyed, and are then bought freely, even though stamped "color added." Even an item such as barbecue sauce has to meet the color standard of the familiar brands. A packaging firm which developed an aerosol pack for this flavor item discovered that the bubbly aerosol product was enough lighter in color, due to the bubbling, that consumers rejected the product until it was suitably colored to the same dark level as the existing bottled sauce.

Probably one of the more extreme examples of confusing the color cue with the reality of taste is the sale of cellar-"ripened" tomatoes in northern United States markets in the winter. To permit easy shipment and storage during distribution, the tomatoes are picked while dead green, before they develop any real flavor. They are then "ripened" in cellars before packaging for market—that is, they are held under the right temperature conditions to develop the expected red color, but they still have no flavor when sold (at good prices).

Even minor clues of package design can affect sales. When the makers of the Arm & Hammer brand of baking soda decided to modernize its label design, the familiar picture of an upraised arm holding a hammer was omitted. Sales started a nosedive which was reversed only by a retreat to the original design. Similarly, when Camel cigarettes tried a market test of a modernized new label design to replace the rather uninspired old one, the sales results forced them to drop the whole idea.

For matters of taste and appearance preference, the basic test applied by consumers to a wide range of products is "how close is the item to the one I am accustomed to using?" For some such products, the similarity must be close to identity. But, for others, some degree of variety may be tolerated or even sought. Cake mixes, for example, must be sold in a variety of flavors—all of which must, however, be within range of expected flavors for a cake. The family thus gets a change (satisfaction of the drive for stimulus variability). Similarly, ready-to-eat cereals need to be made in a variety of flavors, for the same reason. Some people, as already noted, switch face soaps periodically because of the phenomenon of adaptation—they need to change the perfume to be able to smell it (but every type must be a properly familiar "soapy" perfume). Housewives also have been observed to switch brands of detergent because of the need for novelty (stimulus variation) in their lives; so detergents are given different appearances—green crystals, variegated brown particles, a blue tint, and so forth. But the variation must not be a clue to quality, and the deviation must not stray from the familiar.

In labeling these instances as due to simple familiarity, we are implying no original search for alternatives. But, just as clearly, the consumer does not start life with a set of familiarities. At some point the item was not yet in this category. The patterns of the familiar could only come out of the culture, or by accident, or a combination of the two.

## The Sources of Familiarization

For the individual, and for most matters of taste, the source of the familiar goes back to his first experiences within the family of origin. The Hawaiian prefers poi for breakfast because this has been an important item of his diet from earliest infanthood. The United States southerner goes big for grits for the same reason, and the northerner rejects them as unfamiliar. The southerner likes the bitter taste of chicory-blended coffee because that is the flavor he grew up with. The Briton much prefers the taste of reconstituted "tinned" milk (diluted evaporated canned milk) to that of the fresher variety because that is the only kind most have ever known. And the metropolitan consumer in the United States would reject the taste of milk straight from the cow because it has not lost normally present flavor elements (particularly milk sugar) which the bottled or cartoned product he buys at the supermarket has lost by the time it reaches him.

In other words, the familiar becomes such because that is what the geography, economics, or even accidents of the situation in which the culture has developed have made available over the past. Great Britain, for example, can not, on its tiny area, produce nearly the milk consumed by its teeming industrial population. The deficit had to be made up by imports from distant areas, and the only form in which this was economically feasible was the evaporated canned variety. The Polynesians who came to Hawaii had learned to use the taro root as a source of carbohydrate, southerners in the United States had to depend on corn for the same purpose, while the northern tier of states used wheat and oats, and thus the breakfast customs of each area reflect the agricultural technology of the past. Furthermore, much of southern United States was for long an impoverished area, and coffee was an expensive import. But if a mere pinch of the extremely bitter, and easily raised, chicory root, roasted, is added to the ingredients for one cup, the amount of true coffee used can be cut as much as one-half.

Red apples came to be preferred because nearly all of the apple varieties which could be stored well over winter were red. Yellow types were poor keepers. Canned pineapple juice was long the only kind available the year around, or even available at all. The same was true for grapefruit juice. Thus the accidents of the technology of storage made the processed product the standard.

Egg color preferences are an excellent example of pure accident—the accident of breeder choice. New Englanders pay a premium for eggs with brown shells, New Yorkers, and those in many other parts of the country, pay best for white-shelled eggs. There is no difference in the chemistry or the flavor of the contents. But it happened that New England poultrymen long developed and used brown egg breeds, such as the Rhode Island Red. Thus brown eggs were perceived as locally produced, for New Englanders, and thus were more likely to be fresh than white eggs which came from elsewhere. Similarly, New York poultrymen tended to favor the Mediterranean breeds, such as the White Leghorn, and so for New Yorkers, a white shell was a cue to freshness, a brown egg a cue to probable staleness. Such cues were never too reliable, and have been made meaningless for two generations by the universal use of dependable official grades. Nevertheless, the regional biases still exist.

Childhood usage is not the only source of familiarization, of course. Were such the case, most adults would have a narrow set of taste preferences indeed. Other products become familiar through initial introduction by acquaintances in reference groups, are initially accepted to conform to reference group norms. The very act of conforming leads by the principle of cognitive balance, to an attitude of liking and continued consumption which then becomes a preference fixed through familiarity.

It is clear that a great many purchase choices, but not all, are made upon the basis of simple familiarity. Which kinds of products and services are most likely to be chosen on this basis?

### Conditions Under Which Familiarity Is the Deciding Motive

As important as simple familiarity may be as a purchase motive, it is easy to find examples for which some other kind of motive must be dominant. In buying a dressy garment, for example, the consumer clearly tends to seek out something different in design, often radically different, from anything bought recently. If familiarity were the dominating motive, annual automobile model changes would not be so profitable, and we would not have fashion cycles of any kind.

If we reexamine the examples cited above, and any others which come to mind, we note a set of common characteristics in all products for which the only visible explanation of preferences seems to be simple familiarity:

1. The consumer does not risk much loss of possible physical benefit in rejecting unfamiliar alternatives to the accepted familiar items.
2. All such items tend to be relatively standardized staples of consumption, purchased very frequently at relatively low prices, and thus tend to be something akin to commodities, which need not vary much from one seller to another.
3. The use motives tend to be utilitarian in nature. None of the items are likely to be important in satisfying either value-expressive or ego-defensive attitudes.

The differences between the accepted familiar and the rejected unfamiliar tend to be matters of aesthetics—matters of taste in flavor, appearance, musical sound, and so forth. The physical benefit of the accepted familiar is not much different from the possible physical benefit of the rejected. The tasteless red apple is likely to have the same calorie value and amount of vitamin C as the tasty, juicy, yellow apple which is passed over. The brown egg the Bostonian prefers will make as good an omelette or angel food cake as the white egg he discounts (and if he had no preference, his eggs would still cost the same).

Moreover, the purchase frequency of the total of such items is such that the consumer would have no time for really important consumption choices if he spent much time and effort comparing various alternatives in every instance, nor would he gain much in terms of total satisfaction. If we look at the approximate volume of such purchases, we should note that it involves nearly the whole of the food, beverage, and tobacco budget to some considerable degree (about 28 percent of total personal consumption spending in the United States, according to the 1960-61 Bureau of Labor Statistics studies), and most household operation supplies, health and personal care items, reading materials, recreations, and automobile operating supplies (another 15 percent or so of the consumption budget). Thus simple familiarity accounts for something not far from half of the dollars spent for personal consumption. In terms of items, however, the low prices of such items and the frequency of their purchase (weekly and oftener in most cases) are such that they must account for well over nine out of ten choices consumers must make. Clearly, routinization of such choices is imperative, and failure to ever investigate the unfamiliar risks very little, for items like these. For other types of relatively frequent consumer choices, it is important to investigate alternatives at some point, but routinize purchases thereafter, and consumers usually do.

## Routine Choices Based on An Initial Comparison of Alternatives

As already noted, patronage loyalty is commonly based on utilitarian comparison of alternative sellers. (Patronage loyalty can also, of course, contain some element of value-expressive satisfaction for some people. A Saks Fifth Avenue or Marshall Field label carries more prestige than quite a host of others.) First confronted with the need to find a satisfactory source of purchases (as in moving into a new community), the consumer tries out a number of sellers in the community to find one which comes closest to offering the fit to the price/quality/brand assortment she prefers. She reads all of the ads carefully, scrutinizes them as much for clues as to the store, its merchandise quality, and its services, as for specific price quotations, and she confers with acquaintances who seem to have similar tastes. In the process she would probably seek out familiar chain outlets, but shop them with a more critical approach than she would have previously. Finally, she will narrow her patronage to one or a few outlets, classifying those she had shopped into "best for most items," "the place to get some special brands or qualities," and "not worth shopping" from her point of view, and routinize her shopping accordingly.

Similarly, an industrial or institutional buyer would normally conduct a similar search when first confronted with a new procurement situation, such as materials and supplies for a new process or product line. Such large buyers would also come to narrow the alternatives to a select few sources, although almost never a single one for key items, and thereafter routinize ordering, granting a slightly larger participation to the "best" supplier in terms of assortment available and service, and another fixed participation to specific other suppliers. The alternatives among which such choices are made are normally substantially differentiated. Stores do carry different assortments. Industrial suppliers do differ in their services.

Routinization of the initial choice becomes the rule for specific items as well as for choice of suppliers, both at the final-consumer level and at the industrial level. Faced with a different mix of coffee brands, the housewife will search until she finds one with the familiar flavor she prefers; the industrialist may initially try a number of kinds, qualities and forms of needed raw materials. Once a choice is made, the routine purchase becomes the familiar, and any new alternatives have great difficulty gaining a test. This is as true of—in many cases more true of—the industrial buyer as it is of the housewife. For the buyer, in fact, the familiar becomes imbedded in his process structure and in his workmen's habits, and any change can be extremely disruptive of both production efficiency, and often of industrial relations.

For example, both copper and aluminum are good electrical conductors. Copper is better than aluminum in terms of current carried per unit of conductor cross section, and thus makes for a more compact conductor. But aluminum is superior to copper per unit of weight, which makes a difference in the spacing of utility poles, for example. Up until World War II, copper was the cheaper of the two, but the tremendous capacity for aluminum production spawned by World War II aircraft needs brought the cost of aluminum below that of copper. Utilities, however, were very slow to shift over. As late as the early 1950s, copper had lost only one-third of its utility line market, even though the differential made copper cost nearly half again as much as aluminum. One reason was that working with aluminum conductors required new procedures for making connections, for example, and the workforce would have to be retrained, with all the learning curve costs that implies.

Likewise, when a price rise was needed to get scrap platinum on the market quickly during the Korean conflict (for use in stepping up high octane gasoline production), the two principal western suppliers of platinum would not follow any rise in the allowed ceiling price for the new material. They were afraid that their principal industrial users would search too hard for substitutes, and they might, as had happened two decades previously, lose principal markets they could not easily regain.

Familiarity, then, and routine buying without a continuing search for alternatives, covers another large segment of purchases of all kinds. In the case of consumers, it accounts for nearly all patronage loyalty, both of merchants and of purveyors of personal service, from the beauty operator to the physician.

As strong as is the tendency to hold with the familiar, brand switching and even alternative product switching does occur, and in the case of some kinds of consumer items, especially, is far from uncommon.

## Brand Switching Among Routine Purchase Items

The tendency to stick with the familiar and shun the unfamiliar would seem to be incompatible with frequent brand switching in the case of routinely purchased items. But if such were the case, Procter & Gamble would be a very modestly sized firm, since it lives largely by entering established markets only, with new brands of products which are the very epitome of the routine purchase based on familiarity: toiletries, detergents, cooking fats and oils, coffee, paper towels and toilet paper, and cake mixes. Furthermore, the tremendous display of ready-to-eat cereal brands which every supermarket must carry, and the parallel wide offering of brands of detergents and other cleaning items are too great to be explained by simple market segmentation. People obviously do switch from brand to brand, and from flavor to flavor, and probably back again, for a considerable number of routinely purchased items. Indeed, it is possible to classify products bought on a familiarity basis into three groups on the basis of their resistance to brand switching:

1. Highly resistant—new brands sampled only under risk-free conditions
2. Moderately resistant—consumers tend to be brand loyal, but will

tend to substitute other brands when the supply of the preferred
brand is missing (the typical convenience good)
3.  Brand and flavor switch prone—a large proportion of the con-
    sumers frequently switch brands and have no real favorites.

We might expect brand loyalty to be very high and brand switching
relatively uncommon in the case of those products which were substantially different from competing brands in actual performance characteristics and a single variant as the familiar one. But this would have to be
a rare situation when, as posited above, the products were relatively
standardized, frequently purchased, priced low, and utilitarian in
function. However, a somewhat lower degree of brand loyalty, but still
a high one, would be the case for products in which the market was
segmented in relation to quality or other performance characteristics
and quality available covered a perceivably wide range. In such cases,
we might expect some occasional brand purchase deviation, but a
general condition of brand loyalty.

Coffee would be a good example of the latter type of offering. Bought
for its flavor, the flavor is segmented within a market, and does vary
widely between brands, although some brands have similar flavor to
others. Brand loyalty studies do, in fact, show coffee to have such a
market position. Brown (1953), for example, in an analysis of consumer
purchase diaries for nine common food and health items, found coffee
and all-purpose flour at the very top in terms of loyalty, with 95 percent
of the families showing some degree of loyalty in each case, varying
from undivided loyalty to fluctuating switches between two favored
brands. All-purpose flour is another product in which there are major
performance differences between brands, and if the housewife buys it
for baking, her recipes must be varied by brand to get uniform results.

On the other hand, soaps and sudsers—all of which accomplish
about the same results—and ready-to-eat cereals, were at the bottom of
the Brown list, with only about 17 percent of the families and 12.5
percent, respectively, purchasing a single brand with undivided loyalty.
Both of the latter belong to a group of products in which brand and
type switching is so common, for motives of stimulus variation, that the
supermarket must carry a disproportionate variety of types and brands.
Banks (1950), using a different loyalty measure, also found coffee
heading his list, and ice cream and potato chips at the other extreme.

"Positioned products"—products whose preferences are due purely to
emotional associations created through advertising—would be expected
to win an intermediate degree of loyalty. Some segment of consumers
would be fairly brand loyal, but not hesitate to substitute another
brand if unable to obtain the desired brand at the planned place of
purchase. Such, for example, is the case with products such as beer

and cigarettes. Most cigarette smokers (but not all) do have some favorite brand, but few can identify it on a blind test. Likewise, many beer drinkers do have a brand preference, but cannot identify their own brand in a blindfold test. In both instances, the consumer will normally substitute rather than search for a different source of purchase.

Because of the nonobjective basis for the preferences of the positioned product, such brands and products are especially vulnerable to gaps in distribution or inventory. The consumer will try whatever substitute is available, and if the substitution continues for any substantial period, the new brand becomes the familiar, and thus the preferred one. Such products must have extensive and intensive distribution to gain or maintain a market position. Pepsi-Cola, for example, never threatened the position of Coca-Cola very much until it extended and intensified its distribution structure. Likewise, the strong market niche occupied by Coors Beer on the West Coast dates back to a prolonged strike at the breweries of its major competitors in that area, when it became for a while the only major brand readily available.

[Did you ever wonder how a nation in which the coffee house occupied the important place it did in the England of Addison and Steele (late seventeenth and early eighteenth centuries) became a nation of tea tipplers? The cause was a disease which nearly wiped out the principal variety of coffee in the areas from which England then imported its coffee, forcing the nation to turn to tea. It never switched back.]

Finally, we might expect frequent brand switches among those products for which a wide variety of variations were in the acceptable familiar range of flavor or other taste difference, in which none exhibited substantial differences in functional performance other than a mild flavor or other taste difference, and with little strong product positioning. Because used almost daily, and because all variations are reasonably acceptable, we might expect the drive for stimulus variation to stimulate frequent brand or flavor switching. As already noted, such indeed is the case for general-purpose detergents, ready-to-eat cereals, and cake mixes.

To gain and maintain a substantial market share with such an offering, the seller must promote several brands or varieties within the brand simultaneously, and anyone familiar with any supermarket is aware of the multiplicity of brands of detergent put out by the same manufacturer, and likewise for cereals. The store shelf space-hogging by these two types of products is paralleled by the space required to sell cake mixes in all of their varieties.

The consumer may decide to switch routinely bought brands for substantive reasons also, especially if the original choice was made after a consideration of alternatives. The incentive to switch must be strong enough to overcome the attraction of the familiar, but will occur if the currently preferred offering has a noticeable attribute defect of which the consumer is continuously conscious and believable information reveals the possibility of a substantially better fit to the performance desire-set. Thus, frozen orange concentrate easily replaced the use of fresh oranges, at a time when the fresh flavor was the familiar one, because of the nuisance of squeezing the oranges, and cleaning the squeezer afterwards, both of them nuisance steps with no visible benefit attached.

Switching will also take place whenever the currently purchased offering begins to vary significantly from the previous norm and some promise of better quality and/or uniformity appears. Both the final consumer and the industrial plant have a strong preference for uniform performance from their purchases and will actively search hard to get them if variation becomes too great. The lack of quality control in their own house brands of foods undercut the leading position two food chains once had in the midwestern area, leading to a drastic curtailment of their operations. The drive for certainty is one reason quality-controlled brands gain a strong market share and why brands can fail through quality-control slippage alone. For a similar reason, a product which is designed to be relatively tolerant to lack of precision in use will gain a stronger niche than one which must be used with precision. Without much question, the triumph of Taster's Choice freeze dried coffee over the General Foods Maxim brand was due partly to the need for adherence to exact proportions in using Maxim, and the lack of any such need in the case of Taster's Choice.

The preference for the familiar is nearly always a factor in the acceptance of any new offering, even revolutionary ones, but is far from being a dominant one in the case of products bought infrequently, but filling a continuing need.

## Choosing Periodically Purchased Shopping Goods

An important part of the total spending is for goods which are high in cost and relatively durable, so that purchases are relatively infrequent although meeting a continuing need, such as the purchase of clothing, automobiles, and housing, either rental or for direct ownership. The budgetary importance of such purchases justifies and usually gets considerable advance planning and a conscious search for and consideration of some range of alternatives. Furthermore, the situation generally contains one or both of two conditions rending duplication of past purchases either impossible or unwise:

1.  The product is not a standardized staple, but a fashion item, the design of which varies with time, and the assortments of each seller vary in a not wholly predictable manner. Also, the question of suitability to the buyer's personal needs can usually be settled only by direct inspection of the item under consideration. Such is the case with garments, furnishings and accessories, and jewelry.
2.  The design may vary somewhat with time, but more important, the desire-set itself almost inevitably is modified by time, and the price involves an element of bargaining or barter, as in the purchase of an automobile or home.

Advance planning and consideration are common also because the initial cost and durability of the item means that the customer "will have to live with" his purchase for a considerable period of time—he is committed to it, once he makes the purchase. And the desire-set to be fulfilled always is complex enough to contain some elements so incompatible that no one choice will completely fulfill it.

Most of what has been written about the process of consumer decision in such matters is pure speculation by middle-class intellectuals who are bound to be biased by their own habits of expenditure, and can only, in any case, base their conclusions on rather general observation. No really extensive research is available. But that observation does reveal that quite a large portion of the consumers of all classes do go through some similar steps in making such decisions.

The first step, not widely recognized, but easily recognizable from observation, might best be designated as *passive continuous evaluation of alternatives*. The purchaser of a house, a woman's dress, a man's suit, a car, or any other highly infrequently bought expensive durable, knows from the day of his purchase that he will sooner or later be in the market again. Consequently, many people are constantly looking for information against that next time—looking over the new car models or reading the fashion news, talking with friends about their experiences with different models and alternatives, becoming alert to problems in the design-compromise decision they had to make. For the most part, this information is simply stored and evaluated against possible needs, but not pointed toward any specific decision until some event or situation triggers awareness of a problem which must soon be solved. It does, however, serve to narrow the list of alternatives which will be given consideration when the need to act arises.

*Recognition of an imminent problem* to be solved is a second step which initiates a *purposive active search for information on alternatives*, and also some degree of thought concerning the *makeup of the desire-set* which is to be fulfilled, and which elements in that desire-set have the highest priority in view of future needs foreseen. The owner becomes aware of a too frequent need for repairs on his automobile, or it becomes apparent he will need a full set of tires and perhaps a battery soon. A special occasion arises and the woman finds her wardrobe more dated than she likes. Or the family becomes aware that the children are growing to a point where the present home is cramped. Some event or situation arises which causes the consumer to say to himself, "I had better start shopping for a new one soon," and he begins his active search for information, building on what he already has stored from his previous passive search. The process of reaching this point may be quite gradual, marked by growing dissatisfaction which some climactic event finally crystallizes. In this more usual case, actual shopping and purchase may be postponed for a lengthy period of consideration.

How lengthy the weighing of the decision will be, and how much information will be sought, and from where, will depend greatly on the personality of the consumer, his interest and expertise in the purchase area involved, and also on the degree to which incompatible objectives for the purchase must be reconciled. There is also some limit on the time, effort, and cost of the information and shopping search. Assuming that these may be relatively flexible, the consumer has available and may use quite a number of sources: personal acquaintances whose information is valued either because of more information or at least more recent information and some degree of recognized expertise, media published by independent product rating services such as Consumer Research or Consumer's Union, specialized publications (such as fashion magazines, handicraft periodicals, motor periodicals, shelter magazines, and so forth) or special sections in general circulation media (such as the fashion, automobile, and home sections of newspapers, mass advertisements, and even dealer literature and dealer advice).

Even when time and effort permit, it is probable that only a minor fraction of consumers consult all or even the majority of these sources. At least one set of studies indicates that those who are most likely to conduct an intense information search can be described as being in the middle-income category, possessor of a college education, white collar, under thirty-five years of age (Katona and Mueller, 1955). Like most things which are "most likely," however, this does not tell us much. Not all those fitting this description are persistent searchers of information, and among those who are, many would not fit the description above. A much better description would be that he is one who is highly discriminative of values in the kind of purchase involved (and, of course, this description itself is of help only in pointing out media which are of most value in promotion). Those with high interest in a particular field of purchase, and highly discriminative to values in this area, are also those who are likely to be in the forefront of adoption of new products, as will be seen later. And they are the ones to whom other consumers look for information in the area of their interest.

Most consumers probably use some sort of personal source when considering a major purchase, and many may use no more than this. One case observed was that of a middle-class professional woman whose job required use of an automobile. When she decided to get a new one, she simply called a close friend and asked her about her car (a middle-priced foreign make), with which she was familiar. The latter told her, "I like it very much, but the service dealer is thirty miles away. You might look at the S_____ (a lower-priced foreign make). My husband likes his." The shopper called her friend the next night to announce they had bought a S_____, and to say how much she liked it.

Quite obviously, this woman's interest in automobiles was purely utilitarian, and not very discriminative, or she would have conducted a more intensive search. But it is also probably true that large numbers of consumers do not dig deeply. Those who go beyond personal sources probably are most likely to scan the feature news section of mass media, at least when the time for decision approaches, and perhaps read some advertisements. But the circulations of media specializing in areas of major purchases (fashion magazines, automobile periodicals, independent consumer-rating services, and so forth) is such as to indicate that the majority do not make *direct* use of such sources. That does not mean they do not have a very large indirect influence, through their readership by those with a high interest. It is known, for example, that an outstanding or adverse rating by one of the consumer services can have a noticeable effect on sales.

Of course, the circumstances may not permit time for such information search. The car has a major breakdown or is in a serious wreck and must be replaced. The husband gets a sudden notice of immediate transfer to a distant city, and a home must be bought. In such cases, the search is necessarily limited to some quick shopping, aided by whatever personal advice is quickly available, modified by use of whatever of the previous passive search information is applicable.

A search of any kind is paralleled by a weighing of alternatives against the complexities of the desire-set. Rarely, if at all, can any major purchase yield all of the benefits one could wish for in a single package. Some of the benefits desired will be physically incompatible with the realization of others in the set, and the consumer must decide on which are most important of fulfillment, and which must be sacrificed. Once this decision is reached, the purchase is a matter of comparing the values available from different sellers, and making the purchase.

Such shopping and comparison of the actual items on sale is an inevitable step, may be prolonged over a period of time, and may end by postponing the purchase until a better desire-set fit can be obtained, perhaps with some kind of temporary substitute purchase to tide the consumer over until a better choice, or one more within the desired budget, is available. The family may rent an apartment in the new community instead of buying a house, thus limiting the expense and financial commitment until mortgage rates come down. The car may be repaired after all, and kept for another year. The dress may be foregone, and a few new accessories bought to freshen the current wardrobe instead. In the latter case, the consumer and a great many of her like may well decide that the designers have guessed wrong on the direction in which she wished to go, and Seventh Avenue may have a bad season. All of these goods represent a postponable type of purchase, and the consumer will exercise the option to postpone if not attracted by the designs or value offered.

Because of the necessary desire-set compromise, the choice process does not end with acquisition of the purchase. The making of a compromise creates some degree of cognitive dissonance. Consequently some kind of *post-purchase information search* may occur—greater scanning of advertisements for the item and make purchased and also favorable opinions from acquaintances. This may well be the point at which the advertising becomes most effective, and paves the way for the next purchase.

Some authors have speculated on how sellers might spark problem recognition, but beyond what would normally be the goal of promotion and product design, it is difficult to envision any specific course of action which could be effective. Most of the forces which lead to the decision, or to its postponement, are outside the power of the seller. The one thing he can do is to raise the level of dissatisfaction with the current deteriorating possession by creating a geater benefit gap, by means of a well-chosen design, by making potential buyers more aware of the existing gap by intense promotional effort, or by accenting the value gap temporarily, by means of special sales. All of these, of course, are normal commercial practice, and do succeed, at times, in speeding up the day of purchase. The automobile industry's experience, for example, is that sales tend to be greater in years of major model changes than in years in which the new models have only cosmetic differences. But it is also true that the changes must be in the right fashion direction, as is shown more fully in the discussion of fashion. Special sales do create temporary sales volume, but they must be timed to hit a period of increased awareness, also. Beyond these normal trade practices, it would seem unlikely that any kind of effort would penetrate the selective attention and selective perception filters by which the consumer shuts out efforts not directed to a need he is already aware of. He must be ready to search for information before he will pay attention to it. That search is more likely, and more likely to be extensive, in the case of unforeseen purchase needs, and those which are so infrequent that past experience is not too relevant.

## Choosing the Unusual Purchase

Some purchase decisions are both costly and so infrequent, or under such new and unique conditions that little or no prior experience or passive information search is possible. The consumer starts with little more than some generalized desire-set of specifications and some kind of allowable budget. In such a situation, his search is likely to be more extensive than he would make when meeting a continuing need for something purchased at long intervals. Among such would be purchases like those of a house in a new part of the country, the choice of an important gift, and most role transition related purchases.

As the need for such a purchase looms, the consumer is much more likely to mine many sources of information, starting, as usual, with friends and acquaintances considered knowledgeable, but very likely going beyond them to authoritative print sources, including specialized publications, and not excluding advertising. It is no accident that periodicals covering such periods (especially those of role transition, such as bride's magazines) have a ready reception and have no trouble getting advertising. The advertising gets read.

Furthermore, once the purchase is made, after-purchase information search is almost certain to continue, because of the high level of cognitive dissonance. Most of the purchases involved are costly. But even when the cost may be relatively moderate, as it may be for a gift, or for baby items, in the case of the first newborn, the risk factor is normally large, in terms of social visibility for the gift, or in imaginable dangers in the case of the first baby.

The degree of perceived risk is unquestionably one of the major factors stimulating information seeking, and risk considerations shape all purchase strategy.

## Consumer Choices and Risk

Every purchase or exchange implies some degree of perceivable risk, and every consumer choice process includes some effort at risk reduction. Every exchange exacts some sacrifice; almost always some relinquishment of money resources, some loss of time in consummating the purchase, and frequently, as noted in the next chapter, some commitment to spend considerable effort and time necessary to learn the use-system required to gain the desired benefit. The consumer can seldom be really certain in advance that the desired benefit will be forthcoming, nor which of the various alternatives would yield the best benefit/cost ratio of return (Bauer, 1960).

The degree of risk is commensurate with the sacrifice. For this reason, the consumer may readily try a low-price offering whose promise is "too good to be true" (Maloney, 1963). Indeed, for such low-cost purchases, he seems to adopt a strategy of approximation, sticking to the familiar to save search and comparison effort, so long as the familiar remains dependable. He finds a suitable source for his assortment, then stays with that source or those specific sources, minimizing the shopping effort and time risk.

On major purchases, most consumers adopt a different time-and-effort minimizing strategy. They seek out trusted acquaintances whose knowledge of particular purchases is perceived as somewhat superior, first of all, then use other sources later, if at all.

The extent to which dependence is put on personal advice by even those thought to be most careful was headlined by two alleged major swindles which came to an end in 1974. One in particular involved top officials of some of the largest corporations in the country, as well as leading entertainment figures and their advisors: a "tax shelter" drilling fund firm. That those who bought participations in six figures obviously conducted no real investigation became apparent when one prospective investor who did, two years before, discovered that the fund did not meet a standard test of sound investing on the basis of publicly available information on contract terms and background (Egelhof, 1974). Even a reading of SEC reports would have warned them.

Extensive research has shown that such a person-to-person information chain is the principal means whereby products which have some degree of the new in them gain adoption. In one sense, of course, major purchases of fashion items always involve buying something that is new. The really new product, including the new fashions is, of course, the highest risk class of purchase. This class of purchases, and this diffusion process are the subject of the following chapters.

Besides these strategies which are specific to the product class, consumers often adopt certain generalized purchase choice strategies. These include:

1. Always buy the cheapest item. This minimizes the financial risk, but increases the risk that performance may not be up to specifications of the desire-set, and in some cases may even be a high cost solution, if low price is realized by sacrifice of too much durability.

2. Always buy the highest-priced item. This minimizes the risk of poor quality, but increases the financial risk, and may result in paying for premium attributes which are of no value to the specific purchaser.

3. Always buy the most-heavily advertised and best known. This is a parallel strategy to buying the most expensive, and often is the same thing. The risks and gains are similar and, in addition, the best advertised may be even less likely to be the best fit to the individual's desire-set, since the volume sale implied means a mass market, usually for less than premium quality.

4. Stay with the familiar until it is no longer available on the market. This minimizes the learning costs, but it sacrifices the added values of new advances for too long a period and, in matters of fashion, has social deficits.

3. Concentrate on "classics," particularly in fashion matters. This minimizes the risks of value depreciation, and probably minimizes the financial risk overall. Whether or not it decreases total satisfactions depends on whether the consumer has any strong desire for excitement and attention.

6. "Never be the first by whom the new is tried, nor yet the last to lay the old aside," to quote the English poet. This is clearly the strategy of the vast majority of consumers. It minimizes the risk of disappointment, sacrifices the flow of added value which accrues to the early adopter.

7. Constantly seek out information on the new, and make limited trials of whatever new items promise substantial added values. This is the strategy of the innovator and early adopter in those specific product areas of most importance to them. They gain a longer lifetime of total added values from their successful discoveries, and the least time depreciation of the durables they discover. In addition, when the product attributes include social visibility, as in fashion, they gain attention value. They sacrifice the time and effort involved in their constant search for the new (but this clearly has interest values for them or they would not undertake the task). And they almost always pay the high prices for early purchases almost inevitable during the market development period of new products.

8. Commit purchase choices neither to the most expensive nor to the cheapest, nor to any other level arbitrarily, but carefully match

desire-set attributes against product attributes, in terms of value sought and paid. This unquestionably really minimizes financial commitment relative to the benefits obtained, but it costs time and effort to learn how to analyze purchases, and time in making comparison when buying. It is worth while only if the purchase cost is sizable, or performance critical.

Manifestly, which strategy is adopted is heavily dependent on the personality of the consumer. What we know about new product adoption indicates that most people seek especially to avoid the risks of innovation, prefer to let others make the initial trials, then rely on their experiences.

## Summary

1.  The amount of planning and comparison of alternatives involved in consumer choices varies from an almost mechanical routine purchase in the case of some items, to a prolonged search for information on alternatives, comparison of them, and eventual comparison shopping of various competing offerings in the case of other items.

2.  The great majority of all choices are routine.

3.  A very large portion of these routine purchases are chosen on the basis of simple familiarity, with rejection of the unfamiliar in almost any detail of flavor, appearance, or other surface characteristic.

4.  Consumers come to associate familiar superficial clues of appearance with specific desired qualities, and may purchase on the basis of such clues even when the desired attribute is notably absent.

5.  A great deal of the familiarity is cultural in origin, growing out of initial experiences in the family of origin.

6.  Other products become habitual and finally familiar because of trial and consumption to conform to group norms.

7.  The cultural biases themselves can usually be traced to accidents of geography or economic condition, or even of technology, and usually outlive their origin.

8.  Simple familiarity tends to become the deciding motive for choice whenever the item is a low cost standardized staple, used for utilitarian motives, and the differences between the familiar and the unfamiliar are mainly aesthetic, not functional.

9.  Such simple familiarity probably accounts for close to half of the final consumer expenditure budget, and well over 90 percent of the items purchased, involving most food, beverage, and tobacco choices,

as well as household operation supplies, recreation, health and personal care items, and automobile fuel and operating supplies.

10.   Another large group of purchase choices are just as routine in nature, but are more likely to be based initially on a conscious choice between alternatives. Nearly all patronage loyalty is of this sort, as are also the choices of many frequently bought goods, both industrial and final consumer, and most personal services.

11.   Even when the purchase is habitual and based on familiarity, resistance to brand switching is not guaranteed.

12.   Brands highly resistant to switching are usually found among products in which major performance differences are common, such as coffee, in which the customer has become accustomed to a single variation.

13.   Positioned products—products differentiated by advertising on the basis of emotional associations—tend to be moderately resistant to switching so long as distribution is extensive and intensive. But they are convenience goods—the consumer will substitute another brand if the preferred one is not conveniently available. If such substitution is prolonged, the substitute item may become the entrenched brand. In this class are such items as cigarettes and beverages.

14.   Products for which most or all variants are within the accepted familiar range (detergents, ready-to-eat cereals, cake mixes) are normally subject to frequent brand and variety switching as a matter of course, to satisfy the drive for stimulus variation.

15.   Switching may also occur if the product has or develops a noticeable defect of which consumers are fully conscious, or if quality begins to slip or vary widely.

16.   Periodically purchased durable shopping goods, for which there is a continuing need, form only a very small proportion of the items bought, but involve a substantial part of the budget. Typically, these are nonstandardized items such as fashion items, in which the designs available change over time and also may differ from seller to seller. Also included are items for which the desire-set complex may change over time.

17.   For such products, the consumer is always aware that he will need to replace past purchases at some time in the future, and so tends to maintain a passive continuous search for information on new alternatives.

18.   At some point in time, some incident or situation triggers an active consideration of possible alternatives and some recourse to sources of information concerning the merits of possible alternative choices. Trusted personal acquaintances are probably the most widely used of such sources. Others include specialized publications, special

feature sections in mass distributed media, advertising, and dealer promotional materials and salesmen.

19. Only a minority of consumers are likely to make a really thorough investigation, and then typically for products of the sort in which they have a strong personal interest.

20. The culmination of the search is almost always a comparison of the offerings of several sellers, and the consumer may decide to postpone purchase at this point if a good value and a good fit to his desire-set is not found.

21. Whatever the intensity of the information search, it seldom ends with the actual purchase, if any. Most such purchases involve both substantial risk and a considerable degree of compromise in the desire-set. A post-purchase search for information helps resolve the resulting cognitive dissonance.

22. Some purchase choices are made under conditions in which past experience has very little relevance of any kind: choices in unique or very infrequent situations, especially choices related to role transition periods. These choices carry a very high perceived risk, and normally trigger a more than usually intense investigation as a result.

23. All consumer choices are perceived as involving risk, and all choice procedures include some kind of strategy for reduction of the perceived risk. This explains the preference for the familiar in some instances and the search for added information in others.

24. The adoption of new products obviously carries the highest degree of risk.

## Chapter 11 Exercises

1. Looking at your own spending, how much of the total budget would you estimate goes for items and brands bought routinely, with little attention to new brands?

   For how much of this can you remember ever making a careful brand search and comparison at some time in the past?

2. If you smoke, do you have a favorite brand? If so, how did you choose it originally?

   If a non-smoker, ask the above of some smoking friend.

   Do the same for beer, for soft drinks.

3. Are there any routine purchases you make for which you often

deliberately change brands? Why do you switch when you do? How much significant difference do you perceive between the various brands you have used?

4. What foods do you especially like? Where and how did you learn to like them? What beverages (hard or soft) do you use and prefer? Where and how did you learn to like them?

5. What are your favorite recreations and hobbies? How did you get introduced to them or choose them?

6. Consider the last three major purchases you have made. How did you go about deciding on what to choose?

7. One of your larger purchase decisions in recent years was your choice of schools. How many different colleges and universities did you consider? What sources of information did you use before deciding? What was the basis of your final choice?

# The Adoption and
# Diffusion of Innovations
# and The Learning Requirement*

*The material in this chapter is largely adapted from Chester R. Wasson, *Dynamic Competitive Strategy & Product Life Cycles,* Challenge Books, St. Charles, Ill., 1974, by permission of the copyright holder.

DIFFERENCES IN RATES OF DIFFUSION

THE SOCIAL PROCESS OF DIFFUSION

The Five Classes of Adopters
Diffusion as a Chain of Personal Communications
Consistency of the Roles of Those in the Chain
Personality Characteristics of Early Adopters
The Need to Predict the Expected Acceptance Pattern

DIFFUSION AS THE GROWTH PHASE OF THE PRODUCT LIFE CYCLE

The Phases of the Product Life Cycle, and the Differences in Cycles
Marketing Tactics Appropriate for the Differing Acceptance Patterns

THE LEARNING REQUIREMENT AND THE PRODUCT ACCEPTANCE PATTERNS

THE LEARNING REQUIREMENT AND THE PRODUCT ACCEPTANCE RATE

Habit Change as a Prerequisite for Adoption
Relationship of Acceptance Rate to Degree of Habit Change Required

POSSIBLE TYPES OF HABIT CHANGE REQUIREMENTS: MOTOR HABITS, VALUE PERCEPTION HABITS, ROLE PERCEPTION HABITS, USE-PERCEPTION HABITS

NO-LEARNING PRODUCTS: FADS, MISSING LINK PRODUCTS

As NOTED EARLIER, of the two instant foods which were introduced after World War II, orange concentrate met such a ready reception that the sales demand outdistanced both production of the necessary oranges themselves and the distribution facilities for shipping and display in stores during the first few years, but instant coffee met a relatively lukewarm market reception. Despite the fact that instant coffee was already known to the market, demand grew relatively slowly, reaching a full potential only sixteen years after initial postwar promotion.

Another postwar product, the original monochromatic (black and white) television also rose rapidly to success, and was selling at the rate of over 7,000,000 sets per year less than four years after the initial introduction, even though there was extremely limited evening-only programming on the air and no national networks during the first couple of years it was on the market. When color television came out later in 1954, it not only did *not* displace monochromatic television as the industry had expected, but had difficulty reaching any significant sales volume for eight years. Far from displacing black-and-white television, color television sales only reached parity with monochromatic television sales eighteen years later, in 1972 (see Figure 12-1).

As these two examples illustrate, no product starts out at full potential, but reaches that potential only after some period of time. As they both also illustrate, in addition, the period of time for a product to reach its full potential can vary widely even for products which seem to have a very similar function in the consumer spending patterns and desires. Since the expected speed of acceptance of any product must be a major factor in planning the introductory strategy and in anticipating the amount of competition that will be met, it is obviously important that we find some way to predict the relative degree of acceptance in advance.

Both the fact that the demand for any innovation must build up gradually and the fact that the speed of the build-up varies widely between products result from (1) the nature of the product itself as a part of a consumer use-system, (2) the process of consumer-to-consumer and group-to-group communication about the value of new

**Figure 12-1.** The Contrasting Market Growth Patterns of Monochromatic TV and the High Value-perception-learning Color TV

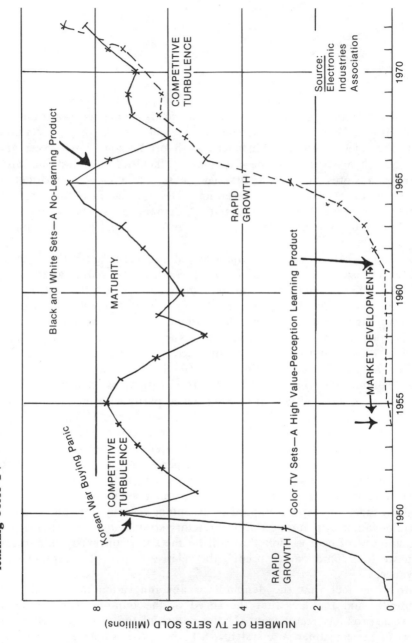

products, and (3) the existence of established habitual use-systems into which the product will fit.

We know a great deal about the process of diffusion of innovations throughout the market from studies initially developed by sociologists working, first, in the rural field and, later, among urban families and on home-use products. Although the research applied mainly to new products and ideas, the pattern seems to be the same for most purchases requiring an individual decision each time.

## The Social Process of the Diffusion of Innovation

The process of diffusion of innovation would be a growth pattern even if there were no social factors involved. The very problem of communicating the availability and the benefits of new products would insure this. No communications medium reaches the whole market. Even for that part of the market which it does reach, the process of selective attention would tend to limit greatly the number of people who would learn of it early. Since only a few of these would buy initially, the product itself would have only minor visibility at first and it would take time for word of the product to reach everybody in the potential market. Thus, even fads have a growth pattern, although a very explosive one.

However, every new product involves far more than the mere problem of communication from the seller's point of view. Very few people will adopt a product purely on the basis of an advertising or sales message. Most people wait to see what the experience is of the few venturesome innovators and early adopters among their social contacts, to legitimize the claims being made for a new innovation (or even for a major purchase or investment of an established offering). Studies of this process indicate that product awareness is general long before the growth is well on its way (Rogers, 1962). Sociologists studying the history of a number of innovations have been able to divide the market into five groups along the time continuum from the entrance of the product on the market until maturity into five role groups—innovators, early adopters, early majority, late majority, and skeptics.

They class as *innovators* those who comprise the first 2 to 3 percent of those adopting a product and found that these people were inclined to seek out and pioneer the use of new products even before release for general use. They are actively searching for whatever it was they had first adopted, but are so far ahead of their neighbors, they have little direct influence.

*Early adopters* (variously designated by some as tastemakers, peer group leaders, opinion leaders, key communicators or influentials, and others) constitute the rest of the first 12 to 15 percent of adopters. This group of people tended to adopt shortly after the first public availability of an offering and also were people whose expertise in the areas of the satisfactions involved by the new product was respected by their neighbors. They were looked to for assurance that the promised satisfaction value was there and their trials were closely watched by their nearest friends. These were the first channels of communication depended upon by the associates for an understanding of the benefits being offered and the value of these benefits.

The rest of the first half of the adopters have been labeled *early majority*. Each wave within this group depends on their earlier adopting associates for trial and legitimation of their offering. The title of *late majority* has been given to another one-third or so of the market which is even slower to adopt the new and accounts for the maturing slowdown of the market. The label of *laggards* or *skeptics* was applied to the last 12 to 15 percent to adopt as the market approaches saturation.

Although sometimes referred to as the two-step process of adoption, the process of diffusion has been shown to be a chain phenomenon, with early adopters first picking up the product, and others, only slightly less venturesome, picking up the news of the product and purchasing it once their close friends among early adopters have signaled that their trials indicate a worthwhile buy. In turn, the second wave of adopters is watched by another slightly less venturesome group (and also probably somewhat less interested in the benefits initially) to legitimate the claims being made in the advertising and other communications of which they are already aware. Thus, the process becomes a chain reaction, with something like a geometric growth curve during the first phase of the growth cycle of a product. Once the midway point in the market is reached, the growth tends to slow down, if only because of the physical limitations of the size of the remaining market, and the market itself levels off as the last of those for whom the product has some potential value finally enter and purchase.

The titles of innovators, early adopters, early majority, late majority and skeptics are, of course, in themselves purely descriptive. However, certain very fundamental behavioral patterns underlie these titles. All studies have shown, for example, that innovators are consistently innovators or early adopters for all products within their field of major interest and expertise, that indeed all of the groups tend to be some easily identifiable groups in terms of personality. As Figure 12-2 shows in the farm field, the early adopters, majority and later adopters are easily identified in terms of their economic state in farming, their age, and their sources of information and in the degree to which they expose themselves to possible information about new products.

**Figure 12-2. The Adoption Cycle, Adopter Characteristics, and Information Sources**

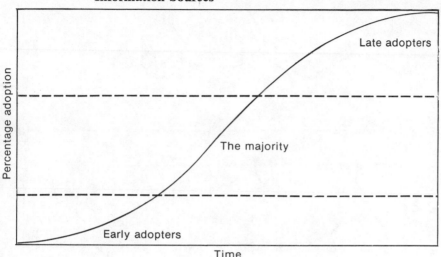

| Early adopters | The majority | Late adopters |
|---|---|---|

*Distinctive Characteristics**

| | | |
|---|---|---|
| Large farms | Average farms | Small farms |
| High income | Average income | Low income |
| Take risks | | Security-minded |
| Usually under age 50 | Age 50 to 60 | Usually over age 60 |
| Actively seeking new ideas | Receptive but not actively seeking | Complacent or skeptical |
| Participate in many nonlocal groups | Participate in some local groups | Seldom participate in formal groups |

*Sources of Information Used***

| | | |
|---|---|---|
| College and other research sources | Adoption leaders and other farmers nearby | Other local farmers and adoption leaders |
| Agricultural agencies | Farm papers, magazines and radio | Farm papers, magazines and radio |
| Mass media sources | Commercial sources | Local dealers |
| Other highly competent farmers far and near | Agricultural agencies | Almanac |
| Commercial sources | | |

\* In relation to characteristics of those in adjoining categories.
\*\* Listed in estimated rank order of use.

Source: Reproduced by permission from Herbert F. Lionberger, *Adoption of New Ideas and Practices*, © 1961 by The Iowa State University Press, Ames, Iowa, page 34.

# Figure 12-3. Theoretical Product Adoption Patterns Compared With Some Actual Adoption Patterns, 1945-1958

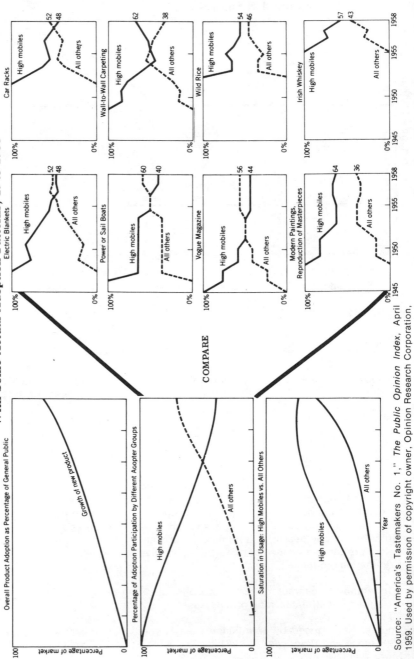

Source: "America's Tastemakers No. 1," *The Public Opinion Index*, April 1959. Used by permission of copyright owner, Opinion Research Corporation, Princeton, New Jersey.

Later research outside the farm field has corroborated most of these findings. One very intensive survey, of an upper-middle-class suburban community, found that all of those who were early adopters of some 160 products during the preceding ten years were people who were in the highest one-fourth on a mobility scale (Opinion Research Corp., 1958). These early adopters were found among those families who had been exposed to the most change in their lives and to the most new ideas. They had greater mobility, job-to-job and generation-to-generation occupational mobility, greater mobility across religious, ethnic or class lines in marriage, and greater personal exposure to an ever-widening contact with various sources of new ideas, particularly, in published materials.

As Figure 12-3 indicates, the actual adoption patterns of these 160 products were very similar to what was to be expected—that the early market for all such new products was made up entirely of members of the high mobile quartile of the population, and the other three-fourths of the market entered much later.

We would expect such a result purely because different individuals have different levels of interest in different kinds of products and benefits on the market. Some recent research also indicates that there may very well be a biological bias toward early acceptance or early rejection of new experiences. As already noted much earlier, psychiatric studies have established that from shortly after birth until well into the teens, at least, individuals can be grouped into those who are very favorable to any kind of new learning experiences, those who resist such experiences initially and finally accept them, and finally those who resist such experiences entirely until forced by circumstances to adapt to them.

However, the analysis of the Opinion Research Corporation study showed that every high mobile was not an early adopter for every offering. The high mobile is an early adopter only for products in classifications which hold an unusual interest value for the given family, when the product is one of importance in his value systems, fitting into the life styles and use-systems of high value to him. He is most likely to be an innovator or an early adopter for products playing simultaneous roles in several of his high value use-systems (Opinion Research Corp., 1958).

Which use-system would cause the adoption of a specific product could be inferred from the physical nature of the products part of the time, but not always. It was found, for example, that the adoption of exotic coffees (such as espresso), was more closely related to a high interest in politics than to a high interest in foods. Adoption of boats and boating was related to a high priority for family recreational use-systems. We can, thus, describe the early adopter as a person who seems to have a personal bias toward new learning situations, who perceives less learning costs in change, and who highly values improvements in some area of his special interest and style of living.

These aspects of his personality may have some correlation to income for some kinds of satisfaction areas, as in farming, for example, in relation to farm practices which could be expected to improve production efficiency. But income is not closely correlated with the early adoption of many other kinds of innovations. It was the relatively young, whose incomes were relatively modest, who early developed and adopted the specialized recreation vehicles, such as dune buggies and dragsters, because high interest in such mechanical toys tends to be centered among the young. In industrial markets, the small outsider is often the best prospect for a really new advance, perhaps because he has no stake in current designs and production processes and thus no relearning to do and no need to scrap the heavy investments in the product being replaced.

The only segment of the established electronic industry that was interested in the transistors, when first developed in 1948, was the hearing aid industry. The sharp reduction in bulk and operating costs raised the perceivable value to buyer so high the industry could not ignore the product improvement involved. Even the military services, whose interest in portability should be extremely high, had not incorporated transistors in a single major item as long as seven years after release of the development from Bell Laboratories. The first market entries were entirely new enterprises, mostly in Japan, which carried the transistors forward into practical use. They made the transistor a force in the further expansion of the radio broadcasting industry.

It was also a smaller new steel company that first introduced the oxygen processes to the United States. Where the older steel companies were still making facilities requiring an investment of $300 per ton of capacity per year, the Kaiser Permanente organization in California introduced the oxygen converter, whose investment cost was only fifty dollars per ton capacity, and thus gained a cost advantage over their much larger competitors. Only after Kaiser Permanente had shown the value of this new process did it begin to spread among the larger steel companies to the point where it eventually would probably replace much of the older types of facilities.

As all studies have shown, and as common observations will also reveal, the growth rate of acceptance varies extremely from one product to another. Thus, if you will refer back to Figure 12-3, we can note that electric blankets took ten years for the 75 percent lower mobile market to catch up in market importance to the high mobiles in the adoption of this product. Car racks, on the other hand, took only a couple of years until parity was achieved. As we also noted early in the chapter, the acceptance pattern of one instant food, orange juice concentrate, was quite different from the very gradual acceptance pattern experienced by instant coffee. (This, incidentally, was despite the fact that instant coffee had already achieved some market share before World War II, although a minor one, while orange juice concentrate was completely new.) Similarly, black-and-white television was widely adopted even before much programming was available, but color television took eight years to get off the ground.

It is crucial that such differences in early market acceptance be anticipated, because the implications of rapid growth, for competition and for the necessary market plans, are quite the opposite of the implications for marketing plans for a product which will undergo a very slow and difficult growth period at the beginning. It is thus important to understand why and under what circumstances early acceptance may be quite rapid as in the case of black-and-white television and orange juice concentrate, for example.

## The Product Life Cycle and Its Early Growth Phase Implications

The study of the diffusion of innovations is essentially a study of the growth phase of a product life cycle. All products sooner or later go through some kind of complete cycle of growth, maturity and decline, the important aspects of which will be discussed later. The full cycle can be viewed as in Figure 12-4, starting with the initial periods of development and preparation for manufacturing and market launching, then going through a period of relatively small sales during a market development period, speeding up during a period of rapid growth, and then slowing down as the market begins to exhaust its potential for expansion. Sales eventually reach a lesser or greater plateau of market saturation and finally enter a period of decline, as the product meets the competition of new innovations capable of doing a better job of meeting the benefit needs of customers. As Figure 12-4 indicates, the expenses tend to far outrun the sales revenue during a market development phase, whereas profits grow extremely fast during the period of rapid growth and then begin to lessen as the product approaches maturity.

But not all products need to undergo any significant market development. Some start out with a relatively rapid growth rate from the very beginning. Such was the case of black-and-white television, and very much earlier it was also the case of the automobile industry. Furthermore, not all products enjoy any extended period of peak sales. Fads

**Figure 12-4.   The Full Product Life Cycle**

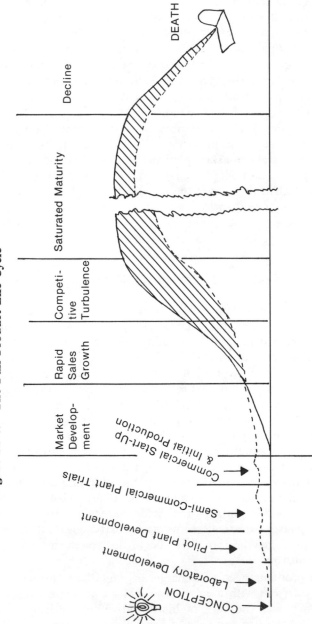

From Chester R. Wasson, *Dynamic Competitive Strategy & Product Life Cycles*, Challenge Books, St. Charles, Ill., 1974.

are a common phenomenon whose market disappears at the very crest of their popularity.

Furthermore, the growth is not necessarily that of a single smooth curve such as shown in Figure 12-4. We often have pyramided cycles in which, just as the growth slows down, some development gives an added spurt to the market. The automobile industry was an excellent example of this, with the initial growth beginning to level out in 1908, then receiving renewal as the development of mass production of relatively moderately priced cars was started by Ford in 1908, and receiving added impetus later from the publicity surrounding the value of trucks on the military front in Europe in 1914 and the development of roads in the 1920s (see Figure 12-5).

As this automobile history indicates, the extreme ease of selling automobiles in the early years immediately attracted a large number of competitors into the field. Growth period profits are extremely attractive and actually create competition. In the case of the automobile industry very little working capital was needed to get into the business at the turn of the century. The owner of a machine shop could start manufacture without much in the way of working capital. Advance deposits from dealers would furnish half of the capital and supplier credit take care of most of the rest.

Thus, in the case of any product in which rapid early growth is anticipated, the firm must be ready to meet strong competition from the first. This dictates quite a different distribution policy from that for a product which will have to undergo an extended period of market development as color television did. With the demand already visible for all the dealer can sell, it is important that every potential outlet be fully supplied as early as possible. Otherwise dealers and distributors will seek out and actually encourage new entrants into the field.

On the other hand, when market development is slow, it is necessary to concentrate what volume there is in the hands of a very few outlets in order that that volume have perceived value to the outlet itself. Moreover, it will be necessary for the dealer to undertake a very aggressive sales and promotional effort and he must be protected in this effort or he will not do so. One of the reasons color television was so slow in gaining growth was that the policy of using selective or exclusive distribution for color sets was not followed by RCA during the early years of the market. The result, according to an unpublished study made for the author, was that most dealers were not interested in selling the color sets even when they had them on the floor. It was easier to sell black-and-white at a lower price, and there were few of the service problems involved in handling the black-and-white sets that were present with color.

# Figure 12-5. The Automobile: A No-Learning Product With a Pyramided Life Cycle

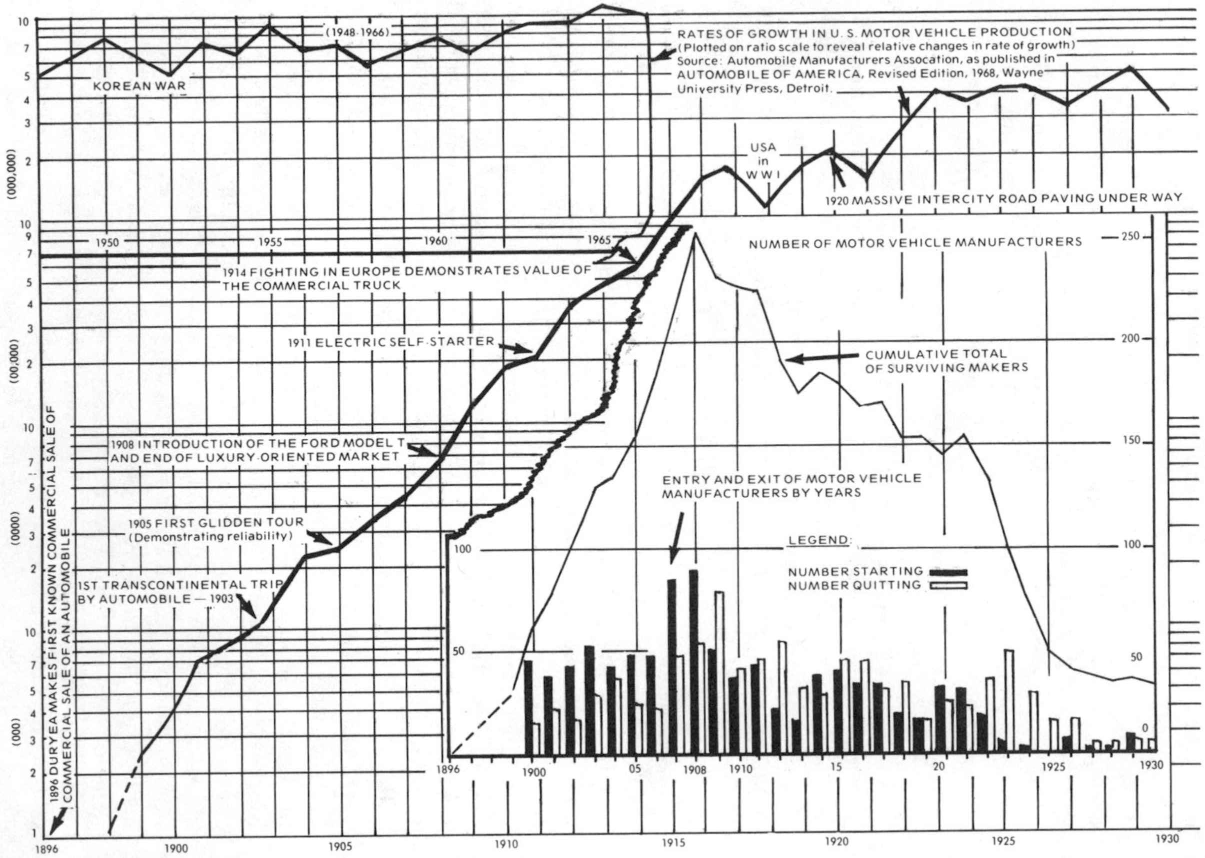

**1896:**

Duryea made the first commercial sales. The way for acceptance had already been prepared by the publicity attendant on the exhibit of European makes at the Columbian Exposition and by a long history of the use of mechanical power in stationary engines and locomotives. Furthermore, the first horseless carriages were just that—familiar carriages which now needed no horse, with the attendant problems of stabling and daily care and feeding. Within a year, other manufacturers followed suit. Entry was easy: dealers' deposits alone almost financed a maker, and supplier credit furnished the rest of his working capital. Sales were no problem. By 1900, 30 manufacturers were in business, and the number climbed to over 250 by 1908.

**1903:**

Sales appeared to be leveling off but got a new shot in the arm with the publicity of the first transcontinental tour over the roadless landscape of that day, demonstrating the reliability of the auto.

**1905:**

The start of the industry-sponsored Glidden tours furnished an annual publicity demonstration of reliability just as the market seemed to be leveling off again. By 1908, acceptance was so strong, many manufacturers discontinued advertising of their lower-end models. As yet, all sales were for cash, and mostly for luxury models.

**1908:**

Growing symptoms of the saturation of the luxury-model market were masked by the spurt in unit sales occasioned by the market-broadening tactics of the Ford introduction of the Model T, a car with features found only in other makes twice its price. The renewed upward spurt of the market did not prevent a shakeout of competition. Exits from manufacturing exceeded entries for the first time in 1909, with those quitting making high-price cars, and the newer entrants competing at the lower end.

**1911:**

Introduction of the electric self-starter improved the serviceability of the automobile and gave the sales curve another upward boost.

**1914:**

Trucks and commercial vehicles start to spurt, with the demonstration of their value on the war front.

**1920-24:**

Saturation set in anew in 1920, only to pyramid upward by the paving of intercity roads, after which the industry market again exhibited symptoms of maturity (and a Depression-induced decline) until after the end of World War II and the beginning of the urban sprawl which, by the end of the 1950 s, had virtually enforced a two-car standard for many families, resulting in the last major pyramidal step.

Other implications of the shape of the product life cycle will be discussed in later chapters. It should be obvious, however, that it is extremely important to find some means of predicting the acceptance rate of a product early in the design, research and development period. Such prediction is obviously not the result of the general nature of the product. Both orange juice and instant coffee were equally useful, convenient foods, and both involved a very similar simplicity of preparation. Nevertheless, orange concentrate was characterized by a market with such explosive growth, bringing in so much competition initially, that only later reduction of the orange crop through freezing restored any degree of profitability once it reached its peak. Instant coffee, on the other hand, grew so slowly that it was a half dozen years before a second brand came on the market.

Similarly, black-and-white television spawned numerous electronic manufacturers overnight, many of which had to be shaken out as the product reached maturity. Color television, on the other hand, with its slow market growth, discouraged everyone but the initial proponent of the accepted system, RCA, which had the market to itself for the eight long years it took to reach a take-off period. In the interim, RCA incurred deficits of millions of dollars per year to develop the market. A knowledge of some of the concepts we have discussed in earlier chapters, however, provides us with a system for explaining these differences and for predicting them as early as the product concept stage of any innovation. The key to that prediction is the simple question as to the degree of learning required by the product.

### The Learning Requirement and Its Relationship to the Product Acceptance Rate

Every innovation requires some degree of change in the habitual use-systems of the individual acquiring it. As noted in the beginning, all products release the satisfactions desired by the user only in terms of some habitual use-system. Thus, all products involve some kind of learning process, some kind of operant conditioning of a complex set of procedures as well as perceptions of value. The prospect must first become aware of and learn of existence of the product and acquire an understanding of what "new" satisfactions the introduction promises. He must learn for himself, by direct study or from others, what the promised "new" in the new product means to him and what value it has in the relationship to his current use-system or possible use-systems. Finally, he must learn to change his habitual procedural use-system to some degree. It is the degree in the change in use-patterns and perception of value which determine the potential speed of growth and market acceptance in sales.

For the great majority of highly advertised new innovations on the market, what the seller means by "new" is that he has developed a slightly different version of something already familiar to the buyer. It is either a somewhat improved copy of some successful competitor's offering, or a variation of one of his own established lines. In the case of such emulative or adaptive new products, the prospect may only be required to perceive that some previously unavailable attribute he already desired, valued and understood was available in a form which fit into his habit pattern. The direct opposite of such emulative and adaptive products are the completely unfamiliar offerings which combine a new bundle of satisfactions, whose meaning and need the buyers must learn to perceive and value, and which will require any purchaser to undertake a prolonged process of developing new habits.

Between these two extremes are all degrees of variation of learning requirements, and it is the prediction of the kind, degree, and intensity of that learning that must be undertaken if the market plan is to fit the probable acceptance pattern.

Estimating the learning requirement is not necessarily easy, although, as will be pointed out later, the outlines of the process are relatively simple. What the customer perceives as new and the degree of that perceived newness is not related to the technological novelty involved in the physical design of the offering nor is it involved in the degree of complexity of its use. The system of use into which the product is initially perceived as fitting will determine that requirement. A product is new, from the revolutionary standpoint, if it requires some significant degree of learning: learning of some new use-system, of some new kind of satisfaction source, of a new role for a product in an otherwise similar system or of a new level of value for some major product attribute.

Technologically, black-and-white television was a highly revolutionary development in electronics. In the customer's perception, however, it fitted into his entertainment use-patterns, particularly that of movies, and was perceived as a highly improved source of this type of entertainment. Color television, on the other hand, was technologically a relatively evolutionary development from black-and-white television. But it required a level of value perception which customers were not habituated to as yet—it cost three times as much just to get the added attribute of color. And color was not considered necessary, as the film sales of any camera shop even today will demonstrate.

One of the problems of prediction is that the use-systems the customer will perceive as appropriate cannot be completely predicted. The use-system may be substantially different from the one foreseen in developing the design and in many cases will include quite unforeseen possibilities.

Whatever the use-system, an introduction may require any or all of four kinds of learning on the part of prospect:

1. Motor learning—a change in habitual muscular use-system sequences
2. Value-perception learning—learning to value the improvement as greater than the cost of acquisition
3. Role-perception learning—learning to accept a change in the user's social role as a result of product use
4. Use-perceptual learning—involved in crediting a new satisfaction source as a reliable and improved fulfillment of a given desire-set

Every product involves some form of habitual sequence of motor or muscular reactions. As pointed out earlier, learning is not a one-step process, but a gradual one which takes place over a considerable period of time. If the product can fit into such an established sequence or simplifies a system without major change of sequences, obviously no learning problem is likely. The orange juice concentrate mentioned at the beginning of the chapter fit into a simplified use-system for other products of which the user was already aware and replaced a much more cumbersome one which was considered as "work" and not necessarily the source of any major benefit, that of squeezing and reaming out orange juice from a number of oranges. The frozen concentrate fit into the usual process familiar to any modern housewife —that of opening a can and emptying it (and perhaps, as in the case of soup, diluting the product with some water). The use of orange concentrate thus was able to fit into an established routine and established set of appliances within the kitchen.

Theoretically, instant coffee should have also fit into a similar use-system. The problem with instant coffee was not the physical use-system, but another matter, that of role perception (discussed below). Thus, it should be expected that the use of frozen orange concentrate would increase rapidly and this was indeed the case, as already noted.

The learning difference required in the sequence need not be great. It may involve a change in a single step in an otherwise already established sequence. Even a single step change requires breaking one habit and establishing a new one. As already pointed out, the breaking of an old habit and the establishment of a new one requires more than twice the time and effort as the mere establishment of a new habit. The process might very well be viewed as in Figure 5-2. The individual must start at the top of his learning curve on one habit and gradually break it down, then go through a period in which he consolidates this break in habit before he can start to develop a new learning curve and climb up again. This was one reason for the prolonged market development period of the electric typewriter, which took from the time of its introduction, in 1926, until as late as 1948, to attain a mere 6 percent of unit sales penetration.

The change-over from a manual to an electric would seem to be relatively minor. The keyboard of the electric typewriter is identical to that of a manual typewriter. It has the advantage of not needing nearly as heavy a touch on the key as the manual typewriter and thus should diminish the fatigue of a person who types all day. Moreover, it produces extremely uniform copy and thus upgrades the quality of the work of the typist. But it also required a change in a well-established habit pattern for any typist accustomed to using a manual machine. On the manual machine she had been trained to rest her fingers on the middle row of the alphabetical keys. She now had to avoid touching *any* key at all until she wanted to register it on her copy. The slightest touch of a key in passing would cause the type bar to print. The result was a great deal of spoiled copy until the typist had unlearned a relatively simple finger position that had become a habit, learned to be extremely careful of how she moved her hands. A learning period of approximately two months was not unusual for a person changing over from a standard typewriter to an electric typewriter.

Indeed, adoption of the electric typewriter was very slow until it had reached enough importance to get schools to use it as a training machine, an event which occurred around 1950. Thereafter, the electric typewriter rose rapidly in sales to 26 percent of units in 1955, 42 percent in 1960, and to 47 percent by 1961. Since the typist had to learn initially on some kind of machine, it was no more difficult to learn originally on the electric machine than on the manual. But once the typist started using an electric machine, the change-over to a manual instrument now required a relearning process and a very annoying fact—the manual typewriter takes much greater effort on each key and required thus a new motor procedure.

For many products, the requirement of a different motor procedure can cause complete failure of the introduction. This was the case of the quality dehydrated soups introduced by both the Knorr brand of the Best Foods Division of CPC International, and by a similar product under the Red Kettle brand, by Campbell Soup in the early 1960s. Both Knorr and Campbell overlooked the change in use-system habits required by the new soup, as shown in Figure 12-6.

**Figure 12-6.   Comparison of Use-Systems for Dehydrated Soups and for the Established Canned Types**

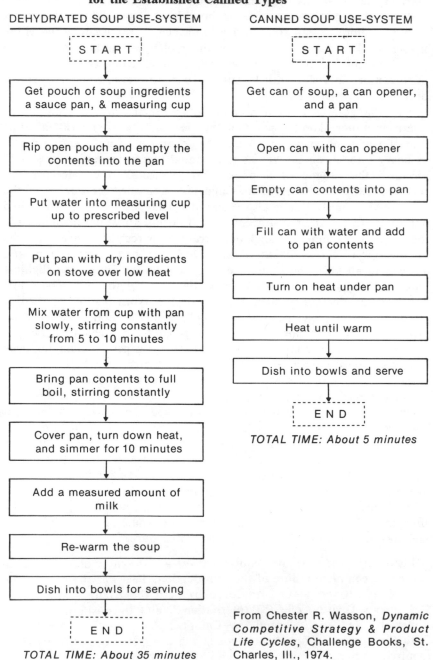

DEHYDRATED SOUP USE-SYSTEM

START

Get pouch of soup ingredients a sauce pan, & measuring cup

Rip open pouch and empty the contents into the pan

Put water into measuring cup up to prescribed level

Put pan with dry ingredients on stove over low heat

Mix water from cup with pan slowly, stirring constantly from 5 to 10 minutes

Bring pan contents to full boil, stirring constantly

Cover pan, turn down heat, and simmer for 10 minutes

Add a measured amount of milk

Re-warm the soup

Dish into bowls for serving

END

*TOTAL TIME: About 35 minutes*

CANNED SOUP USE-SYSTEM

START

Get can of soup, a can opener, and a pan

Open can with can opener

Empty can contents into pan

Fill can with water and add to pan contents

Turn on heat under pan

Heat until warm

Dish into bowls and serve

END

*TOTAL TIME: About 5 minutes*

From Chester R. Wasson, *Dynamic Competitive Strategy & Product Life Cycles*, Challenge Books, St. Charles, Ill., 1974.

Within the United States, most soup, even that served by many restaurants, is prepared from the condensed canned variety by merely opening the can, diluting it, warming it, and serving it. By contrast, as can be seen from this figure, the production of a bowl of soup from a pouch of the Knorr or a can of the Red Kettle dehydrated product required a lengthy procedure and constant attention. Given the place of soup in the menu systems in the United States—an emergency meal served principally to youngsters—no housewife would undertake this tedious process.

It is true that the Knorr soups were already popular in Europe, from which Best Foods imported them. But in Europe, soup occupies a completely different niche in the menu system of the European culture. The alternative there is not the opening of a can and warming of the diluted contents, but the preparing of soup from scratch ingredients, a process that often takes hours. The soup itself is used in a completely different meal system. In Europe soup can be a main dish at a meal. In the United States, on the other hand, the primary use of most soups is as a quick emergency meal for children. Thus, the use-system being replaced was a completely different use-system, with a completely different context of value. Had either Knorr's or Campbell's diagrammed the use-systems involved, as we have done in Figure 12-6, neither would have pursued further development of the product. Both of them would have rejected the concept from the start. Unfortunately, they did not, and Campbell's lost a published $10,000,000 on their enterprise, CPC International a reputed $15,000,000, before both acknowledged failure.

In the soup case, a problem of value perception was also involved. There are times when the prospect will undertake some degree of learning, and at least some degree of added effort, if the value to be obtained is perceived as greater. Such was the result in the case of angel food cake mixes. The first such mixes introduced contained all the necessary ingredients, including a package of dehydrated egg whites. One manufacturer had the insight to see that a great many people did not consider dehydrated eggs to be the equivalent of fresh eggs, and so introduced a cake mix without the egg package. His advertising told the housewife she could "use her own fresh eggs." The result was a high degree of successful market penetration. In the case of soup, of course, the problem was that the product introduced was not perceived as such high value.

Color television is an excellent example of a case in which the learning required was primarily that of perceiving a new level of value where few people had perceived any before. Black-and-white television did what no home entertainment system has previously been able to do, show picture together with sound. The alternative was to go to a local movie theater, stand in line, buy tickets, find a place to park, and do this every time a new show came on. Black-and-white television brought this process into the parlor at the click of a switch, and the shows were free once the set was bought. Color television, on the other hand, offered nothing that the black-and-white television did not offer except color and it cost three times as much to buy (as well as manufacture).

Furthermore, there is a great deal of evidence that color is not conceived as being all that much better by everybody. Indeed, one of the principles of good entertainment is that it involves some degree of closure, as we noted earlier. In effect, people added the color by their own perception. The process of closure tends to give a higher value to the perception of a situation than the lack of it. Also, it is still true that much of the film handled by camera stores is black and white two generations after the introduction of color film. Even today, some forty-odd years after the introduction of color movies, many movies are shown in black and white. Thus, it should have been obvious that color would not be immediately perceived by a great many people as being a substantial added value. (One woman of the author's acquaintance used to see the black-and-white commercials of Hamm's Beer, touting "The land of sky blue waters" in full blue color, on a black-and-white screen.)

Nevertheless, color had potential value for a great many people, but one that took determined selling and seeking out of the best prospects, at a time when they would be perceptive of these values. In one such instance, known by the author, an aggressive television merchant foresaw that a specific medical program would be of a great deal of interest to possible physician customers and persuaded ten physicians of his acquaintance to let him put sets in their homes on consignment and adjust them in time for the program. The result of this effort was the return of only four of the sets. The other six were purchased. But as this example also shows, the learning of value requires experience and often hard selling to get people to make the try.

Since all products involve a role for the user thereof, the question of what the product does to this role can also be extremely important. We have already noted that instant coffee had a very slow acceptance at first. The problem does not appear to have been in the product itself. The product first introduced on the market in 1946 produced practically as good a coffee as the product did ten years later.

The difficulty apparently came from a different direction. Studies showed that instant coffee was associated in the housewife's mind with careless housekeeping. Two panels of women, for example, were shown two different shopping lists that differed only in a single item. In the one case, the shopping list called for roasted canned coffee of a familiar brand and in the other case the list called for instant coffee. When asked to describe the person who had composed each of the shopping lists, most of the housewives looking at the instant coffee list proclaimed her "a slovenly housekeeper who did not care for her family."

Unlike orange juice, in which no skill is attached to extracting the juice itself from the orange, coffee is a product to which women attach a certain degree of skill in the making, as the current ads for many brands still show. The housewife who viewed her main role as that of housekeeper and cook for the family could not acquiesce in such a downgrading of her family role. However, coincident with the growth in the use of instant coffee was the growth of participation of women in the work force. As we noted earlier, this led the housewives themselves to downgrade the importance of their homemaking role in relation to their outside job, and instant coffee became acceptable.

Any product which tends to downgrade the skill of the person who must use or prepare it will meet some greater or lesser degree of resistance, particularly if the product is in an industrial setting. Paint rollers received extremely widespread use among homeowner painters long before professional painters were willing to discard their brushes and adopt this time saving and productivity producing tool. Computer typesetting has a great many advantages over linotype operation, but it has a great disadvantage in that it downgrades the skill of a typesetter. It eliminates much of the need for the knowledge and skills of the linotyper, and so has met stiff resistance from the unions. Automatic transmissions are often taken for granted today, but when first introduced in the late 1930s, it was not a widely-sought-after option. It is probably no accident that it became important mainly after the residential shift to the suburbs and the two-car family, where women had to become the family chauffeur. A very large number of women are not mechanically oriented and dislike the use of a standard gear shift. Skilled drivers, on the other hand, resisted the automatic transmission to the point where the "stick shift" became a prestige item worth a premium on sports cars.

Finally, many products require the buyer to acquire some degree of *use-perceptual learning*. He must learn to perceive a new satisfaction source as both reliable and an improvement over a different preexisting one in the fulfillment of a specific desire-set. One case of such a product was the small foreign sedan, introduced from Europe with the return of the veterans of World War II. Although first on the market in an organized way in 1949, it took eight to ten years before the volume got to be such as to require the big three in Detroit to develop their own "compacts." Although Detroit felt reasonably safe in increasing size and gaudiness of their products thereafter, the introduction of these small sedans eventually eroded the market of Detroit's product to the extent where the erosion in public interest became visible at the time of the oil shortages of 1973 and 1974, catalyzing a shift which had already begun to take place in public demand in relation to car size.

## No-learning Products

The corollary of the learning requirement is that a product which fits into a going system and whose value is already perceived as high, will have very rapid market acceptance—it will be a no-learning product. Monochrome television was just such a product. It fitted into the most popular entertainment system of the period, the movie—but was a considerable improvement over that product in terms of its availability. It made possible the viewing of true movies at home in the parlor.

All fads are no-learning products, primarily because a true fad requires no learning of any consequence. Although the physical form of the product itself may be new, it fits into some existing use-system and its sole added benefit is one which is always in demand—that of pure novelty. This is also the reason for its instant demise on obtaining full popularity. Novelty, or to give it a psychological label, stimulus variation, ceases to be novelty or variation once established.

Sometimes the use-system is established but the product itself is missing. Then the mere development of the missing link is all that is required for market success. Essentially this was the case with monochrome television. The public had already long before learned to switch on the radio to bring comedy, drama, and news into the home, but it had to go to the movies to get the picture. The picture tube simply added a new and highly desired dimension to radio and permitted the broadcast medium to fill a need previously available only from two different sources. The development of rubber tires for tractors was another such product. The tractor itself had long been in use on farms but had been highly limited because the steel wheels used for driving these tractors tended to compact the soil in the fields—an undesirable effect—and also made it impossible to drive the vehicles over normal roads without removing the lugs. Rubber tires did away with both the soil compaction and the prohibition against driving on public roads. Within a very short period after the introduction of rubber tires, both the steel wheel tractor and the horse disappeared from farm motive power.

The supermarket was a systems-completing product arising from the development of two preceding systems, the use of the motor car for transport and the development of home refrigeration. With automobile shopping, one-stop purchasing became preferable to the door-to-door visit to several shops in the area, previously needed to acquire a market basket of food. The automobile itself made possible the transport of a full week's supply of groceries to a home in which the mechanical refrigerator would keep the product in eatable condition for that length of time.

The almost impregnable position in the computer market obtained by IBM was not the development of the computer (which had already been the work of others), but the development of something needed to make the product of value to the user, the program library and programming services.

Thus it is that the adoption and diffusion of new products depends first on the communications within the reference group of which the consumer is a member and second, the speed of that acceptance, both by innovators and by others, depends on the extent to which the product requires the change of the established habit systems or the acquisition of new ones, whether the habits be those of muscular procedures, or perceptions of value or perceptions of the individual's social role within the groups of which he is a member.

One very special kind of new product is fashion, which we will explore in the next chapter.

## Summary

1.   All new products take time to reach full potential sales, but the speed of the sales climb is extremely variable, with some products requiring years to reach growth and profitable volume.

2.   Such a gradual build up in sales would be inevitable if the only factor were that of reaching all of the market with communications about the benefit. However, adoption lags well behind awareness due to the fact that adoption and diffusion is a social process, depending heavily on a chain of personal advice.

3.   Only limited numbers of consumers—the true innovators—will try new products on their own when first available. Others wait to see what the experience of these earliest adopters is before making any trial.

4.   Diffusion depends on a chain of person-to-person communications, with each successive layer of consumers adopting on the advice of slightly more venturesome acquaintances, then passing on advice to those slightly less venturesome than they. Sociologists studying this diffusion phenomenon have rather arbitrarily divided new users into

five classes: innovators, early adopters, early majority, late majority, and skeptics.

5.   Extensive research indicates that both the innovators and early adopters have substantially different backgrounds and personalities from the later adopters. Generally speaking, they have a wider experience with changes in their lives.

6.   Early adopters are consistently so for a wide class of products, but only for products important in their value systems. For other types of products, they follow the lead of others.

7.   Early adopters of new farm practices tend to be those with higher income, but income and size of operation are not closely correlated with early adoption generally.

8.   High interest in the class of products involved is the only apparent distinguishing mark for consumer goods. In industry, the small outsider is more likely to be on the alert for new processes and products than the largest established firms.

9.   The study of the diffusion of an innovation is the study of the growth phase of the product life cycle. All products pass through some kind of cycle of growth, maturity, and decline.

10.   The changing phases of the product life cycle are conventionally divided into those of market development, rapid growth, competitive turbulence, maturity, and decline. Some products, however, never require any significant period of market development, entering a sharp rise in sales growth almost from the day of introduction. Other introductions go through a series of pyramided growth cycles before reaching final maturity. Still others linger in an extremely prolonged phase of expensive, resource-consuming market development for years. Advance prediction of the expected pattern of acceptance is an essential to rational market planning.

11.   The key to prediction of the differences in rate of acceptance lies in an analysis of the relearning of habits required to gain the benefits of the innovation.

12.   Emulative or adaptive copies of widely accepted products pose no such learning requirement.

13.   The learning requirement is completely unrelated to the degree of technological advance represented by the new design. It hinges entirely on the degree to which the consumer must acquire new habits of action and perception.

14.   Any one or more of four kinds of habit relearning may be required: motor learning of the physical use-system, new value perception, new role perception, and new use-perception learning.

15.   The motor learning requirements can be analyzed by a simple comparison of the flow charts of the new system and of the old one

being replaced. Even a single change in a single step means the relearning of a complete new habit system.

16. Several kinds of new products skip the market development phase because they require no relearning. These include fads, whose only new benefit is stimulus variation, and missing link products needed to complete systems already being adopted.

17. Fads and fashions constitute important special classes of new products worthy of study in themselves.

## Chapter 12 Exercises

1. The first major field research on the diffusion of innovations concerned the introduction and adoption of hybrid corn seed, now the almost universal farm practice. Hybrid corn is planted, cultivated and harvested in exactly the same way as is ordinary cross-pollinated corn. The most important benefit is much higher yields per acre, and thus more profit—a difference which was about 25 percent even at first, and has grown much larger. The only difference in the farmer's procedures was a switch to purchasing new seed every year. Previously, the farmer generally saved some of the old crop and replanted it, but this could not be done with hybrid seed, since it does not reproduce true. Despite the well-validated promise of greater production and the heavy barrage of publicity in farm journals and from the agricultural experiment stations, and strong sale efforts on the part of the seed companies, only 6 percent of the farmers had tried it by the end of the first six years. Why?

2. By contrast with the hybrid corn experience, the automobile industry took off on a rapid sales rise from the beginning, despite the fact that all sales were strictly for cash for years, the price was equal to as much as two or three years' pay for a skilled workman, and most did not normally buy other personal transportation (horses and buggies), unlike the corn farmers who had to use some kind of seed in any case. Why?

3. Draw a use-system flow diagram for seeing a show at the movie and the diagram for seeing a show on television. Why was television so quickly successful?

4.   Draw the use-system diagram for a pitcher of orange juice prepared by squeezing fresh oranges (one dozen approximately equals the yield from one can of frozen concentrate) and for a pitcher made from orange concentrate. What do you conclude would be the consumer's first reactions in this case?

5.   Classify your friends according to the 5 classes of adopters. Is there any in the list who is usually earliest with respect to any kind of new purchases? Is there anyone who tends to be last?

6.   Select some one important introduction of recent decades (for example, the lightweight motorcycle). Diagram the use system. What product did it displace, or what product was it competing with? Diagram the use-system for that product.

Look up the sales history of the introduction (usually available from some trade association).

7.   Many magazines and newspapers regularly run lists of new products. *Advertising Age* publishes one such monthly, for products of the highly advertised consumer type. Look up several such lists. How many are "really new" in the sense of being more than a variation of some established product?

8.   Why would a firm normally avoid pioneering new products, as P & G does?

9.   Why would a firm deliberately seek to develop and introduce high learning products?

# The Unending Pursuit of
# Stimulus Variation:
# Fashion and Fads

WHAT IS FASHION?

THE REACH OF FASHION AND FADS

Not Just Garments but All Sorts of Consumer Offerings
Fashion Cycles in Business Management Practice
Fashion Cycles in Ideas

DO DESIGNERS CREATE FASHIONS?

Fashions Which Failed Despite Promotion
Fashion Which Succeeded Despite Designer Disapproval
Inability of Merchandising Experts to Foresee Acceptance

PREDICTABILITY OF FASHION

A THEORY OF FASHION

Psychological Basis for Fluctuations
Reference Group Basis for Norms and Over-Adoption

THE CLASSIC: THE STYLE WHICH NEVER GOES OUT OF FASHION

FASHION AND THE PRODUCT LIFE CYCLE

FASHION AND PROFIT

FADS: THE EMPTY PRODUCT

In 1968 AND 1969, the "in" girl or woman wore skirts hardly covering her groin. By 1973, the hem of the evening gown of any woman with a claim to elegance reached the floor. Meanwhile, the fashion world had attempted to introduce a mid-calf length skirt, the "midi," in 1970. It was a complete and dismal failure despite every effort by the most prestigious shops to press it upon their customers. Instead, women opted for a style that had been sneaking into evening wear since 1964, the pants suit. Ever since, the pants suit has remained a basic item in the woman's wardrobe regardless of style changes. It has become a classic.

## What Is Fashion?

Fashion is one area in which the psychologist in his animal laboratory can give us very little help. One obvious element in fashion is the drive for stimulus variability. It is true that animals much lower than man also exhibit this drive to some extent. But nothing corresponding to the wave-like fluctuations of conformity in clothes, and very many other fields of human behavior, is exhibited in the animal world.

Fashion, first of all, is a social phenomenon. There are certainly clear group and class norms as to what looks good, at the moment, and what is dowdy and "dated." Fashion is a life cycle phenomenon. Fashions come in slow, through acceptance by a small group of innovators and early adopters, rise to general acceptance, then gradually fade out over time. They are not to be confused with fads, as will be explained below at some length. The fad comes in quickly, rises to a peak, then fades overnight into oblivion. The fad is a no-learning product. Fashion acceptance requires some considerable degree of learning.

Finally, it should be quite obvious that fashion is not limited to clothes. Fashion involves very many areas of human consumption, including many areas of the supposedly cold bloodedly, rational industrial purchasing and design field.

**The Reach of Fashions and Fads**

Fashion is often considered synonymous with women's clothes. Any book with fashion in its title turns out to be devoted almost exclusively to women's clothing. It is certainly true that a great deal of print paper and writing is devoted to the obvious turns of women's tastes in what is acceptable and where. Whole series of magazines have nothing else for their topic. Nevertheless, fashion is quite obviously a far more widespread phenomenon than garment style fluctuations. One need not be a very long term student of automobiles to realize that the popular shapes and styling of automobiles change almost as frequently as the waist line and hem line of women's dresses, and in just as cyclical a manner. Anyone with knowledge of house designs over the years can date a home by the details of its exterior styling and note the ebb and flow of popularity of design elements that reach back over the centuries, just as in women's and men's clothes design elements. Nor is fashion limited to the consumer world, as these examples might seem to indicate.

Styles of management have their ebb and flow of popularity among corporations, with organization charts having their own cycles of "in" and "out." The wave of popularity of such mechanical aids to management of computers is an excellent example of a fashion cycle. Computers often were adopted for jobs for which they were very ill-suited and much more expensive than the clerical labor they displaced. For a time, exaggerated claims for the computer rivaled those claims made for the Delphic Oracles centuries before. While computers remain around in some form or another, just as dresses and garments always have, the wild rage for a monopolistic share of management decision credit has long ago subsided.

Even in the world of ideas, we can trace clear examples of fashion. A colleague once measured the space devoted in religious magazines to various theological topics and found a typical wavelike concentration of interests in specific theological ideas much like the concentration of interest in women's dress silhouettes.

The author has shown clear evidence (see Figure 13-1) of similar fashion cycles in the commercial promotion of market research methods to the consulting market. Quite clearly, fashion is a very widespread phenomenon important to product design and to the marketing men. It is also a phenomenon responsible for a great deal of pure mythology as to our ability to manipulate our fellow man or woman. The greatest of these myths is that fashion is an artificial creation of commercial interests.

**Figure 13-1.    The Swings in Research Techniques Fashions**

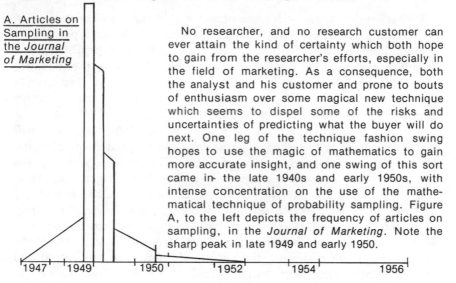

A. Articles on Sampling in the *Journal of Marketing*

No researcher, and no research customer can ever attain the kind of certainty which both hope to gain from the researcher's efforts, especially in the field of marketing. As a consequence, both the analyst and his customer and prone to bouts of enthusiasm over some magical new technique which seems to dispel some of the risks and uncertainties of predicting what the buyer will do next. One leg of the technique fashion swing hopes to use the magic of mathematics to gain more accurate insight, and one swing of this sort came in the late 1940s and early 1950s, with intense concentration on the use of the mathematical technique of probability sampling. Figure A, to the left depicts the frequency of articles on sampling, in the *Journal of Marketing*. Note the sharp peak in late 1949 and early 1950.

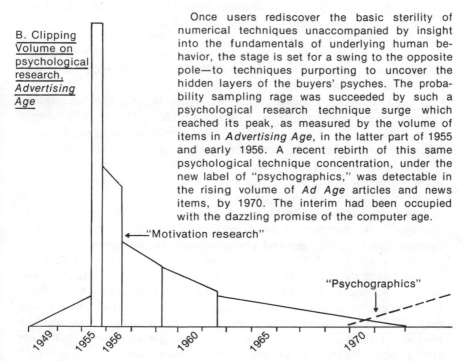

B. Clipping Volume on psychological research, *Advertising Age*

Once users rediscover the basic sterility of numerical techniques unaccompanied by insight into the fundamentals of underlying human behavior, the stage is set for a swing to the opposite pole—to techniques purporting to uncover the hidden layers of the buyers' psyches. The probability sampling rage was succeeded by such a psychological research technique surge which reached its peak, as measured by the volume of items in *Advertising Age*, in the latter part of 1955 and early 1956. A recent rebirth of this same psychological technique concentration, under the new label of "psychographics," was detectable in the rising volume of *Ad Age* articles and news items, by 1970. The interim had been occupied with the dazzling promise of the computer age.

From Chester R. Wasson, *Dynamic Competitive Strategy & Product Life Cycles*, Challenge Books, St. Charles, Ill., 1974.

### Do Designers Create Fashion or Do Fashions Create Designers?

Perhaps no myth has wider acceptance within the world of commerce than the myth that women are forced to wear the fashions put out by leading designers. The myth dies hard and is still widely held, despite a wealth of evidence that fashion is most clearly forced on the industry, not the reverse. This is well illustrated by the events of the last decade and decade and a half—particularly the history of two women's garment styles—those of the midi and of the pants suit.

The midi was introduced on the market in late 1969 and early 1970 as the successor to the then popular mini, which had dominated the market for the previous couple of years. The mini was, itself, the epitome of the desire for emulation of youth—a style which was highly suitable only for a person with a figure of an early adolescent—leggy and still not well developed sexually. Whereas the ultimate of the mini style, the micro-mini skirt, ended barely below the crotch, the midi skirt ended midway between the floor and the knee. From the standpoint of the designers, the specific designs that they introduced with this particular skirt length should have been the answer to women's desire. With a highly unusual degree of unanimity, almost the entire industry concentrated on this single style.

This unanimity was almost unique. A simple leafing through the fashion news of previous years would show that, generally speaking, designers went in a number of quite divergent directions until it was found which direction would gather popularity.

In the case of the midi, that was not done. With almost unanimous support, the whole industry, including retailers, threw their weight behind the midi style. The result was a complete catastrophe, even though some of the most prestigious shops insisted that their clerks show only the midi. Despite all their pressure from industry and the fashion press, the midi died a quick and well-warranted death.

The results are obvious in one of the few cases we have of measurement of style cycles—a series of store advertising linage throughout the summer of 1970, conducted by the George Neustadt, Incorporated organization and commissioned by the Bureau of Advertising, the results of which are shown in Table 13-1. Retailers, of course, adapt their advertising to what is selling, and as these tabulations show, the midi appears to be something that was not selling. Interestingly enough, what was selling was a product that had received only left-handed blessing, at best, from the designers, for quite a number of years, until women had shown major interest in it despite various obstacles from social pressure—the pants suit.

Unfortunately, the only way to trace the history of the pants suit is through the news items appearing in various items of women's fashion

Table 14-1.   The Midi Style Dies A-Borning: Percentage of Chain and Department Store Dress Advertising Devoted to Each Garment Style, 16 U.S. Cities, Summer and Early Fall, 1970

| MONTH 1970 | PERCENT OF TOTAL LINAGE DEVOTED TO EACH STYLE | | | | | |
| | Midi | Mini | Maxi | Pants Dresses & Suits | Knee Length | Undes-ignated Style |
| --- | --- | --- | --- | --- | --- | --- |
| JULY: all prices | 13.5 | 13.0 | 2.7 | 20.3 | 32.3 | 18.2 |
| Higher pr. lines | 30.6 | 3.0 | 10.1 | 27.4 | 21.2 | 7.7 |
| AUGUST | 10.5 | 13.6 | 3.1 | 29.0 | 31.7 | 12.2 |
| SEPTEMBER | 10.9 | 6.3 | 4.2 | 38.0 | 30.8 | 9.9 |
| OCTOBER | 5 | 7 | 7 | 41 | 27 | 13 |

Source: Measurements by George Neustadt, Inc., commissioned by Bureau of Advertising, A. N. P. A., and published in Bureau of Advertising News Releases.

news. One of the problems of any discussion of fashion is that the industry is so committed to the myth of created fashion that no one has bothered to keep figures of any sort until recent years, with the exception of the mail order houses. Even those figures that have been accumulated in recent years by a commercial service are not available for public consumption, nor do they reach back to the time of the first clear indication of pants suits desires among women in the year 1964.

Long before 1964, of course, women had been wearing pants of one sort or another, for casual wear. Culottes are one item of women's casual wear that has come in and gone out of fashion for centuries. During the fifties and sixties, a great many suburban women had adopted one form or another of pant-like attire for casual daytime wear—jodphurs, shorts, toreador pants, ordinary slacks, and denim slacks. The widespread use of these costumes, however, had no counterpart in more formal or dressy wear until sometime in the early 1960s.

The first recorded instance that can be found of dress-type slacks was in 1964. One major Paris designer, Courreges, introduced a line of severely English tailored type women's pants suits. There is not much evidence that this type of pants suit attracted much attention amid the much frillier and "feminine" dress offerings of his fellow designers. Nevertheless, articles appearing in magazines devoted to upper-class tastes noted frequent use of various kinds of pants costumes by some women of the so-called beautiful people "jet set" around the world.

While most of the news items seemed to concern the use of these for semidress casual wear, there was more than a little sign that some of the women were going further than this, to the expressed dismay of eminent designers who sold them some of these garments—sometimes, apparently, at the customer's request. Emelio Pucci, for example, who had concentrated on feminine type pants suits, is quoted by *Vogue* as "frankly dismayed" at the use of pants in the city: "This most casual of looks is the most severe of frames; elegance, after all, is conforming to one's surroundings." Women, however, paid little attention, although they began to have problems when they started wearing such outfits in public places. A well-known actress, Suzanne York, found herself barred from lunch at the Colony Restaurant when she showed up wearing a high fashion pants suit in October, 1966, and at that time, Chicago's Maxim's Restaurant and Manhattan's "21" nightclub maintained a rigid ban on such items (*Time*, Oct. 14, 1966, pp. 87-88). However, there was evidence that by this time, some of the upper-class restaurants were beginning to change their standards. According to *Time*, restauranteur Stephen Crane of Beverly Hills, California, who owned a chain of restaurants in Los Angeles and seven other cities, set a national policy at this time with the guidelines "if the whole party is sufficiently 'cocktail' or black ties, women with pants suits would be allowed to be seated." Upper-class women by this time were apparently beginning to adopt pants suits in large numbers. By 1968, the major designers were succumbing, having been pressured by clients to design items specifically for them in previous years.

Probably the major event of 1968 was the decision of St. Laurent, of the House of Dior in Paris, to give a New York showing of city pants at $145 to $175. The result was such great popularity that new clothes had to be shipped in by air to keep the showing in stock (*Time*, Sept. 27, 1968, p. 63). Nevertheless, neither the trade nor various employers were quite ready to relax their ban (on a style that certainly was much more modest than the mini skirts which were allowed full sway in both high-class restaurants and in offices). One department store buyer, for example, appeared quite dubious: "Will my customers pay $400 for St. Laurent pants copies while couture clients pay $1,500 for originals?" Apparently they did.

Employers had mixed reactions. Macy's, New York's largest department store, insisted "we don't allow it." Garfinkel's, Washington's upper-class store, grudgingly said "if it becomes accepted our employees would be allowed to wear pants to work." Bullocks, Incorporated, in Los Angeles, gave a similarly grudging approval "we would probably go along." Citizens Southern's National Bank in Atlanta "we would not want to be among the first to initiate acceptance." But the

First National Bank of staid Boston admitted "we would allow our women employees to wear pants if they continue to act like women." Chase Manhattan Bank of New York had an absolute dictum "we don't hire women wearing pants" (*U.S. News and World Report*, Sept. 12, 1968, p. 79). By 1970, however, retailers were glad to have the pants suit, with the complete collapse of the midi, and by 1974 the pants suit had become an item that was considered a must alternative in every well-dressed woman's wardrobe, although no longer the dressiest number.

By 1974, other items had taken over the dominance of the dressier area, but a pants suit is just as acceptable at the opera as ever. It had become a classic, despite all forms of social pressure and all the frowns from the designers. Clearly, fashion originates, at least in part, with the women themselves.

Probably by far the best example of the final collapse of all opposition to the pants suit is evidenced by a memorandum of the United States Department of Justice, quoted in the *New York Times* on November 30, 1970, addressed to the ladies of the U.S. Attorney's office and their bosses: "Subject: Fashion Bulletin" (see Figure 13-2).

**Figure 13-2. The Siege Ends: Even the Government Bureaucracy Bows to the Pants Suite**

Form DJ-150
(Ed. 4-26-65)

UNITED STATES GOVERNMENT DEPARTMENT OF JUSTICE

*Memorandum*

TO : The Ladies of the U.S. Attorney's Office and Their Bosses

DATE: November 20, 1970
ERN:np

FROM : Edward R. Neaher
United States Attorney

SUBJECT: Fashion Bulletin

In view of the growing recognition that pantsuits are "on the scene" to stay — at least for a while — many offices are now permitting their lady employees to wear these for business purposes.

While this office is firmly dedicated to femininity, nevertheless we stand ready to permit you to wear pantsuits to the office if you wish to do so.

We are confident that in doing so, we can count on your usual good taste, so that visitors will not mistake the office for a Greenwich Village coffee house.

Your attention is called to the attached order of

The office memorandum that gave official blessing to the wearing of pant outfits to work

Source: *New York Times*, November 30, 1970

Interestingly enough, the office memorandum shows the signer of the memorandum conferring with his secretary, already in a pants outfit. Obviously, the secretary's pressure had something to do with it. Just to show they were not against longer skirts, many women began to design and sew really long skirts for themselves, before fashion houses offered them, and the ankle length skirt began a comeback (Norris, 1971).

The fashion press, of course, wrote off the fate of the midi as simply an expression of a completely new trend among women to buy what they pleased. A study of available history, however, indicates quite the opposite: that fashion has probably never been something forced on the women. The author became aware of this many years ago when he was asked by the buyer for a mail order house to develop a means of predicting the relative demand within a line for which the cataloguing was complete, but not yet issued. The buyer admitted that he was unable to determine which of the styles he was promoting really would sell well.

Table 13-2.   Sales Record, Relative to the Average Item, of Misses Dresses Given Feature Catalog Treatment, 21 Seasons for Which Data is Available, a Major Mail Order Catalog House, 1937-1967

| Kind of Feature Treatment Given* | Total Number of Items | Below Average Item Sales | | Above Average Item Sales | |
|---|---|---|---|---|---|
| | | No. | Range as a % of Average | No. | Range as a % of Average |
| Front cover | 4 | 4 | 35-53 | -- | -- |
| Only item on page Inside front cover | | | | | |
| left-hand page | 4 | 3 | 27-81 | 1 | 175 |
| right-hand page | 2 | 1 | 63 | 1 | 224 |
| Other locations | 11 | 2 | 17,83 | 9 | 132-450 |
| Only two items to a page | 20 | 12 | 13-79 | 8 | 126-637 |
| Layout emphasis | 55 | 41 | 10-90 | 14 | 102-408 |

*"Featuring" is defined as giving more attention value to the presentation of a style, as compared with the presentation of the remaining styles listed. Normal treatment of the other items consists of giving equal treatment on a page to from 3 to 5 items. Feature treatment to a presentation can take one of 4 forms:

1.  Use as the cover illustration
2.  Giving a full page over to a single style
3.  Giving a full page to only two styles
4.  Giving more space and a preferred position to one of the several styles on a page

Recently, the author has been analyzing a series of data from another mail order house and has found the rather interesting relationship between promotional pressure and actual sales shown in Table 13-2. (Mail order house data is used because this seems to be the only type of retail organization which keeps accurate data on consumer demand.) It should be noted that the styles analyzed for Table 13-2 were all within the limits of the currently acceptable in the fashion world. If sales were the result of promotional pressure, the featured items should have been the best sellers. As Table 13-2 shows, this was not the case. Even though the company's styles were their own, the great majority of the styles that received the greatest promotion did much worse than those which were not so promoted. This could be interpreted, of course, as meaning that the women were perverse, that they decided to buy something other than what was promoted. If such were the case, however, we would not have the rather dramatic exceptions that this table shows—in a couple of seasons, the most popular of all styles were those being heavily promoted. The explanation probably lies elsewhere —that the fashion buyer's knowledge of industry trends tends to bias his estimate away from the tastes of his customers, and they buy what they want, not what someone else thinks they should want.

There are other observable instances in which fashion promotion has not succeeded in selling the customer. The automobile industry, for example, fell into such hard times with Detroit's promotion of over-stuffed automobile sizes in the late 1950s that only a crash program to build compacts for the 1960 season was able to rescue the industry from even heavier inroads by small foreign cars.

We need not, however, rest our argument on instances in which promotion is a factor. If promotion really were a factor, it would then be true that fashion would be found only in the cases of offerings for which some form of concentrated commercial promotion of styles would influence acceptance. Such is not the case with the home building field, or other forms of architecture. Yet there are obvious fashion waves in the type of house design that sells best in a given period. During the fifties and early sixties, it was the ranch house—the one-story design— which occupied most of the market. Earlier it had been the Cape Cod colonial. During the 1970s the false Mansard roof became the popular style. Yet there is probably no field in which the seller is more sensitive to the trends of the market than in the production of houses for speculative construction, and none in which the commercial promotion of design is less prominent.

Nor can we explain the fluctuating popularity of various kinds of religious ideas and religious enthusiasms by commercial promotion, because for the most part none is involved.

Obviously then, fashion arises from some form of internal drive. Most of the garment industry itself is willing to agree with this fact, but still holds doggedly to the belief that fashion arises from purely whimsical causes. As a result the industry has shown little interest in backing any kind of systematic study of trends.

### Is Fashion a Whimsical Phenomenon and Completely Unpredictable, or Can the Trend be Traced and Predicted?

Just as deeply imbedded as the myth that fashion is created, is the myth that fashion is something that is wholly unpredictable and only can be arrived at intuitively. This is the general feeling among most experts in the area. It feeds their ego, of course, but it happens to be quite wrong as shown by a number of proprietary studies that proved the validity of at least short-run predictions. The author, among others, was able to devise such a prediction system for a mail order company, as early as the 1940s, and others have had somewhat similar results with somewhat similar problems. Probably an outstanding example of prediction ahead of the market was made by a dominant maker of home permanents. During the 1950s the research department of this firm periodically conducted random telephone surveys of women around the U.S.A., asking one key question, "How are you going to have your hair done the next time you go to the beauty parlor?" At that time, the highly curled coiffure was the dominant fashion. However, toward the end of this period, this survey revealed a developing trend toward much more casual styles, a trend which had not yet manifested itself in sales. As a result, the firm developed a number of products suited to this trend and was able to maintain their own company's volume of business, and thus shift the burden of the downtrend in sales of their standard product to competitors.

Much earlier, the Opinion Research Corporation had run a number of studies of fashion acceptance in the fields of rugs, shoes, and popular phonograph records. As early as the 1930s, they had demonstrated that it was possible to predict the relative popularity of a rug design before it got beyond the designer's sketch stage. Later, according to those in charge of the research, they had similar success with the prediction of acceptance of men's shoe styles. Finally, they found that by a rather imaginative approach to juke box operations, they were able to predict whether or not a new record would do well and also whether this record would have a slow steady growth and a solid market for a considerable period ahead, or whether it would have a very fast growth and die out rapidly as a fad.

Among the unpublished studies is a master's thesis by Marvin Oakes, on the shoe sales of a mail order firm over a six-year period. In shoes, we have an excellent means of measuring fashion in that most of the basic styles tend to be carried over from year to year and it is the relative sales that change and not just the offerings themselves. As Figure 13-3 shows, these data reveal a very definite progression over this six-year period, from one style trend to quite the opposite. The change is far from being whimsical. Unfortunately, there are few such publishable studies based on actual sales data.

If, as the discussion above indicates, fashion is neither created by forces external to the groups and individuals involved, nor a whimsical matter, then it must be based on natural forces and be predictable within useable limits. Having cleared away the myths, we are in a position to see what behavioral knowledge can contribute.

## The Nature of Fashion

Observation indicates that fashion can be defined in terms of the following:

1.   It is one form of product life cycle but with a difference. It is a product life cycle in which the life goes through many reincarnations or repetitions.
2.   Fashion involves, primarily, the superficial and observable aspect of a product—the aspects that might be involved in people's judgments of those owning the product. It has social visibility.
3.   Fluctuations are from one extreme to another.
4.   The fluctuations are normally complex, involving clusters of traits, rather than one single attribute of the basic product.

Fashion is clearly one kind of product life cycle. Acceptance of the fashion starts with a few innovators and early adopters and diffuses through the population in an expanding acceptance pattern exactly the same as any other product with some degree of learning content. It reaches a plateau of maturity of saturation and then declines slowly, giving way to a competing fashion.

The competing fashion itself is always one that is clearly opposite in many respects to the one it replaces. In most respects, it satisfies an opposite desire-set from those fulfilled by the basic characteristics of the previous fashion. Fashion changes, however, do not affect the basic core function of the products involved. The new fashion in garments still protects the wearer from the elements and remains within the limits of what is considered socially acceptable in exposure of the

**Figure 13-3.  An Example of the Continuity of Fashion Trends:
Percentage Distribution of Shoe Sales by Selected
Style Traits, A Major Mail Order Company, Spring-
Summer Seasons, 1964-69**

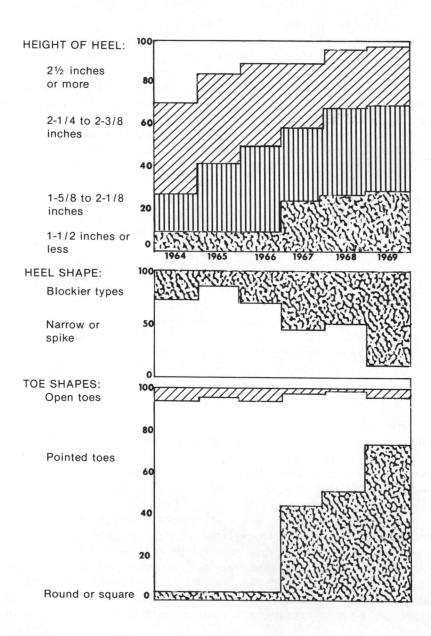

human body. The newly popular style of automobile still furnishes the same basic transportation as did the old one, within the limits of performance normally needed by the individuals buying them. The newly popular style of house normally has the same capacity for individuals and quite often has essentially the same internal layout as the previously fashionable style.

What changes are made are in characteristics which are highly observable to outsiders and may form a basis for judging the taste of the individual concerned. One corollary is that products which are not observable enough to influence the opinions of others in reference groups are not very likely to be subject to style or fashion fluctuations.

The fluctuations themselves involve more than a single characteristic. When the dress styles change they do not just fluctuate from a hem line above the knees, for example, to one below the ankles. The entire silhouette changes. The micro-mini, and its many predecessors over the centuries, did not just lengthen to become the succeeding longer skirts. (Indeed, it may have been a lack of sufficient change in the related elements that was responsible for the sorry record of the unmourned midi. Judging by later developments, women obviously desired longer dress lengths, but the specific designs introduced were obviously considered quite distasteful.) The micro-mini, for example, involved a dress with little or no waist line accent and gave minimum prominence to the development of a woman's upper abdomen. The micro-mini, in other words, was a style which accented the youthfulness of those who had a youthful, immature, leggy figure. Succeeding styles emphasized the attractive characteristics of the mature woman.

To understand fashion, then, we must have some kind of theory based on what we know about human behavior in general, and which explains all of these elements. Only such a theory can furnish a basis for useful analysis of fashion trends and for prediction of where any given trend is likely to end up, and what general kind of style will replace it.

## A Theory of Fashion Useable for Prediction of Future Trends

Fashion is clearly a socially and psychologically based phenomenon even though it is not externally created. A useable theory of fashion, therefore, should be constructable on the basis of what we know about human psychology and human social behavior. Such, indeed, is the case and we need only a few of the extremely well-established concepts from psychology and social psychology already discussed to understand this phenomenon. These concepts are:

**Figure 13-4. The Automobile Design Puzzle: How to Get As Much of What the Driver Wants in a Single Design**

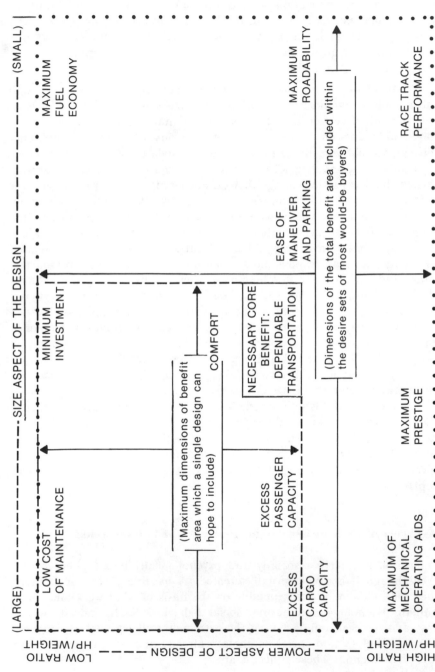

1. *The principle of design compromise:* All products must be designed to satisfy simultaneously a wide variety of desires at one and the same time, and the satisfaction of some of these desires is physically incompatible with the satisfaction of other desires within the limits of what can be obtained by any single design. The individual and the group must, therefore, compromise on what they will accept, sacrificing some attributes in order to get other attributes.

---

### Design Compromise and the Desire-set

Nearly all purchase situations involve the search for a complete bundle of satisfactions designated as a *desire-set*. The consumer must satisfy a large number of desires in every purchase he obtains, or his resources of time and spending power would not be able to get a very large portion of his desires fulfilled in any degree at all. Generally speaking, all of the various attributes he desires in an offering are individually obtainable, but it is equally true that all of them are not usually simultaneously attainable in a single offering. Moreover the specific desire-sets of one consumer for a specific type of physical product will vary from the desire-sets of other consumers and the degree of personal emphasis on each of the attributes will differ from one purchaser or one group to another.

The compromise he chooses will depend on his own hierarchy of needs at the moment. If economy is the most salient of those needs, economy characteristics will be the hallmark of the design he chooses. If he seeks first of all a car that has status symbolism—one that proclaims to the world that he has "arrived," then he will sacrifice the economy aspect of his desire-set, and with it a great many of the virtues of the small maneuverable automobile unless he opts for an expensive sports model.

It is easy to analyze almost any important purchase in the same terms. In clothing, for example, a woman may desire a style which shows off her figure to best advantage and also hope for a great deal of comfort at the same time, along with other attributes important to her personally. But figure-conforming styles and comfort do not go together and she must make a choice. In buying a house, the purchaser must make compromises between costs, quality of neighborhood, style to suit his tastes, and style which will easily be resold, among other items.

This is most easily seen in the case of a mechanism like the automobile. The complete desire-set would include some degree of satisfaction of all of the following items:

1. Dependable service, free operation, and an almost universal network of service facilities available at a moment's notice
2. The greatest possible ease of maneuver and handling
3. High cargo capacity and substantial passenger capacity whenever needed
4. Compactness of external size to make parking extremely easy
5. Extreme frugality of fuel consumption
6. Highly responsive performance
7. Quick acceleration
8. Low initial cost as well as low maintenance cost
9. A smooth luxurious ride, rugged durability under almost any degree of maintenance or lack of it
10. Attractive styling

Even the most superficial inspection of this list indicates the impossibility of getting all of these attributes to the fullest degree in a single offering. The buyer cannot get high acceleration and fuel economy at the same time. He must sacrifice some passenger and cargo capacity if he is going to get a really compact small vehicle, especially one with ease of maneuver and handling. He cannot get a highly unique personal vehicle and at the same time expect to get one with the mass service network of a major selling car. He cannot expect the highest degree of durability and dependability and low cost at the same time. He cannot have both easy parking and a large car. In short, the customer must compromise, choosing a design meeting some of his desires more adequately than others. Figure 13-4 illustrates some of the designer's problems.

2.  The concept of the *hierarchy of needs:* all of the desires of an individual are in some form of hierarchy and this is true of the desires within a given desire-set. Some are at the moment more highly desirable than others, primarily when the item most desired is least well satisfied.

3.  The principle of *priority of satisfaction of the topmost* need in the hierarchy and the principles of *stimulus variability* and *adaptation.* Buyers will tend to seek out designs which contain attributes capable of satisfying the desires least well satisfied at the moment. Once such a design is found, the novelty of the design itself becomes a source of stimulus variability, but after a period of time, it no longer serves this purpose and by the principle of adaptation it becomes no longer interesting.

4.  *The principle of satiation* and subsequent restructuring of the hierarchy of needs: the attributes sacrificed previously in order to obtain this new design now begin to reach the top of the desire hierarchy and a search for a new design begins. The new design will, of course, tend, by this very fact to have attributes quite opposite from those which it replaces.

Thus, we can explain the individual side of fashion adoption by the principles of design compromise and the multiplicity of desires within a desire-set, by the principle of hierarchy of needs, and by the principles of stimulus variation, satiation, and adaptation.

But this explanation by itself does not explain why one style becomes the socially acceptable item in a period and gains widespread use, even by those to whom the style is not well-fitted objectively. To explain fashion, we must also explain why individuals will adopt a fashion ill-suited to their needs. We must explain the phenomenon of *over-adoption.*

*Over-adoption* is a phenomenon of the growth and even the early maturity period of nearly all new product diffusion. Early adopters and innovators pick up a product or design because it is well suited to their needs. But those late in the adoption cycle often choose it simply because it is the accepted thing to use or do, even when ill-suited to their needs. Early students of agricultural adoption cycles, for example, found that farmers with operations not suited to large scale equipment were, nevertheless, purchasing such equipment because it was in style. Those who watched the miniskirt fashion of clothes could not help but remember the large numbers of girls and women whose high bust development, or whose ill-shaped legs, lent themselves poorly to the style. One of the longer dress styles that came in later, the "Prairie" style, was obviously ill-suited to the youngsters, and yet became popular in spite of this fact because of its similarity to their mothers' dresses.

Firms whose need for calculation was far below the ravenous appetite of a computer often spent more for computer rental than a simple clerical operation would have cost them.

Clearly, we must turn to social psychology and sociology for an explanation of the product life cycle and over-adoption aspects of fashion. Again we can explain these aspects of fashion by a few principles already discussed concerning diffusion of innovations and the motives for adopting products:

1.  Since *all fashions involve some learning* of the ability of the product to satisfy the desires and some risk that it may not, initial adoption will be by a few innovators and adopters. They will also be few, because such adoption must be by those freest from the pressures of the group to conform, *those at the very top of the pecking order* in society.

2.  As these people prove by their trial and adoption that the product is acceptable and does meet these needs, they will be imitated by those next to them in this pecking order and thus also a little freer than those below to act in ways that are not in full conformance with those in their groups. Thus, by diffusion, the initial adoption will be, as in all product life cycles, an expanding geometric progression for a period of time, until the halfway point is reached. After this point there will be a decline in the rate of growth due to a lack of adequate population to support a geometric progression.

3.  Later adopters will be responding to *the need to conform to the group* and not to their own desires or needs. Among those responding, now that the product has become that which is "good taste," will be those to whom the product is very ill-suited. Thus, by the time the fashion reaches maturity, those who are adopting the fashion are doing it out of pure conformity motives plus, perhaps, some need for stimulus variation which any new fashion can furnish.

4.  By the time the fashion reaches full maturity and has become the reigning taste, those who adopted early will have fully satisfied their need for stimulus variation and the item will no longer satisfy this attribute of the desire-set. They will, therefore, be seeking something else that is new. The acceptable something else that is new will be a design which satisfies items in their desire-set which were least well satisfied by the previous design. Thus the innovators and early adopters will begin to set in motion a new fashion cycle, buttressed by the need, of those to whom the old fashion was not well suited, to gain something they urgently desire.

## The Classic: The Style That Is Always Acceptable

One other aspect of fashion is not fully explained by any of the above. This is the fashion that never goes out of fashion: *the classic*. In every area in which fashion reigns, such classics will be found—designs which will always have a solid, predictable market of considerable size and which change little or none at all. In garments, we find such classics in the tailored suit with a knee length skirt and now also, apparently, in the pants suit. In colors, which are also subject to fashion cycles of their own, we find these in the more muted shades. In automobiles, for example, a car that is somewhat slightly off-white is always attractive to a considerable segment of the market, and the European automobile makers have proved that certain types of body designs need not be changed over very long periods. In general, these seem to be designs very similar to those of the postwar Studebaker, powered adequately, but modestly, relative to the extremes of the market.

Observation thus indicates that the classic is a mid-point design. It does not reach flamboyantly to either side of the extreme and thus gives in full measure all of the basic core functions of the product and some measure of the other functions. Clearly it does not satisfy the need for stimulus variation in and of itself except, perhaps, in some minor detail such as fabric and textile pattern in a garment.

The market for classics is generally rather predictable. It is clearly best-suited to a certain type of personality, and a large portion of these people are those who have characteristics very similar to those innovators and early adopters. That is, they are people who do not feel extreme social pressure to conform exactly to the extremes of the newest in styles. They are also obviously people who value very highly the core functions of a product and see little need to be different in an exhibitionist manner.

Generally speaking, sellers are aware of what constitutes classics in their field, particularly since such classics are often consistently high volume sellers. In women's shoes, for example, the standard unadorned pump is always in style and always dressy and always also among the high-selling styles.

Generally speaking, classics themselves are seldom the reigning style but frequently a style may come in and establish itself as a classic. Such, as already noted, was the case of the pants suit which has come to be virtually a necessity in most women's wardrobes, although not constituting the bulk of the items in their closets. A classic should be identifiable in its early adoption period by the very fact that its principal value is that it has a high degree of relatively quiet attractiveness and is extremely functional in its performance.

## Relationship of Fashion to the Product Category Cycle

Although fashion itself is a form of product life cycle, it is also clearly a type of graft upon the life cycle of the basic product category itself. Indeed, there is some reason to speculate that in the case of many products, fashion occupies a limited place in the life cycle of the product category. The growth of sales of European type cars on the American market, for example, would indicate that the tendency is toward emphasis on the functional aspect of a product as it moves well along in maturity. And the value of styling and fashion declines much earlier than the decline of the product itself.

## Fashion and Profit

One last note concerning fashion: although fashion itself is hardly creatable, it is obviously something whose recognition can be a major source of profit. The fact that the designers cannot tell women what they are going to wear does not mean that designers should stop trying to find designs that will meet new needs for stimulus variation and new unsatisfied desire-sets. In fact it is the ability of the designer to sense just these things that makes him successful. Even when operating within the limits of the essentially classic, the designer has a lot of elbow room for his creativity. One of the most famous and earliest of really capable American designers, Norell, created designs that are always essentially acceptable still, and are always recognizable classics. Nevertheless, each new design was a fresh success.

On a much simpler level, one of the major sellers of cake mixes operates on the assumption that the line consists of two basic classical elements, chocolate cake and white cake, and that all of the other flavors and types are sure to go through fashion cycles of one sort or another. The result is that the firm constantly introduces a handful of new flavors on the market, and withdraws the old as their popularity declines, only to introduce them five or six years later, when they can again satisfy a new need for stimulus variability. Thus they are able to keep a relatively small inventory of types at any one time, all of them high-volume sellers. Whether or not this is, technically, the manipulation of fashion may be questioned. Social visibility is not involved, but the seller can have some leverage on adoption. But it follows many of the same rules.

Ignoring the fashion trends can be just as disastrous as insight into the trend can be profitable. One example, out of many, was the disastrous design mistakes of the Chrysler Corporation in 1950 when it ignored the growing popularity of the "long, low, and sleek," and again in 1962, when its Dodge and Plymouth lines came out in highly sculptured body shapes just when the clean-lined models were getting the market. The garment field, of course, is littered with bad guesses every year. One observer claims that 85 percent of women's dresses eventually sell for less than their initially ticketed price. This sounds exaggerated, but the number is clearly substantial.

Fashions are often confused with fads, and fads are sometimes defined as a short-lived fashion. Observation of the general course of events of a fad, however, shows that it is a quite different kind of phenomenon from fashion—it is an empty product.

### Fad: The No-learning Empty Product

Fashions come in slowly over a period of time just as any other product with a considerable degree of learning content. Fads enter a period of rapid growth very shortly after their introduction. Once established, a fashion reigns supreme for a very considerable period, then slowly fades out. But the fad, once it reaches the peak of its growth, suddenly loses all value altogether, except in cases where sales decline to a point where they come from some small segment of the market which finds the offering to have substantive value in meeting a specific desire-set.

Fashions reign because they satisfy very well the kind of desire-set not previously well satisfied. A fad comes in with no predictable substance in content, for most of those who adopt it. Its only value is that it appeals to stimulus variability. The result is that while fashion trends may be predictable, the content of a fad does not seem to be. Fashions have an evolutionary history that is related to the preceding fashion. Fads really do go off in directions that are highly unpredictable and seem to be more related to the general mood of the population at the moment than to the nature of any preceding product.

Fashions rise slowly in popularity because they do contain some degree of learning content and they tend to persist partly because they become part of the group norms. Nobody, however, brings any pressure on anyone to adopt a fad, except possibly the general feeling, of very limited extent, of a desire to conform to what everyone else is doing within the face-to-face groups to which the individual belongs. Although it is impossible, on the basis of anything we know, to predict the content of any future fad, it is possible to predict the content of an incoming fashion.

For both fads and fashions, however, it is possible to identify the item once popularity begins to grow. Careful analysis of any fad will show that it satisfies no need, beyond that of stimulus variability, which is not already satisfied by some other product available to the buyers. The only added value is that of novelty.

The quite different lengths of the life cycles of fashion and fads, and the very different market growth speeds, require quite different strategies of market entry and exit. It is possible, and indeed it is usual, for competitors in the fashion field to copy the early introducers long after the fashion is well on its way to growth. It is still possible to profit from the introduction.

In the case of fads, however, those who get in late nearly always lose their shirts. To profit from a fad, one must get in very early in the period of rapid growth. The exit must also be timed somewhat *prior* to the very peak of success. Otherwise the seller is almost certainly going to be left with extremely huge inventories and canceled orders.

These differences are far from being merely academic. In certain industries, for example, both fashions and fads are common. One such is that of popular music records. Some popular records take hold relatively slowly, but remain popular for years. Others reach an early peak and are dead within months. Such is also true in food fields such as snacks. It is, therefore, extremely important that the nature of the demand for the product be assessed in advance, if possible, and certainly very early in the period of its introduction.

It is quite possible to make a great deal of money from a fashion. It is equally possible to profit greatly from a fad, provided all the elements of correct procedure are observed and the timing is precise.

In the case of a fad, for example, there should be no substantial investment in special production facilities and, if possible, production itself should be contracted out in order to minimize the total investment involved. Once the fad has caught on, promotion should be stripped to the minimum, but distribution should be made as intense as possible. If the latter is not done, competitors will take over any vacant spots in the distribution chain and may even garner most of the profit. All resources in the promotion of something identifiable as a fad should be committed to the very minimum.

Quite often something that is actually a fad will be written off as a failure. Such was the case of a potato chip product called Schmoos, introduced in the special shape and name purely to get something different to appeal to the market. Test markets showed a life cycle of about six weeks, but during this six weeks the sale was reasonably satisfactory. Had the product been identified as something whose only appeal was novelty—which was, of course, the case—it might have been possible to plan this introduction together with a whole series of later introductions of similar characteristics, and build a shifting market of some profitability.

## Summary

1.   Fashion is a social phenomenon as well as a form of moderately high learning product life cycle.

2.   Fashion fluctuations are not limited to the garment industry, but can be observed in many areas of product acceptance, including automobiles, architecture, business management practices, and religious ideas.

3.   Fashion is not the artificial creation of designers, but arises out of the drives of consumers themselves.

4.   Nor is fashion a whimsical, unpredictable, trendless phenomenon. Proprietary research, scattered over a variety of product categories, has proven successful at predicting shortrun trends and at least one piece of available research clearly reveals definite trends.

5.   Observation indicates that fashion can be defined as a product life cycle which tends to repeat itself in complex ways, fluctuating from one extreme to the opposite, affecting clusters of traits rather than single attributes of design, and involving primarily the socially visible aspects of the product.

6.   The generally observed character of fashion fluctuations can be explained by means of four basic principles: the necessity for design compromise, the hierarchy of needs, and priority of satisfaction of the least well satisfied in the hierarchy, adaptation and satiation, and the drive for stimulus variability.

7.   By themselves, these principles do not explain the phenomenon of over-adoption—the acceptance of the fashion by those for whom it has doubtful value. This is the social, or conformist, side of fashion.

8.   The social aspect of fashion is explainable by the fact that fashion is a moderately high learning introduction which is, as in all matters of new product acceptance, first adopted by the innovators at the top of the pecking order, who are relatively free from pressures to conform. Through them, it diffuses to successively lower layers in the

group hierarchy, until it is adopted by those on the lowest rungs, who are extremely conformist.

9.  No explanation of fashion is adequate which does not also explain the classic—the style which is never out of fashion.

10.  Observation indicates that all recognized classics are near-mid-point compromises which give a full measure of functional value at some sacrifice of excitement and attention value. They would thus tend to be the choice of the self-assured who feel little need for either.

11.  It appears probable that fashion, besides being a type of product life cycle in its own right, may be an aspect of the growth phase of some product life cycles, fading out of the scene as the category cycle reaches full maturity.

12.  Fashion can be an important source of profit when trends are correctly recognized and the designer's creative imagination works within the trend.

13.  Although fads are often confused with fashion, they represent two quite different types of product life cycles. The fashion cycle normally exhibits the slow initial rise of sales characteristic of a market development period. Fads start off with a rapid sales growth from the earliest period, then collapse at the moment of maturity—they are one clear type of the no-learning product.

14.  Because of the very rapid rise in sales and subsequent collapse of the market characterizing the fad life cycle, market entry must be very early in the cycle, or not attempted at all. Exit is best timed prior to the peak in sales to avoid large inventories of worthless merchandise. Distribution must be as intensive and extensive as possible from the very first, and commitment to specialized production facilities held to the very minimum.

## Chapter 13  Exercises

1.  The text makes a point that fashion is not just garments, and mentions architecture, automobiles, religious ideas, and management practices as examples. Can you mention any other areas of consumption in which there are obvious fashion fluctuations? What seem to be the nature of the extremes in each case?

2.  The author has included ideas as fashion phenomena. Do you perceive any evidence of this in the college culture?

3. The highest paid buyers in any merchandising operation are usually the fashion buyers, and for a very good reason: his mistakes can be very expensive. Last season's left over fashions have very little value. Yet the text shows that the judgment of these experts is not very good, at least not much better than the weatherman's forecasts. If fashion is as predictable as the author claims, why don't these experts discover the secret?

4. If you were in the position of one of these buyers, how might you go about discovering what is just beginning to be popular? (Note that at this stage, the majority of consumers would not be ready to accept the style—only early adopters.)

5. If you were in a business such as popular music recording, where successes may be either fad-like or fashion-like, how might you determine early in the cycle which you have, if either, before sales are enough to give a clue? (Note that if a record is actually a fad, immediate volume production and distribution are a must!)

6. Can you think of any kinds of product in which continuous rotation of new variants (color, flavor, sound, pattern, etc.) are the best way to stay on top of the market?

7. If stimulus variation is a key drive, why would there be a market for classics, as there provably is?

8. If you had to make a projection as of now, what would you say is the coming style trend in women's clothes? In men's? Why?
   In men's hair styles? In women's hair styles? Why?
   In automobiles?
   In _____ (choose your own area)?

# PART V.
# The Managerial Implications of
# Consumer Behavioral Tendencies

THE MANAGERIAL IMPLICATIONS of most of the individual concepts discussed in previous chapters have been noted. Part V looks, in addition, at the combined meaning of all behavioral tendencies for each major aspect of market planning.

The effect on product planning is naturally central, since the offering is the aspect around which the behavior of both consumer and seller are structured. Both business experience and behavioral knowledge agree that, except for the very limited case of commodities whose production is highly fragmented, the structure of competition can only be differentiated. Any attempt at direct competition with offerings which are truly identical is doomed to inevitable failure. Each seller must aim to serve those segments of the market for which his experience and skills best fit him, whether he be manufacturer or distributor. The distributor is, in fact, another kind of producer. In addition, both theory and experience indicate that the seller must always anticipate trends in taste and value perception, and plan ahead to adapt to them.

The effectiveness of the communications mix is limited by the selectivity of the audience, by audience perceptions of the source and its credibility, by the method of presentation, and by the choice of media. The potential productivity of promotional effort varies with the phases of the product life cycle.

Finally, our knowledge of human behavior requires us to extend the definition of price to every negative aspect of the offering, not just the monetary side. The seller's use of price is severely limited by consumer perception patterns, and the decision is far more complex than is generally recognized in economic discussion, always involving product or merchandise mix issues, and multiple decisions in the channel of distribution.

# Adapting Product and Distribution Assortments to Consumer Behavior

## BASIC PREREQUISITES FOR SUCCESSFUL PRODUCT COMPETITION

Being First to Get Attention
Product Differentiation
Keeping Up with the Product Life Cycle
The Limited Area of Direct Competition

## INDIVIDUAL DIFFERENCES AND THE BASIS FOR DIFFERENTIATION

## THE MANY AVENUES TO DIFFERENTIATION

Product Positioning
Functional Performance
Physical Styling with Psychological Connotations
Associated Services
Implied Guarantee of Source
The Context of Assortment

## DIFFERENTIATION AS ASSORTMENT

Products As Assortments, Assortments As Products

## ASSORTMENT DESIGNING AS A LEARNED SKILL, CREATING SPECIALIZATION

## ASSORTMENT BIAS AND DISTRIBUTION CHANNEL RELATIONSHIPS

## THE NEED FOR SELLERS TO CLUSTER TO MATCH DESIRE SETS

## PRODUCT LIFE CYCLE AND PRODUCT DESIGN REQUIREMENTS

## PRODUCT LIFE CYCLE AND DISTRIBUTION REQUIREMENTS

WHAT IS THE SECRET of successful market entry? Consider the following examples.

The toothpaste market is obviously a very attractive market, yielding very large margins above product costs and creating a sizeable sales volume for the successful seller. As a result, companies in the drug and toiletries field are continuously vying for a share of the market and new entrants frequently come in, even though the market itself is a mature one. One major entrant within the last generation was Procter & Gamble. Their first effort, Gleem toothpaste, was a substantial success. Functionally, Gleem did nothing that other toothpastes did not do, but P & G managed to position Gleem as a favorite of those who felt guilty about their tooth cleansing habits, with the claim that Gleem was for "those that could not brush after every meal." This covers, of course, nearly 100 percent of the population, but not all of the population feel guilty about this fact. Substantial numbers do, however, and by offering some solace for this guilt, P & G gained a substantial market niche. Later P & G developed another toothpaste, one that built on recent dental research to add a quite objective value that other toothpastes were not yet able to claim—addition of a fluoride compound that, through careful clinical tests, had established itself as an effective deterrent to dental caries among children. Building on the clinical tests, they were able to get the American Dental Association's seal of approval and then launch Crest as the toothpaste which guaranteed fewer cavities. This also was a success, and did not completely displace their own Gleem brand, but took substantial shares from various brands then on the market.

Jealous of the Crest success, a drug company, Bristol-Myers, decided to enter the same market. They also added the fluoride compound to the toothpaste Fact, and also went through clinical trials necessary for American Dental Association approval, acquiring the coveted seal. After spending $5,000,000 trying to get a foothold in the market, however, they withdrew their Fact without making enough of a market impact to be noticed.

In a hitherto unpublished local study of supermarket shopping in a middle-class-suburban area, Bell and Wasson (1971) found that, for four of the five stores in the area, shoppers had relatively definite expectations as to merchandise, quality, and prices, and that no two store managements had quite the same image. The fifth store, however, could not be characterized either by type of customer or by special perceived qualities of value. It obviously had a much lower consumer traffic, on the basis of the count taken during the short period of the survey, and the purchases within the store averaged less than the averages for the other four stores. Within a year, this fifth store closed, along with many other units of the same chain in the same metropolitan area.

When the foreign car invasion began to assume threatening proportions in the late 1950s, all of the automobile manufacturers went into crash programs to develop "compact" cars—cars that were roughly fifteen feet in overall length and much more economical of gasoline in the current Detroit models. Ford's Falcon captured the largest initial share of the market but mostly at the expense of Ford's own large cars. General Motors brought out a unique kind of car for the American scene, a rear engine, rear wheel drive model—the Corvair—which, after an initial stumble, caught on as the "sporty" Monza model by the inclusion of bucket seats. The Corvair's advantage for General Motors was that the market did not seem to come out of the general market share of the larger General Motors cars but captured pieces of markets from various segments, including probably some of the foreign makes. The result was not viewed with a great deal of joy by the Ford Motor Company. Jealous of the ability of General Motors to capture a significant market for their new small car without losing out on their other larger models, Ford directed the research, which it had been pursuing for some six years previously, toward finding a small-car design which would get the Corvair market. The research revealed that a long hood and a short rear deck, with cutout fenders, spelled "sports" to a great many people. The designers then came up with the Mustang, which they and the Ford management perceived as a direct competitor of Corvair.

Fortunately, for Ford, this did not prove to be the case. The Mustang was an instant success, twice as successful as the research had predicted, and did succeed in doing what the Falcon did not. It captured a segment of the market without cannibalizing Ford's own share with its other cars. However, it did not get much of the Corvair market. Like the original Corvair, it drew its market from so many segments of other makes that Ford was not clear what aspect of competition was being hurt.

Now it was General Motors' turn to be jealous because the Corvair had never sold that well, and General Motors set about to design a

Chevrolet equivalent of the Mustang. When the General Motors Camaro was introduced, it was just that—a General Motors Mustang with lines extremely similar to that of the Ford entry. Although the Camaro obtained enough market share to justify some sales effort, particularly after the dropping of the Corvair models from the line because of adverse publicity, the model never proved to have more than a fraction of the market that the Mustang had attracted.

In another series of design moves, General Motors started early in the fifties to concentrate on larger and larger models and more and more powerful engines in these models. At the time in which this move was initiated, this proved a very popular move, and GM strengthened its market position. However, about that same time, the foreign small-car invasion also began to be serious. The total sales of foreign cars in 1954 were enough to start Ford on a course in investigating small-car design, a direction which GM neglected. The first results of this research were the Falcon and the Mustang, and later the Maverick and the Pinto, all of which, in their own ways, were successes, although the Falcon was a limited one as noted. When the 1960s compact models hit the market, Chrysler had its entry also, the Valiant, and later added an equivalent of the Valiant, the Dodge Dart, to its line.

Meanwhile, the foreign car market share did little more than pause for breath at the time of the Detroit compact entries, and the well-distributed makes continued to strengthen their hold on the market through the late sixties and early seventies. By the early 1970s, some of the relatively popular models of the foreign cars were among the luxury and semiluxury makes. Mercedes-Benz had acquired a substantial share of the market and Volvo and Audi had begun to eat into the type of trade usually dominated by Pontiac and Oldsmobile. As an answer to some of Ford's smaller entries, GM had early introduced a model called the Chevy II, which was almost line for line the same as Falcon, and then had continued a luxury model designation of this, the Nova, as the "small" car of the Chevy line. By 1973 model year, GM had extended the Buick, Oldsmobile and Pontiac class under different labels, using essentially the same body shell as the Nova. In the case of all of the so-called small models, however, a large portion of the mix being offered to the market was with heavy V-8 engines and the size of the cars was, to the foreign car prospect at least, no longer small in any sense except for lack of internal space. Starting in the middle sixties, GM's share of the market began to erode slightly. Typical of the decline phase of produce life cycles, the large car erosion was not precipitous until the fall of 1973 and the winter of 1974, when the Arab oil boycott suddenly turned people's attentions to the extreme fuel thirst of the large cars. For a few months, the market for large cars almost completely dried up.

Chrysler's policy of continuing the Valiant and Dart line had built up close to 50 percent of Chrysler's share, so that Chrysler was not hurt nearly as badly as General Motors, and Ford was also less badly hit because of the extent and number of small lines it had. General Motors, in the meantime, had developed a car somewhat more powerful than the economy models of Japan and Europe, but in the same general size range, the Vega. Unfortunately, the Vega production volume was not adequate to the demand in this period and the engine plants of General Motors were so heavily committed to V-8's that the more economical six-cylinder option on their "small" large cars was not able to take up the slack. GM had been getting a larger and larger share of what had started to become a smaller and smaller market.

Much earlier in the period of the fifties, the Hoover vacuum cleaner had been in a similar position to GM. Hoover had come to dominate the upright vacuum cleaner market so thoroughly that other makes were almost completely in the shade. However, home furnishing trends had changed the demand pattern for vacuum cleaners. Wall-to-wall carpeting had become fashionable and the so-called canister or tank cleaners, introduced by Lewyt and General Electric, had begun to be quite popular because of the flexibility of their off-the-floor cleaning attachments. Finally, Hoover's dominance of the market had become so absolute that it had most of the upright market but the market itself was declining. Much too late, the company woke up to the situation and developed their own canister, but their late introduction of the canister model never achieved the share of the canister market that their upright had obtained in the upright market. They introduced their models too late.

The above illustrates three of the imperatives of profitable marketing made necessary by the pattern of consumer reaction to market offerings of various kinds: (1) the need for substantial differentiation of the offering—of the benefit assortment implicit in all kinds of offerings, (2) the importance of being first, and (3) the importance of the need to adjust to changing consumer preferences with the passage of time in the product life cycle.

## Satiation, Selective Attention and the Inevitability of Differentiated Competition

The central focus of every exchange transaction is the product or, more accurately, the total offering, which includes many values outside the physical product, including the distribution values, the services inherent in the chain of sales. Success or failure of any offering initiative depends on the product design of the offering, on effective communication of the perceivable values offered, and timing. No exchange initiator can succeed without the correct offering. No trick of communications techniques will help a badly designed product. However, the most effectively designed offering may also fail because the values are not communicated effectively and the introduction of the design must be timed right in relation to competitive entries and to the product life cycle. The key to perceivable consumer value is a substantial perceived difference in that value. Satiation, perceived consumer risk, and selective attention rule out the possibility of direct head-to-head competition in the traditional economic sense.

Bristol-Myers' introduction of Fact toothpaste, Ford's introduction of the Mustang, and General Motors' introduction of the Camaro were all predicated on the assumption that competition was direct and head on—an attitude sanctioned by much of economic and legal theory, but quite contrary to the facts of human behavior. Each of these was an attempt to compete directly by introducing a new entry which the seller perceived as closely similar to one already established on the market. Two of them—Fact toothpaste and the General Motors Camaro—were short of their market target because the designers came too close to their design target.

Ford, fortunately for the firm, did not design a car that consumers perceived as a Ford Corvair, but as something quite different and, thus, a design error led to a major success. Research on early customers for the Mustang showed that the appeal of this make was largely to the family man who could not afford the luxury of two cars and who still yearned for something with some semblance to sports car image that could take care of the transportation of a young small family. Although the Mustang doubtless drew some consumers who had been buying VW's and other small foreign economy sedans, a large portion of the market seems to have come out of the total market for larger cars and for used cars (especially since the initial price was low relative to the market). The market share was made up of consumers who wanted something that looked sporty and was economical in operation. The Mustang was a car that would enable them to compromise the inner desire for a sports car and the practical need for a family vehicle.

GM's Corvair, on the other hand, had offered the first automobile on the American market with design connotations that appealed to many as a personal car in the European image. The rear engine conformation suggested the foreign sporty image, to people who were not really seeking a sports car. The size was small enough to appeal to them as a highly personal vehicle which offered modest economy of operation as well as economy of size. General Motors' Camaro, on the other hand, offered nothing new to those who were looking for a Mustang desire-set except the GM label, which some few customers would prefer to a Ford label. This was the market GM got.

Bristol-Myers' Fact was offering nothing that P & G's Crest did not already offer. It was a fluoride toothpaste just as the established brand Crest was. It had the American Dental Association seal of approval, which the P & G's Crest had. The only difference was a different label and a different manufacturer which, in the case of toothpaste, was not a sought-for benefit.

The error of the food chain which failed to attract much patronage was not an unusual one. The firm did not have any particular market segment in view at all. Instead, it seemed to consider the merchant's job to be one of simply promoting store traffic by featuring a few cut prices, without paying attention to the desire-sets of any major market segment that the promotion might attract. When no substantial segment found an offering assortment close to its desire-sets, promotional effort lost all of its attention value and repeat consumer traffic did not materialize.

All of these examples underline a major aspect of consumer behavior, the consumer's search for satisfaction of a bundle of benefits in a single purchase. They also underline the differences in the desire-sets of different groups of consumers and in the values assigned to the items included in their individual bundles. Once they find a value close to the desire-set, they stop their efforts at further search—they are satiated. As a result of satiation they tune out any further efforts to gain their attention for a similar package.


### Direct Competition Versus Differentiated Competition

The difference in desire-sets and the principle of satiation requires that competitive efforts be structured around differentiated offerings for any mass produced item. Direct competition in the traditional sense is not possible for any mass produced item for which all of those in any one market segment with a single similar desire-set can be satisfied by the output by a single producer.

Direct competition of identical or closely similar offerings can succeed when and only when all of those seeking to satisfy the same desire-set can not have their needs filled by one or two producers—that is, when production is fragmented relative to any one market segment. In such a case, every offering can appeal to the same desire-set, and only in this case. Such, in fact, was long the situation with agricultural commodities, although with large scale farming operations of modern times, this is becoming much less so.

When production capacity is not highly fragmented in relation to the needs of any one market segment, the first producer perceived as filling the desire-set of a given segment will get its business. All later entries perceived as identical or similar will get no attention, and will not even be perceived as identical because not yet tested and familiar—they represent a purchase risk and, therefore, a lesser value. The difference of entry or timing differentiates their value negatively. New entries must, therefore, find some positive means of differentiation. They must offer perceivable and substantial added values to market segments who do not as yet find any currently available offering as adequate to their desire-set. These market segments will be composed of the fringes of the offerings of several producers as a rule, and will try a new entry only if the differentiation is perceived by them as quite substantial, due to the j.n.d. principle. Such fringes exist because of the wide variation in desire-sets among consumers due to major individual differences of many sorts.

## Individual Differences, Design Compromises and Differentiated Competition

As indicated in earlier chapters, desire-sets are certain to vary from place to place within the market, from class to class, and from individual to individual, due to differences in tastes and also due to differences in degree of satiation of a particular desire element because of the competition between different product classes. A sailboat or prestige car may both very well satisfy the need for some form of status-seeking, for example. The man who has a sailboat is, therefore, unlikely to be searching for the status element in a prestige car, although he may have other reasons for buying such a vehicle.

Thus, many of the benefit attributes which draw particular market segments to a product will be of little interest to other market segments, who nevertheless buy the product for some few of the benefits in it. They may very well be seeking some other kinds of attributes instead. As a result, every seller's market segments, even some of the more loyal, contain large numbers of people who can be attracted by a substantially different design requiring different kinds of design compromises from them.

The principle of design compromise has already been discussed earlier. It should be noted that design compromises have two sides, the seller's side and the buyer's side. On the seller's side, he must develop a design compromise with wide enough appeal to take in a number of different market segments. The result will be that only a small portion of his market will perceive the design as being completely adequate to the fulfillment of all of their desires. Nearly every purchase involves some degree of design compromise for the buyer also. Some of those compromises are inevitable, as already indicated. No single physical design can satisfy all of the desires in a given desire-set. Some of them are physically incompatible with others.

As already indicated, once the customer gets the design which satisfies his uppermost desires at the moment, these desires themselves tend to change their position in his hierarchy and he has a built-in source of dissatisfaction. In addition, none of the designs on the market may really come as close as possible to meeting the desire-sets of quite a few of the people on the fringes of each market segment. They are therefore looking for a new design compromise which better fulfills their desire-sets. This is the condition that makes it possible for a new competitor to enter the market. His opportunity lies in developing a product which has a substantially different design compromise built in and thus attracts the fringe segments of a number of existing sellers. This really is what GM did with its Corvair and Ford did with the Mustang. The GM Corvair was perceived as something not then available from American manufacturers, a relatively personal car with design elements that had the connotation of some of the sporty European models, the rear engine conformation, for example. In addition, it was made by an American manufacturer and serviced by a widespread American automobile service network. It thus gathered some of the business that, lacking an American design which fulfilled this need, would normally have gone to foreign makers, and also won over various individuals who had been buying Americn cars and did not wish to risk a foreign car purchase but had longed for these elements.

Ford's Mustang probably took some of the fringes of the Corvair segment, but also took over fringes of the used-car market as well as the new-car market which had been searching for a small, personalized *family* car with sporty attributes.

Both the Corvair and the Mustang succeeded because they offered highly noticeable differences over current offerings. The General Motors Camaro failed because it did not offer a substantially perceived difference from most offerings on the market. There are many such sources of differentiation, not all of them involve physical design and not all of the physical design is accepted because of its functional values.

## The Forms of Offering Differentiation

There are many forms of differentiation and even for the same general product class, one seller may use one form and one may use another. Differentiation may simply be a form of promotional positioning, as in the case of a great many small low-ticket consumer items such as beverages, toiletries, cigarettes and the like. The difference may be in functional performance, as also happens in these fields and in nearly every field in which the purchase price is quite high. Differentiation may be a matter of physical styling which essentially communicates connotations and thus is really another form of positioning. It may be a matter of associated services rather than in the product itself, as it is indeed in the field of industrial supplies and in many consumer items. It may be simply a matter of the warranty against risk implied by a source perceived as more dependable, or it may be a matter simply of the accompanying assortment.

Differentiation by positioning was illustrated earlier in the case of Marlboro cigarettes. This is the basic form of differentiating for many of the minor consumer purchases. All toothpastes, for example, will do about the same functional job of cleaning teeth. Until the introduction of fluorides, about the only real difference between the various dentifrices on the market was in packaging and flavor. Nevertheless, a great many consumers have and still do have their preference in toothpaste and it is possible for a new seller to gain a substantial and relatively loyal share of the market as P & G did with its introduction of Gleem, whose only differentiation was a perceived position which enabled those with a guilty conscience to feel better. On the other hand, there are times, even in fields like these, in which the differentiation is as much a matter of physical function as positioning. Crest established itself as basically a medicine, a dental caries fighter, by adding a fluoride which had provable benefits in preventing decay among children's teeth. It gained credibility for its story by obtaining the American Dental Association's seal. Colgate defended its market by becoming a fluoride toothpaste, but one that still tasted good. When Bristol-Myers introduced its Fact, however, it did nothing to differentiate it from any other toothpaste in terms of either function or perceived psychological position. It had no appeal for any special market segment different from that of any other toothpaste. Close-Up aimed at those who were looking for a mouthwash and the pleasant feel in the mouth after brushing teeth, as the name implies, although neither the advertising or the label claim prevention of bad breath.

In the case of most toiletries, beverages, cigarettes and other consumer products in which the physical differentiation possibilities are extremely small, advertising must carry much of the load of establishing differences between their different offerings. But in other kinds of products, such as automobiles, the position must be carved out in terms of objective physical design differences, some of which may simply carry psychological connotations attracting specific market segments. The original model of the Corvair did not really sell very well, but then GM introduced a luxury model with bucket seats and this immediately spelled "sporty car" to a great many people and became an overnight success as being the first American offering of an individualized foreign type of car. Mustang's design was based on a long series of research which showed that cutout fenders, a long hood, and a short deck spelled sports to a lot of people. And thus Ford took a design that was basically the Falcon and transformed it into a spectacular market success.

On the other hand, the small economy foreign sedans carved out their market segments by design differences that had specific functional values for customers. Economy of operation, ease of handling, and the return of fun in driving became major appeals and still remain so. Although a very small portion of foreign car buyers participate in "rallyes," the rally itself signifies certain characteristics of these cars, their feeling of personal attachment, for example, that none of the major Detroit manufacturers have been able to capture with their offerings. No one ever entered a Cadillac or Buick or Chevy Monte Carlo in a rally.

Some of the functional differences, of course, are matters of taste and design with a functional basis. 7-Up sells itself as a beverage which is different from Coca-Cola, as it is quite definitely, in flavor. The building developer attempts to sell a type of development layout and a set of home designs which have physical characteristics somewhat different from those of other nearby developers. The machine tool manufacturer puts out a new mechanism that does some jobs in a way that no other mechanism on the market accomplishes the task.

On the other hand, there are many products on the market in which the offerings of the different competitors are physically identical. For example, the industrial abrasives made by any firm are not essentially different from those of a number of their competitors. Competition in such cases is based on accompanying services. In the case of industrial abrasives, it involves both engineering advice in the use of abrasives (some of which sometimes recommends against the use of something the customer might otherwise buy, and thus gains a great deal of credibility for positive recommendations for use when they are made). In other cases, of course, it is a matter of pure availability of a local distributor who keeps a wide assortment in stock.

IBM gained its major lead in computers by its pioneering of program libraries, even though IBM computers themselves were not always physically superior to those of their competitors. Other computer manufacturers have obtained a niche in the market by designing special use computers for very specific kinds of sophisticated operations.

Sometimes the only differentiation the seller has is that he now has a product identical to those from other sources, but it is in an assortment that is much broader and much better tailored for a particular type of customer than the other sources offer. And thus it is that the assortment makes the difference.

Finally, a great many firms simply rely on their reputation as building the most solid and durable equipment and having a wide service network to gain a niche in the market. John Deere relies on this in the farm tractor field, for example, and Caterpillar tractor has long been able to avoid pioneering new designs because when it does bring out a design, it is generally considered as one of top quality.

In one sense, of course, all forms of differentiation are a form of assortment differentiation. The product does not sell because of the single differentiating characteristic, but because the total assortment which includes this differentiating characteristic is seen as more valuable than some other assortment of benefits frozen into a different single physical design. As already pointed out, much of the value perceived in the offering of many sellers comes from the various assortments of goods and services. The major perceived advantage of American manufacturers, in the minds of most automobile buyers in the United States, is simply the fact that the service network of the domestic manufacturers is wider than those of the foreign sellers.

## Product Is Assortment and Assortment Is Product

Literally speaking "product" is defined as something somebody has produced or manufactured. However, from the consumer's point of view the physical product is just a possible cue to an assortment or bundle of potential use-system benefits. What the factory turns out is merely junk unless the customer perceives the end product as making possible the answers to several of his desires at one time. For this reason, the term *offering* has been used throughout this discussion because the cue which the consumer perceives is far more than that of physical design, even in the case of physical products. It includes associations built by society, by promotion, or by both. The offering includes utilities of place and time, of implied collateral services such as repair service, and comprehends the insurance values of trusted labels and trusted distribution channels. Finally, the offering includes directly the matter of assortment choice, the ability to choose between patterns, models, colors, sizes, and so forth to find one coming closest to the desires of the customer.

For many products, industrial as well as consumer, the buyer is always seeking to gain a major assortment of benefits in every item purchased and also a chance to purchase a number of different items at the same time. Since he needs many items at a given time, for supplementary or even unrelated uses, he is always on the lookout for a seller who can supply as many of the items desired as possible in the grades, types and sizes desired.

What complicates the seller's problem is the fact that every consumer has a somewhat different set of desires to be satisfied than any other consumer, both in terms of the bundle of satisfactions desired in a single offering and in terms of the assortments of items, grades and qualities to be purchased. He needs an assortment and every manufacturer, as well as every merchant, must, therefore, do a merchandising job. The steel companies differ not a bit in their price of a specific item, as a rule. But no two steel companies turn out the same assortment of steel forms, shapes, alloys, and so forth. Likewise, the range of models that Chevrolet offers is not the same as the range of models that Ford offers.

If the total offering embodied in any product is a satisfaction assortment, so also any specific offering of a merchandise assortment is a product, not just an aggregation of individual items and services. The patronage loyal consumer is "buying" that specific assortment in exactly the same sense as the brand loyal consumer is buying the individual brand of product. This is one of the reasons why distributive arrangements are just as much a part of the total offering as are the details of physical design. The successful merchant assembles the particular kind of assortments desired by a major group of segments in his market. A majority of the items and services in that assortment may be no different physically from those offered by other sellers in the same market area, but the difference in the composition of the rest of the assortment will automatically attract certain customer segments based on their desire-sets.

*Assortment Bias*

At first thought, it might seem simple for a merchant to carry just any combination of items and services he wishes to, in whatever width and breadth of assortment he desires. This is not the case.

Although no individual consumer may be in the market for even a majority of the components in that assortment, all of the components included represent a single merchandise and service bias. That bias may be a certain level of quality. It may be a specific type of design where applicable, catering to a specific type of taste (nearly always a social class bias in the case of consumer goods). The simple theme of that bias may be strong emphasis on price promotional goods. It may be on wide and individualized offerings. In some kinds of selling, the emphasis may be on ready availability in time and place as it is, for example, in the case of the convenience store or the all-night service station. Whatever the basis, a specific group of market segments have learned that this is the merchant who has the assortments that they are looking for, and they have an "image" of him (as it is sometimes called) which indicates that this is the kind of product he sells.

Learning to build a specific kind of physical product fitting a certain type of buyer segment and learning to build a certain specific kind of merchandise assortment involves the learning and specialization of skills, and almost invariably rules out the acquisition of skills of a different sort. Sellers really have no choice but to undertake a certain degree of specialization, and this is what makes for competition.

## Market Segment Specialization and Product Differentiation

Both manufacturers and distributors or merchants must and do become habituated to searching for or developing items of greatest importance to the particular set of core segments they learn to serve. Learning to fit their own customer needs is almost certainly trial and error in part but, however developed, both the successful merchant and the successful manufacturer acquire a very specific bias and skill of some sort through long practice and a feeling of what will work and what will not.

Once the merchant or manufacturer becomes established in a specific market niche, consumers learn to associate the seller with his specific merchandising bias and will not seek him out except when they desire products and services represented by this bias. They acquire patronage habits paralleling the seller's merchandising habits. Efficiency in production or in merchandising requires organized learning of skills just as efficiency does for the individual worker. Skills have internal incompatibilities just as product design does. The machinist who is very efficient in turning out precision custom designs is awkward at low tolerance assembly line production, and vice versa. Executives who are in the habit of always looking for spectacular promotions are seldom good at careful planning of relatively unspectacular matters such as store location or the design variety desired by upper-middle-class consumers. Changing these habits within an organization is just as difficult and just as prolonged a process as is the changing of any individual's habits.

Sometimes, unfortunately, the market segment itself shrinks and the seller has to find some means of getting into what is, in effect, a new business. This is very difficult for a seller to do for two reasons. In the first place, it means a change in habit with all the difficulty this entails. In the second place, it involves a change of perception on the part of his customers as to his ability to furnish them what they desire.

In both cases, of course, it involves changes in habit, a very difficult process, as has already been noted. Very few merchants have ever succeeded in changing their market segment radically. When it was accomplished, it was done under circumstances in which they were serving new markets which had not acquired any specific perception as to the merchant's niche, and under new managers who had not yet accustomed themselves to the merchandising habits of the older managers. The development of such merchandising and manufacturing habits means that both the manufacturer and the distributor have limited freedom in choosing their relationship.

### The Symbiosis of Manufacturer-Distributor Relationship

Manufacturers and distributors rely on each other. They thrive best together and the only conflict likely is that inherent in all aspects of the economy—that of who gets what share of the final price paid. Even the monetary source of conflict is easily exaggerated. The relationship of manufacturer and distributor is that of any buyer and seller except that, in distribution, the alternative choices open to either one are very limited in number, so the distributive margins tend to settle at customary levels profitable to both parties. Each needs the other because each is aiming to serve the same market segments. The manufacturer must seek out and attract those distributor customers into whose service and goods assortments his offering best fits. Otherwise he will fail to gain the market he needs. The distributor must seek out sources, services and goods assortments that best fit the needs of his customers; otherwise he will fail to gain the trade that he is aiming for.

However well or poorly the merchant constructs his assortment, a large proportion of consumers he does attract will perceive that assortment as being deficient in some essentials of their desire-set and will seek out and use additional source or sources to complete their desire-sets. Thus, the merchant must seek out a location which gives consumers that opportunity.

This is one reason why many kinds of merchants cluster in specific locations. The shopping center itself, by bringing together many kinds of merchants, enables the customer to buy a much broader assortment than he hopes to get from any one merchant. Moreover, many consumers will need a variety of choice they cannot expect to find from one particular merchant with his particular merchandise bias.

Food store centered shopping centers have all found that the other stores in the center, as well as the food stores themselves, tend to do better if there are at least two supermarkets in the center with complementary assortment biases. Likewise, even the department store sponsored large regional shopping centers try to get at least two and preferably more department stores in the same complex. Women's dress shops generally do poorly unless they have at least two other "competing" shops in the same shopping district.

All of these combinations are necessary in order to attract the widest following of customers who are interested in at least part of the assortment bias involved. A small scale example of how this structure of competition works is illustrated by the accompanying summary of a hitherto unpublished study of shopping patterns for one week in the middle-class-suburban areas of Geneva and St. Charles, Illinois conducted in 1971 by Chester R. Wasson and the late James A. Bell, Jr.

---

**A STUDY OF THE SUPERMARKET PATRONAGE STRUCTURE
IN THE ST. CHARLES-GENEVA AREA, 1971**

James A. Bell, Jr. and Chester R. Wasson

AREA POPULATION: Trade Area, approximately 33,000. Over one-third professional, technical and managerial class, another one-sixth middle-class clerical and sales, and one-fourth craftsmen, foremen and kindred. Orientation of schools and other institutions middle-middle class and upper-middle class.

AREA LOCATION: Currently on the western fringe of the Chicago metropolitan area. For a long time, essentially an exurbia, with substantial industry employing skilled help, and has had commuter connections with central Chicago since early in the century. In the middle of the Fox River Valley, midway between the satellite industrial centers of Elgin and Aurora.

ESTABLISHED SUPERMARKETS STUDIED: 5 in all. Questionnaires passed out to shoppers on one Saturday afternoon and returned by mail. Total responses 805. For locations of the following, consult the map on page 339.

EAGLE DISCOUNT SUPERMARKET. A regional subsidiary of Lucky Stores. 10,000 sq. ft., with a cramped parking lot, 5 blocks east of the St. Charles main business district, near the east end of town, on Main St. (State Route 64). Everyday low discount price policy, only modest promotion, no price specials except marked "key buys." About 7,500 items.

BLUE GOOSE. Single store independent, affiliated with a cooperative wholesale, but not carrying its identification. 12,000 square feet, adequate parking lot, one block south of Main street in the heart of the St. Charles main business district. Minimum promotion, featuring a few specials each week, but no price emphasis. Store layout unusual in that the path to the rest of the store leads the customer through the produce department (which carries an unusual variety of fresh produce, including some exotic items), then past the meat department (whose breadth of offerings is also unusually wide). 9,000 items.

JEWEL STORE, ST. CHARLES BRANCH. Leading chain in the region. 10,000 sq. feet, located in a modern shopping center near the northwest corner of the main residential area of the city proper, near the intersection of State Route 64 and a main local artery, Randall Rd. Other stores in the center: Kresge, a large drug store, TV dealer, liquor store, shoe store, jeans store, laundromat, travel agency and finance office, large Sears catalog and paint store (formerly an A&P supermarket), bicycle store. Highly promotional chain, carrying multiple weekly advertisements in every available local medium, with some deep cut specials weekly. About 7,500 items.

JEWEL STORE, GENEVA BRANCH. Same chain. 10,000 square feet near west end of main Geneva shopping district on State St. (State Route 38). Parking lot barely adequate. About 7,500 items.

NATIONAL SUPERMARKET. National chain. 14,000 square feet, large parking lot, one block further west than the Jewel Store in Geneva, on the opposite side of State St. Highly promotional. About 7,000 items, heavily weighted with store brands.

All stores were food supermarkets, with no extensive nonfood departments.

Number of respondent families: 805

Food expenditure for the week studied: Mean value, $36.50
                                        Median       35.00
                                        Mode         30.00

Distribution of Patronage: One store only: 36%
                           Two stores      47
                           Three or more   15

**Figure 14-1.  Locations of the Supermarkets Surveyed**

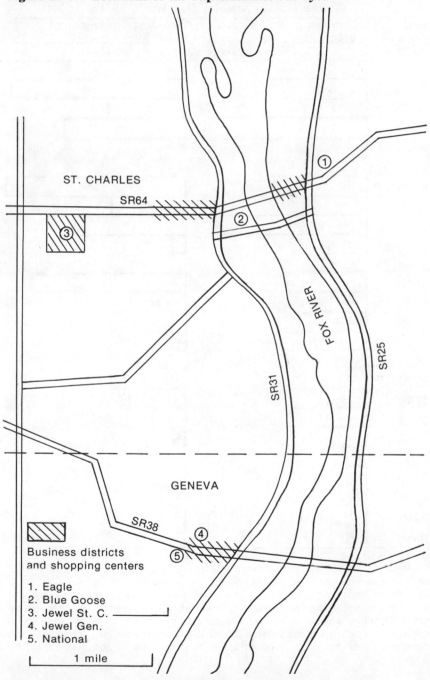

**Figure 14-2.  Patronage Patterns for Five Supermarkets in the St. Charles-Geneva Area for One Week, 1971**

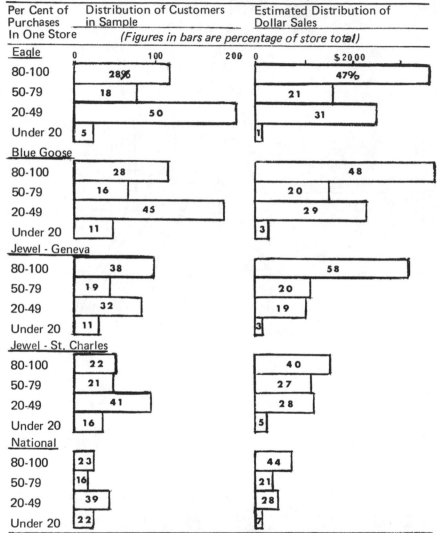

| Per Cent of Purchases In One Store | Distribution of Customers in Sample | Estimated Distribution of Dollar Sales |
|---|---|---|

*(Figures in bars are percentage of store total)*

**Eagle**
- 80-100 : 28% / 47%
- 50-79 : 18 / 21
- 20-49 : 50 / 31
- Under 20 : 5 / 1

**Blue Goose**
- 80-100 : 28 / 48
- 50-79 : 16 / 20
- 20-49 : 45 / 29
- Under 20 : 11 / 3

**Jewel - Geneva**
- 80-100 : 38 / 58
- 50-79 : 19 / 20
- 20-49 : 32 / 19
- Under 20 : 11 / 3

**Jewel - St. Charles**
- 80-100 : 22 / 40
- 50-79 : 21 / 27
- 20-49 : 41 / 28
- Under 20 : 16 / 5

**National**
- 80-100 : 23 / 44
- 50-79 : 16 / 21
- 20-49 : 39 / 28
- Under 20 : 22 / 7

COMMENT: Note that the similarities in the patronage patterns of the five markets are far greater than the differences in the percentage distributions. Only a minor fraction of the patronage attracted by any store is strongly patronage loyal. The larger numbers of loyal patrons attracted by the stronger stores bring with them a proportionate number of only partly satisfied fringe patrons. The patronage pattern of the weakest of the five stores has much the same pattern as those of the two leaders. Thus the best designed assortments (or products) are as vulnerable to competition as the weakest.

**Table 14-1.    Patronage Pattern by Store**

| | | | Percent of Total Customers | | |
| Store | Total number of patrons* | Median amt. spent in store | Spending 100% in this store | Spending 80% or more here | Designating store as favorite |
|---|---|---|---|---|---|
| Eagle | 404 | $19.50 | 11% | 28% | 50% |
| Blue Goose | 413 | 19.00 | 20 | 28 | 53 |
| Jewel-St. C. | 235 | 17.50 | 18 | 22 | 46 |
| Jewel-G. | 262 | 20.00 | 27 | 38 | 61 |
| National | 115 | 13.00 | 17 | 23 | 52 |

* Although the patron count was not intended originally as a measure of total business, observation indicates that it is a useful approximation of the relative volume of the respective markets. National's weak position was confirmed by a later closing of the store.

PATRONAGE PATTERN BY STORE: PER CENT OF WEEKLY BUDGET SPENT IN THE STORE. See Figure 14-2.

**Table 14-2.    Supplementary Store Choices, by Favorite Store**

Supplementary Store Choices, By Favorite Store

| | Percent supplementing purchases at: | | | | | | |
| Favorite Store | All Stores | Eagle | Bl. G. | J-SC | J-G | Natl. | Other |
|---|---|---|---|---|---|---|---|
| Eagle | 100 | xx | 53 | 17 | 12 | 4 | 14 |
| Blue Goose | 100 | 47 | xx | 23 | 20 | 6 | 4 |
| Jewel-SC | 100 | 40 | 44 | xx | 6 | 4 | 6 |
| Jewel-G | 100 | 16 | 35 | 10 | xx | 22 | 17 |
| National | 100 | 17 | 18 | 10 | 43 | x | 12 |

NOTE that the two strongest stores—Eagle and Blue Goose—also have the strongest attraction as a supplementary source for the patrons of the other.

**Table 14-3.    Merchandise Attraction of Each Store, As Perceived by the Very Light Supplementary Shoppers and by the Patronage Loyal**

| | Selected because of selection and quality of: | | | | |
| Store | Fruits & Vegetables | Meat | Bakery & Delicatessen | Frozen Foods | Canned Goods |
|---|---|---|---|---|---|
| Shoppers spending less than 20% of budget in store: | | | | | |
| All stores | 100% | 100% | 100% | 100% | 100% |
| Eagle | 9 | 8 | 3 | 19 | 29 |
| Blue Goose | 57 | 50 | 50 | 41 | 19 |
| Jewel-SC | 14 | 20 | 31 | 19 | 23 |
| Jewel-G | 14 | 10 | 16 | 7 | 10 |
| National | 6 | 12 | -- | 15 | 19 |

Table 14-3. (continued)

Shoppers spending more than 80% of budget in store:

| All stores | 100% | 100% | 100% | 100% | 100% |
|---|---|---|---|---|---|
| Eagle | 24 | 24 | 16 | 28 | 31 |
| Blue Goose | 34 | 33 | 43 | 33 | 30 |
| Jewel-SC | 10 | 10 | 10 | 10 | 10 |
| Jewel-G | 25 | 25 | 25 | 21 | 20 |
| National | 7 | 8 | 6 | 9 | 10 |

## Table 14-4.

### Service Reasons for Shopping the Store, All Patrons

| Service mentioned | Percent of mentions by all shoppers | | | | |
|---|---|---|---|---|---|
| | Eagle | Bl. G. | J-SC | J-G | Natl. |
| All services | 100% | 100% | 100% | 100% | 100% |
| Location | 29 | 22 | 36 | 33 | 34 |
| Rapid check-out | 21 | 26 | 18 | 18 | 20 |
| Friendly, courteous service | 33 | 25 | 30 | 30 | 26 |
| Neat, roomy aisles | 17 | 27 | 16 | 19 | 26 |

COMMENT: As might be expected, shoppers who spend nearly all of their budget in one store see less difference between departments than do those who merely patronize it for supplementary reasons. Comparing all of the tabulations above, it seems clear that Blue Goose and Eagle are shopped more for merchandise reasons than the other stores, with Blue Goose perceived as especially good for those items most important to middle-class shoppers: quality meats, vegetables, bakery, delicatessen, and frozen foods. Eagle's strong point seems to be the staples, as represented by the canned goods rating. The other 3 stores show a high locational rating for their patronage. Although the Blue Goose had less check-out stands than any of the other stores, the high rating for rapid check-out seems, by observation to be objectively correct. Measurement indicated no significant difference in aisle width nor any greater clutter, with one exception: Blue Goose' last aisle has a real bottleneck due to some island displays. Nevertheless, Blue Goose is *perceived* as having neat and roomy aisles!

## Table 14-5.

### Market Segmentation by Store: Family Life Cycle Position of Customers and Employment and Education of Housewife

| Favorite Store | | Stage of family life cycle: | | | | | |
|---|---|---|---|---|---|---|---|
| | | Married, all stages | No children | Oldest child at age: | | | |
| | Single | | | 0-5 | 6-12 | 13-18 | 18 yrs. + |
| Total, all stores | 100% | 100% | 100% | 100% | 100% | 100% | 100% |
| Eagle | 20 | 29 | 23 | 33 | 30 | 28 | 23 |
| Blue Goose | 44 | 27 | 37 | 13 | 24 | 23 | 38 |
| Jewel-SC | 15 | 14 | 8 | 23 | 13 | 27 | 19 |
| Jewel-G | 16 | 21 | 24 | 18 | 16 | 13 | 16 |
| National | 6 | 8 | 8 | 13 | 8 | 9 | 4 |

### BY EMPLOYMENT AND EDUCATION OF HOUSEWIFE

| Favorite store | Employment | | | Education | | | |
|---|---|---|---|---|---|---|---|
| | Full time | Part time | none | Less than High Sch. | Graduated High Sch. | Attended College | Graduated College |
| Total all stores | 100% | 100% | 100% | 100% | 100% | 100% | 100% |
| Eagle | 34 | 31 | 30 | 32 | 29 | 25 | 23 |
| Blue Goose | 39 | 19 | 25 | 27 | 30 | 27 | 31 |
| Jewel-SC | 12 | 17 | 15 | 18 | 18 | 26 | 24 |
| Jewel-G | 16 | 26 | 23 | 11 | 14 | 16 | 16 |
| National | 9 | 7 | 8 | 12 | 9 | 6 | 6 |

COMMENT: As might be expected from its merchandise strength in staple foods, the Eagle's strongest attraction is to families with relatively young children, whose tastes run more to hamburgers and hot dogs than to aged steaks, and to peanut butter than to kumquats and artichokes. The slightly heavier bias toward the less well educated housewives also suggests that some of the trade is from the blue collar classes, with less interest in the fancier foods. That the Eagle's appeal is merchandise was later confirmed when the firm built a large supermarket on the other end of town, in a center less than one-half mile from Jewel-St. C. The store did extremely well from the start, and when the old store was closed and a new tenant moved in, the latter obviously obtained only a fraction of the old Eagle traffic.

The Blue Goose, as might be expected from its reputation in quality meats, produce and baked goods, attracts families at both ends of the family life cycle: the singles and young marrieds, and those whose children are old enough to have learned to like the finer foods, as well as the empty nest families. The higher proportion of the more highly educated also shows a more middle- and upper-middle class customer bias.

> The two Jewel stores' patrons apparently represent the neighborhood composition. The Geneva store is in an older part of town with a relatively normal family composition, the St. Charles store surrounded by relatively new homes and middle class family apartments, with a preponderance of young families.
> The only obvious strength of the National store is among the more poorly educated, a very minor element in this area.

Note the following points about these study results:

1. There is a broad spread in customer-attracting ability among the four supermarket managements in the area and between the five stores, with two of the stores extremely successful and one of the five quite obviously failing. Somewhat more than one-half of the patrons of every one of the five were buying more than one-half of their food items for that one week in any one store. If we define patronage loyalty as buying 80 percent or more of the food at a given store in one week, less than one-half of the customers at any of these markets could be considered loyal, and those who do all their shopping at a single store are relatively few in number. In general, however, most consumers found two suppliers adequate.

2. Consumers perceive differences in the offerings of the four managements, with two stores clearly preferred for the merchandise assortments and the other three apparently depending in part on locational convenience.

3. Patrons who prefer one of the two leading stores are more likely to use the other leading store for some purchases than any of the other three stores.

4. The store whose patronage is least (and which later was closed) occupies a very poorly defined position in the perceptions of the consumers of the area and the two leaders have the most clearly defined niches.

Manifestly, each merchant is selling a product as much as is the manufacturer (who nearly always is, in truth, himself merely a distributor of many of the items he assembles into his final-consumer product—the "original equipment" items he purchases).

Just as clearly, the manufacturers who supply these merchants need to find distributors who serve their own specific kinds of customers. When the manufacturer seeks distributors he is seeking someone to add specific services, including the assortment services needed, to match consumer desire-sets. He is adding a *place value* desired by the segments he serves.

Because the perceived value of product changes over the product life cycle the most profitable product design and distribution policies also vary with time.

## The Product Life Cycle and Product Policy

Consumer perceptions of the value of the product decrease with the product life cycle as they become adapted to its value and the product loses its stimulus variability elements. One of the dangers of success for any manufacturer or merchant is to fail to recognize the declining value of his offerings in consumer eyes and the need to take on or develop products that will be in a growth stage. This was the error that the Hoover Company made with its vacuum cleaners when it failed to perceive the effect of changing house furnishing patterns on these desire-sets of customers. The increased use of wall-to-wall carpeting and of draperies increased greatly the relative value of the newly developed canister cleaners and Hoover did not move into this field until other makers had acquired a major share in the market structure.

Likewise, General Motors was so successful with its policy of selling "more car per car," and constantly enlarging and increasing the power of the smaller models they introduced in the 1950s and 1960s, that it overlooked the growing trend toward smaller and more compact and functional automobiles until the 1973-74 oil embargo crisis suddenly catalyzed the switch in public favor. Indeed, even earlier, this policy had made some difficulty for General Motors in introducing its smaller Vega model which was designed to attract many of the customer segments buying foreign cars. The dealers accustomed to selling their customers larger cars, and upgrading them into even larger models, did not appear to enter wholeheartedly into the Vega promotion, and there is even some suspicion that many of the executives at General Motors saw the Vega as merely a sop to a small-car portion of the market, not as an entry into the growing markets of the future. GM apparently had similar dealer service problems in the promotion of its German-made Opel and the firm quite obviously did not see the need for giving the Opel the same quality of parts availability that it did to its larger cars, if we judge by consumer complaints.

One of the major problems of any seller is the constant updating of a product line or its assortments to include items which are not yet even close to the volume of those in the mature stages, but which, because they are market development or early growth stage products, contain the elements of future profit in the rapidly growing or soon to rapidly grow segment of the product life cycle. The very success of the leader in a market is likely to blind him—to cause him to overlook the changing desire-sets of his customers and the changing opportunities of technology, and the need to build for the future rather than to build on the successes of the past. Thus all of the established makers of desk calculators ignored the potentials of integrated circuit electronic devices and thus lost dominance in the market in 1973 to rank outsiders and their introduction of the small electronic computers. Any seller must constantly monitor the profit life cycle position of each item and adjust his general product strategy and his general distributional strategy to correspond. He must also carefully consider the category product life cycle stage of any product that he introduces into the market.

### Introductory Design and the Product Life Cycle

Products may be, and are, introduced at any stage of the product category life cycle, except possibly the decline phase. Each stage poses quite different design requirements.

Relatively high-learning products, which must undergo a prolonged period of market development before rapid sales growth appears, must be so designed as to minimize every aspect of learning and especially of relearning.

High-learning products should, if possible, be so designed physically as to fit into an existing use-system with as little modification in that system as can be attained. The first mass-produced farm tractors, for example, did approximately the same job as a good team of horses. Had today's mammoth power plants been the initial design, it is doubtful that they could possibly have succeeded. Similarly, the first mechanical refrigerators of the 1920s period had a capacity of four cubic feet, and freezer capacity only for ice cubes. They were thus only about the size of the larger ice-boxes they replaced. When Europe also began mass purchase of mechanical refrigerators in the 1950s, Europeans bought mainly this same limited size box, not the fifteen-to-twenty cubic foot combined freezer-refrigerator models that American consumers now found necessary in their own modern use-systems.

The introductory design for the high-learning product should also minimize any value-learning to whatever extent this is possible. Early acceptance of the farm tractors was made possible by a price which was about that of the team of horses it replaced.

Since the customer's main interest in such a high-learning product is for the new core function itself, the introductory design need be only a single model. Model variations will be needed only when understanding of the benefits has laid the groundwork for acceptance and growing sales. Henry Ford's policy of selling only one body model of his revolutionary 1908 Model T was justifiably successful, in the 1908-14 period. His only mistake was maintaining this policy, with only the most grudging modifications, through the growth period into a mature market phase, long after the initial search for the basic mechanical transportation was satisfied and other items in the hierarchy of needs were rising to the top.

By contrast, low-learning products, or any new brand launched in the early growth stage should be designed to meet varying desire-sets with many model variations to match both physical content desire differences and value-level perception differences. The basic design should also appeal to a very specific set of segments in a market now becoming, or soon to become, quite segmented—to be aimed at developing a specially differentiated market niche.

Finally, a product launched in a mature market can hope to succeed only if a gap in desire-set coverages can be found and exploited. The market potential exists only if enough people are on the fringes of existing segments, with a relatively common unfulfilled set of desires. GM's Corvair was such a product, as were the first Ford Mustang and both Gleem and Crest toothpaste. Bristol-Myers' Fact toothpaste was not, nor was the GM Camaro.

Launching a product in the decline phase of the product life cycle would seem to be a project doomed to failure. Even poor brands still on the market are attracting less and less attention, as new products take over their functions. No substantial number of potential customers have any unfulfilled needs to be met by the basic category.

## Distributive Policy and the Product Life Cycle

The appropriate distributive values needed in the offering mix also change with the changes in the phases of the product life cycle. Because initial total sales volume is certain to be quite low for any high-learning product in the market development phase, the seller must concentrate such sales in a few distributive outlets, through an exclusive or selective distribution policy, as the price of getting the aggressive promotional efforts he must have from them. He will have to keep consumer search effort down by substituting aggressive personal and mass promotion, as well as the maximum of obtainable publicity.

If the seller does mistakenly attempt to gain intensive distribution, as RCA did initially with color television, he will find dealers little interested in carrying out the kind of aggressive sales and promotional effort required, partly because the sales volume for each outlet is too meager, and partly because the kind of aggressive promotional and sales effort is an unaccustomed one for most such distributors.

Once the growth stage is reached, however, every attempt must be made to develop an extensive and intensive distributive system. Potential buyers are by now thoroughly aware of the promised benefits, understand their value, and convinced of their credibility through the testimony and trials of their tastemaker friends. At the same time, no brand will have yet established a strong habitual following, so the brands most readily available will gain most of the sales.

Moreover, by the time sales growth is obvious, potential dealer customers will be strongly attracted to the offering and the potential profits, and if they fail to get adequate supplies from one brand, potential distributors will actively seek out other sources to cash in on the boom. In such a case, they will really create competitors, and usually also create production capacity which the mature market cannot support. This is why the last phase of the growth period is one of competitive turbulence, when weak sellers get shaken out.

Part of the over-capacity can be caused by stock-short dealers. Lacking an inventory of a "hot" item, they will buttonhole every possible supplier, promising orders. Since they make the same promise to each, the apparent market potential becomes highly inflated, and the introducer may lose out to new competitors.

This is what happened to the firm which introduced the Japanese Hibachi to the barbecue market in the U.S. The firm permitted a contract supplier to let shipments lag, and soon found itself pushed out of the market by a multitude of sellers who were eager to give immediate delivery.

The seller can survive the later shakeout of the turbulence stage, and meanwhile gain a strong market position, only by obtaining a leading position in the preference of customers during the early growth stage. Sellers who have not succeeded in developing a strong market niche for their offering during the early growth stage, and strong distribution availability, will be among those dropped by dealers when the competitive turbulence stage leads to a surfeit of sources and the need to drop the weaker brands with no established positioning in consumer expectations.

With the end of the period of rapid growth, the quality and strength of the dealer and service network assumes an ever more important role in the maintenance of market share. The stimulus variability value of the product is now gone, and customers have also now acquired well established brand patronage habits. They are not easily switched to other brands unless their favorite is so poorly distributed as to require a high search cost, or after-sales service is deficient.

Until product cycle decline becomes evident, therefore, the seller must ardently court his immediate customer—the dealers and service outlets. Once decline sets in, this is no longer necessary nor worthwhile. The offering no longer has any attraction for either dealer or final end users, other than the change-resistant laggards, and only that distribution need be sought which remains marginally profitable.

## Summary

1. Because of the nature of fundamental consumer behavioral tendencies, product introductions can succeed only when they are the first of the designs to get attention, when they are perceived as substantially differentiated in some way from other entries of the same category, and can continue to succeed only if design and distribution are kept in consonance with the changing phases of the product life cycle.

2. Only substantially differentiated offerings can hope for success because too-similar offerings will not get attention from market segments already satisfied with current offerings.

3. Direct head-to-head product competition succeeds only when production is so fragmented that the output of a great many sellers is needed to satisfy any one or a few major buyers. Only then can every producer design for the same desire-set.

4. Differentiated competition is possible because the wide psychological differences between individuals and the degree of the satiation of their desire-sets mean that no one offering can fulfill those desire-sets. Moreover, the economics of mass production mean that large fringes of every seller's market segments are certain to be relatively unsatisfied with the available design compromises.

5. Different kinds of offerings may be differentiated in at least one or more of several ways: psychological positioning, functional performance, physical styling with positional connotations, associated services, the implied guarantee against risk of a more dependable source, or by inclusion in an acceptable assortment.

6.   Purely psychological positioning is mainly confined to low-physical-difference, low-ticket consumer items such as toiletries, cigarettes and beverages. But functional performance differences are sometimes available even in such cases.

7.   All forms of differentiation are, in essence, assortment differentiation, since differentiation in the case of the individual product is a difference in the internal assortment of benefits.

8.   Likewise, all item assortments are essentially products, just as the individual product is an assortment of benefits.

9.   Every consumer, industrial as well as final buyer, is searching for the satisfaction of a somewhat different desire-set in every purchase, and different combinations of items in every merchandise assortment. What the consumer is buying is not just an invoice of specific items but the assortment closest to his needs.

10.   Every successful assortment has its own specific theme or bias, and consumers become habituated to perceiving that bias as the seller's market niche.

11.   Fitting the needs of a specific set of market segments is a complex skill developing out of a long learning process. The resulting habits of manufacturing and merchandising confer a special advantage on the seller in serving that particular niche, but make changing the bias as difficult a process as any other habit change.

12.   All skills, whether of manufacturing or merchandising create incompatibilities of habit with the learning of different kinds of skills, making changes in market direction extremely difficult.

13.   Because of market segment specialization, large numbers of buyers must utilize multiple sources to fill their needs.

14.   The assortment principle means that the distribution channel choices of any manufacturer are severely limited, and so are the merchandise source choices of the merchant. Both need the other to serve their special market segments, and the relationship is symbiotic.

15.   Since any single assortment leaves many partially dissatisfied fringe segments, merchants tend to cluster to give consumers the best possible desire-set fit. Consumer perception of the value of any offering changes with time and the fading of the stimulus variation values in the offering, resulting in the product life cycle. Sellers

who do not keep up with the changing value-perceptions and changing desire-sets lose market position eventually.

16. The design of new market entries must take account of the current phase of the category product life cycle. If that phase is the market development stage, design and value must be minimum learning oriented. If at the growth stage or later, it must provide for multiple models to fit many variations of desire-sets.

17. The appropriate distribution policy also changes with the phases of the product life cycle. Selective distribution is a must for the market development phase, extensive and intensive distribution for the later phases.

## Chapter Fourteen Exercises

1. In the Bell and Wasson study, Blue Goose seemed to be perceived as having roomier, less cluttered aisles than its competitors. Yet actual measurement indicated that all stores had about the same aisle widths, and that Blue Goose actually had a bottleneck in one aisle while the other stores did not. Moreover, it had greater customer traffic than 3 of the other stores, which would have meant more people clutter. What reasons can you give for the widespread *perception* of greater roominess at the Blue Goose?

2. Asking people what they would like in a new product nearly always gets merely an echo of what they already own (and are unlikely to buy the next time). Similarly for a store. More than one book based on instructor questionnaire answers has proved to be a flop.
   Given this situation, how would you go about entering an established market with a product (or a store)—how would you discover a differentiation which would be successful?

3. A publisher once confided to the author that he was trying to find a way to get more instructors to really examine his new books when they got them, and some of the followup mail professors regularly receive on new books obviously is aimed at this goal, without much success. Why?

When and under what conditions would you expect an instructor would really examine new texts?

4.  If you were instructing text book salesmen, what kind of information would you teach them to gather and pass back to headquarters to help you decide on choosing new manuscripts, and even to whom to pass out sample copies to?

5.  Describe the assortment bias of the two most successful supermarkets in your community.
    Describe the assortment biases of General Motors, Ford and Chrysler. What unique elements in their offering mix gives each its niche in the market?
    Describe the assortment biases of the two leading department stores in your community.

6.  Radicals and reformers have long complained that there are no differences between the two major political parties except that one was in when the other was out. Is this really so? If so, why do most voters perceive differences? If it is not a correct view, what are the differences and why do they seem similar in so many respects?

7.  How does Ford differ from Chevy?

8.  Why did foreign cars gain a strong foothold in the U.S. market at a time when independents were dying out like flies sprayed with DDT?

9.  Why does any firm find it almost impossible to change its product mix overnight when popularity shifts? Why, for example, was GM hurt so badly in 1974 when the demand trend to smaller cars suddenly accelerated?

15

Consumer Reaction to
Informative Communications

THE FOUR COMPONENTS OF COMMUNICATION: AUDIENCE, SOURCE, MESSAGE, MEDIA

THE FIVE KINDS OF AUDIENCE SELECTIVITY

Exposure
Attention
Perception
Appeal
Response

AUDIENCE MULTIPLICITY

Different Segments of Final Users
Channel Intermediaries
Others

EFFECTS OF PERCEIVED MESSAGE SOURCE: CREDIBILITY, TESTIMONIALS AS SOURCE, MEDIA AS SOURCE

MESSAGE PRESENTATION EFFECTS

Presenting Both Sides
Perils of Fear Appeal
Value of Asking for Big Attitude Changes
Recency and Primacy in Presentation
Value of Stating Conclusions

MEDIA EFFECTS

Select Audience
Perceived as Source

PROMOTIONAL EFFORTS AND THE PRODUCT LIFE CYCLE

Investment Value of Promotional Effort in Market Development
    Stage
Building Market Share During the Growth Phase
Defensive Value During Maturity
Ineffectiveness During Decline

INFORMING THE CONSUMER of what is for sale and getting him to act require a different kind of communications mix in each situation. Consider the following:

A young woman who had a highly disfiguring facial birthmark developed a camouflage cosmetic which enabled her to face the world without embarrassment. She then decided to put the cosmetic on the market and the product was introduced in major department stores with quite a burst of publicity. Unfortunately for her enterprise, very few women have facial blemishes as gross as hers, and so the product died on the shelves. Later, a television specialty mail order entrepreneur, looking for new products to exploit, came upon this now dormant cosmetic. He had the insight to note that though few women had gross facial disfigurement, many had minor blemishes which gave them an inferiority complex. To promote the item, he developed a specialty television mail order campaign based on thirteen minutes of cosmetic advice and two minutes of demonstration. The latter noted that even "glamorous" Hollywood stars often have facial blemishes which were not seen on the screen because of a make-up similar to his. The new promotion developed sufficient volume that department stores were glad to put the product back on the shelves for regular sale.

The A. O. Smith Company developed an automatic unloading silo consisting of a glazed steel enclosure, a vinyl cap, which sealed out the air on top and prevented spoilage, and an automatic unloading device at the bottom. The total device was more than twice as expensive as an ordinary silo, but it had a major advantage. By means of its use, it was possible to take the cattle out of the pasture, where they destroyed two-thirds of the forage they were grazing, pen them up, and feed chopped forage through the new silo without loss of nutrient. The result was, in effect, a tripling of the yield of feed from pastures. The firm initially attempted the sale of this new silo through farm equipment dealers in a number of areas with zero results. They then appointed contractors, with exclusive distributorships for specific territories, who had to invest over a quarter million dollars for erecting equipment. These contractor salesmen then developed a widespread market for their product, a product which mere display and advertising brochures had been unable to tap.

The cotton growers of the United States lost a major market for their fibre when rayon cord displaced cotton from tires during the early 1940s. Looking around for new markets, the Cotton Council, decided that the best potential lay in wider use in women's dress clothes. Up until that time, cotton had been used in only the cheapest of women's house dresses, products made without style and of textiles whose dyes faded and whose size shrunk. The Council hired some major designers to develop fashions based on cotton textiles which had been sanforized (to limit shrinkage) and whose dyes had been tested for tub fastness and sun fastness. Then they launched a widespread publicity campaign to promote the new dresses. A key element of the campaign was a beauty contest in which a "Maid of Cotton" was elected, who then traveled from city to city exhibiting these fashions in the department stores. The department stores, of course, cooperated with advertisements, and the newspapers gave wide play to the new fashions by new designers. The result: within a few years cotton had taken over equal billing with rayon in women's dresses.

The above three incidents illustrate the vital part that the proper communications mix plays in linking the seller and the buyer and also the need to adapt the communications mix to the problem in hand. The purpose of communications, of course, is to persuade the prospective buyer to purchase and try the seller's offering. The process involves, however, more than a message or a medium. The source of the message itself is part of the communications, and the state of the receiver, the person who gets the message, profoundly influences both whether or not it will be received at all, and if received, what meaning will be read into the message. Moreover, the product itself must live up to expectations, as the Cotton Council wisely foresaw.

Effective communications thus involve four components—the audience(s), the source(s), the message, and the medium—and the loudest message about the product, positive or negative, is communicated by the product itself. Each of these components affect whether or not communication will take place at all and, if it does take place, what the communications convey. The most important of these components is the audience or the audiences.

## Communications and the Audience

The audience, or more likely the different audiences, determine whether or not communications take place at all. Without an audience, the seller is talking to the wind, and this is not a rare event.

The audience limits communications through five different kinds of selectivity: selective exposure, selective attention, selective perception, selective appeal, and selective response.

*Selective exposure* is basically a corollary of selective attention and selective perception. People expose themselves to possible information about matters in which they have a significant interest and only to sources perceived as being of this kind. The Oldsmobile owner reads Oldsmobile advertisements, the sports car driver reads only sports car news, a Republican political rally draws only Republicans and Democratic rallies only Democrats, and the fence-sitters both groups hope to reach stay away from both meetings. People who do not have a deep interest in automobile performance do not pick up any automobile magazines or read the test results. For this reason any would-be persuader's success is limited to that audience composed of those that are already persuaded, for which the message is mere reinforcement, and of those whose drives are active and which he can meet or can be perceived as meeting. No message is likely to register without some preexisting basis for a real interest. Nor is it likely to get the chance. Persuasion persuades only those who are ready to be persuaded.

Selective exposure helps the seller who takes it into account, but it limits his audience to those who have already bought his product and to those who are already searching to fill a drive which it can be perceived as fulfilling. As pointed out much earlier, the tendency of people to reduce their cognitive dissonance by reading ads of products they have already purchased is important to the seller. When the audience limits itself to sources of information on items in which they have a high degree of interest, it enables the persuader to choose the audience by choosing the medium to which such people will expose themselves, thus limiting the waste coverage he might otherwise have. All successful media choices are planned to appeal to a specific audience which has some related group of unsatisfied drives. If the sellers' message is clearly labeled as addressed to a particular subsegment of those he can serve, he has some assurance they will respond, provided these people are actively searching for a solution to a personal drive.

*Selective attention* further limits the audience the communicator can reach. Even though he may put his message in a medium which reaches the audience he desires, he must so construct his message that it will attract their attention on the basis of some interest they already have, and for which they are seeking satisfaction. This is one reason why none of us pays much attention to most of the advertisements even in those publications or on those broadcast media which we select as being close to our interest, as noted earlier. Even when the item being advertised, for example, is known to be highly attractive to the audience of a given publication and even when it is offered free, a response of as much as 3 percent is a very high response, as the distributors of highly-prized merchandise catalogues long ago discovered.

Finally, what the message conveys to the audience is limited by *selective perception.* Those who pay attention to the message perceive its meaning in terms of their own expectations and also what they consider important to themselves. In gestalt terms, only that which the viewer expects to find and which he considers important are figure. The rest of the message is ground and is not really received. The woman looking over the new releases in fashions in the women's section of the newspaper, for example, notes only those ads and those characteristics in the ads which appeal to those apparel needs which are at the top of her hierarchy of interest at the time. She sees a trend developing in the direction in which she desires and ignores all of the other diverse kinds of offerings in both the advertisements and in the news columns.

*Selective appeal* refers to the fact that communications are more effective in gaining attention when they are perceived as explicitly addressed to the receiver's specific group or market segment than when it is addressed to the public at large. Thus it is that a small two-inch, one-column-wide advertisement in the back of a magazine can get attention and deliver a persuasive message. By clearly headlining itself as addressed to "Air Travel Bargains for Students," it immediately flags the attention of students desiring to travel, despite its small size. Properly handled, it becomes figure and the rest of the page becomes ground.

The *method of appeal* and *method of presentation* can also affect the selectivity of the appeal. Generally speaking, high IQ audiences tend to respond better to appeals relying mainly on impressive logical arguments and tend to give a poorer response to appeals consisting of unsupported generalities or false, illogical, or irrelevant arguments aimed at an emotional appeal. On the other hand, those with lower intellectual achievement tend to be persuaded in a reverse manner.

One of the problems of many advertisers of mass consumption items is the need to appeal across class lines. The tendency of advertisers to use a single type of appeal, fitted to the lowest common denominator of the intellectual level of the audience, may be one explanation of the irritation that many middle-class people exhibit with the institution of advertising. Although it obviously takes more effort, and may be somewhat more costly to tailor different appeals to different segments of the market, the added effectiveness of doing this might very well prove more profitable in the end than the overall approach used by most advertisers.

A parallel phenomenon is that of the *selectivity of response.* Different kinds of personalities seem to respond differently to different kinds of appeals. People with different group membership patterns will respond differently because of the different standards of the groups to which they belong and the importance of the group membership to that individual. Different individuals will respond differently because of their different use-systems into which they perceive the product as fitting, and the different hold of habit on their adoption if the product is really new. The response will also differ because of the different degree of satiation of the particular drive involved.

Research seems to indicate rather marked differences of response by different kinds of personalities. These studies seem to indicate that formal authority figures should be shown as the ostensible source of the message—as in testimonials, for example—to appeal to those with authoritarian personalities (that is, people who tend to act in a dominating manner and who hold unquestioned respect for those in position of formal authority). Market subsegments consisting of receivers who are relatively unsusceptible to social influence, those with aggressive personalities, should not be appealed to in terms of majority opinions.

Fortunately for most sellers, most of their efforts in promoting new ideas and new products concern matters which are really in harmony with group standards in the target audience. When the objective of the communicator is to secure acceptance or support that goes contrary to such existing standards, however, he has the difficult job that any missionary faces: he must attempt to change the standards of the group itself. His first converts will come from those on the fringes of the group, from the isolates to whom group membership is relatively unimportant, and through them he may hope to reach others who are more closely affiliated with the group. The existence of sharply defined group standards is one factor in the difference between the relative ease of introduction of the evolutionary new products and the time and energy that it requires to promote a truly revolutionary one.

Moreover, what may be perceived as revolutionary depends on the rigidity of the accepted practices in the target group. To most people in the United States at the time the automobile was adopted, the horseless carriage was a welcome advance over the horse-drawn type. It was much more easily cared for and housed, and gave much greater freedom of movement and greater speed. But to those in the Amish communities in various places in the United States, it is still a product to be avoided. The Amish perceive the automobile as a very revolutionary violation of group standards.

**Audience Multiplicity**

So far, "audience" has been treated as though it were a singular phenomenon. But for many sellers, indeed for most sellers, the audiences are multiple. Even mass-sold, simple consumer products attain a major market share only by satisfying a number of different kinds of market subsegments. Moreover, few products reach the final user directly from the buyer. In between are distributor or processor customers, each of whom must be appealed to, and often also other people in the local community whom he must sell. Thus an official of Celanese Corporation—a major producer of man-made fibres—has been quoted as remarking that there are forty points between his factory and the final user at which the sale of his product could be killed: forty different receivers which his communications must persuade to use his fibres or products made from them. Some of those points are relatively obvious to anyone with any knowledge of the textile industry. Figure 15-1 sketches the seven most important stages of the fibre-to-garment-to-user flow which is involved and also indicates at least three sets of communication lines which must be designed to cover targets not directly concerned with product purchases: investors, technical people employed in quantity, and the community and the electorate. Every one of these ten possible sets of message receivers has its own unique goals relevant to Celanese's objectives. Celanese must persuade the receivers to see their respective goals as congruent with the corporation's own goal, which is the use of a Celanese product in seven of the cases, and some other kind of support for the corporation in the other three cases.

The Celanese example may seem extreme, but it is otherwise typical of the communications problems of most firms. For a great many of them, establishing all of the following targets and perceptions would be important.

1. *Final buyers:* to perceive the seller's wares as the preferred source of satisfaction for a given set of needs and to develop the habit of seeking them out.
2. *Merchants and distributors:* to perceive the firm as the best source of profit for a group of items in their merchandise mixes.
3. *Industrial buyers:* to perceive the seller as the most valuable source of materials, components, or supplies—that is, of supplies and components which will add the greatest value to their own products.
4. *Prospective employees*, particularly in the scarce categories: to perceive the firm as offering the most attractive work opportunities.
5. *Financial institution and investors:* to perceive the firm as a sound investment with a bright future and thus one worthy of money at a somewhat lower return than they might expect from one they did not so perceive.

**Figure 15-1.   Some of the Communications Audiences to which a Textile Fibers Producer May Need to Appeal**

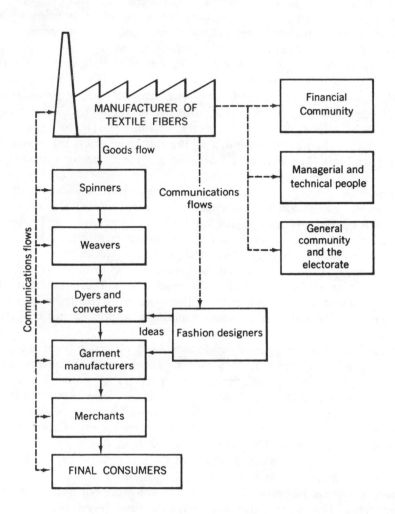

6. *The general public and especially the voters:* to perceive the firm as a valuable adjunct to the community's economy and which should, therefore, be defended from attacks by competing special interests.

Communications must develop a perception among final buyers that the product offers greater satisfaction than any competing product bundle for the needs which they have, considering the relative avoidance costs in money, shopping effort, and other penalties. Since shopping effort is an important part of the equation, communications must aim for the optimum distribution-created utilities needed, by persuading dealers and distributors to stock the item and promote and display it well. Distributors must perceive the product as being highly demanded by customers. They are, of course, more direct customers of the seller than the final customers themselves, but the physical product they buy satisfies a quite different drive for them than it does for the final user, the drive for profit.

The merchant is interested in only one attribute in any product—its profit opportunity attribute—either directly or indirectly. The product bundle can deliver that profit directly, as total margin on sales, or it may enhance the merchandise mix so that other products sell better, or it may do both. The source of increased sales may be the outstanding attraction of the physical product, but it is more likely to be a combination of the product and the communications mix accompanying it, plus the expert aid the salesman renders in helping the merchant carry out operations. Some of the value for the merchant may be due to the prestige element in the brand reputation, a reputation which may help him to bolster the perception that possible customers have of all of his offerings. Unless the merchant perceives the product as offering such an extra profit opportunity, the consumer will not find it in the outlet. Some of the communications, therefore, must really be aimed at the merchant himself even when seemingly addressed to the final consumer.

Industrial buyers also seek only some kind of profit potential, and such potential may come from a better price because of the product's reputation with final buyers, which they perceive as a built-in part of the consumer advertising. Thus the consumer advertising needs to convey a message to these intermediate industrial buyers, as well as the message which seems to be directed to the customers. Celanese, for example, undoubtedly sells some considerable part of its textile fibres because of the right to use the "made of Celanese" label on a garment.

However, most industrial purchases lose their identity in the manufacturing process and even if they did not, are perceived as so relatively unimportant that they could not influence final buyer perception of value. Nobody buys a Ford Maverick because it happens to have Goodyear Tires. For industrial buyers in such cases, the perceived differential of value motivating the industrial purchase must come from other elements in the design of the product bundle—in the distribution or in the technical services—and these values must be communicated in some manner.

The first job of the communications program is, of course, to move goods in some way or another or to help move them. Few better sources of good public relations or advertising exist than a highly popular brand. However, it is very rare that a product delivers this message of satisfaction well to everyone who might invest in the firm's securities, go to work for it, or vote on taxes or other political matters directly related to its welfare. Some parts of the communications mix must take the satisfaction of needs of people in these other roles into account.

It is not enough, of course, that the message reach the audience and be perceived by it. The message itself must have credibility, an attribute perceived as coming from the source and not from the message itself.

## The Influence of the Perceived Source on Communications

Communication messages do not stand on their own feet. The impact is affected by the source and by the manner of presentation. And the message itself can influence the audience's opinion of the perceived source. Credibility is a critical component of any form of communications and no tricks of wording or visual association can accomplish this end.

Part of the credibility depends on the readiness of the audience to believe the message before they even receive it, but a great deal depends on the perception of the audience as to the credibility of the source. The more the audience perceives the source as credible, trustworthy or prestigious, the greater the immediate credence given to the message and conclusions communicated (Hovland and Weiss, 1951). A new product, introduced by a manufacturer whose brands are well known and well liked, is much more likely to be tried than one promoted by an unknown newcomer to the market. Source credibility is one basis for manufcturers' use of family brands—brands applied uniformly to all products of a given class put on the market by the firm.

The good will value of a trademark, or simply the backing of a trusty merchant, are essentially matters of credibility of source. An advertisement by Marshall Field's, by Wannamaker's, or by Macy's gives a product claim more credibility than a similar advertisement by John's Bargain Store.

On the other hand, a poorly presented message can itself lower the credibility of the source. The political candidate who makes a single slip of temper can lose the election already seemingly in his grasp (as Dewey may have in the 1948 presidential campaign). The firm whose products always live up to the claims gains credibility for future messages, while advertising of a type viewed by the specific audience as exaggerated can actually cost expected sales for a merchant normally viewed as credible (as was indicated in the mattress sales incident quoted from Martineau earlier). Although we have discussed the source in the singular, the source of most messages is usually viewed as multiple by the audience. While the manufacturer cannot escape the responsibility for being one of those sources for his own brand, the outlets for his products are also seen as a source for products advertised through them, and the medium carrying the messages also is perceived as a source, even in the case of advertising.

The credibility of the medium depends on the attitude of the specific audience toward that medium and also the compatibility of the medium with a particular subject to the message. A dress design advertised in *Vogue* is likely to be considered a higher quality dress design than the same design would be advertised in *TV Guide*. Furthermore, the vehicle within the medium can be seen as a source. Advertisers always seek to get placement adjacent to compatible editorial matter—food advertising in the home section of the newspaper, automobile repair and parts advertising in the sports section, and so forth. Part of this is simply a matter of being sure that the right audience sees it, but part can be a matter of credibility. Some tests made by commercial agencies seem to indicate that some kinds of TV programs detract from the impact of commercials for specific products and other kinds of program adjacencies can enhance the message (*Advertising Age*, 1960). The young teenager may spend many of his working hours listening to rock and roll on his little personal transistor radio, but he may pay little attention to advertisements for grooming aids on this kind of station.

The multiplicity of perceived sources is one reason for the successful history of testimonial advertising. Lux soap long dominated the facial soap market because of the movie starlet testimonies on its radio programs. The name of a teenage idol is often enough to guarantee a market for any teen consumption item, from wigs to records to haircuts. To a certain degree, corporation promotional characters such as Mary Blake and Betty Crocker become authority figures, capable of lending some degree of credibility to the firm's advertising messages.

One of the major assets of good publicity is that the medium is the perceived source, lending vastly more credibility and even greater attention value, than a paid advertisement.

The method of presentation can also affect the credibility of the source. When the audience is inclined to be critical, or even potentially hostile, it is often well to start out the message by agreeing with the audience. The classic case in literature is Shakespeare's rendition of Mark Antony's funeral oration for Caesar, in which he starts out calling Caesar's murderers "honorable men" and ends up indicting them as villains. The Bekin's moving firm ran ads starting with a picture of a mover holding up a broken plate and the headline "we goofed!", and proceeded with a message intended to convey a picture of an extremely careful mover. Avis ran a long series of ads admitting that they were not the biggest automobile rental firm, and used this to get across the message that they might give better service by "trying harder."

## The Relationship of the Message to What Is Communicated

The meaning the audience gets out of a message, and its tendency to act on it, are not as simple as the amateur may suppose. The effect of the message will be related more to the experience and feelings about the subject of the messages felt by the audience that receives it, than to the precise content of the message itself. It will also be affected by the total situation surrounding the message and by selective perception. In any communications exchange situation, the purpose of such a message is to either strengthen a favorable attitude toward the seller's offering, in the case of an old established product, or to change attitudes to those favoring a new offering. The message itself can only hope to accomplish one or more of the following:

1. Attract the attention of the target receiver for the satisfaction cue being offered.
2. Build within a specific receiver or group of potential customers a comprehension of the potential differential value for them of the attributes of the offering.
3. Create added service in the product bundle itself.
4. Induce trial of the offering.
5. Reduce cognitive dissonance among those who have bought to render them more favorable to future purchases.

Only by doing one or more of these tasks can the communications accomplish its main purpose of adding value to the offering by changing the approach/avoidance balance. We have already discussed the problem of attracting attention. The depth of the difficulty naturally varies with the subject of the message and its degree of potential interest to the audience.

Tricks can be used to attract attention but the tricks themselves will not necessarily get people to study the message. Some years ago, a major manufacturer of men's socks ran a centerfold advertisement in *Esquire* magazine with the advertisement decorated by a full length picture of a typical *Esquire* girl. A later research study of the ads in that magazine showed that a great many readers remembered the advertisement, but that none of them remembered what was being sold.

Even when the message succeeds in getting attention in a manner relevant to the message itself, the communications may not necessarily have created a sale or exchange of any sort, or moved customers much closer to action. Research has shown, for example, that most possible target prospects are well aware of revolutionary new products before the market development period is over, but that only habitual innovators and very early adopters buy. It is necessary to go beyond attention to develop a full comprehension of the value of the unique benefits in the new offering and thus increase either the approach tendency to purchase, or to reduce the avoidance factor, or both. Usually, of course, one of these avoidance factors is the fear of not getting what the customer expects in the new product.

One task of the communications mix may be to add actual values or services in order to change the approach/avoidance balance. For many products, the salesman's advice is often as much a part of the product bundle as it is communications. Any publicity which builds up knowledge of the firm, and respect and confidence in its operations, adds meaning to the implied warranty of its label and thus may lower the avoidance barrier. Advertising and label may develop associational services: the campaign which successfully links an illusion of enhanced sexual attraction to the new aftershave has increased the service content of the bundle as much as the laboratory which developed the basic chemical formula.

Even when communications have succeeded in making an initial sale, no more has been accomplished than to gain consent for a trial. What happens next depends upon the buyer's perceived experience with the product bundle itself. If that experience seems to deliver a higher than previously available value, the product itself will have built the first real step toward an approach habit. Such sales promotional tools as sampling and warranties aim at the reduction of the avoidance barriers to initial trial. The product itself has to accomplish the rest of the communications job.

The role of the communications program does not cease with that initial trial. Quite often the buyer has some doubts about the wisdom of any substantial expenditure he has made because of the inevitable compromises he must make between competing satisfactions and competing offerings. The complete communications mix must include elements intended to reinforce his perceptions of satisfaction after purchase. As a matter of fact, such a reduction of cognitive dissonance may be the greatest actual result of any advertising campaign and is the one most easily accomplished because the buyer now really wishes to reassure himself that he was right.

## The Effects of Method of Message Presentation

Research into the effects of the specific content of messages have revealed a number of principles which are not always taken advantage of in commercial communications:

1. *Presentation of both sides*: Whenever the audience may start out in disagreement with the source or may hear or experience the other side anyway, it is best to present both sides of the argument to show the problems as well as the advantages of the offering.
2. *The fear backlash:* Strong appeals to fear tend to arouse such emotional tensions as to effectively inhibit any kind of action. Milder appeals are more likely to result in getting that action (Janis and Feschbach, 1953).
3. *Ask more, get more*: The more extreme the change of opinion asked by the communicator, the more actual change he is likely to get.
4. *Argument position*: The beginning or ending arguments or points are more likely to stick in the memory than those in between. (This is a simple corollary of the gestalt principle that the outstanding items draw more attention, the principle of *recency and primacy*.)
5. *Conclusion drawing*: It is best to state conclusions specifically rather than let the audience draw its own (Hovland et al, 1953).

Most sellers and politicians apparently feel that the other side is too likely to be presented anyway, and they often forfeit an opportunity to get the audience on their side by agreeing that what they have does not suit everyone's tastes or needs. However, a few advertising campaigns furnish refreshing examples of admitting what the customer is likely to know or learn anyhow, and thus increase the effectiveness of their campaign.

The Avis campaign "we are only number 2, we have to try harder," is one way of turning a weak spot into an appeal to the underdog tradition, and there is a great deal of evidence that this series of ads proved to be very effective. The Dow Chemical Company 1966 business journal advertisements headlined the kind of product failure to which the poor use of plastics could lead. The aim would seem to be overcome some of the prejudices against the use of plastic materials (of which

Dow is a major supplier) which arose from earlier ill-advised applications. Headlines such as "Don't look now, but mother's plastic blender just laid an egg," with the illustration showing a cracked blender jar spilling 'contents over the counter, seemed well designed to attract an industrial customer's attention. Then the value of getting expert help from Dow sales people could be driven home with the implied assurance that only a suitable plastic would be recommended. Similarly, when Renault came back on the market in the United States with a highly improved car, their admission that their first entries in the 1950s were poorly designed for America were an attempt to build on known previous weakness to get attention and credibility for their new story.

Probably the best evidence for the wisdom of not using too strong an appeal to fear comes from the public reaction to the medical evidence clearly linking smoking and lung cancer. Shortly after the surgeon general's report, sales of cigarettes dropped for just over a month, but were higher than ever within three months. When the danger is pictured as too great, the mind refuses to perceive the truth. Later publicity and advertising directed against smoking was a little wiser in emphasizing some of the less dramatic but far more frequent debilitating effects of smoking.

It is often necessary to appeal for a drastic change in attitude whenever attempting to get really new ideas accepted, whether in the buyer-seller situation of commercial advertising or dealing with social and political ideas. Otherwise the screening effects of selective perception may eliminate those parts of the message the audience is not ready to believe. Maloney has stated that his research indicates that a claim which is disbelieved because it is "too good to be true" has often proved conducive to "nudging the consumer along the path" to trial and adoption of a product, in the case, of course, of products which are relatively inexpensive (Maloney, 1963).

To accomplish such an end, the claim must be specific enough to be subject to test and the source must be certain the claim will later stand up to the test of experience. This principle would seem to imply also that the easiest kind of product to persuade people to try is one which appears to offer a very substantial additional satisfaction value, not something that is just as good or even better.

The research on the necessity to draw specific conclusions seems to indicate that when the audience is deeply interested, this may not be true. But most commercial offerings involve matters which are not of a great deal of deep interest to consumer and it is usually better in such situations to tell the prospect, in effect, "when you need . . ., get . . . ."

## The Influence of the Medium on Communications

The medium tends to select the audience because each possible communications medium is designed to appeal to a rather specific audience and various market segments expose themselves to quite divergent media. For most products, a mixture of media must be employed because even the most widely used media may reach only a portion of some segments. Not all men read the sports pages or are ardent sports spectators, and many in the upper classes tune in to television only occasionally. On the other hand, audiences of different media tend to overlap. Those selecting to expose themselves to one type of medium are more likely to expose themselves extensively to other similar media or other types of media carrying similar kinds of editorial matter. Because of this, the message tends to get multiple supplementation because of the selective exposure of the audience. As already pointed out, the medium itself is, to some degree, seen as one of the sources of the message and it is always part of the general context in which the message is received.

The real media for the communication of the benefits of a product is a far wider group of things than just the formal print broadcasting and personal sales media we think of in this connection. By far the most important medium to communicate the benefits of an offering is the offering or the product itself. It is the product which is perceived as delivering the reward for the search for satisfaction. All other forms of communication can only hope to get the individual to try the product. It is true, of course, that the various media and the messages of communication can provide a setting and furnish the buyer some guidelines within which to perceive the benefits. And in the case of some products in which the benefit is really some form of emotional association outside the physical product itself, the advertising or sales person may actually determine what is perceived as the benefit.

If the communications message, through whatever medium, leads the prospect to expect a certain benefit, this may be all that is necessary for the product to render that benefit. Thus the young girl who is persuaded by the sales woman that she looks more beautiful in a certain type of eye shadow and a certain tint of lipstick may feel more beautiful, and because she has a greater poise as a result, really be more attractive.

If the television advertisement delivered by a man in a white coat convinces the viewer that he will get really fast relief from his headache by taking the pill advertised, he may very well feel relief from his headache by taking the pill advertised, and he may feel that relief within seconds after taking the pill, even though the medication would actually require as much as one-third of an hour to take effect physically. Medically, this is known as the *placebo* effect. It is known, for example, that as many as one-third of those given an ordinary harmless sugar pill, with the suggestion that the pill could grant the desired relief from arthritis, will actually lose their arthritis pains. Medical corpsmen at the battle front have occasionally relieved battle field suffering by injecting pure distilled water after their supplies of morphine have run out.

Thus, in matters in which the perception involves some purely emotional experience, the communications message delivered through the right medium in the right manner may very well confer the sought-for benefit. However, this is true solely of benefits that are emotional or affective in content. It is not likely to occur when the benefit is cognitive in content—when it is a matter of objective observation. Trying to sell a large gas-hungry car to people during a period of gas shortage by quoting unusual tests that it delivers "fifteen miles to the gallon" is not going to get the customer to perceive that it does so when his eyes tell him, after purchase, that his gas gauge is empty when he has driven only far enough to have gotten seven miles to the gallon.

The value of the product itself in delivering a convincing message is the basic reason for the use of the various forms of sales promotion that aim at getting customer trial: various means to gain direct sampling, such as direct-to-the-home distribution of free samples, or distribution of free samples in stores with or without demonstration, coupon sampling, full or part refund offers, demonstration parties such as the wine tasting parties put on by wine makers, tie-in packaging, grouping the item with related products and offering (the combination deal at a drastic temporary price reduction, contests and sweepstakes coupled with temporary price reduction coupons, merchandise premiums or premium coupons packed in a package, guarantees to lower the perceived risk of buying the product, cents-off deals, and others.

Pricing can also be a medium for delivering a message about the product. A price which is below the normal market level for other similar products tells the customer, "don't expect too much from this item—this is a low-end product, and should not be expected to deliver premium benefits." Customer experience has long shown that, in general, the premium products deliver greater kinds and degrees of satisfaction than the low-end products, and the customer will act in accordance with these habitual perceptions.

Thus, a novelty firm that had produced a novel form of barbecue, a "Tiki-bachi" consisting of a clay jar with a grinning ugly face in which the mouth, eyes and nostril holes furnish the air intake, found that the product did not sell well at $2.95 but did quite well at $4.95. The reason: research showed that most of them were being bought by women as gifts for their husbands and it is a group norm that people do not give gifts that cost substantially under $5.00. To paraphrase the slogan of a greeting card manufacturer, a price under $5.00 carries the message that the gift "shows that the giver does not care enough to give the very best."

Promotion, like every other aspect of marketing effort, must also vary with the product life cycle.

## The Promotional Effect and the Product Life Cycle

Each stage of the product life cycle requires a different set of communication objectives and carries with it different media opportunities and different media requirements. For a high-learning product going through a prolonged market development period, the only thing that can be expected of mass communications of any sort is to create awareness and understanding of offering benefits among the mass of the potential market. The only sales that can be hoped for are trial purchases by early adopters.

During this market development period, publicity is normally highly available and also highly desirable. Publicity is available because the novelty and the new benefits offered by the new product bundle are of possible interest to a great many people and therefore, can be treated as valid news by the various media. Any actual sales obtained, however, will normally have to be through aggressive personal sales. Only the personal salesman is in a position to search out the risk questions in the mind of the prospect and to show to each prospect how the product best fits into his own desire-sets. Only the personal salesman can search out the other questions in the prospect's mind and give them a convincing answer. Even then, sales will be made only to those who are innovative by nature and highly value the added benefits of the new offering. The purpose of mass communications during this phase of the cycle is to transmit an awareness of the product to the main population and to secure some degree of understanding of the benefits involved, laying the groundwork for future diffusion and market growth.

There are situations, of course, in which the personal sales effort is not economically feasible. The size of the individual purchase may be too small to justify the cost of a personal sales call. Then some other personal advice device should be sought, backed up by overwhelming mass communications. Such was the case of the first Toni home permanents which came out at $1.75 a kit. It was obvious to Toni from the first that their product would not sell itself. It required a great deal of learning with respect to the feasibility of doing one's own permanent and the safety of such an attempt. To meet this need, Toni mounted a saturation radio and newspaper campaign, concentrated expenditures at any one time on a single market. In addition, the salesman persuaded the girl behind the cosmetic counter to try a kit herself so that she could become a positive sales woman.

Once the market development period is ending, and, of course, with any product that starts out with no need for a significant market development phase, the major objective of the communications must be to create brand preference among both the trade and the final users. Some publicity may still be possible at this stage, and is always valuable because of the high degree of credibility imparted by the perceived source—the medium itself in which the news item appears. Generally speaking, however, the communications medium emphasis must be shifted to various kinds of mass advertising media, supplemented by dealer promotions to encourage the dealer to stock the item and thus make it more available and more widely on display.

During this period, the dollars invested in advertising and sales promotion should be viewed as an investment in a permanent market share. Getting the early majority adopters to try the product for the first time places all later competitors in the position of having a riskier product, a product with an element of the unfamiliar, once these early majority adopters become satisfied with the offering. Advertising dollars spent during the growth period should normally return both immediate sales profits and a solid head start in the market share. Personal sales to final users are much less important during this period, since the benefits of the offering are now widely understood. Instead the main emphasis must be on making the product as widely available as possible, to back up the communications investment.

By the time the competitive turbulence phase of the product life cycle is reached, the main objective becomes to maintain the consumer franchise by continuous reminder of the benefits they are receiving from the product and the indirect value of this advertising in strengthening dealer ties. Consumer interest is no longer nearly so high, now that the stimulus variability aspect of the product (its novelty) no longer exists. Extensive distribution becomes increasingly valuable, since consumers are less likely to actively search out sources for the product.

During this phase, the main communications channels of value are mass media advertising, both to reach and maintain the share of market already gained and to impress the dealers with the value of the firm's efforts in their behalf. Sales promotions to gain sampling are less important than in the earlier period of rapid growth but still have some value, since during this period some of the brands that came in during the early growth period will be dropping out of the market and their consumers will be searching for new sources for a product which has already become part of their use-systems.

During the maturity phase, the main problem is to keep the consumer reminded of the value of the product and to maintain trade loyalty. Almost all of the communications need to be in terms of mass media. Extra effort thrown into communications during this period normally gains only a temporary effect which subsides once the extra effort is withdrawn (see Figure 15.2).

During the decline phase, there is little point to putting much into communications at all. Consumers will not pay attention because interest in the product is already disappearing, and thus there are no significant numbers of potential new customers to be obtained. The decline has arrived because some different kind of competing offering is widely perceived as having significantly greater benefits and the remaining customers are mostly the laggards who are both late to adopt and last to drop a product. Their dislike of change is greater than their interest in added benefits. What studies are available indicate that whatever effort is put into extra advertising and sales promotions during this period is almost pure waste and a drain on the profits without any offsetting benefit.

Thus, the variability of the effect of promotions with the product life cycle is one reason no simple rule-of-thumb can be given as to the proper level of advertising for a product. During the early growth period, perhaps the only reasonable standard is that all advertising that can be afforded should be done. During the decline period, the obvious standard is that no advertising can be afforded which does not return an immediate profit of some kind.

## Summary

1. Communications mix results are affected by four factors: the audience(s), the source(s), the medium, and the message.

2. Five kinds of audience selectivity limit the effect of any communications: selective exposure, selective attention, selective perception, selective appeal, and selective response.

3. Most sellers must try to reach several audiences, appealing to different motives in each. Besides the different end-user market segments, messages must also be designed for the attention of intermediary buyers and even to stockholders, potential employees and the general public.

### Figure 15-2.  Effects of Temporary Bursts of Promotional Activity at Different Stages of the Product Life Cycle

A. During the Rapid Growth Phase: an extra burst of promotional spending can be an investment in greater future market share by attracting and winning buyers just beginning to sample the product category.

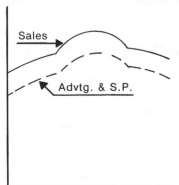

B. During Maturity: heavy promotional campaigns during the saturated market phase may attract some temporary sales gain, but the added sales are likely to disappear with the end of the campaign. Most buyers have already made a choice of the brand they prefer, if any, and are unlikely to be switched by mere promotion.

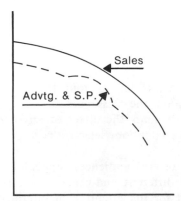

C. During the Decline: any apparent gain from added promotional effort is more likely to be due to mere coincidence than it is to the promotional effort. Most buyers have already lost interest in the product and will pay no attention to promotional messages.

From Chester R. Wasson, *Dynamic Competitive Strategy & Product Life Cycles*, Challenge Books, St. Charles, Ill., 1974.

4.   Whatever or whoever is perceived as the source of the message also affects its reception. The original credibility of the message is derived from the credibility of the source.

5.   A poorly presented message can reflect back on the credibility of the source itself.

6.   Sources are usually perceived as multiple. In addition to the manufacturer, the outlets and the media are also perceived as sources.

7.   Testimonials in advertising are one device for using prestigious or otherwise believable independent individuals as perceived sources.

8.   Well-done publicity is extremely effective because the medium is perceived as the principal source.

9.   Credibility is also affected by the method of message presentation.

10.   Presentations to hostile or skeptical audiences do better by presenting both sides.

11.   Very strong fear appeal presentations risk a backlash, and tend to inhibit action rather than stimulate it.

12.   Requests for extreme changes of attitude are more likely to cause change than requests for mild changes.

13.   Because of the principle of recency and primacy, beginning and ending arguments are most likely to be remembered.

14.   It is normally best to state conclusions specifically rather than let the audience draw its own.

15.   Media both select audience and are perceived as message sources.

16.   Media audiences tend to overlap and thus give the message additional supplementation.

17.   Delivery of the message through a prestigious medium may have a placebo effect—it may make the message self-fulfilling.

18.   The product itself is one of the most effective media for delivering the message concerning its benefits.

19.   The phase of the product life cycle is an important element in the effectiveness of promotional efforts.

20.   Publicity is especially available and particularly valuable in promoting awareness during a market development period, but personal sales is the only really effective means of gaining the necessary early adopter trials of high-learning products.

21.   The rapid growth phase of the life cycle requires heavy emphasis on mass media messages intended to stimulate trial and establish brand preference. Well-designed promotion during this phase tends to create relatively permanent gains in market share. Sampling is an especially valuable means of promotion during this phase.

22.   The communications goal during the period of competitive turbulence and the succeeding maturity phase is to maintain strong

distribution and hold market share. Special promotional efforts during the maturity phase tend to produce only temporary gains in market share, in the absence of a really substantial product improvement.

23.   Promotion has little or no effect during the decline phase. The benefits are no longer being sought and consumers pay no attention.


## Chapter 15  Exercises

1.   If all of the 5 kinds of selectivity are a fact of life for the advertiser, how can he plan his advertising and how can he manage his sales operation to minimize the cost implications of each one of them? (In advertising, for example, he pays for the whole circulation of a periodical or the whole audience of a broadcast program regardless of how few he really reaches.)

2.   How many audiences must a golf club manufacturer reach if he is to be successful in marketing his line? What kinds of media would you suggest for the manufacturer of a quality set of clubs, and why?

3.   How many audiences, and which ones, would a manufacturer of an insect spray for general consumer use have to reach, and why?

4.   Getting a product onto dealers' shelves and even keeping it there, once on, is not easy. No store manager ever has the amount of display space he could wish for. How does a manufacturer with a new product appeal to this distributor audience, and how does he get some degree of credibility for his story?

5.   Classify all of the broadcast (TV and radio) commercials you are exposed to in one day for their method or level of appeal (logical reasons why, or irrelevant emotional appeals). Check the ads in *Newsweek* and *Time*. How do these classify? Why, in each case?

6.   What kinds of selectivity render personal selling the most effective communications medium for a revolutionary new product? Why?

7.   What means does a wholly new market entrant, without an established reputation and with a new product, have to gain credibility for his communications, especially his advertising?

8.   Find 3 current advertising campaigns which seem to attempt to present both sides. Why do they do so, in each case?

9.  What method must a mail order seller use to gain and maintain credibility for his claims for products which the consumer must first order before he can inspect them?

10. In what sense may the distributors and dealers be part of the communications strategy of a firm (in addition to the advertising such outlets may perform, that is)?

    In the case of the quality golf club manufacturer, what does this mean with relation to his preferred distribution strategy?

11. In trying to maximize the return on his promotional dollars, what should be the general policy about allocation of communications funds and efforts to various elements in the product mix? Why?

# Avoidance Reactions to the Various Prices Exacted in Exchange*

---

*This chapter is based mainly on material in Chester R. Wasson, *Dynamic Competitive Strategy and Product Life Cycles*, Challenge Books, St. Charles, Ill. (1974), by permission of the copyright owner.

PRICE AS ANY PURCHASE INHIBITING FACTOR

THE EIGHT DIMENSIONS OF PERCEIVED PRICE

Monetary Cost
Time Availability
Place Availability
Use-time
Search Effort
Dissatisfaction Risk (3 Types)
Learning Cost
Design Compromise

CONSUMER PRICE PERCEPTION PATTERNS

j.n.d. Effect
Price Lining
Price/Quality Inference
Reversed Price Perception
Cost/Price Judgments
Fair Price Reference Points and Engineering to a Price
Price Aura Effect
Quotation Effect

COMPLEXITIES OF THE PRICING DECISION

Need to Shift Policies With the Changing Phases of the Product
Life Cycle
Need to Price an Assortment at a Variety of Margins
Need to Purchase Distribution Services

MARKET ENTRY PRICING

MERCHANDISE MIX PRICING

DISCOUNT STRUCTURE DETERMINATION

ADJUSTMENTS NEEDED WITH CHANGES IN THE PRODUCT
LIFE CYCLE

WHEN ADAPTING HIS OWN behavior to get the buyer to give him what he wants, the seller really works with just three basic variables:

1. *His offering*—a bundle of perceivable positive values, including the place and time values created by his distribution system
2. *Communications*—all of the attempts to inform customers of the benefits in the values he is offering to them
3. *Price*—the various methods of limiting purchases of offerings to those willing to give some kind of value in exchange, adequate to justify his making the offering

The term *price* has two general definitions in common use and most people use both definitions at different times. One definition is extremely narrow. It is the monetary sacrifice needed to acquire an offering. The other definition is extremely broad. Price is used to designate any sacrifice of time, effort, material goods, or even of some kinds of desired satisfactions necessary to gain a highly-desired satisfaction.

Most economic theory has focused on monetary price alone, but this has led to something far less than a satisfactory understanding of consumer decision behavior in any exchange situation. From a psychological point of view, price can only be properly defined as any attribute of an offering which tends to inhibit the consumer's desire to acquire it and limits the amounts of his purchases. Thus a psychological definition would correspond with the very broad one in general use. Briefly, price should be understood as including any perceived avoidance characteristic in the offering.

In the pigeon experiments mentioned much earlier, the pigeon was led to limit his seeking of corn by means of an electrical shock, causing him to approach the button which would yield the corn only when he was extremely hungry. Thus, the electrical shock was for him a price.

## The Multiple Dimensions of Perceived Price

There are at least eight different aspects of price involved in the consumer's decision as to when, where, and from whom to acquire an offering:

1. The monetary cost
2. The time availability
3. The easy accessibility of the place at which the purchase must be made
4. The time required to put the product into use
5. Search effort
6. The risk of dissatisfaction
7. The learning cost
8. The necessary design compromise

Economists and lawyers try to get around some of this by defining time and place utilities as product attributes. But anything less than here and now is negative in value, so that these are really sales inhibitors, not positive utilities. The lack of complete availability at any time of the day or night is a negative attribute and the psychologist would have no hesitation in labeling them as avoidance attributes in an offering. Neither economists nor attorneys have any explanation for the fact that consumers recognize as different products the gasoline sold by an independent service station under its own label and the physically and chemically identical fuel sold out of the pumps of the American Oil Company. Nevertheless, the customer undeniably treats the two as being different offerings and, under normal conditions of relatively free supply, the unrecognized brand must sell for two to three cents less per gallon than the recognized brand and, even then, only a minor segment of the market will purchase it. The source credibility of the unknown brand is less than the source credibility of the recognized brand, and thus involves a risk of dissatisfaction. Similarly, the convenience store which is open at 11:00 at night can charge quite a bit more for the same carton of milk than can the supermarket down the street which closes at 9:00 P.M. And the nearby corner store can hold to a higher price than the discount house across town.

It is true that all three of these items—timing, place, and risk dissatisfaction—can, to some degree, be translated into monetary terms, as our own example showed. But many of the other ones are not so easily translated. One of these is the *time cost* of using the product. It is true that the buyer's supply of money is always limited relative to the totality of his desires and his monetary resources, forcing him to choose which desires will be fulfilled first, and to what extent.

*Time costs*, however, are often more important than the monetary price, since the buyer must allocate his available hours as carefully as his monetary resources. For many a buyer, the time available is more inelastic than his monetary income. A great many people can find ways to increase their monetary resources to some appreciable extent if forced to, but no one has yet added one millisecond to the twenty-four hours of the day. For this reason, many buyers put a very stiff premium value on any offering perceived as costing less time than its substitute.

One of the more spectacular examples of this time price effect has been the degree to which the private automobile has driven mass transit virtually off the road, even when the mass transit cost is much less in money than automobile operation. The automobile enables the individual to make more flexible use of his time, especially when the alternative is a bus line caught in the same traffic jams. The only mass transit lines that have been able to survive and gain traffic have been subway and commuter rail lines moving over privileged rights of way on convenient schedules, and thus able to best the time cost of the private automobile for substantial market segments.

Another testimony to the value of the time cost has been the rather spectacular growth of sales of the time-saving, so-called "convenience foods" in the last generation. Quite often, the quality of these is somewhat lower than the "scratch ingredient dishes" for which they substitute, and their money cost is frequently substantially higher, but they enable the working housewife to make better use of her limited time for meal preparation than does the processed produce which has begun to displace the sale of fresh produce in most supermarkets.

The standard marketing classification of goods into convenience goods, shopping goods and specialty items is testimony to the importance of *search cost* to the customer. The fact that a customer will freely substitute a different brand for his preferred one, if the latter is not in stock at the place of purchase, is proof enough that *search effort* is a perceivable cost. Indeed, one of the reasons that people tend to be patronage loyal to a given store is the fact that it is much easier for them to find what they are seeking within that store than in a different store with a somewhat different layout. Much of the total expenditure of advertising takes place in order to reduce the consumer's search effort, to inform him of where the satisfactions he desires are readily available.

There are really three different kinds of *risk costs* perceivable by the customer—the risk that desired satisfaction will not be forthcoming even after the other prices are paid, the risk of lack of future supply when desired, and the risk of continuity of supply over a period of time.

The buyer seeks for information clues which will help him evaluate the risk that his desires will not be satisfied, to help him to determine whether the promises of fulfillment made for the product are likely to be kept. From past experience, he is certain that such promises are not always completely credible. He will, therefore, discount the other prices by the degree of perceived risk in the purchase—by shopping at a store, for example, whose choice of merchandise is dependable, by choosing a brand he knows to meet his needs, and so forth. The market shows many examples of such dissatisfaction risk discounts—cut rate gasoline, private brand retail items sold at less than the regular brand price, the reluctance of people to substitute a new item with much higher satisfaction value for one with which they are familiar, and others.

The *risk of lack of future supply* when desired is also a major factor in many purchases. For most of our purchases, we are looking for a dependable source of a series of similar purchases of indefinite duration. We pray for a continual supply of our *"daily* bread," not just today's bread. We want a continuous supply of wholesome water, not just a safe drink and warm bath today. We look as carefully at the service network that the manufacturer maintains as we do at the design of his car, in order to be insured that the service will be restored whenever interrupted by mechanical breakdowns we know are certain to occur. We may purchase our gasoline at a certain station which we know charges more than others in order to be assured of mechanical service when we need it.

The *risk of continuity of supply* is especially important to the industrial purchaser. He does not wish to have to close down a multimillion dollar assembly line because a shipment of abrasive wheels has been delayed. He will, therefore, limit purchases to sources of supply which experience has proven most reliable in furnishing offerings of known dependable content and assurance of steady adequate supply, and will usually insist on having at least two or more such suppliers as added insurance.

New competitors who seek entrance into markets, in which the perceived risk of supply interruption is considered important, must first seek buyers to whom the risk of such an interruption is of less importance than the much higher values they perceive in the offering. The first European sports cars imported into the United States were sold in very small numbers to enthusiasts who placed a very high premium on the sensitivity of their handling characteristics and were willing to pay a high out-of-service interruption cost to get these attributes.

An earlier chapter has discussed the importance of the *learning need price* as a barrier to the ready acceptance of new offerings. One industrial example of the height of such a price premium was the slowness with which aluminum electrical conductors took over from copper cable among major utilities. When the equivalent amount of aluminum conductor cost only two-thirds as much as copper, a great many utilities continued to use the copper, in part because the switchover to aluminum would require them to retrain their work force in different methods of making electrically conductive connections.

All purchases of any great importance require some degree of *compromise on design* attributes. The quite different composition and evaluation of the desire-sets of individual prospects are so varied that all customers could come really close to getting what they need only through custom manufacture. In addition, every buyer has desire-sets in which some of the things he desires are not compatible with other elements in his desire-set. The need to avoid the high cost of custom design by designing a few standard models, and the need to make a choice as to which desires are most important at the moment, are both inhibiting elements in the purchase of a product.

The greater the degree of the standardization in the offering, the larger the proportion of prospects who must forego substantial elements in their desire-sets and the larger the number of wished-for attributes they will not receive. This is one reason why a careful analysis of any market will nearly always reveal some niches into which an insightful new producer can move. It is also the reason why the production economies of single-model design must always give way sooner or later to a variety of options. Henry Ford could insist that customers buy "any color as long as it is black" and limit themselves to two or three body models. But his grandson could succeed with the Mustang only because he offered several distinct lines and any combination of seventy different options within the line.

For all of these reasons, the seller must consider far more than the monetary price in planning his marketing operations. In addition he must recognize that the traditional economic viewpoint of the demand curve as a smooth continuous function simply does not exist, that, due to certain inherent psychological tendencies plus various learned expectations, the customer's perception of price does not follow the nice mathematical formulas that economists prefer to use in their texts (see Figure 16-1).

## The Realities of Consumer Price Perception

There are at least eight distinguishable realities of the consumer reaction to price that are not normally taken into account in price theory (see Figure 16-2):

**Figure 16-1.   The 8 Major Components of Buyer Perception of the Price of Acquisition**

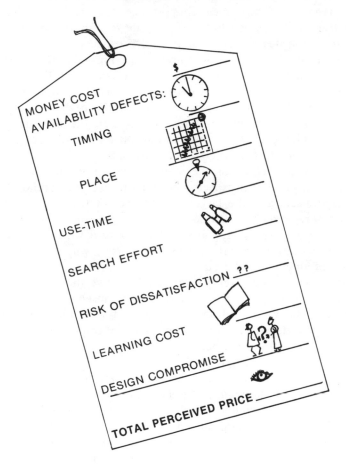

1.   The just noticeable difference effect (j.n.d.)
2.   Price lining
3.   Price/quality inferences
4.   Reverse price perception
5.   Cost/price relationship judgments
6.   Fair price reference points
7.   The price aura effect
8.   The effect of the method of price quotation

**Figure 16-2.   The 8 Principal Parameters of Buyer Perception of Value**

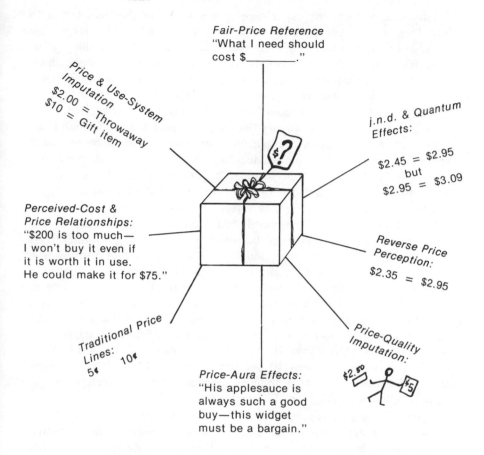

*Fair-Price Reference*
"What I need should cost $_____."

*Price & Use-System Imputation*
$2.00 = Throwaway
$10 = Gift item

*j.n.d. & Quantum Effects:*
$2.45 = $2.95
but
$2.95 = $3.09

*Perceived-Cost & Price Relationships:*
"$200 is too much—
I won't buy it even if
it is worth it in use.
He could make it for $75."

*Reverse Price Perception:*
$2.35 = $2.95

*Traditional Price Lines:*
5¢   10¢

*Price-Quality Imputation:*

*Price-Aura Effects:*
"His applesauce is
always such a good
buy—this widget
must be a bargain."

The *j.n.d. effect* was discussed much earlier in the book, and it was noted at that time that this discriminal threshold is not normally a small difference. This is nowhere more obvious than in price. Merchants long ago learned that in order to move slow-moving goods, or clear out a stock, the price cuts had to be quite deep and quite dramatic. No merchant ever advertises in big bold letters "SPECIAL SALE: PRICES CUT 5 PERCENT." Indeed, it seems certain that price cuts of anything under 20 percent are not likely to be very conducive to much market change. They must be much greater than a j.n.d., which is generally of the order of 8 or 10 percent.

In general, the differences center around round number figures. Thus, the customer may not see any real change in price when it moves up from $2.65 to $2.95, but will react with shock to a price that crosses the $3.00 mark.

This was, in fact, the experience of a small firm that was trying to introduce a new pet product of a premium grade. The large size package of the product originally was priced at $2.65, but the cost of the packaging of the large twenty-five pound size was so much more expensive than that for the smaller sizes that it yielded a much lower profit at this level than did the next smaller size (the ten pound one) at $1.29 per package. The head of the firm then put a suggested retail price of $2.75 on the twenty-five pound package and found no difference in sales response. Such was also the case when he moved it up to $2.85 and $2.95. Finally, deciding that $3.09 was still a bargain relative to the $1.29 for ten pounds, he put a suggested list price of $3.09 on it. At that point, the demand disappeared completely.

The just noticeable difference effect also seems to be true even in industrial purchasing. An unpublished study by a colleague, of the reactions of buyers of tin plate (all of them very large manufacturers, mostly in can manufacturing), found that a difference of five cents a base box was not viewed by the industry as a difference at all, but a "chisel" and not one which would cause them to change their source of supply. Only a difference of some ten times as much, fifty cents, was viewed as the least amount of price difference that would be significant. The result of this effect is a quite different kind of demand curve than economic texts show—that is, the demand within quite a range of prices, somewhat less than 10 percent of the total involved, is completely inelastic and then changes abruptly once a certain round number value is reached (see Figure 16-3).

Related consumer reactions to pricing are the phenomena of *traditional pricing* and *price lining* and the need to conform to a specific level or set of levels of prices in the market and to design the product to accord with these levels. Consumers approach the purchase act with some obvious expectation of paying a very specific price per unit of purchase and tend to ignore offerings that do not come at these price levels. Candy bars must be either five cents, ten cents, or fifteen cents and if there is an in-between price involved, it seems that it still must accord with these levels. For example, chewing gum sold from the turn of the twentieth century until 1970 for a price of five cents per package of five sticks, with very little variation and those only in terms of a small volume of carton sales and in very large packages at lesser prices. Finally, however, ingredient costs forced a price increase. The industry then went to a ten-cent package for a seven- or eight-stick pack rather than seven or eights cents for the standard five-cent package. There is no question but that the industry was basing its decision on previous

**Figure 16-3.   Price-Demand Patterns: As Taught in the Traditional Economics Classroom, versus Experience in the Actual Marketplace**

A. THE PRICE-DEMAND PATTERN AS TAUGHT IN THE ECONOMICS CLASS-ROOM. Quantity demanded and the elasticity of demand are presented as continuous functions of price. That is, it is assumed that the slightest shift in price will produce a corresponding shift in the quantity sold, and always in reverse relationship, with no definite limits on the relationship.

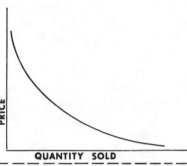

B, C & D. PRICE-DEMAND PATTERNS AS THEY ARE FOUND IN THE MARKET-PLACE

B. *The Most Common: a Typical Result of the j.n.d. and Reference Point Phenomena.* (When sales are confined to established use-systems)
Demand is a discontinuous quantum function of price, and is characteristically lower both below and above some reference point.

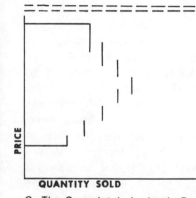

C. *The Completely Inelastic Demand.*
Up to some specific quantity limit, whatever quantity is available can be disposed of at a single specific price, and none will sell above that price. Above the limit, none can be sold at any price.

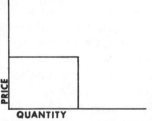

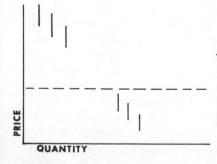

D. *The Use-System Elasticity Pattern.*
Within a single set of related use-systems, demand is relatively inelastic, but a price below some specific critical point uncovers new and larger markets, also relatively inelastic.

attempts to charge a price in between the five-, ten- and fifteen-cent points for other confections.

*Price lining* is really an extension of the same phenomenon. By price lining we mean the selling of somewhat similar products in the same category at widely separated, very sharply defined, specific price quotations. In such a system, each price line point represents a sharply-defined perceptible quality level. Most of us are familiar with this practice in clothing and in canned goods in the supermarket, as well as in automobiles. What may not be so obvious is that any seller who tries to build a product at some point in between these price lines has very great difficulty in moving his wares, as one men's suit maker discovered, when he tried to design a suit to sell between two different quality levels.

In general, of course, the quality differences between lines have an objective physical basis for the perception of difference, although the untrained buyer may not always be able to judge these differences directly. When such price line situations are common within an industry, the range of quality between makers within the same price line tends to be quite narrow. The rather superficial approach to pricing, that of talking about pricing "at the market," "above the market," or "below the market," does not accord with the way consumers react. The lower price item is not lower priced but a lower end good. The man who buys a Robert Hall suit for $65 has no illusions that he is buying the equal of a $200 make. He just does not desire to put that much into the kind of extra quality that he knows is there. He may not be personally able to judge the difference in the tailoring in the store, but he has learned from experience that a real difference exists, and the differences are reflected in price. He does not tend to investigate clothes at a lower price level than he customarily buys because observation and experience has taught him that the price sacrifice to which he is accustomed is needed to obtain a corresponding level of desire fulfillment. On the other hand, he is seldom tempted to pay a higher price than his habitual level because he does not value the extra satisfactions which the higher price tag brings with it.

It is true that price line judgments probably can become somewhat circular. Having learned that the expected bundle of satisfactions comes only at a specific price level, the buyer perceives the price itself as a partial cue to expect a given level of quality. Thus we have the phenomenon of quality being judged from the price, including the well-known anomaly that intrigues many economists—the fact that a good perfume sells much better at a higher price than at a lower one.

The perfume example is not nearly so anomalous as many economists would like to believe. It results really from two different extremely common reactions to price. The first is group standards as to the value of the product in a given use-system. Most expensive perfume is purchased as a gift, and one does not give cheap perfume. The other is a much more general principle, and that is that the customer approaches almost every price situation with some kind of fair-price reference point in mind. The fair-price reference point has been demonstrated under artificial laboratory situations as well as in the market place.

Thus, Tull, Boring, and Gonsier (1964) found, in an experiment with students, that the amount that would be purchased at a price which the students were told was the usual price they would pay, was greater than the amount at prices either above or below. Similarly, in a market test of a product that did not seem to be moving very well for a large hard goods chain, an unpublished study showed that the product was much more attractive to customers at $1.09 than at either $.89 or $1.29.

The price elasticity on which economists lay a great deal of quite justified emphasis results from a somewhat different phenomenon than they generally concede—the fact that different price levels tap different market segments and thus different use-systems in which the product has different value. In almost no case is it ever true that the elasticity is a smoothly changing phenomenon. A market test of potential dealers for a fisherman's specialty product—a trolling speedometer, for example—showed that the demand at a retail price above $5.00 (note the round number effect here) was far less than sales at a retail price under $5.00, and that the degree of elasticity on both sides of this $5.00 break was rather low, indicating that the correct selling price (which they adopted) would be $4.95, just below the $5.00 level. Apparently, dealers thought customers would view the offering of the item below $5.00 as one subject to some degree of impulse purchase, but that a price above $5.00 would require more consideration.

These *fair-price points* and other discontinuities are not so mysterious as they may seem to be. When a product enters the market, it is competing with some other product performing a somewhat similar function. The value of this other product determines the initial reaction to the price of the one being newly introduced, even when the product does not seem to be the same type of product at all.

The trolling speedometer was, functionally, a means of improving fishing luck, and could thus be compared with the cost of another lure.

Such a comparison proved to be the case of a special soil conditioner that a small company tried to introduce on the market. The product had a great many values, one of which was that it really did stimulate growth, quite substantially, both in the open and the greenhouse. However, it was not a fertilizer and contained no plant food elements at all. But in the customer's mind, a fertilizer which stimulated growth or a soil conditioner which stimulated growth were similar functionally, and should have cost the same. The company found that it had to hold its price in line with fertilizer because it was sold in the same department and performed a function which customers perceived as being quite similar.

*Fair-price relationships* form the basis for a phenomenon that is completely ignored in most economic texts, that of *engineering to a price*. By engineering to a price is meant that the seller initiates the design of his product with a given selling price in mind, and then works out a design that comes close to meeting the performance specifications of the market and yet can be produced and sold at a profit at the target price.

This, of course, reverses the normal traditional view of pricing, in which the product is first produced and then sold at what the market will bear. Such a system would be completely unworkable in any industrial economy because of the long lead times between design and sale. A manufacturer cannot design an automobile and build an expensive assembly line for it and then simply hope that it will sell at some profitable figure, especially since the design must start some three years before the sale and involves a heavy investment. Such long lead times are not limited to the automobile industry. They are indeed a fact of life even in products as simple as greeting cards.

A phenomenon closely related to the fair-price reference point is that of *cost/price relationship judgments*. Manufacturers have found that they cannot obtain a premium for an option on a design such as, for example, power steering on a tractor, that has been normal on the market, if the design that they produce is obviously much simpler and cheaper to build (even when it does as good a job or a better one than the options on the other designs). Customers seem to feel that it is "not right" for a seller to make a higher than usual profit on an item and thus will reject as too expensive an item which they believe is selling too far above cost.

*Reverse-price perception* is a result of a different kind of experience by sellers—the phenomenon that it is often true that a price just above the lower end of a dollar bracket, for example a price such as $2.35, may be rejected by buyers, when they will pay a price of $2.95 more readily. This may be due to a fair-price reference point, but may also be due to the fact that buyers have become accustomed to seeing prices just under the upper end of a range set by the just noticeable difference. The unusual price is then viewed as either a cut in quality or as an attempt to pass off a quality that would normally sell at a lower price, just under the previous dollar mark. In any case, unusual and unaccustomed price levels do not normally bring in more business.

The customer does not always approach every single item of purchase with a clear picture in his mind of what he can expect to pay for it on today's market. As a result, he looks for clues as to what he should pay. This is, of course, one of the reasons why the soil conditioner sold for the price of the fertilizer, even though clearly labeled as not a fertilizer. The fact that it was sold in the same department might well have been viewed by buyers as a clue as to what it should sell for.

One result of this is what is clearly a *price aura effect*. If a store is seen as a good place to buy a number of items of rather frequent use, the customer is likely to believe that the other items in the store are equally good buys and to question the price much less. This is one reason why stores can juggle their price mix in order to make a profit and why the Joint Food Commission appointed by Congress discovered that it is never possible to determine which food store in town has the lowest prices, since a shift of a few items in the market basket will shift the relative ranking of the stores. It is also one basis for the heavy price promotional approach of some stores who appeal to people who may be somewhat less careful shoppers, by quoting quite deep cut special prices in some items, quite out of line with the rest of their prices.

Finally, the *method by which a price is quoted* can greatly affect the consumer's reaction to a price. One of the more common of these differences is the tendency for people who buy on the instalment plan to look only at the cost of the individual instalment and not at the total price of the product. A great many unpublished studies have all shown that such is the case, that the standard for determining whether or not the purchase can be made is the size of the individual payment and not the total price.

It is also true, moreover, that people often look at only one major component of the price and not at the price of additional items of optional equipment coming with it, as in automobiles. Thus, the automobile companies will feature the stripped price of the low-end model quite prominently in their ads, but the customer, to buy the car he needs, may pay 50 percent additional, or even more. It is also one reason why the optional equipment may very well carry much higher margins than those on the basic item itself.

All of these reactions result in creating a very complex decision process for the seller in arriving at his price.

### Some of the Complexities of the Seller's Price Decision

The typical classroom discussion of price assumes that the seller has only a single price decision to make, at a single point in time. Such is not the case. He always has to solve the problem of product mix and merchandise mix decisions, and must, in addition, always take into account the discounts necessary to obtain the distribution structure that he desires. Furthermore, his freedom to set price is obviously limited by the considerations we have just discussed—those of expected price lines, just noticeable differences, and of price reference points. Moreover, pricing, like every other aspect of marketing decision, must be related to the product life cycle and a price quotation that is correct for one aspect of this cycle can be quite inappropriate at a different phase of the cycle (see Figure 16-4).

### Market Entry Pricing

The seller probably has more pricing freedom at the time he enters the market with a new product than at any other time in that product's career, but even at that point in time, his freedom to price is far less than is sometimes assumed. He must always take into account the probable reference point which customers will use in judging his product.

A great many pages, and perhaps even volumes, have been written with regard to pricing on a cost plus basis or on a basis of return on investment. Essentially, these discussions have assumed that the calculation of cost plus or return of investment comes first and the price is then determined. Such is really not the case. What the seller does, if he has any knowledge of the market, is to first ask himself what value the consumer will perceive in the offering and thus at what price he can hope to sell the item. He then judges whether the difference between this price and his roughly estimated cost justifies market entry or whether the return on investment which this price seems to indicate justifies entry, assuming the validity of his sales volume estimate. The decision is really, as one Scottish economist has observed, a *price minus* decision and not a cost plus (Smyth, 1967). Furthermore, it is made prior to market entry and thus never can be a very accurate estimate, since profit and cost are more directly related to volume than to unit variable expense.

If the entry is into an established market where price lines are already set, the price decision is essentially a product decision—a decision as to which niche in the market is most open to exploitation by the new entrant, whether low end, somewhere in the middle, or at the premium end of the market. The seller then must design and distribute a product to meet with the specifications necessary to fill customer

### Figure 16-4.   The Complex of Considerations Involved in the Pricing Decision

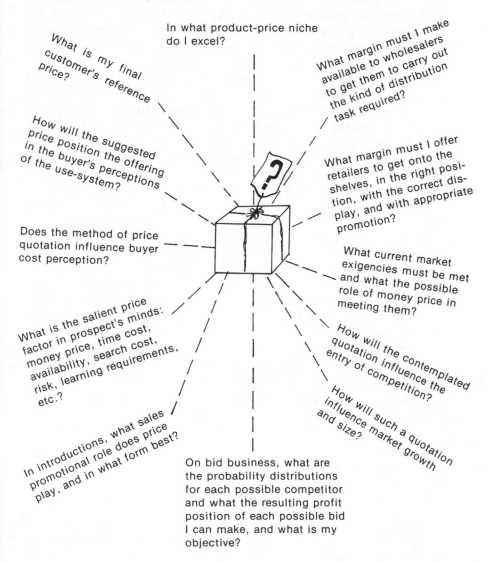

In what product-price niche do I excel?

What is my final customer's reference price?

What margin must I make available to wholesalers to get them to carry out the kind of distribution task required?

How will the suggested price position the offering in the buyer's perceptions of the use-system?

What margin must I offer retailers to get onto the shelves, in the right position, with the correct display, and with appropriate promotion?

Does the method of price quotation influence buyer cost perception?

What current market exigencies must be met and what the possible role of money price in meeting them?

What is the salient price factor in prospect's minds: money price, time cost, availability, search cost, risk, learning requirements, etc.?

How will the contemplated quotation influence the entry of competition?

How will such a quotation influence market growth and size?

In introductions, what sales promotional role does price play, and in what form best?

On bid business, what are the probability distributions for each possible competitor and what the resulting profit position of each possible bid I can make, and what is my objective?

expectations as to what they should get with the product in this market niche.

Finally, he must determine what use-system is most likely to be readily accepted in relation to the product and most likely to yield a profit, since the price itself will be used as a cue by the buyer as to the probable correct use-system of the product. Examples have already been cited earlier as to the need to price any item intended for gifts, or likely to be used for such at a level which people perceive as correct for gift items. But gift giving is not the only use-system which must be taken into consideration. The improper choice of use-system can greatly limit the market the product can hope to obtain.

One of the major errors in the introduction of plastic dinnerware was to foster the sale of this dinnerware as low-priced promotional items at supermarkets before it had become well established. Such dinnerware can actually be made in a number of grades and the higher grades are quite durable and could well have competed with much chinaware for acceptance. However, once the promotional use was pushed, market expectations were established which defined the plastic ware as cheap enough to be almost a throwaway item or to be used in place of the cheapest crockery (such as might be used in families with small children who are likely to take such dishes out into the yard and lose or break them). With such a use-system established for the product, it proved impossible to develop the quality market for the higher-quality product, and thus a great portion of the most profitable end of the market was sacrificed in order to obtain a short-run profitable volume.

The introducers of stainless steel tableware made no such mistake. The first major promotion of this product was in high quality, well-finished designs competing directly with sterling silver tableware. Medium- and low-end price lines were introduced only after this quality niche was thoroughly established. The latter then swept up much of the market which previously had been held by cheap silverplate items. Thus the introducers of stainless steel tableware were able to market a full product mix, each segment of the line of which brought a corresponding profit. Product mix and merchandise mix considerations are an important part of nearly every seller's decision structure.

*Product Mix and Merchandise Mix Decisions*

It is really a rare seller who offers a single fixed package of one item and related services. And when he does, he is normally at a disadvantage and must operate through channels which will supplement the limitations of his too-narrow offering. Buyers normally are seeking to obtain an assortment of satisfactions, a bundle of related items from each seller with which they deal. They need to minimize their transaction costs of both time and money by getting as much of each desired assortment and of each desire-set as possible from a single seller. The result is that those sellers get their business whose offered assortments come closest to their assortment needs in satisfaction content and value. The real offering of any seller is, therefore, his assortment of merchandise and services—what the manufacturer thinks of as his product line and accompanying services and the storekeeper views as his merchandise plan, not the individual items within those lines.

It is true that each buyer will differ somewhat from others in the extent and content of his assortment desires, and different items in the line will have a different degree of salience for different buyers. The importance of price and quality will thus diverge from one buyer to another and even more from distinguishable market segment to segment. As noted in our illustration in the supermarket, some housewives, for instance, may be more interested in fresh meat and produce quality in their store, and pay much less attention to cold-cut meats and bakery goods. Some are ·interested more in the prices and breadth of assortment they have available in staples and not really very much interested in the less common cuts of meat or the more unusual forms of produce. For this reason, any business district has heavier customer traffic and prospers more if it has department stores or supermarkets under more than one management. And for the same reason, all of the "competing" department stores in the shopping center prosper and each has a well-defined core clientele of its own. This also explains why there is no single definable "lowest price" merchant, except in terms of a particular segment of customers.

Each seller must offer some specific assortment to fit the desire-sets of a group of market segments if he hopes to be successful and make a profit. He will thus try to plan his product mix or merchandise mix of quality/price combinations to be most attractive to his own kind of customers, and feature those items highest in the desire hierarchy within their assortment desire-sets.

On the other hand, every seller must carry some kinds of relatively standardized items which are purchased frequently and are identical in practically all customer assortments and thus must be promoted by all sellers at approximately the same quality level and the same price level. In the supermarket, for example, these are items such as sugar and the popular soup brand; in the department store, women's nylons; in the industrial markets, standard carbon steel nuts and bolts; and at the meat counter, the hamburger. Because customers perceive little or no differentiation between such items bought from different sellers, and because they must buy them often in volume, such items are important in the purchasing patterns of a large number of buyers in all segments, and the seller must meet the market. Because of their purchase frequency, such "traffic items" must be heavily promoted regardless of cost and thin profits because any price which is higher than expectations for them tends to give buyers a perception that other prices may be out of line, due to the aura effect. The purpose of such items in the mix is merely to bring in customers and any profit is, therefore, indirect. The promotion is intended to generate sales of the other items in the product line or merchandise mix.

A successful seller must balance his profit margins in such a way that the low margins on his traffic items are compensated by higher margins on those items whose quality level design and price are highly salient for his own specific target segments, who would then willingly pay more to get precisely what they want. With an adequate margin, high turnover among heavy user buyers makes such items profitable even though the margin may be merely average. The seller will also have some items in his assortment which have a relatively low frequency of purchase and low attention value. He can compensate for low turnover of such items by much higher percentage margin levels and he may offer specialty items or specialty options on his products which bring much higher than normal margins.

This method of balancing the product mix or price mix may make the seller a lower cost outlet in fact as well as perception, for his target segments, and a higher cost outlet for those segments whose market basket requires a quite different mix.

As a result of the divergence in desire-sets and desire-assortments, product line and merchandise mix pricing require a carefully managed mix of price margins which takes account of three factors:

1.  The product desire-assortment of the target market segment, in terms of items and quality levels which they can discriminate and of the degree of salience of each item to the members of the target segment
2.  The frequency and volume of each purchase, the extent to which it is part of the desire-sets of all segments, its degree of standardization and, in consequence, the price sensitivity of customers in relation to that kind of item
3.  The turnover of the item when purchased by the specific target market segment the seller hopes to or does obtain

Traffic items, defined as high turnover, universally bought offerings, will normally be priced very close to or at the same level as quoted by competition and expected to yield minimum margins over cost. Their purpose in the offering assortment is to bring in customers for other items in the line.

Highly differentiated items demanded by and selling in good volume to the seller's own target segments, the quality of which will be obvious to them at their level of discrimination, will be priced at a level which yields a good to very good margin over cost but also a price which will be perceived by those for whom the item is salient as giving a high ratio of value to cost. These items will form the backbone of the profit structure.

Items which are handled as a convenience for the target segment but not particularly salient in their perceptions, nor bought frequently in quantity, will be priced to yield substantial margins.

The margin mix is just as much a problem for the seller who is offering a large single-item purchase such as an automobile, a home, a printing press, insurance, or the like. The sellers of such large ticket purchases must also offer an assortment, a choice among partly competing items, in order to serve well a large enough segment of the market. They also must devise a price mix which will be both attractive and insure the possibility of a reasonable profit. They, too, must offer some choices at very modest margins in order to attract segment fringes and other choices which can sustain a more robust mark-up. In the case of such internally competing assortments, the rules for successful pricing are parallel to those for the supplementary item assortment such as a supermarket or the department store carries.

Such single-choice assortments are normally composed of a broad range of perceivable quality levels. Generally speaking, also, the cost range of producing the various models is much narrower than the perceived quality range, at least for those buyers interested in the higher quality items. (It is said, for example, that the actual factory cost of a Cadillac is only about $300 more than the cost of a large Chevrolet.) The core of the market segment for such a seller is composed of buyers who seek and see high value in more of the possible product differentiating attributes than do those at the fringes of the segment, because those in the fringes perceive significant value only in the core product attributes. The seller is in more direct competition with other sellers for the business of such buyers than he is with respect to the business of those seeking the higher-level models with a differentiating characteristic. Thus, his stripped models become his traffic attracting items, although not in the sense of sales volume.

The low-end buyer—the buyer of what has come to be called "the stripped model," is not interested in many of the refinements which caused this differentiation. He is seeking a replacement tire or replacement automobile battery which will keep his car on the road for another year of moderate service, an automobile which will give good dependable transportation service but not necessarily some of the aesthetic satisfactions which go with decoration and various special accessories. He does not see very much added value, therefore, and will not pay a price proportionate to cost for accessory attributes. Because of his value perceptions, he is interested mainly in the core attributes and thus perceives very little value difference between the offerings of different sellers.

Most possible buyers, on the other hand, do perceive real value in the differentiating attributes of the products of one or another of the sellers, and will pay a reasonable price to obtain them. Some smaller segments will perceive even higher value in the unique attributes and will pay a very good price to get extra differentiation of their purchase. The pricing of the internal competing line, therefore, usually aims to:

1. Offer a relatively unattractive low-end line with a highly competitive, very thin margin low-end price. The effect on average profit is kept at a minimum by means of "plain Jane" design.
2. Offer a middle-line group designed to be the best compromise in relation to the desire-sets of the main body of the target market segments. The margin between price objective and design cost is aimed to yield target margin objectives on the average.
3. Offer a premium line with all the accessory options for those valuing highly the maximum satisfaction package, designed to yield a very high margin between target price and design cost.

It is seldom wise to treat the low-end line as a design stepchild, even though it must be kept relatively unattractive to the main market segment. It should attract the fringes of the same segment as does the main line. Thus every seller has a complex balancing act in terms of his product/value mix. He must start with a choice of feasible average profit margins, then balance low-end offerings of traffic items yielding thin margins, but gaining customer attention and patronage, with main line items at or near target margins, and high-end items with a robust contribution to profit. His main guidelines must be the content, proportioning, and salience of the desire-set assortments sought by target market segments.

End use consumer pricing is not the only problem the manufacturer or seller must face. Unless he is dealing directly with the end customer, he must also consider the various customers in between. Those dealer and distributor customers are his channels of distribution to the end users, and he must make allowance for adequate prices to buy the services of these intermediaries so necessary to his market success.

### Discounts Needed To Attract Distributive Customers

The end customer's perception of value determines the right price for which a product must be designed, but the seller rarely deals directly enough with this end customer to get all of this price. He must take into account any intermediary customers who will purchase the product in order to move it further along toward this final customer. Each of these, in their roles as distributors, has a perceived value for the service they are rendering and this perceived value must be taken into account in setting the discounts that will be quoted by the seller or the "mark-ups" which he expects the distributor to take. (These terms, *mark-up* and *discount*, are exact synonyms and are calculated in the same manner: both are the result of dividing the total margin over the buying price of the customer by the price at which the customer will sell the product.)

Distribution discounts are, therefore, really purchase prices—an offering of a specific portion of the final end user's perceived value, in return for a number of value additions made by the intermediary. Such distributive intermediaries add four basic types of user perceived value to the manufacturer's product:

1. *Time and Place Utilities*: Maintenance of inventories where most convenient to most buyers at the times the buyers desire them and the quantities needed by buyers
2. *Communications Services*: Local advertising, attention-getting displays, personal selling services—all needed by the end user.
3. *Financing Services*: Paying for the inventories the distributors carry and the assuming of credit risks
4. *Objective Production Services*: Assembling of use-related items and services to meet customer assortment-desires and matching their needs; performing fitting, altering, and other services designed to adapt the physical product more closely to customer desires; provision of parts repair and maintenance services which are a necessary part of the package in the customer's desire-set; furnishing of instructions for use and maintenance; adding a close-to-the-buyer warranty of value

It has already been pointed out that a considerable part of the price perception of the final customer are timing and place utilities. Gasoline in the storage tanks of the Indiana refinery are not of much value to a customer whose tank is running dry in the middle of Iowa. The buyer may pay a high price rather than wait until stores open the following morning at 9:00, for milk that he finds he needs at 10:00 in the evening.

The advertising and display services performed by distributors are direct value to the customer himself, as it relieves him of a great deal of his search effort costs. By far the most important function of the dealer or distributor, from the customer's standpoint, is the assembling of assortments to meet his own desire-sets. Another important function, of course, is the final fitting of the product to those needs. He is not interested in cattle carcasses, but in steaks. The man likes to have his slacks cuffed at exactly the right point in relation to his ankles. None of these can be well carried out by the manufacturer and all of them are important values to the final customer.

In general, of course, the seller accepts the discount dictated by general trade practice for the given category of goods he is distributing, for each member of the channel. However, there are times when he must make an independent decision in this matter and decide whether or not the services that the distributor can perform are adequately paid for by his margins or even overpaid for at times. A proper level for such discounts will vary with the phases of the product life cycle as must many other aspects of the price mix.

### Product Life Cycle Price Adjustments

Each phase of the product life cycle requires a different set of pricing and price mix objectives because each phase of the product life cycle brings in a different level of customer value perceptions.

With high learning products, the pricing of the introductory market development stage of the life cycle can be quite critical. It is important, of course, to so design the product as to require the minimum of value-perception learning and also to match the value reference perception of the most receptive market segments. During this period also, at the very point of introduction, it is important to recognize the phenomenon of imputing value from price, in positioning the product in relation to some specific use-system. Moreover, the initial offering price becomes the value reference point for much of the rest of the life cycle. Setting it too low may not only position the product in the wrong use-system but will certainly limit the room for price maneuver later.

The immediate profit cannot be a major consideration in setting this price level, since it will be necessary to incur high promotional costs to bring the introduction to the attention of innovators and early adopters, and volume will be low for a considerable period because of the small proportion of these in the total population. The proper level is probably one that takes full account of the cost reduction which the experience curve will bring some time well after the first items come off the assembly line. Once this point is reached, the experience curve should be followed downward in price in order not to furnish a motive for additional early competition as soon as profits really become visible. Price lines can be quite simple, however, because at this point in the product life cycle, the perceived values lie in the core function itself. There will be little incentive to hunt for variations at first.

On the other hand, distributors will require extremely high discounts in order to perform their role in the heavier promotional effort needed to put across any revolutionary new product.

Once the take-off point of the growth stage begins to emerge, and selling becomes directly profitable, price lines need to be broadened to cover as many major segments of the market as can be economically accomplished. Dealer margins, on the other hand, should normally be cut during the growth stage, since it is no longer necessary to gain dealer support in order to sell the product. At this point, dealers will be motivated to take on a product merely because it is growing and is profitable.

The correct price structure and the amount of room for price maneuver depend on the character of the introduction and the point of the cycle at which it is introduced. The emulative or adaptive product, introduced well along in the growth phase or later, must fit into existing price expectations. The only choice open to the seller is the price niche at which he must aim. This niche should always be the one containing market segments least well served so far, and the niche will create its own set of best fitted segments.

It is unfortunately true that many late comers into the growth phase market assume that the best niche is the extreme of the low end—that the best introduction is a product which is cheaper than those already on the market. Such is not necessarily the case and is often quite wrong. There are even times when the most vulnerable niche is the ultra premium level with a product engineered to appeal to an especially discriminating segment not currently satisfied with available use-values. Thus, among American auto manufacturers not often recognized as existing, is one making very expensive copies of classic cars ($75,000 in the case of the deluxe version of the Stutz Black Hawk). Pepperidge Farm breads built a major market share by introducing a quality well above any then on the market.

The introduction of the Polaroid camera exemplifies an excellent choice of introductory pricing tactics and later adjustments. The first item introduced, a single model, was design-targeted to appeal to the nonprofessional photographer interested mainly in a single print. The camera was released at the upper edge of the popular camera market (about eighty dollars), with generous retail margins to furnish an incentive for stores to inventory and sell them, and it was introduced only at special outlets and department stores where buyers would expect a quality offering. Once the product was well established in acceptance, it was followed by low-end models to broaden the market and by precision models useful mainly for scientific work at higher prices. Meanwhile, of course, trade discounts were lowered because it was no longer necessary to sell the Polaroid camera. It was bought whenever available.

Once the product reaches maturity, the entire aim of the pricing system must be defensive, to preserve the product category franchise. At this point, most of the market will be well satisfied with the different models available and the remaining dissatisfactions will be primarily those which the product design itself is not capable of handling. Customer search, therefore, will be for a different kind of product which meets the needs not met by the product being priced. It is, therefore, necessary to keep this search effort low by maintaining relatively low margins on the product to preserve the advantage of being the familiar.

Once the decline phase is reached, there is no longer any necessity for using price to maintain or expand a market. The decline itself is coming about because superior products are already on the market and only the skeptics and the laggards in the consumer cycle will still be purchasing the product. Pricing should, therefore, for the first time in the cycle, be primarily profit oriented and any effect on market share should be completely disregarded. The product is being purchased only by those who put a high value on not having to change their habits at this stage.

A profitable level price is one which takes full account of all aspects of price, as every aspect of the marketing effort must, of customer perceptions, of value, and of customer habits and attitudes toward change.

## Summary

1.   Price is one of the three variables the seller can utilize to influence consumer behavior, but a negative variable, an avoidance factor used to offset the positive attractions of the offering and the communications.

2.   Behaviorally, price must be defined to include any aspect of the offering which inhibits the consumer's desire to acquire it.

3.   Perceived price has eight possible dimensions: monetary cost, time availability, place availability, use-time demands, search effort requirements, risk of dissatisfaction, use-learning cost, and design compromises.

4.   Although time and place are sometimes defined as utilities, they must be viewed as negative, since they are always less than desired.

5.  Use-time demands often override considerations of monetary cost.

6.  One of the primary purposes of much of advertising is to reduce the costs of search-time effort.

7.  Risk costs are of three kinds: dissatisfaction risk, risk of loss of future supply, and risk of supply continuity.

8.  The learning cost requirement is, as already indicated, a major cause inhibiting new product acceptance.

9.  The need for the consumer to accept design compromises is what renders all market positions vulnerable to creative competition.

10.  The consumer's perception of the price also has eight facets: the j.n.d. effect, price lining, price/quality inference, reversed price perception, cost/price relationship judgments, fair price reference points, the price aura effect, and the price quotation method effect.

11.  The combination of the j.n.d. effect and the presence of price reference points invalidates the simplicity of the demand curves so popular in elementary economics texts.

12.  Price lining severely limits the flexibility of the designer.

13.  The price aura effect is what enables the merchant to balance his low margin items with higher margins on other items.

14.  The pricing problem of any seller is far more complex than generally recognized in most economic theory. He almost never is in a position to price a single item independently, nor to limit the effect of that quotation to one point in time. In addition to observing the limits set by consumers' perceptions, the seller must usually plan a profitable price and merchandise mix for a complete assortment of offerings, in relation to each other. He must also decide on appropriate discounts needed to obtain necessary distribution services. Moreover, his price policies must change with the phases of the product life cycle.

15.  Market entry pricing is often a crucial decision, and is never truly solved on a cost-plus or return-on-investment basis. Neither cost nor return can be readily predicted, and neither recognizes the only valid decision starting point—the value perceivable by the consumer and what his reference price is.

16.  In determining his possible entry price, the seller must analyze the possible use-systems and then engineer the design to be priced for the use-system with the greatest long run profit potential.

17.  The seller must nearly always construct a balanced product/price structure, with differing margins for different items which average out to a target profit margin.

18.  When he is selling the consumer a complementary assortment of items, he must balance the minimal margins obtainable on traffic items with target margins on those items perceived as salient by his

market segments and with premium margins on specialties sold to his core market.

19. When the consumer will be making a single-item choice out of an assortment of graded models, the merchandise price mix must be constructed of "plain Jane" stripped models to be used for competitive comparison, with minimum profit margins on these bulwarked by average profit main sale volume models for the bulk of the market segments being served, and sweetened with high margin options for the core segments interested in premium aspects.

20. The total price possible is determined by the end user's perception of value, but this end price must be shared with the intermediate buyers in the distribution chain. The trade discounts made available to these intermediaries are compensation for the added values which they are in a position to contribute to the final end offering: time and place utilities, communications services, financing service, and customer-fitting production services.

21. Each phase of the product life cycle has a different appropriate pricing strategy. The market development period for the high-learning product calls for a design requiring minimal learning coupled with a price requiring the least possible change in value perception. Growth phase policy demands a variety of price lines and models to satisfy different developing market segments. Mature markets need defensive pricing to maintain the market against the potential inroads of new kinds of offerings. During the decline phase, immediate profit is the only valid consideration, with complete disregard to the effect on market share.

## Chapter 16  Exercises

1. The text makes quite a point about the different kinds of non-monetary "prices" or avoidance factors in the offering. For each of the other seven factors he mentions, give at least one example of your own of a situation or offering in which that factor clearly overrides the monetary factor to a significant degree.

2. Take some market basket list, such as your own list of purchases for a two week period. Comparison shop the local supermarkets with this list. Are all items priced the same in every store? If not, are all of the differences in the same direction? How big are the

individual differences, percentagewise? How can the stores with the higher prices, in each instance, sell the items involved?

3. Check some multiple price line clothing or department store, or some general mail order catalog (where the different quality lines are labeled as "good", "better", or "best"). What is the size of the percentage price difference between price lines?

4. What are the implications of "engineering to a price" for anti-trust law?

5. Visit a gift shop. What are the prices of items clearly intended for gifts of some importance?

6. Tabulate and graph your summary of the garment prices (for garments under $150) in one Sunday edition of a metropolitan newspaper. Do you get an even spread of prices, or do they cluster in some manner? If they cluster, around or near what points do they cluster?

   How much difference is the price spread within clusters, percentagewise?

   Does there seem to be any particular spot in the cluster for each different class of store, such as discount markets and prestige stores?

7. What does the text mean by the "defensive pricing" recommended for products in the mature stage of the cycle?

8. What is the difference between "selling below the market" and selling a low-end product?

9. Can a premium product, sold at a premium price, be physically identical to an average product sold "at the market"? If so, then what is the distinction between "selling above the market" and selling a premium product?

10. Firms have been sued under the Sherman Anti-Trust Act for selling a product under a private label (distributor brand label) for less than the same product under their own well-advertised brand. What would be your defense of the practice, based on known behavioral principles?

11. Some states have laws prohibiting sale of products below cost, and even specifying a minimum markup which must be followed. These are aimed at the below-cost pricing of traffic items and are usually the result of lobbying by small merchants and aimed at their larger competitors. Do such laws really help the smaller merchant compete better, and why or why not? Are they likely to

make any real difference in the customer's market basket cost, and why or why not?

12. At what points of the product life cycle is pricing policy most critical, and in what sense in each case? Why, in behavioral terms?

13. If you were entering the market with a new toothpaste, detergent, or breakfast cereal, how would you determine the initial price? Why?

14. If you were to develop an entirely new synthetic textile fiber, with unique and important new properties, how would you price it?

15. What pricing tactics can help broaden a market, once the growth phase of the cycle is well along? How do they work, in terms of consumer behavioral principles?

# PART VI.
# Epilogue: Some Questions

THE PREVIOUS DISCUSSION has dwelt entirely on the tools for understanding consumer behavior which are available from current knowledge of consumer behavior. Tools themselves have no morals or ethics, and they can be just as effective in producing harm as good. Unfortunately, the choice between good and evil is seldom a clearcut one, and the following chapter raises some questions which are answerable, and many others which only the student and marketing man can answer for themselves.

Some Questions of Whether
or Not and Where Lines
Should Be Drawn

## WHAT ABOUT MANIPULATING CONSUMERS?

Widespread Belief in Possibility
Answers From Psychological Knowledge
Answers From Business Experience

## MISPERCEPTION, SALES VOLUME, AND SOCIAL WELFARE

What About Harmful Products Which Are Desired?
What About Exploitation of the Placebo Effect?

## PARASITIC MARKETING STRATEGIES

Exploitation of the j.n.d. Through Package Clipping
Use of Advertising Muscle to Take Over Markets Pioneered By
    Others

## PREDATORY MARKETING PRACTICES

Preying on Fears and Anxieties

## THE OTHER SIDE OF THE COIN: MARKETING AND BEHAVIORAL TOOLS CUT BOTH WAYS

THE STUDY OF ONLY those forms of human behavior which can be classed as consumer behavior definitely implies some intention to influence consumer behavior in an exchange situation. This could and probably should raise some questions as to whether or not all such attempts at influence are ethical and if not, where ethics dictates drawing the line.

To put the question in its worst light, as some people quite certainly do, should we try to "manipulate" consumers? This is really the easiest question to answer because it is the wrong question. It assumes that all exchange situations are one-way streets with a consumer a passive puppet. As our review of psychology shows, such can never be the case. There are some harder questions, however, as to what uses of our knowledge of consumer behavior are in the best interest of society as a whole and of the consumer. These questions allow for a great deal of gray area in which the individual will have to search his own conscience for the answer, and also gray questions as to what can be done effectively to curb practices which are clearly not in the interest of society as a whole.

## What About Manipulating Consumers?

It is obvious that a great many very well educated middle class consumers, at least, are convinced they are being victimized by marketing efforts, in particular, by advertising. Unless this were so, such books as Vance Packard's *The Hidden Persuaders* (1957), Ralph Nader's *Unsafe at Any Speed* (1965), and their many predecessors would never catch the attention of enough people to make publishing worthwhile, nor agree well enough with the perceptions of those who did read them to make best seller lists, as they invariably do. Nor would their highly unbalanced and generally superficial presentations hope to gain much acceptance or fame for the authors.

The basic theme of all these books, starting at least with Stuart Chases' *Tragedy of Waste* (1929) and continuing through Nader's books, is that marketing efforts are basically parasitic and unsocial, or at least, that the unsocial effects of marketing are what produced profit, by forcing people to buy things they do not want.

Is there any basis in either theory or business experience to justify these charges?

Let us start by recognizing that people are sometimes led to purchase decisions they sooner or later regret. One need go no further for confirmation of this than the daily news, with periodic revelations that people are regularly robbed of their life-time savings through various swindles including the oldest of all, "the pigeon drop" (give me your $5,000 to show your good intentions and you will be able to claim the $50,000 inheritance from the uncle you never heard of), and extending to the most sophisticated forms of chain letters and "investment" in new magical get rich real estate or commodity speculation schemes. Illegal as these all patently are, if any of them could be shown to result from pure external manipulation of the buyer, without any corresponding internal drive for power and profits, then manipulation is not only possible but probable in more legal operations.

Turning first to theory, what we know about drives, attention and perception definitely excludes the possibility that even the grossest swindle of these sorts could succeed without the cooperation of the buyer. He must first have some drive, some wish, to gain a return above any he knows to be available to the public generally, without exerting any skill or effort of his own. Otherwise, selective attention alone would eliminate him as a possible victim—he would not listen. All perceptions are based on experience and such an offer is so counter to all his experience that he never gets something for nothing, that he would not perceive the offer to be valid.

What does experience say? The testimony of every confidence man is in full agreement—their endeavors never did succeed except with people who "had larceny in their hearts"—or to put it more mildly, were too greedy. Most people do not prove to be prospects at all, only a small minority even listen or respond. So experience agrees with theory. Consumers are not puppets, at least in this most extreme of cases. But we have even better evidence than this in the many failures well within the limits of legitimate marketing.

No area of selling has available a better battery of sales pressure devices than the feminine fashion industry has. Whole series of publications have devoted droves of readers avidly awaiting each new issue of news and authoritative dictum on what the best dressed woman will soon be wearing. Every large metropolitan daily carries at least a weekly section devoted to the same end. Moreover, merchants, whose prestige and authority are well earned, cover pages of the papers with their offerings of the new. And in the "better" shops the sales people are not mere clerks, but knowledgeable advisors on whom customers do depend in part.

Generally, of course, the fashion offerings available in any given season, are really quite diverse. In one instance cited earlier, however, that of the midi introductions of 1970, such was not the case. For once the industry spoke with one strong voice. If customers were manipulable, the midi should have been a smashing success. As already indicated, however, it was pure disaster, and one fashion that caught on strong that season was one which both designers and merchants had been rather reluctant to sell—the pants suit.

Other major failures have been noted already. Twenty million dollars of promotion and advertising should buy a lot of manipulation if any is possible. It did not for either Knorr or Campbell in their abortive attempt to sell gourmet grade dehydrated soups. Sixteen million dollars backed by the most consistently successful advertiser in the consumer field—P & G—should help break open a market. It failed in the case of the P & G home permanent attempt. The list could be extended indefinitely, for no area of marketing is more strung with the bones of failure than that of new product introductions well backed up with promotion.

Thus it is that both theory and business experience are clear on one point—the consumer will buy only when what is promised appeals to some internal drives strongly enough that he perceives the promises believable and the cost worth what he gets. This does not mean that the consumer's perception cannot be so defective that what is purchased does not really live up to the promise. The perceptions can be tricked, as theory, experiment, and experience all agree.

However, the economics of mass production guarantees one partial safe-guard: if the misperception does not persist after purchase, industry does not benefit from the results. The flow of new suckers is never massive enough to produce the needed volume of sales. Only continued repeat purchases by customers whose drives are satisfied can support a mass production sales effort.

But are sales themselves a social justification?

## Misperception, Sales Volume, and the Social Welfare

It should be clear that all exchange process transactions of any kind—commercial, political or even religious—take place when what the seller offers is perceived by the consumer as meeting an active internal drive. Furthermore, it should be equally obvious that unless the result of the purchase is perceived as satisfying, the consumer will not repeat the purchase, and will quite likely also advise his friends to avoid it, guaranteeing eventual failure for any kind of mass produced offering.

But it is also true that what is perceived is not always the same as what actually is. Whether or not success is justified and success itself proves that the "true interests" of the customer are served is not so easily answered on the basis of objective evidence. Clearly, in a great majority of cases, the customer's interest and society's are both well answered, but is also true that there are a great many cases in which society is harmed and there are some in-between points where only the individual's conscience can give him an answer.

At one extreme, some of the judgments will still seem to be based on accepted standards of social welfare. Without question the great bulk of opinion would condemn the business of promoting heroin drug addiction. Consequently, this is not only generally illegal in most western countries, but the bulk of objective evidence clearly indicates that the damage to the social welfare has no offsetting benefits for either the individual consumer or for society as a whole.

But what about the production and sale of cigarettes? The threat to the general health of nearly all users is pretty well established. In addition, smoking in public places is an unmitigated nuisance to those who do not smoke—that is, the minority are trampling on the rights of the majority who do not smoke. There is also accumulating evidence that smoking mothers inflict damage on the developing fetus, a matter which is not outside the purview of societal concern. On the other side of the case, a large minority of the population are sufficiently addicted to cigarette smoking that they find it extremely difficult to break the habit. Immediate stoppage of production and sale are clearly impossible from either a political or practical standpoint.

But what about the individual whose best potential for farm income is the growing of cigarette types of tobacco? What should the stockholder do who own shares in R. J. Reynolds or some other cigarette company? What should the advertising agency do which has the opportunity to land one of the more lucrative cigarette advertising accounts?

If these questions still seem easy to answer, let us consider a question a little further toward the middle of the scale—the question concerning the gaining of profit from the production, promotion and sale of alcoholic beverages. Unlike tobacco, which yields no provable positive benefit for the user, alcohol is one of the oldest of tranquilizers and when consumed in moderation, as it is by about nine out of ten users, is a very mild tranquilizer with no known deleterious side effects to offset the relaxation conferred. Few other tranquilizers in common use can equal this record. In addition, alcohol has culinary and social values, especially in diluted and lighter forms such as wines and beer. But for some important fraction of the population, alcohol in any form is an addicting drug when used to excess. When so used, it leads to personality changes and to direct dangers to health. It is a proven factor in death by cirrhosis of the liver.

Whatever many people may feel about the alcoholic beverage industry, complete prohibition of production and sales was a disastrous and corrupting failure. Any policy to restrict sale by regulatory action is difficult to enforce. Again what should the individual do concerning his part in the production, promotion and sale of alcoholic beverages?

Moving well up the scale toward the other end, what about the use of promotion to cause people to perceive a desirable benefit which is not physically present, but belief in which can yield the benefit? What about deliberately exploiting the placebo effect, commercially? For example, no drugs sold over the counter without prescription really can relieve a headache or other pain without considerable passage of time—approximately twenty minutes or more. But "fast" relief is the major theme for all such drugs and the unstated implication of all advertising is that relief comes much more quickly than it physically can—say in one or two minutes. Moreover, a great many people who believe such advertising are certain to feel relief within such a short time. Is this right?

Or consider the use of the placebo effect on the matter of a pain much less physical than most headaches: the pain of doubt the teenage consumer may feel about his or her social acceptance. Should advertising be so designed as to induce such a person to believe that the right aftershave, perfume, or lipstick will confer greater social acceptance? Without question, many believe such implications and the result is the relief of anxiety through use of the products being promoted and probably even a greater degree of attractiveness because of this relief and the greater poise resulting. At least such is the conclusion of Mayer in his discussions of the added value of advertising, in *Madison Avenue, U.S.A.* (1957).

In all of the kinds of actions cited above, the individual does have a desire for which the product is perceivable as a cue to satisfaction. In every case, promotional efforts play an important part in developing sales volume, and the methods in most cases, except possibly those of the drug pusher, are within the bounds of what would be considered generally acceptable. This is particularly true of those involved in advertising. Advertising is by far the least aggressive of all promotional tools. It cannot force attention nor promote perceptions the consumer is not fully ready to accept. Nor does advertising succeed by stepping over the bounds of good taste. It does, however, sometimes develop perceptions of something the consumer does not get unless he believes what the promotion implies. This placebo effect is characteristic of the promotion of some of the most solid of social institutions, including conspicuously, nearly all religions. If you wish to accept some items along this scale and reject others, where would you draw the line?

Witch doctors, priests, and many other kinds of leaders made use of the placebo effect, probably long before the dawn of history, and most of the other uses of misperception were well understood before the study of psychology ever came into being. It is rather unlikely that a wider understanding of consumer behavior would lead to any greater exploitation of the consumer on this basis than now occurs.

The results of actions involved in two other types of marketing also have a history but seem more prevalent in modern society, and the greater understanding of human behavior could well tempt even more people to take advantage of the buyer in these other ways. Two classes of such marketing practices might, in their extreme form at least, be labeled as parasitic marketing, and predatory marketing. Both of them involved gray areas rather than simple black-and-white decisions, and each individual needs to search his own conscience to find the border line.

**Parasitic Marketing Strategies**

Two extremely common marketing strategies can be labeled as parasitic under at least some specific extreme forms. One is best designated as package-clipping, to take advantage of the j.n.d. The other is the attempt to take over markets built up by others through skill and investment in market development, by the "knock-off" or other devices.

*Package-Clipping*

In earlier centuries, rulers sometimes offset their treasury deficits by trimming small amounts of the precious metals from the edges of the coins that came in for payment, and some of the less scrupulous citizens also increased their incomes in a similar manner. Soon, of course, the only coins available were the debased clipped variety whose value was also less. The observation that such debased coins soon drove out the full value ones has been called Gresham's Law, named after

Queen Elizabeth I of England's treasurer, who noted that "bad money drives out good."

Gresham's Law is also valid in marketing: skimped packaging eventually drives out good and the parallel principle also applies: those who debase the packaging gain a profit thereby.

In the case of packaging, the incentive to do so rests on the j.n.d. principle. As already shown in Figure 6-5, a small change in all three dimensions of a package can result in a very substantial change in the content without immediate perception of the difference. In Figure 6-5, for example, it was shown that a contents difference of nearly 15 percent could be removed by decreasing each dimension by 5 percent without any perception that the package is smaller.

This principle rewards the initiator of such package debasement with a very substantial cost advantage, and adds to the consumer costs. Initially, the consumer has to pay as much for the short count package as for the full one. Eventually, of course, the shortfall package drives out all full count ones, but the initiator has been able meanwhile to use his profits to gain market share, and the proportionate cost of packaging materials has been increased, since the surface does not shrink as much as the volume.

In the middle ages, the laws in some countries penalized short counts rather severely, so the "baker's dozen" became thirteen in order that the baker be on the safe side, for example, in selling his rolls. But while modern states would penalize any attempts to claim and charge for twelve and sell eleven, nothing is done about the seller who sells what looks like a three-pound package but which contains only two pounds ten ounces, so long as the fine print (never read by the consumer) designates the correct contents. This, for example, is what happened to the standard three-pound box of oatmeal, now two pounds and ten ounces, the Number 2 can of vegetables (four cups), now replaced by the Number 303 (three-and-one-half cups), the quart-and-one-half (forty-eight ounce) can of fruit juice, now forty-five ounces, and many other examples.

Sometimes whole industries change package size in order to avoid a break in traditional price lines when costs change. Such was the case with the once five cent candy bar which started at two ounces, shrunk to one-and-one-half ounces, then had to be raised in price to ten cents and finally fifteen cents, as of 1974.

At other times, individual firms seem to have a definite policy of package clipping to muscle into somebody else's market. One major advertiser has used some such device successfully on at least three occasions—when it sought a share of the cooking oil market, of the peanut butter market, and of the potato chip market. At the time that this firm introduced its cooking oil, the standard containers were cylindrical quart bottles (thirty-two fluid ounce), and pint bottles, (sixteen fluid ounce). The firm had the insight to see that such a cylindrical bottle of oil could be slippery and so developed a wasp-waist bottle—a real benefit for the consumer. But the firm also noted that the irregularly shaped bottle could be as tall as a quart bottle and as wide or wider at the base, and hold only 75 percent of a quart (twenty-four fluid ounces) without the customer perceiving that the bottle was smaller. So they introduced their brand in this off-standard size, at the quoted price of a quart, with their usual massive introduction advertising (at least partly financed by the short fall in contents). By now, of course, all brands are irregularly shaped twenty-four ounce bottles, but the initiator gained one of the top two positions in the market by his apparent deception.

A similar ploy was used to carve out a major niche in the peanut butter market. Again, their research turned up the need for the minor package benefit. The standard twelve-ounce jar had right-angle corners between bottom and sides, and people had trouble getting the last bit of butter out of the corners. So the firm designed its jar with rounded-bottom corners. Well enough, but again the firm clipped the package from twelve ounces to eleven ounces without consumer perception of the short weight. (The label, of course, gave the actual weight in fine print but most housewives probably didn't read the label even on their old packages.) The result: a major market niche and no more twelve-ounce jars.

In the potato chip case, the firm was introducing an obviously much smaller package. They had developed a wavy chip similar in appearance to the natural potato chip but made with a uniform shape by holding and frying potato meal. (The molded type of chip, made in other shapes, had been pioneered by another large firm.) Such chips could be stacked compactly in a relatively small metal cylinder to be kept fresh and it was so treated. Now this package was clearly smaller than competitors. What to do? The decision was made to put even less in the container, nine ounces instead of the twelve ounces in the standard bulky natural chip bag, then in the TV commercials loudly compare the volume in the cylinder with the volume in "this bag" . . . an unidentified bag that looked like the standard one but actually was a specially made nine-ounce bag. In this case the firm relied on the assumption that this bag was another standard size commercial pack and would not be perceived as smaller in the TV illustrations. Again, it gained a major market niche by preying on the perceptions of consumers.

Obviously, such tactics are not in the general interest. It is true that the firm gave consumers some additional benefit in package design but it is also unlikely that their market would have been so substantial had consumers been made equally aware of the stiff added price they were paying for the advantage. Firms who did not initiate such raids on the consumer budget were penalized by loss of market share and to this degree the structure of competition itself was damaged.

But what is the remedy?

The other important form of market parasitism is the attempt to take over markets whose development was financed by more venturesome pioneers and more innovative designers. In the garment, jewelery, and toy industries, this is known as the "knock off"—the emulation of successful designs pioneered by others. Theoretically, such designs are patentable and/or copyrightable, but both copyrights and patents are very narrow in what they protect and most "knock-offs" are variations of the original. In addition, markets are so volatile and ephemeral in all these fields that the imitator may merely copy, take his profit and disappear.

Unlike the case of package clipping, it is possible to argue for some addition to the social welfare in the case of many knock-offs. For one example, a three-piece woman's knit suit was extremely popular one season—an outfit consisting of a knit jacket, knit blouse and knit skirt with a blouse in a contrasting color. One competitor, deciding to cash in on the trend, decided to knock it off with a cheaper version—a skirt, jacket and dickey instead of full blouse. Another competitor went one step further. He designed a two-piece outfit, which looked the same, by knitting a contrasting panel in the neck of the jacket instead of furnishing either a blouse or dickey—at a lower price, of course. In a case such as this, each seller was really aiming for a different market segment. And those who knocked off the original were actually spreading the availability of the design within the limits of what would be perceived as attractive and worthwhile by the buyers in these other segments. In the fashion field also, it can be noted that the knock off is a two-way street. Everybody copies to some extent.

But not all popular product emulation has as much positive benefit from the standpoint of the welfare or of the general consuming public. One major firm in the toiletries field indoctrinates its trainees to avoid innovation. This firm's policy is apparently to let other firms carry the burden of pioneering market development, then step in with another version of the product and capture a major market share through massive promotion. The policy often succeeds, but part of this success is due to the attempt to find weaknesses in the product or marketing plans of the pioneering brand and add some improvement to the product. The firm also fails sometimes when smaller and faster moving competitors take countersteps.

Regardless of the product improvements and failures, such a follow-later policy obviously could decrease the incentive for others to pioneer in the area of their interest and could thus deprive consumers of the benefit of the new products. Curiously enough, the antitrust laws, as interpreted by the U.S. Justice Department, favor this practice, since the department frowns on the buying out and merger of firms in the same field and insists that the firms enter their own brand instead. Were they allowed to buy out those that did the pioneering, the pioneers might very well prefer to take the initial market growth profits and put them to other use.

It is obvious that some, at least, of these parasitic practices take advantage of the principles of perception to damage the basic structure of competition with no visible offsetting benefit to consumers. But the history of regulating "unfair competition," from the 1890 Sherman Act on, indicates that it is unlikely that regulatory action promises much help in protecting consumers from the effect of such practices.

The long-run effect of parasitic practices on consumer welfare is indirect by increasing the cost of the irrelevant part of the offering—the package—relative to the whole, and the extent to which sometimes, at least, it discourages creative innovation. But other marketing practices prey directly on anxiety and fear and directly affect individual consumers.

## Predatory Marketing Strategies

A tendency to exploit the fears, anxieties, and aspirations of role transition periods characterizes a number of marketing strategies still practices by a minority of sellers. The practices range from the outright swindle or confidence game to the borax credit operation.

Confidence games are a form of marketing, but one in which the seller promises and collects for satisfaction he has no intention of delivering. The range for the sale of the Brooklyn Bridge (or its equivalent) to the offering of grossly mislabeled goods. The law and consumer education have drastically reduced the scope of all such forms in the field of commerce, but no laws hinder those promoting ideas in every area from politics to religion. Some small confidence operations remain on the local small enterprise scale, largely in such areas as fake home improvement sales on a door to door basis and occasionally on a grand scale in the investment field. For the rest, labeling and brand laws have been reasonably effective, and since mass production must depend on repeat sales, the market place itself has largely eliminated the sales of the outright shoddy goods.

But very little has been done to inhibit appeals to fears and anxiety, especially to the anxiety states of those in role transitions. One such case is that of those who migrate to cities from relatively primitive rural areas, settling in the slums and ghettos. Such consumers are often willing victims of those who use "borax credit" to promote the sale of goods which appeal to their aspirations. (The term borax credit refers to the sale of goods whose quality is much lower than implied by the description and by the high prices asked, on extremely high-cost credit terms.) Such borax credit sellers—principally of furniture, house furnishings, appliances and garments—appeal to the high anxiety aspirations for the fiscally innocent with "easy credit" "low-down payment" offers of goods at prices far above those paid for similar quality by informed buyers, at usurious interest rates. At times, in fact, the down payment may actually cover the merchant's cost, and any payments received are profit. If the payments cannot be met, the goods are repossessed and the buyer, under current laws, at least, still is left with a debt hanging over his head. Often many such buyers are driven to loan sharks who exact a further pound of flesh before bankrupting the consumer completely.

Some of these practices could be ruled out by law, at least those of repossessing goods on which money is owing and still continuing to collect. Much of the rest of it, however, grades into the wide use of consumer credit in society, a practice which is widely approved and which in some degree at least, has a great deal of justification.

Another less easily condemned practice is that of exploiting the anxieties of those in the role transition periods of adolescence and early adulthood. At the one end of the scale are the practices of a great many sellers of door-to-door goods, of what are often of reasonably good quality but far higher in price than similar goods sold through normal channels. These goods are sold, however, not on their appeal as physical products but as symbols of the status into which many young women desire to move, that of a well-established married matron. The "canned" sales approach which salesmen are trained to use appeals to the woman's desire to move into this role by pointing out how the product being sold would help fit her for the role of gracious hostess.

At the other end of the scale are products whose major appeal is to the problem of role transition from child to adult, but which are not directly so promoted. The heavy users of cosmetics tend to be in the range of upper adolescence and early adulthood and a great deal of this purchase is undoubtedly related to role transition anxieties. Indeed, it is quite possible for many types of firms to gain a major benefit from these transition periods, as pointed out earlier, without any definite aim to do so. Again, where should a line be drawn?


## The Other Side of the Coin

All of the examples above point to cases of which some, at least, would normally be condemned by most people. But the same principles used in exploiting consumers' fears and anxieties and moving into markets developed by others may be used for beneficial results as well. Even the toiletries firm cited above as one with an apparent parasitic policy has always made its moves to grant some positive appeal to its products and this is a major part of the reason for their success. Indeed, as already pointed out, competition succeeds best when it offers additional value for the consumer. The j.n.d. principle can be used to block an invader as well as to finance an invasion, at least under some circumstances, as already pointed out in an earlier chapter. Like all tools, the use of the principles of human behavior can be beneficial for the market or it can, in what is, fortunately, a very minor part of the cases, be used to give the customer much less than he has a right to expect. The history of the industrial revolution and of the years from then until now indicates that for the most part, the tool is beneficial and, as with all good tools, a greater understanding by the sellers would be of a great deal of value to the consumer himself, by decreasing the waste inherent in poorly planned products and poorly planned promotions, the cost of which must eventually be borne by the consumer himself.

# References

*Advertising Age*, "Puritanism Still Lives in the East, Sociologist Says," *Advertising Age*, May 2, 1966, p. 76.

_____, "Too Lively TV Show Kills Ad Effect: Schwerin," *Advertising Age*, Apr. 5, 1960.

Asch, Solomon E. "Opinions and Social Pressure," *Scientific American*, November, 1955.

Atkin, K. "Advertising and Store Patronage," *Journal of Advertising Research*, Vol. 2 (1962), pp. 18-23.

Banks, Seymour. "The Relationship Between Preference and Purchase of Brands," *Journal of Marketing*, Vol. 15 (October, 1950), pp. 145-157.

Bauer, Raymond A. "Consumer Behavior as Risk Taking," *Dynamic Marketing for a Changing World*, ed. Robert S. Hancock, Chicago: American Marketing Association, 1960, pp. 389-398.

Bell, James A., Jr. and Wasson, Chester R. "A Study of Supermarket Patronage in the Geneva-St. Charles Area, 1971," unpublished.

Bexton, W. H., Heron, W. and Scott, T. H. "Effects of Decreased Variation in the Sensory Environment," *Canadian Journal of Psychology*, 1954, No. 8, pp. 70-76.

Bralove, Mary. "Most People Have No Taste; It's Been Lost in the Process," *Wall Street Journal*, April 30, 1974, p. 1.

Britt, Stewart H. *Social Psychology of Modern Life*, New York, Holt, Rinehart and Winston, 1949.

Brown, George. "Brand Loyalty—Fact or Fiction?" *Advertising Age*, Vol. 24 (January 26, 1953;, pp. 75-76.

Brown, Robert L. "Wrapper Influence on the Perception of Freshness in Bread," *Journal of Applied Psychology*, Vol. 42 (Aug. 1958), pp. 257-260.

Brown, Wilson B. and Motwani, Ramesh. "The Influence of Family Relationships on Marketing: India and America Compared," unpublished manuscript, 1972.

Bruner, J. S. and Goodman, C. C. "Value and Need as Organizing Factors in Perception," *Journal of Abnormal Psychology*, 1947, No. 42, pp. 33-34.

*Business Week*, "Europe Goes Shopping," *Business Week*, May 18, 1963, pp. 58-72.

Cohen, A. *Attitude Change and Social Influence*, New York, Basic Books, 1964.

Crutchfield, R. S. "Conformity and Character," *American Psychologist*, Vol. 10 (1955), pp. 191-198.

Dutton, David, "Does American Marketing Strategy Work Abroad?" in *New Ideas for Successful Marketing, Proceedings of the 1966 World Congress, American Marketing Association*, June, 1966, pp. 680-693.

Egelhof, Joseph. "Would-Be Investor Escapes Oil Swindle—Thanks to Pro's Advice," *Chicago Tribune*, June 28, 1974, Sec. 3, p. 11.

Erlich, D., et al. "Post-Decision Exposure to Relevant Information," *Journal of Abnormal Psychology*, Vol. 54 (1957), pp. 98-102.

Epstein, A. N. and Teitelmann, P. "Regulation of Food Intake in the Absence of Taste, Smell, and Other Oro-Pharyngeal Sensations," *Journal of Comparative Physiological Psychology*, Vol. 55 (1962), p. 155.

Ferber, Robert, Blankertz, Donald F., and Hollander, Sidney, Jr. *Marketing Research*, New York, Ronald Press, 1964.

Festinger, L. *A Theory of Cognitive Dissonance*, Stanford University Press, 1957.

Frank, Ronald E. "Is Brand Loyalty a Useful Basis for Market Segmentation?" *Journal of Advertising Research*, Vol. 7 (June, 1967), pp. 27-33.

Harlow, H. F. and Harlow, M. K. "Social Deprivation in Monkeys," *Scientific American*, No. 207 (1962), pp. 136-146.

Helfgott, M. J. "The New Package Research," presented to Marketing Workshop, American Marketing Association, Mimeo, Lippincott and Margulies, Inc., 1960.

Hodge, Robert W., Siegel, Paul M., and Rossi, Peter H. "Occupational Prestige in the United States: 1925-1963," *Class, Status and Power*, eds. Reinhard Bendix and Seymour Martin Lipset, 2nd ed., New York, The Free Press, 1966, pp. 322-334.

Hovland, C. I., Janis, I. I., and Kelley, H. H. *Communication and Persuasion*, New Haven, Conn.: Yale University Press, 1953.

_____ and Weiss, W. "The Influence of Source Credibility on Communication Effectiveness," *Public Opinion Quarterly*, Vol. 15 (1951), pp. 635-650.

Hunter, W. S., "Habit Interference in the White Rat and in Human Subjects," *Journal of Comparative Psychology*, 1922, No. 2, pp. 29-59.

Kagan, Jerome and Havemann, Ernest, *Psychology: An Introduction*, New York, Harcourt, Brace and World, Inc., 1968.

Kassarjian, Harold H. and Cohen, Joel B. "Cognitive Dissonance and Consumer Behavior," *California Management Review*, Vol. 8 (Fall, 1965), pp. 55-64.

Katona, George and Mueller, Eva, "A Study of Purchase Decisions," *Consumer Behavior: The Dynamics of Consumer Reaction*, ed. Lincoln H. Clark, New York, New York University Press, 1955, pp. 30-87.

Katz, Daniel. "The Functional Approach to the Study of Attitudes," *The Public Opinion Quarterly*, Vol. 24 (Summer, 1960), pp. 163-204.

Krugman, Herbert E. and Hartley, Eugene L. "The Learning of Tastes," *The Public Opinion Quarterly*, Vol. 24, No. 4 (1960), p. 621.

Laird, Donald A. "How the Consumer Estimates Quality by Sub-Conscious Sensory Impressions—With Special Reference to the Sense of Smell," *Journal of Applied Psychology*, Vol. 16 (June, 1932), p. 246.

Lazarsfeld, P. F., Berelson, B., and Paudet, H. *The People's Choice*, University Press, 1948.

Maloney, John C. "Is Advertising Believability Really Important?" *Journal of Marketing*, 1963, p. 1.

Martineau, Pierre, *Motivation in Advertising*, New York, McGraw;Hill, 1957.

Mayer, Martin. *Madison Ave., U.S.A.*, New York, Harper Brothers, 1957.

Meyers, James H. and Reynolds, William H. *Consumer Behavior and Marketing Management*, Boston, Houghton-Mifflin, 1967.

Mills, J. "Changes in Moral Attitudes Following Temptation," *Journal of Personality*, Vol. 26 (1958), pp. 517-531.

Nader, Ralph. *Unsafe at Any Speed: The Designed-In Dangers of the American Automobile*, New York, Grossman, 1965.

*Newsweek*, "A Star-Spangled Swindle," *Newsweek*, July 8, 1974, pp. 56-57.

Norris, Bernardine. "The Midi—Not Long Enough?" *New York Times News Service*, November, 1971.

Nosachuck, T. A. and Lightstone, Jack. "Canned Laughter and Public and Private

Conformity," *Journal of Personality and Social Psychology*, Vol. 29, No. 1 (Jan., 1974), p. 143.

Opinion Research Corporation, "America's Taste Makers, No. 1" and "America's Taste Makers, No. 2," *The Public Opinion Index*, Princeton, N.J.: Opinion Research Corp., April 1958 and July, 1958.

Packard, Vance. *The Hidden Persuaders*, McKay, 1957.

*Printers' Ink*, "Key to Asia: Respect for Differences," *Printers' Ink*, Feb. 21, 1964, pp. 41-54.

Rainwater, Lee, Coleman, Richard P., and Handel, Gerald. *The Workingman's Wife*, New York, Dobbs Ferry, 1959.

Riesman, David and Roseborough, Howard, "Careers and Consumer Behavior," in *Consumer Behavior*, ed. Lincoln H. Clark, New York, New York University Press, 1955, pp. 1-8.

Riker, H. A., Jr. and Besharaty, M. "Tchamanzar Dairy Company (B)," *Cases in Buying Behavior and Marketing Decision*, ed. Chester R. Wasson, St. Charles, Ill., Challenge Books, 1969. Also available from Intercollegiate Case Clearing House as an individual case.

Rogers, Everett M. *Diffusion of Innovations*, New York, The Free Press, 1962.

Schiele, George W. "How to Reach the Young Consumer," *Harvard Business Review*, March-April, 1974, pp. 77-86.

Seifer, Nancy. *Absent from the Majority: Working Class Women in America*, National Project on Ethnic America of The American Jewish Committee, New York, 1973.

Sherif, C. W., Sherif, M., and Nebergall, R. E. *Attitude and Attitude Change*, Yale University Press, 1961.

Smyth, R. L. "A Price-Minus Theory of Cost?" *Scottish Journal of Political Economy*, June, 1967, pp. 110-17.

Social Research, Inc., *Working Class Woman in a Changing World*, Social Research, Inc., May, 1973.

Stridsberg, Albert. "Great Differences Within European Common Market, Expert Warns," *Advertising Age*, Jan. 20, 1961, pp. 75-79.

Thomas, Alexander, Chess, Stella, and Burch, Herbert G. "The Origin of Personality," *Scientific American*, Vol. 223, No. 2 (Aug. 1970), p. 102.

Tucker, W. T. "The Development of Brand Loyalty," *Journal of Marketing Research*, Vol. 3 (August, 1964), pp. 32-35.

Tull, Donald S., Boring, R. A., and Gonsier, H. M., "A Note on the Relationship of Price and Imported Quality," *Journal of Business*, April, 1964, pp. 186-91.

Twedt, Dik Warren. "How Can the Advertising Dollar Work Harder?" *Journal of Marketing*, Vol. 29 (April, 1965), pp. 60-62.

Wasson, Chester R. *Dynamic Competitive Strategy and Product Life Cycles*, St. Charles, Ill., Challenge Books, 1974.

# Index